Vladimir Soloviev
and the Spiritualization of Matter

Oliver Smith

Studies in Russian and Slavic
Literatures, Cultures and History

Series Editor:
Lazar Fleishman (Stanford Universtity)

Vladimir Soloviev
and the Spiritualization of Matter

Oliver Smith

Boston
2011

Library of Congress Cataloging-in-Publication Data

Smith, Oliver, Ph. D.
 Vladimir Soloviev and the spiritualization of matter / Oliver Smith.
     p. cm. -- (Studies in Russian and Slavic literatures, cultures, and history)
  Includes bibliographical references (p.   ) and index.
  ISBN 978-1-936235-17-9 (hardback)
 1. Solovyov, Vladimir Sergeyevich, 1853-1900. 2. Matter. 3. Spirit. I. Title.
 B4268.M35S65 2010
 197--dc22
                                    2010047543

Copyright © 2011 Academic Studies Press
All rights reserved

ISBN 978-1-61811-826-4

Book design by Ivan Grave
On the cover: *The Portrait of Vladimir Soliviev*, by Ivan Kramskoy (a fragment). 1885

Published by Academic Studies Press in 2011
28 Montfern Avenue
Brighton, MA 02135, USA
press@academicstudiespress.com
www.academicstudiespress.com

CONTENTS

Abbreviations used for Soloviev's works vii
Acknowledgments ix
Introduction 1

Chapter I. THE FIRST THINGS 19
    The Early Period, 1873-81 24
    The Material World 31
    I. The Monad 36
    II. Theogony 47
    III. Cosmogony 66
    IV. The Fourth World 79

Chapter II. HUMANITY 91
    I. Anthropogeny and History 96
    II. The Task and the Kingdom of God 105
    III. Christ the God-man 113
    IV. The Body of Christ 122
    V. Death and Flesh 138

Chapter III. PROPHECY 145
    I. Soloviev as Prophet, 1881-1897 147
    II. Soloviev, Authenticity and the Antichrist 163
    III. The Apocalyptic Turn, 1897-1900 176
    IV. Prophecy and the Threefold Office 194

Excursus. THE PRIMACY OF THE THIRD: Soul, Feeling and Reverence . . 207

Chapter IV. THE LAST THINGS 237
    I. Love 240
    II. Beauty 257

Conclusion. ON SPIRITUAL-MATERIAL UNITY 275

Bibliography 283
Principal Works Cited 296
Appendix. Glossary 297
Index 299

ABBREVIATIONS USED FOR SOLOVIEV'S WORKS

FI *Filosofiia iskusstva i literaturnaia kritika* (Philosophy of Art and Literary Criticism), ed. R. Gal'tseva and I. Rodnianskaia, Moscow, 1991.
PSS *Polnoe sobranie sochinenii i pisem* (Collected Works and Letters), ed. by A. A. Nosov, 3 vols, Moscow, 2000-01.
S^1 *Sochineniia* (Works), ed. by A. F. Losev and A. V. Gulyga, 2 vols, Moscow, 1989.
S^2 *Sochineniia v dvukh tomakh* (Works in Two Volumes), ed. N. V. Kotrelev, 2 vols, Moscow, 1989.
SS *Sobranie sochinenii* (Collected Works), ed. E. L. Radlov and S. M. Solov'ev, 12 vols, Brussels, 1966-70.

ACKNOWLEDGMENTS

Without support from the Arts and Humanities Research Council, who funded my doctorate degree at University College London and research trips to Russia, this book would not have been written. I am in their debt for allowing me to complete research on the initial project. I am also extremely grateful to the Carnegie Trust for the Universities of Scotland for their financial assistance toward this publication.

There are many people to whom I owe thanks in the production of this manuscript. I am particularly grateful to Robin Aizlewood, whose gentle yet firm supervision on more than one occasion redirected my attention from paths best left unexplored. For suggestions on additions and edits of various incarnations of this text, I thank Philip Boobbyer, Tim Beasley-Murray, Lazar Fleishman, Pamela Davidson, Geoffrey Hosking, Claire Whitehead and Emily Finer. Many people have contributed to expanding my knowledge of, and appreciation for, Vladimir Soloviev. Jonathan Sutton, who first introduced me to Russian religious thought, has been an irreplaceable source of wisdom and guidance. I benefited greatly from conversations with Soloviev scholars in Russia, especially Nikolai Kotrelev, Aleksei Kozyrev and Sergei Khoruzhii. And I thank all those whose conversation and advice has propelled me in new directions, especially Adam Ure and Brandon Gallaher.

Aleksei Tkachenko-Gastev and Tanya Khramtsova were kind enough to put me up for many weeks of research in Russia, and I thank them for their continuing kindness and friendship. My parents, and my sister Victoria, have been a source of constant and unfailing support, for which I thank them all. The love of my wife, Shelley, has lightened many dark moments in recent years, as well as expunging multiple typos and awkward phrasing from sections of this manuscript. The creature who has presided over the majority of the writing of this book is our cat Eva, whose ability to find comfort on a small desk between tomes of Russian philosophy never fails to amaze me. I thank her, as well as past animal companions James, Tessa and Dylan.

My grandparents were extremely dear to me and unfailingly attentive when I would tell them about the progress of my work. My grandfather once asked what my book would be about and, having listened carefully to the rather convoluted answer, replied: 'No one is going to read that, Oliver.' I dedicate this book to his memory.

*Dedicated to my grandfather,
Horace Abbott.*

INTRODUCTION

The present study began as an investigation of subject-object relations in the work of the Russian philosopher, poet and visionary Vladimir Soloviev (1853-1900). I was interested in which metaphysical premises lay behind his positing of a substantial unity between subject and object, and what consequences these had for the conceptualization of their interaction in lived experience. It became clear very quickly, however, that approaching Soloviev's work from the perspective of the modern Western philosophical tradition, most notably German Idealism, with its accentuation on the problematics of the subject-object divide, would lead to a disfiguration of his theory of cognition. While the Russian philosopher uses the terms subject and object, they are only very occasional visitors to his discourse, and occur mostly when he is discussing the work of other thinkers. Instead, it is the pre-modern distinction between 'spirit' and 'matter,' with roots in classical and biblical thought, which occupies central position.[1] The distinction between subject and object of cognition is retained, but the cognitive process itself is placed within the larger context of the more fundamental interaction between spirit and matter.

Having reached this point, it became further clear that it would be impossible to investigate this interaction without touching upon Soloviev's philosophy of history. The interaction between spirit and

---

[1] For a concise treatment of the main points in the spirit-matter distinction in Greek and Christian thought, see E. McMullin, 'Introduction,' in *The Concept of Matter in Greek and Medieval Philosophy*, ed. E. McMullin, Notre Dame, IN, 1965, pp. 1-23 (pp. 13-16).

matter is understood in his thought not as a temporally neutral sphere open to rational investigation but as a relationship characterized by qualitative changes in its nature over time. These changes taken together amount to a kind of teleology in which the two principles act upon one another in an historical progression where the efficacy of their mutually conditioning activity increases until an ideal interaction is reached. This final goal Soloviev describes as the 'spiritualization of matter' (*odukhotvorenie materii*), whose end he equates with the biblical idea of the coming of the Kingdom of God—the full definition and penetration of the material principle by the spirit and, conversely, the full habitation of spirit in material form.[2] The term may be compared with the Eastern Christian idea of *theosis*—the deification of both individual believer and the created world—although Soloviev ties his concept much more closely to evolution in historical time, and to the 'worldly' spheres of human life, than had Christian writers before him.[3] Moreover, Soloviev understands this process of transfiguration not only as a divine initiative but as the conscious 'task' of humanity, which is called to transfigure both itself, as corporeal form, and the material world around it. The spiritualization of matter is thus an idea that feeds on an entire historical complex of philosophy, theology, and mystical experience. As well as biblical and patristic thought, it resonates strongly, as a recent work has demonstrated, with the religious humanism of the Renaissance, with its emphasis on human

---

[2] For an introduction to the theme of 'spiritualization' in Soloviev's thought, see Jonathan Sutton, *The Religious Philosophy of Vladimir Solovyov—Towards a Reassessment*, Basingstoke, 1988, pp. 72-74.

[3] For an overview of the many aspects of *theosis* in patristic thought and Orthodox tradition, see A. Louth, 'The Place of *Theosis* in Orthodox Theology,' in *Partakers of the Divine Nature: The History and Development of Deification in the Christian Traditions*, ed. M. J. Christensen and J. A. Wittung, Madison, 2007, pp. 32-44. For more on Soloviev's broadening of the concept, see Paul Valliere, *Modern Russian Theology: Bukharev, Soloviev, Bulgakov: Orthodox Theology in a New Key*, Edinburgh, 2000, pp. 160-61; R. F. Gustafson, 'Soloviev's Doctrine of Salvation,' in *Russian Religious Thought*, Madison, WI, 1996, pp. 31-48 (pp. 37-40, 47-48). Paul Collins argues that the 'concepts which Solovyov developed contribute to an understanding that deification is not simply a private concern or experience but something which forms and frames the Church as a believing community in its relationship with God's purposes for the whole cosmos.' P. Collins, *Partaking in Divine Nature: Deification and Communion*, London, 2010, p. 95.

INTRODUCTION

responsibility and agency.[4] It is also very much a product of the ground on which it arose, being perhaps one of the most representative products of the Russian religious mind, whose fundamental conviction Nicholas Zernov has described as the 'recognition of the potential holiness of matter.'[5]

Apart from its multiple layers of meaning, what makes the study of Soloviev's philosophy such an intricate and often perplexing exercise is just how much of the philosopher himself there is in it. No matter how many potential sources of influence one uncovers to explain the provenance of his ideas and ideals, a large part of his legacy remains the province of personal experience, which moves beneath the work in ways not easily discernible, if at all. In the case of his ideal of the spiritualization of matter, while not seeking to deny the significance of the religious and philosophical traditions upon which Soloviev drew, it seems to me crucial to take into consideration from the very beginning three particular feelings, or dispositions, that informed and moulded his reasoning.

The first is the feeling of consonance between the spiritual and material realms, heaven and earth, which was (if we are take his various biographical accounts seriously) given to Soloviev in various moments of his life, but particularly in his final sophianic vision at the Egyptian desert (as depicted in the poem *Three Meetings*) when, as he writes, 'Всё одно лишь было / Один лишь образ женской красоты.'[6] This is, so to speak, the ground of all his philosophizing, the feeling from which all else stems. The second is a kind of antithesis to the first: the knowledge that, despite the experiential primacy of such consonance,

---

[4] See G. M. Hamburg and R. A. Poole, 'Introduction: The humanist tradition in Russian philosophy,' in *A History of Russian Philosophy 1830-1930: Faith, Reason and the Defense of Human Dignity*, Cambridge, 2010, pp. 1-26 (esp. pp. 5-9).

[5] N. Zernov, *The Russian Religious Renaissance of the Twentieth Century*, London, 1963, p. 285.

[6] 'All was only one / One sole image of feminine beauty' [trans.]. V. S. Solov'ev, "*Nepodvizhno lish' solntse liubvi...*" *Stikhotvoreniia; Proza; Pis'ma; Vospominaniia sovremennikov*, ed. A. A. Nosov, Moscow, 1990, p. 123. Unless otherwise stated, all translations of Soloviev's work, and other Russian sources, are my own. His poetry is quoted in the original Russian, with translations in the footnotes, while his prose is translated into English within the text.

it is not sufficient to win victory over the most formidable foe: death. With the same intensity that he felt the consonance of spirit and matter, Soloviev at the same time felt the full weight of that 'bondage to decay' of which Paul speaks in his letter to the Romans.[7] From this feeling derived the philosopher's emphasis on the 'desire for immortality,' which stands so central to his account of spiritual life in his work *The Spiritual Foundations of Life* (1882-84).[8] As a task, the spiritualization of matter is intended first of all as a means of liberation from death, and in this way may be conceived as the active component in what one author has termed Soloviev's 'immortalization programme.'[9] The final feeling I wish to single out is Soloviev's fear of the counterfeit, from which flowed his conviction that there exists an anti-ideal, a form of spiritualized matter and a mode of spiritualizing activity that are so proximate to his ideal as to be virtually indistinguishable. I believe these three feelings to be so important that I have endeavoured to integrate them as fully as possible into the interpretation of Soloviev's work without losing the general focus.

My goal has thus not only been to define the exact nature and parameters of the task of the spiritualization of matter insofar as it relates to human activity in the world in Soloviev's philosophy, although it is this first of all, but also to depict the correspondence between the philosopher's life and his theoretical and creative output. I am not interested in psychologizing Soloviev, or in separating subjective from objective motivations in the hope of arriving at a more scientific picture. Rather, I have tried to understand his thought as a part of the complex of his 'life's drama.' In this I see my own, however inadequate, attempt to follow the ideal outlined in the introduction to Soloviev's remarkable treatment of Plato, *The Life Drama of Plato* (1898), of whom he writes:

---

[7] Romans 8.21. All biblical citations are from the NRSV (New Revised Standard Version) except in those cases where Soloviev advances his own translation, or else where the preservation of the original meaning from the Slavonic Bible directly affects the argument. In these cases, the translation is my own.

[8] V. S. Solov'ev, *Dukhovnye osnovy zhizni*, St Petersburg, 1995.

[9] Irene Masing-Delic, *Abolishing Death: A Salvation Myth of Russian Twentieth Century Literature*, Stanford, CA, 1992, p. 105.

> Life for him was not the peaceful passing of days and years of intellectual labour, as it was for example for Kant, but a profound and complex drama embracing his whole being [...] Plato himself as the protagonist of his own life's drama: this is the real principle of the unity of his work.[10]

In hoping to pursue a similar goal in relation to Soloviev himself, I have used three parallel approaches. On the first plane, the argument follows the general construction of the task of the spiritualization of matter itself. Starting at the 'first things'—the core convictions that lie behind his ideal—it moves on to look at Soloviev's thought on prophecy as that human agency most effective for the task, and ends with the 'last things'—its eschatological realization. Secondly, I have retained a broadly chronological approach in relation to Soloviev's life and work. While I do not restrict the exposition of his ideas to the works of a given timeframe, the themes that are explored correspond to those which were foremost in his work as it developed from the early to the mature periods. There is thus a general movement from the eclectic mix of influences and ideas that characterizes the early period, to the biblically grounded work of the middle period, and ending with the apocalyptic writings of Soloviev's later years. In accordance with this, there are three biographical sections in which I treat some of the events, inspirations, and personal traits that influenced the given theme. Lastly, I have tried to sketch an arc across the whole work reaching from Soloviev's early, negative philosophy to the positive philosophy of the middle period, and ending at the reinvigorated negative philosophy of the later years.[11] Such an arc follows what I see as his move away

---

10 V. S. Solov'ev, *Sochineniia*, ed. A. F. Losev and A. V. Gulyga, 2 vols, Moscow, 1989, II, p. 585. This approach, deriving from Soloviev's own methodology, was adopted by Dimitri Strémooukhoff in his important work on the philosopher. 'It is Solov'ev's life,' he writes in his introduction, 'which allows us to understand the internal rhythm of his thought.' Dimitri Strémooukhoff, *Vladimir Solov'ev and His Messianic Work*, Belmont, MA, 1979, p. 12.

11 The resonance of the terms 'negative' and 'positive' philosophy with the work of Hegel and Schelling, both of whom had a great influence on Soloviev, is intended, although I use them here in a broad, non-technical sense. They should in no way be confused with 'negative theology,' or apophaticism, an important tradition in Eastern Christian thought of which we find very little in Soloviev's work.

from defining his ideal of the spiritualization of matter in contrast to thinkers past and present (i.e. in terms of what it *is not*) in his early years to its positive development (i.e. in terms of what it *is*) in the biblically grounded thought of the middle period, and finally to the emphatic return to the negative development of the theme in his last years.[12] This last approach is synthetic in that it combines the purely philosophical and biographical aspects by charting the personal development of the philosopher in its interaction with his work.

As Xavier Zubiri has written, all philosophy is necessarily pursued from a 'situation,' and to abstract from that situation means to do insufficient justice to the ideas that have their source in it.[13] In Soloviev's case, this situation is all the more important since so much of his thought represented the development of intuitions and revelations received in what can only be described as heightened states of consciousness,[14] or else reacted to threats and dangers he saw in the contemporary world around him. The peculiarity of his antinomic nature, at once entrancing and disconcerting, consisted in the fact that here was a theoretical philosopher of the highest order who was subject to prophetic dreams and diabolic visitations, who looked on philosophical truth with the eyes of an enthralled visionary. As Sergei Averintsev has written:

> The idea of truth and the idea of good aroused in Soloviev not only love, but the state of being-in-love. To fall in love with the Eternal Feminine — this we can understand; but to fall in love with truth! [...] Every time the philosopher returns to his beloved task of the 'justification of the good,' to the explication of moral perspectives, his erudition bursts into life, the

---

[12] This development is seen in the progression between what I see as the three most characteristic works of each period: *Critique of Abstract Principles* (1880), where Soloviev's philosophy emerges, as the title suggests, in its *critique* of other systems; *History and Future of Theocracy* (1886), where he advances his own ideal on the basis of a philosophy of history rooted in the Bible; and *Short Story of the Antichrist* (1900), where in an imaginative landscape his ideal appears as the reverse pole of the anti-ideal depicted.

[13] 'Philosophy, then, has to be done, and therefore it is not a question of an abstract apprenticeship. Like every truthful doing, it is a concrete operation, executed from a situation.' X. Zubiri, *Nature, History, God*, Washington D. C., 1981, p. 26.

[14] For an insightful treatment of the methodological challenges involved in the study of mystical thought, see Sutton, *The Religious Philosophy of Vladimir Solovyov*, pp. 1-15.

INTRODUCTION

movement of phrases becomes light, winged, as if dancing. In this living flame of the ethical Eros is the appeal of everything written by Soloviev, the source of his power.[15]

No wonder, then, that commentators on Soloviev's work have been drawn just as strongly to his biography, seeking to find in the latter some key to unlocking the meaning behind the changes and contradictions in the former. Since the publication of Evgenii Trubetskoi's influential *The Worldview of Vladimir Soloviev* in 1913,[16] many scholars have followed his example by dividing Soloviev's life and creative output into three distinct phases.[17] Although the periodization suggested by these scholars is similar, the precise character given to each period differs, as do the dynamics attributed to the development of Soloviev's philosophy as a whole. Broadly speaking, most are agreed in seeing in Soloviev's early period (1873-80) an emphasis on theoretical questions or *first principles*. Conversely, the middle, and longest, period (1881-96) is characterized by a turn toward practical questions such as the so-called 'Jewish question,' the unification of the churches, and the formulation of a complete ethics. In the final years of his life (1897-1900), Soloviev is understood to have become increasingly absorbed by apocalyptic presentiments, and to have undergone a certain degree of disillusionment with his previous activity. In accordance with such a schema, Trubetskoi divides Soloviev's life into 'preparatory,' 'utopian' and 'positive' periods respectively.[18] Although such a division has some merits, it more ably reflects Trubetskoi's relation to Soloviev than any objective assessment of the changes across the different periods. Another important early writer on Soloviev, Dimitri Strémooukhoff, does away with the traces of subjective valuation in Trubetskoi's terminology, preferring instead the triad 'theosophic,' 'theocratic,' and 'theurgic,' each relating to the ideal he sees inhering in the differing periods.[19]

---

[15] S. S. Averintsev, 'Ontologiia pravdy kak vnutrenniaia pruzhina mysli Vladimira Solov'eva,' in *Sofiia — Logos: Slovar'*, Kiev, 2001, pp. 413-16 (p. 414).

[16] E. N. Trubetskoi, *Mirosozertsanie Vl. Solov'eva*, 2 vols, Moscow, 1995.

[17] The notable exception to this tendency is K. Mochul'skii, *Vladimir Solov'ev. Zhizn' i uchenie*, Paris, 1936.

[18] Trubetskoi, *Mirosozertsanie*, p. 94.

[19] Strémooukhoff, *Vladimir Solov'ev and His Messianic Work*, pp. 12-13.

The solution is certainly preferable to that of Trubetskoi, and in some respects faithfully articulates the shifts of emphasis in Soloviev's life and work. However, one must be careful not to accept Strémooukhoff's terms too readily at face value. The ideal of 'free theurgy' was present very early in Soloviev's work; equally, 'free theosophy' is very much a part of Soloviev's late project. For this reason, I have preferred to use the neutral terms 'early,' 'middle' and 'late,' and seek to trace the more complex developments between the periods. I have, however, adopted the use of the word 'apocalyptic' in reference to the important change that occurs in Soloviev's late period.[20]

Disagreement abounds in how to characterize the development from one period to another. Nicolas Zernov is perhaps in the majority, although no doubt the most outspoken, in viewing the succession of periods in Soloviev's life as a series of cataclysms which befell their subject with supreme inevitability. After Soloviev's visions, culminating in the desert meeting in Egypt, Zernov argues, 'his academic career was ended before it had begun, his relations with other people, especially women, were changed' and 'his philosophical and religious activities took a new and unexpected turn.' Even more striking is Zernov's assessment of the new, apocalyptic vision that asserted itself in later life. It compelled the philosopher, he writes, to adopt a new worldview that '*nullified* the theories which he had previously expounded with such zeal and conviction.'[21] While the subject is ripe for interpretation and reinterpretation, this work insists on the continuity of Soloviev's vision and project, which evinces, in the words of Zen'kovskii, 'genuine evolution rather than abrupt change.'[22]

---

[20] Nicolas Zernov and Metropolitan Filaret of Minsk have described Soloviev's last period as 'apocalyptic,' although, as will become clear, their interpretation of the word differs significantly from mine. See Nicolas Zernov, *Three Russian Prophets: Khomiakov, Dostoevskii, Soloviev*, London, 1944; Mitropolit Minskii i Slutskii Filaret, 'Privetstvennoe slovo,' in *Rossiia i Vselenskaia Tserkov'*, ed. V. Porus, Moscow, 2004, pp. 7-9 (p. 8).

[21] Zernov, *Three Russian Prophets*, pp. 121, 149. See also Trubetskoi, *Mirosozertsanie*, pp. 8-9.

[22] V. V. Zen'kovskii, 'Vladimir Solov'ev,' in *Istoriia russkoi filosofii*, 2 vols, Paris, 1950, II, pp. 11-72 (p. 20).

Even on the question of evolution there is room for considerable debate. From one perspective, Soloviev's work appears to evolve, moving in new directions and incorporating new themes, while from another it appears not to evolve at all, representing but the outgrowth of a series of ideas that were already present early on. It was during his very earliest period that Soloviev experienced his three visions of Sophia, or Divine Wisdom, which eighteen months before his death he described as 'the most significant events to have happened to me in my life thus far.'[23] There is little doubt that, as many commentators have argued, Sophia is the central paradigmatic idea and motivating force behind Soloviev's philosophy. While I can only touch on her influence, Sophia's role as the wellspring of that feeling of consonance between the spiritual and material realms should be remembered as the constant backdrop to his thinking.[24] Soloviev believed there to have been something culminal about his sophianic experience; it is clear from his writing that what he saw in those visions he in some way understood to be the realization of his eschatological goal, the final spiritualization of matter. In a sense, what evolves in his philosophy evolves back toward an adequate articulation, a working through, even a reimmersion, in those past events.

Nonetheless, to deny the multilayered nature of his life's work and reduce all to an undifferentiated perception of absolute reality would be to trespass against the core of Soloviev's philosophy, which saw in an excessively mystical bent the roots of what he called 'abstract clericalism' or 'sham theocracy.'[25] Soloviev was moved not by an exclusionist understanding of an arcane and deeply personal intuition, but by a genuine faith seeking understanding, a faith grounded in his

---

23   Solov'ev, "Nepodvizhno," p. 124.
24   For a fine introduction to Sophia in Soloviev's thought see J. Kornblatt, *The Wisdom Writings of Vladimir Solovyov*, Ithaca & London, 2009, pp. 3-97. As will be argued later, the centrality of Sophia to Soloviev's thought need not be seen as diminishing the role of Christ. Sophiology was intended not as a replacement or supplement of Christology but an integral component of the same.
25   V. S. Solov'ev, *Polnoe sobranie sochinenii i pisem*, ed. A. A. Nosov, Moscow, 2000-01, III, pp. 151-55. Zen'kovskii argues that if 'it is accepted that Soloviev's work had several roots, and that his own inner task lay in the problem of their organic synthesis, we thereby avoid placing his constructions in a Procrustean bed of our own making.' Zen'kovskii, 'Vladimir Solov'ev,' p. 21.

'meetings' with Sophia but nonetheless aspiring to a rational expression accessible to all. When asked whom he would like to be, the philosopher wrote in a friend's album, 'I would like to be myself — turned inside out!.'[26] His philosophy was not a secondary activity but the result of a profound yearning to make known the subjective data of his vision of transfigured nature. According to Paul Allen, the 'desire to communicate to others his most intimate, most cherished ideas, was one of the strongest impulses in Soloviev's life.'[27] The movement of Soloviev's thought demanded that the God who appears to us in mystical experience be not only intuited but also thought. A God who is only thought, though, remains an abstract principle until she is concretely *felt* in the temporal and spatial conditions of our physical reality. The fruitful, if oftentimes confusing, ambiguity of some of Soloviev's key terms stems from the perceived necessity of expressing in purportedly rational discourse both that which is beyond conceptual expression and that which is expressed through the concept.

The focus of any analysis that has endeavoured to take a holistic approach to Soloviev's work has inevitably gravitated toward his late period, especially the significance of his *Short Story of the Antichrist*, which in published form appeared at the end of the dialogic work *Three Conversations* (1900). There is no single work that has been more influential in defining the nature of Soloviev's legacy. Through its lens, commentators have managed to arrive at a multitude of different interpretations as to the philosopher's final relation to his principal ideas. These range from views such as those held by Zernov and Trubetskoi, who are perhaps in the majority in equating the apocalyptic turn in Soloviev's worldview with the renunciation of his former ideals, to milder approaches where an attempt is made to find a degree of continuity between the early and late periods. The question is of central importance for the present study, since the core of the matter rests in the philosopher's final position as regards the nature of

---

[26] N. Kotrelev, "Blagonamerennost' ne spasaet cheloveka": Neizdannye avtografy Vladimira Solov'eva,' *Nashe Nasledie*, 55 (2000), pp. 64-73 (p. 65).
[27] P. M. Allen, *Vladimir Soloviev: Russian Mystic*, Blauvelt, NY, 1978, p. 87.

ideal human activity in the world. If it is accepted, as Trubetskoi argues, that Soloviev ceased to believe in the allocation of any role whatsoever to human agency in the realization of the Kingdom of God,[28] then the spiritualization of matter, as the concrete task of humanity, will be of interest to the scholar as that which is overcome in Soloviev's mature work. If, however, as we will argue, the mature work can be understood as growing organically from that which came before it, then his final relation to the question of the task of humanity will appear to us in a different light.

The spiritualization of matter, as idea, is expressive of the core of Soloviev's extravagant project: to arrive at such an interaction and relation between the heavenly and earthly realms in which both find mutual fulfilment and consummation, a consummation realized in and by a conscious humanity. For Trubetskoi, 'the enduring significance of Soloviev's teaching' was 'not in this idea, not in the utopian merging of what is above with what is below, but in the affirmation of that authentic Kingdom of God, which flesh and blood will not inherit.'[29] It is almost certain that not only would the younger Soloviev have disagreed with this statement, but so would have his mature counterpart. While he never spoke of a 'merging' between the two principles, the philosopher continuously repeated that the essence of his vision of 'All-Unity' was precisely the unity of *all* aspects of human life, including the material, with the divine. No doubt responding to misunderstandings of his own system, Soloviev once wrote the most direct description of his own thought that we now possess:

> My own teaching I cannot claim; but in view of the dissemination of harmful falsifications of Christianity I consider it my duty, from different perspectives, in different forms and in different contexts to explain the central idea of Christianity: the idea of the Kingdom of God as the fullness of human life — individual, social and political — reunited through Christ with the fullness of the Divine.[30]

---

28   See Trubetskoi, *Mirosozertsanie*, p. 95; Filaret, 'Privetstvennoe slovo,' pp. 8-9.
29   Trubetskoi, *Mirosozertsanie*, p. 97.
30   V. S. Solov'ev, *Sochineniia v dvukh tomakh*, ed. N. V. Kotrelev, 2 vols, 1989, II, p. 316.

The theme of the 'counterfeit' (here 'harmful falsifications'), one of the three fundamental feelings that we defined above, can be observed not only in Soloviev's *Short Story of the Antichrist* but in a great many of his works, especially those of the late 1880s up to his death. While the fear that his cherished ideals of good, truth and beauty could be coopted into the service of a corrupted ideal reached an unprecedented intensity in his last years, it had been present long before. Indeed, it informs so much of his philosophy that any account must at least touch upon it. In our case, it is all the more relevant since the spiritualization of matter is defined not only positively, in its concrete parameters, but also negatively, its character emerging in opposition to that which is only its semblance.

Following the arc described above, therefore, I begin by exploring Soloviev's attempt, in the early published work, to overcome the limitations he saw in the work of thinkers belonging to the Western philosophical tradition.[31] While Soloviev himself first appeared to the public in the mould of a critical philosopher of the Western tradition, a huge swathe of unpublished work, the first specimens of which only became widely available to scholars in the late 1970s,[32] as well as the important *Philosophical Principles of Integral Knowledge* (1877), present a very different portrait. Here, visionary experience, novel forms of logic, and much else jostle for position in expansive and restive prose that develops themes from religious tradition and mystical thought, as well as ancient and modern philosophy. The goal is not critique but the attainment of a complete worldview that not only sought a criterion for objective truth but attempted to answer fundamental questions of *meaning*: the goal of the historical process; the vocation of humanity; the interaction of the divine with the creature.[33] In this way, Soloviev's early

---

[31] Soloviev's master's dissertation, defended in 1874, is titled *The Crisis of Western Philosophy: Against the Positivists*. PSS, I, pp. 37-138.

[32] François Rouleau's publication of the unpublished works written in French was a major event in Soloviev studies. See V. S. Soloviev, *La Sophia et les autres écrits français*, ed. F. Rouleau, Lausanne, 1978.

[33] Consider the opening line of *Philosophical Principles*: 'The first question which any philosophy should answer [...] is the question about the goal of existence.' PSS, II, p. 185.

critical philosophy coexisted with the development of a comprehensive religious philosophy in works that remained unpublished, either in whole or in part.[34] Ending the first chapter with his early teleology in these latter, we look forward to the middle period, where Soloviev's thought on the 'task' of humanity within history becomes the defining motif of his writing.

There can be little doubt of the importance of biblical thought in Soloviev's positive exposition of his ideal.[35] Having examined the many influences that had an impact on Soloviev's early philosophy of matter, therefore, I go on to chart the philosopher's biblically grounded anthropology of his middle period, and the central paradigmatic model of his ideal — the spiritualized matter of the body of the risen Christ. Here the relationship between Soloviev's two central philosophical terms — theanthropy (*bogochelovechestvo*), the union of the divine and human natures in an individual human being, and All-Unity (*vseedinstvo*), the union of the heavenly and earthly realms at a universal level that embraces both collective humanity and the material world — is explored in some detail. Representing the intensive and expansive aspects of the spiritualization of matter, these two terms are the philosophical touchstones of Soloviev's unifying vision. Taken as the two aspects under which the perfection of the spirit-matter relationship appears, they represent the fundamentally Christological problematic that the philosopher tried to resolve throughout his work: to explicate how the individual realization of the spiritualization of matter coincides with the realization of the same at a universal

---

[34] This is in no way to claim that the unpublished work should occupy a more important place in the interpretation of Soloviev's early philosophy. His decision *not* to publish these works should be taken seriously, as should his decision to cease the publication of *Philosophical Principles*.

[35] Evgenii Rashkovskii writes that 'in his inner disposition, in the general intention of his thought, he was not so much an academic as a *biblical* philosopher [...] At all stages of his career, the Bible, alongside its reception in Christian tradition, was the source of Soloviev's philosophical interpretation.' E. B. Rashkovskii, 'Bibleiskii realizm, ili "opravdanie" istorii v trudakh pozdnego Solov'eva (vmesto poslesloviia),' in Ia. Krasitskii, *Bog, chelovek i zlo: Issledovanie filosofii Vladimira Solov'eva*, Moscow, 2009, pp. 427-44 (pp. 430, 441).

level.³⁶ One gets the impression that the philosopher is here at the very limits of his discourse, looking for that bridge which would unite the discontinuous spheres of individual and universal being.

It is almost as if the weight of that discontinuity, the split between the truth of the moment of inspiration when the individual soul reached that consonance which was before all separation and the continuing fiat of death in the expanse of the material world, pushed Soloviev away from the positive development of his ideal into an increasingly forceful refutation of those artistic representations and directions in thought that attempted to habituate the void without remainder, to cede to what he considered the deceit of absolute irreconcilability. His late work, from the time that he moved away from his public advocacy of church reunion and social reform, is remarkable not for its divergence from his previous ideals, but for the light that is shed on them by their negative development. Instead of Christ, we have the Antichrist. Instead of the spiritualization of matter, we have the fraudulent shimmering of the ideal on the surface of the real, superficially triumphant yet inwardly barren. Soloviev at this time no longer sought a synthesis between different systems of knowledge. He still accepted what he considered true or beautiful in the works of the artists and thinkers with whom his spiritual journey was inextricably connected, but now attempted to work his way into their thinking and creative process themselves, to uncover that which was either unsaid, misstated or falsified from the perspective of his ideal. Instead of picking up ideas from diverse sources and incorporating them within a patchwork quilt of new construction, he now wished to understand the reasons for the individual artist or thinker's fall from truth, their diminishment of themselves in their ideal.³⁷

---

[36] Stanislav Rotsinskii writes that the 'teaching of All-Unity can correctly be defined as monopluralism, the value of individual being [for Soloviev] is in essence equal to the significance of universal being.' S. B. Rotsinskii, *Vladimir Solov'ev i zapadnaia mysl': Kritika, Primirenie, Sintez*, Moscow, 1999, p. 76.

[37] Rashkovskii has described Soloviev in his last decade as distancing himself from the pretensions of 'universal synthesis,' developing instead a 'more heuristic approach'. E. B. Rashkovskii, *Smysli v istorii: Issledovaniia po istorii very, poznaniia, kul'tury*, Moscow, 2008, p. 189.

INTRODUCTION

Part of the fascination of this period is that it represents the fruit of a long period of reflection on his own personal vocation, and its correlation to the ideal found in his work. It is for this reason that the middle section of the present work looks not only at Soloviev's thought on prophecy as the ideal of human activity (the 'third power') in its configuration toward its goal — the spiritualization of matter — but begins by exploring his own relation to his prophetic vocation, his own individual attempt to live out his ideal. Two biographical sections, relating to the middle and late periods, are here integrated under the aegis of prophecy. To understand the relation between the prophetic thematic of the middle years and Soloviev's late philosophy of love and beauty: such is one of the central goals of the later parts of the work. To this end, the two biographical sections are bridged by a discussion of Soloviev, prophetic authenticity and the Antichrist, which seeks to prepare the ground for the unique constellation of self-doubt, the renewed emphasis on the imperative of discernment,[38] and the concentrated pathos that we find in the philosopher's last years, which are the focus of the final section of my work. After looking at how this concentration finds particular expression in Soloviev's understanding of love, I end this section on the 'last things' with a treatment of Soloviev's aesthetics in which, as Zen'kovskii has written, 'beats the pulse of the end of the history.'[39] By finishing with his eschatology, we end with both the realization of the task, and the height of its conflict with its mirror image. The resolution of the spiritualization of matter appears to us in the intensity of its battle with its counterfeit other.

Soloviev was a man with a remarkable breadth of knowledge and experience. By highlighting only those influences on him that relate to our theme, I do not mean to suggest that these are the only definitive ones, nor do I insist that they are the only way of approaching the

---

[38] 'Soloviev's entire interest,' writes Vladimir Bibikhin, 'was focused on the exposure of insincere thought.' V. V. Bibikhin, 'Dobro, istina i nesushchestvovanie u Vladimira Solov'eva,' in A. P. Ogurtsov (ed), *Blago i istina: klassicheskie i neklassicheskie reguliativy*, Moscow, 1998, pp. 71-95, p. 80.

[39] V. V. Zen'kovskii, 'Esteticheskie vozzreniia Vl. Solov'eva,' in *Russkie mysliteli i evropa*, Moscow, 1997, pp. 278-87 (p. 282).

spiritualization of matter in his work. Likewise, when I use the ideas of others dating to both before and after Soloviev's death, I often do so for the sake of contrast and comparison alone, and they should in no way be taken as proof of having had an influence on the philosopher, unless such is stated.

After a notable drop in the number of publications dedicated to Soloviev after the fruitful period of the early twentieth century,[40] interest in the philosopher began to grow significantly from the 1980s. In Russia, many of his works and articles were published in new editions, often with detailed commentary and analysis. Nikolai Kotrelev, whose meticulous scholarship has illuminated many aspects of Soloviev's legacy, deserves special mention here.[41] Aleksei Losev's major work on Soloviev, completed in 1983, is an important source of reflections and new directions.[42] As far as Soloviev's poetry is concerned, the studies of Zinaida Mints have a depth of analysis that is hard to equal.[43] Outside Russia, Jonathan Sutton's 'reassessment' of Soloviev's philosophy brings many of the dominant themes that have been overlooked or neglected by previous scholarship back into focus. Particularly significant is Sutton's consistent emphasis on Soloviev's critique of absolute dualism, which he proposes as one of the philosopher's central teachings.[44] Important

---

[40] Apart from the works of Trubetskoi, Strémooukhoff, and Mochul'skii, mention should also be made of the important work written by Soloviev's nephew Sergei, who was unique among his early interpreters in having access to a great amount of the unpublished material. The work was written in the 1920s, but only published in 1977. S. M. Solov'ev, *Zhizn' i tvorcheskaia evoliutsiia Vladimira Solov'eva*, Brussels, 1977. Sergii Bulgakov, himself an important theologian in his own right, added much that is valuable to the interpretation of Soloviev's legacy. See especially S. N. Bulgakov, 'Shto daet sovremennomu soznaniiu filosofiia Vl. Solov'eva,' in *Kniga o Vladimire Solov'eve*, ed. B. V. Averin, Moscow, 1991, pp. 389-447; S. N. Bulgakov, 'Priroda v filosofii Vl. Solov'eva,' in *Vl. Solov'ev: Pro et Contra*, ed. T. L. Samsonova, 2 vols, St Petersburg, 2002, II, pp. 618-43.

[41] Many of the volumes Kotrelev has edited, as well as his extensive commentaries, are used in this work.

[42] Aleksei Losev, *Vladimir Solov'ev i ego vremia*, Moscow, 2000.

[43] Z. Mints, 'Vladimir Solov'ev — poet,' in *Stikhotvoreniia i shutochnye p'esy*, Moscow, 1974, pp. 5-56; Z. Mints, 'K genezisu komicheskogo u Bloka (Vl. Solov'ev i A. Blok),' in *Aleksandr Blok i russkie pisateli*, St Petersburg, 2000, pp. 389-442.

[44] Sutton, *The Religious Philosophy of Vladimir Solovyov*, pp. 43-50.

work has also been done by Paul Valliere, who seeks to understand Soloviev's main ideas by fitting him within the broader philosophical and theological context, and Judith Kornblatt, who has illuminated many aspects of Soloviev's sophiology.[45] Of particular consequence for the development of this study has been the article on Soloviev's eschatology by philosopher William Desmond, which laid the ground for a more nuanced approach to Soloviev's later years.[46]

The only complete works of Soloviev were published soon after his death by Sergei Soloviev, the philosopher's nephew, and Ernst Radlov.[47] Radlov also edited a four-volume edition of Soloviev's letters, the last published in 1923; all four were reproduced in one volume in 1970, along with an appendix of other material.[48] Between 1966 and 1970 a facsimile reprint of the second edition of the complete works was published in Brussels.[49] This includes two volumes of additional material including the letters, now compressed into two volumes with additional notes. Despite the formidable achievement of Radlov and Sergei Soloviev, however, the philosopher's early, unpublished work made it into neither the first nor the second editions, and numerous inaccuracies detract from the text. Between 2000 and 2001, the first three volumes of a new, twenty-volume series were published. These volumes are thoroughly researched and annotated, and make available

---

[45] Paul Valliere, 'Sophiology as the Dialogue of Orthodoxy with Modern Civilization,' in *Russian Religious Thought*, ed. J.D. Kornblatt and R.F. Gustavson, Madison, WI, 1996, pp. 176-92; Valliere, *Modern Russian Theology*; P. Valliere, 'Vladimir Solov'ev (1853-1900): Commentary,' in *The Teachings of Modern Orthodox Christianity: On Law, Politics, & Human Nature*, ed. J. Witte Jr and F.S. Alexander, New York, 2007, pp. 33-68. Kornblatt, J.D., *Wisdom Writings*; 'Solov'ev's Androgynous Sophia and the Jewish Kabbalah,' *Slavic Review*, 50, 1991, 3, pp. 487-96.

[46] William Desmond, 'God Beyond the Whole: Between Solov'ev and Shestov,' in *Is There a Sabbath for Thought? Between Religion and Philosophy*, New York, 2005, pp. 167-99.

[47] V.S. Solov'ev, *Sobranie sochinenii Vladimira Sergeevicha Solov'eva*, ed. E.L. Radlov and S.M. Solov'ev, 9 vols, St Petersburg, 1901-07. Another volume was added to the second edition: *Sobranie sochinenii Vladimira Sergeevicha Solov'eva*, ed. E.L. Radlov and S.M. Solov'ev, 2nd edn, 10 vols, St Petersburg, 1911-14.

[48] V.S. Solov'ev, *Pis'ma*, ed. E.L. Radlov, 4 vols, St Petersburg, 1908-23; *Pis'ma i prilozhenie*, ed. E.L. Radlov, 4 vols, Brussels, 1970.

[49] V.S. Solov'ev, *Sobranie sochinenii Vladimira Sergeevicha Solov'eva*, ed. E.L. Radlov and S.M. Solov'ev, 12 vols, Brussels, 1966-70.

the early, unpublished writings. At the time of writing, however, only these three volumes had been published. From *Lectures on Theanthropy* (1878-81) onwards, therefore, the reader has to rely either on the older edition or on more recent, smaller collections of Soloviev's work. I have chosen to cite from a number of different publications, offering the reader where possible a version of the text that is fully annotated, and with the fullest available treatment of its historical context. A list of abbreviations of the publications used can be found after the title page. To avoid unnecessarily long diversions into technicalities, I have also included a glossary of Soloviev's key philosophical terms, with a discussion of issues around translation into English, as an appendix to the text.

Chapter I
THE FIRST THINGS

Very early on in the philosophical career of Vladimir Soloviev (1853-1900), the general tenor and shape of his system of *All-Unity* (*vseedinstvo*) were already forcefully outlined in a series of works remarkable for their formal diversity and audacious scope. Central to his project was the incorporation of matter, understood positively as the potential seat, or receptacle, of divinity, into his philosophical schema. The presence of the material world is felt not only in those spheres commonly associated with it, such as aesthetics and gnoseology, but across the board, representing a vital part of Soloviev's metaphysics, ethics, and soteriology. This chapter will explore Soloviev's thought on 'the first things,' dealing with the emergence of God, the material world, and humanity in turn.[1] In so doing, we will not only concentrate on the content of his teaching but also his method, whose logic (or lack thereof) can tell us just as much about the driving forces behind his philosophy as its expression in print.

---

[1] The category of 'emergence' does not necessarily relate to the historical order. The 'emergence' of God, for example, one of the more problematic aspects of Soloviev's early philosophy, should be understood in a logico-ontological sense. It is both the idea of God, as seen in the entirety of its logical development, and the positive disposition of God toward the possession of the fullness of her essential being. As we shall see in the section on cosmogony, however, Soloviev does tie his concept of God very closely to the temporality of the created world. Yet he does so in an attempt, as with emergence theorists, to conceptualize the simultaneous economy of both an immanent and transcendent divine activity. For comparisons to recent thought on this question, see P. Clayton, *Mind and Emergence: From Quantum to Consciousness*, Oxford, 2006. At one point, Clayton gives the following definition, which concurs with Soloviev's cosmogony in many areas: 'emergence is the theory that cosmic evolution repeatedly includes unpredictable, irreducible, and novel appearances' (p. 39).

Soloviev's God was emphatically 'not of the dead, but of the living';[2] indeed, so closely did the philosopher associate the absolute with determinate being that to some they appeared indistinguishable.[3] The material world as the home not just of the idea but of divinity itself is an integral part of Soloviev's philosophy, and the precise dynamics of the human being's interaction with this world a fundamental problem with which it engages. There is an almost instinctual drive that underlies his philosophy and poetry alike as they search for the expression of a truth that is not only rationally or metaphysically valid but materially palpable, a truth which finds its ultimate vindication through incarnation in the world.[4] It is this 'concern for concreteness'[5] that marks Soloviev out as an idealist thinker of peculiar calibre and draws him close to the materialists and positivists whom he took such pleasure in lampooning.[6]

Despite Soloviev's manifest desire to share his beliefs and ideas through his writings, whether by design or default he often fell far short of the mark. It is remarkable that, during his early period, in which the philosopher had visions of undeniable importance in the formation of

---

[2] Mark 12.27.

[3] The word *sushchee* in Soloviev is synonymous with the absolute yet it also means that which is, or being. See glossary for more on this complicated term in his thought.

[4] Many authors have supposed Soloviev to have advocated a form of pantheism, although the merits of such a label are questionable. See, for example, L. M. Lopatin, 'Filosofskoe mirovozzrenie V. S. Solov'eva,' in *Filosofskie kharakteristiki i rechi*, Minsk & Moscow, 2000, pp. 145-91 (p. 176); Zen'kovskii, 'Vladimir Solov'ev,' p. 43. Copleston mentions, without advocating, the term *panentheism*, according to which though God is not in all things (which would be pantheism) all things are 'in' God. See Frederick C. Copleston, 'V. S. Solov'ev,' in *Russian Religious Philosophy: Selected Aspects*, Notre Dame, IN, 1988, pp. 201-40 (p. 239). See also Clinton Gardner, 'Vladimir Solov'ev: From Theism to Panentheism,' in *Vladimir Solov'ëv: Reconciler and Polemicist: Selected Papers of the International Vladimir Solov'ëv Conference held at the University of Nijmegen, the Netherlands, in September 1998*, ed. Wil van den Bercken, Manon de Courten and Evert van der Zweerde, Leuven, 2000, pp. 119-29. Losev, perhaps, strikes the most appropriate tone with his term *materialistic idealism*, an oxymoron of which Soloviev would no doubt have approved. See Losev, *Vladimir Solov'ev i ego vremia*, p. 90.

[5] I owe this apposite phrase to Paul Valliere. See Valliere, *Modern Russian Theology*, p. 140.

[6] Soloviev's admiration for the father of positivism, Auguste Comte, although deriving from a complex of reasons, is a case in point. See his late essay 'The Idea of Humanity in Auguste Comte' (1898, S^2, II, pp. 562-81).

his worldview, his visitor—Sophia, or Divine Wisdom—appears not once in his published philosophical works. Soloviev's 'eternal friend' fits more comfortably into the symbols of his poetry. Even here, though, he does not address her by name, preferring instead epithets such as *tsaritsa* (queen), *milyi drug* (dear friend) and, most commonly, *ty* (thou).[7] And when, in 1898, he finally comes to write an account of his sophianic visions, he chooses not only the remove provided him by poetic form but the further disguise of humour. Aleksandr Nosov writes that:

> Soloviev loved to talk and write ironically about serious and important matters, a characteristic common amongst overly sensitive people who fear ridicule or even disregard for their treasured convictions. This explains the humorous tone of his poem 'Three Meetings,' which describes the most significant event of his life. It also explains the incessant irony of his overall epistolary style, his need to turn even the deepest of intimate convictions into a joke.[8]

The philosopher's sensitivity made him particularly reluctant to open himself to potential ridicule and acted as a counterweight to the intensity of his desire to lay bare the content of his vision. Yet there is another factor at work here too. Although almost all of his fundamental concepts are already clearly and forcefully stated in the culminating work of the early period, *Critique of Abstract Principles* (1880), Soloviev still seems to be holding back, to go only so far and no further.[9] Dimitri Strémooukhoff writes that, in his philosophical works, Soloviev seems to have 'consciously concealed his thoughts,' providing only veiled expressions of his ideas.[10] His may not be a policy of outright

---

[7] The last two lines of the poem 'Three Meetings' contain both resolve and apology: 'Подруга вечная, тебя не назову я, / И ты прости нетвердый мой напев!' (Eternal friend, I shall not name you, / And you forgive my unsteady song!). Solov'ev, "Nepodvizhno," p. 124. For further discussion of the language used to portray Sophia in Soloviev's poetry, see Samuel D. Cioran, *Vladimir Solov'ev and the Knighthood of the Divine Sophia*, Waterloo, Ontario, 1977, pp. 49-54; and Kornblatt, *Wisdom Writings*, pp. 101-08.
[8] Solov'ev, "Nepodvizhno," p. 4.
[9] In the appendix to *Critique*, Soloviev writes, 'To proceed with an explanation of the objective-creative character of mysticism would force us to touch on subjects of which I consider it *premature* to speak' (my emphases). See PSS, III, p. 339.
[10] Strémooukhoff, *Vladimir Solov'ev and His Messianic Work*, p. 11.

concealment, but there is, early on in his career, a sense in which he believes himself to be revealing only a certain part of his thought, to be consciously delaying the exposition of other areas until a suitable time.[11] Soloviev often informs his reader that a particular aspect of his thinking can only be explicated at some unspecified point in the future, most often without providing a reason for such a postponement. Not only does his philosophy rely heavily on historical argument,[12] its very articulation has a historical basis.

It is to be supposed that the fullness of Soloviev's vision was already, as it were, 'present' to him at an early age. The fact that he was aware of other areas of enquiry which he consciously left untouched is evidence of the same. But the mode of its expression, which drew on many sources, was refined over time. Whether Soloviev was waiting until he discovered an ideal form for the expression of his vision, or whether he saw himself involved in a process of gradual revelation, bringing his reader to a closer approximation of the truth with each new work, is a question we will consider in the course of this chapter.

THE EARLY PERIOD, 1873-81

In 1873, Soloviev left Moscow University to spend the academic year at the Moscow Theological Academy in Sergiev Posad. It was an odd decision that puzzled his friends and aroused the suspicion of the clerical staff at the Academy.[13] But it followed a pattern of rather sudden changes inaugurated by Soloviev's transfer from the university's Department of Natural Sciences, where he had enrolled in 1868, to the Department of History and Philology earlier that same year. Far from

---

[11] We note that the idea of 'free theurgy,' raised emphatically in the closing words of 'The Lived Meaning of Christianity' (1882), was omitted from the edit of the text for inclusion in *Spiritual Foundations of Life* (1882-84). 'Zhiznennyi smysl khristianstva,' in *Filosofskie nauki*, 1991, 3, pp. 63-64. See Chapter 1, note 15.

[12] This point is recognized by most commentators. See, for example, Sutton, *The Religious Philosophy of Vladimir Solovyov*, p. 182.

[13] In a letter to E. V. Romanova of late 1873, Soloviev writes that the professors of the Academy believed him 'to have come with the express intention of disturbing their peace with my critique.' See Solov'ev, "Nepodvizhno," p. 181.

the attraction of monasticism, as some of his acquaintances supposed, what really drew Soloviev to the Academy was an increasingly strong sense of mission, vivified by a reinvigorated Christian faith he had all but lost as a teenager.[14] In a letter to Ekaterina Romanova dated 2 August 1873, which reads like a manifesto for the philosopher's future activity, Soloviev defines the task which stood before him and humanity alike: 'to clothe the eternal content of Christianity in a new and suitable, i.e. absolutely rational, form.'[15] He was preparing himself, he writes, with such grandiloquence as to appear completely earnest, to study 'everything the human mind had produced in the last centuries.' This included reading the Greek and Latin theologians of the ancient church, for which purpose he needed the resources of the Academy.[16]

In March 1874, Soloviev returned to Moscow to work on his Master's dissertation, which he was to defend later that year, as well as to participate in discussions over the future of his career at the University. His mentor, the philosopher Pamfil Iurkevich, wanted to formalize a post for his young protégé prior to the defence of his Master's dissertation so that he could leave on a study trip abroad as

---

[14] Soloviev's childhood friend, Lev Lopatin, wrote of the philosopher in his early youth that he 'was never again to meet such a passionately convinced materialist.' See Lopatin, 'Filosofskoe mirovozzrenie V. S. Solov'eva,' p. 149. In the words of Soloviev himself: '[from the age of thirteen] in four years I experienced one after the other all the phases of the negative development of European thought over the past four centuries. Passing from iconoclasm and doubt about the necessity of external religious practice, I advanced toward rationalism and disbelief in miracles and the divinity of Christ. I became a deist, then a pantheist, then an atheist and a materialist.' At one stage, he writes, 'I surrendered myself to practical iconoclasm and threw out of the window onto a rubbish heap several icons that were in my room.' Cited in S. M. Solov'ev, *Zhizn' i tvorcheskaia evoliutsiia*, p. 37.

[15] This letter is crucial to an understanding of Soloviev's project at the stage of its conception. See Solov'ev, "Nepodvizhno," pp. 173-75.

[16] Ibid., pp. 174, 182. Although it appears as though Soloviev took little from the lectures he attended at the Academy, Pavel Florenskii believed that it was here that the philosopher first encountered the idea of Sophia in discussions with the followers of noted theologian Fedor Golubinskii (1797-1854), whose own teaching on Sophia had been influenced by his reading of Boehme and Swedenborg. See S. M. Solov'ev, *Zhizn' i tvorcheskaia evoliutsiia*, p. 90; I. V. Tsvyk, 'Vladimir Solov'ev i dukhovno-akademicheskaia filosofiia XIX v.,' *Vestnik Moskovskogo universiteta*, 3, 2003, pp. 3-21.

soon as possible, but this was rejected by the university authorities.[17] As a consequence, Soloviev ended up defending his dissertation, published under the title *Crisis of Western Philosophy: Against the Positivists*,[18] in November 1874, and took up the position of senior lecturer in the Department of Philosophy in December, replacing Iurkevich after his death that same month.

Crisis of Western Philosophy proceeds from the contention that Western philosophy, as 'abstract, exclusively theoretical cognition, has completed its development and passed irrevocably into the world of the past.'[19] Despite this negative assessment, however, Soloviev finds the seeds of potential renewal in thinkers such as Schopenhauer and von Hartmann, whose work for him represents the first approximations of a new, integrated philosophy of life directed by the human will.[20] The 'Panlogism'[21] of Hegel is subjected to the fiercest criticism but, behind all the rhetoric, the form adopted by Soloviev owes much to the Western tradition, and betrays considerable reliance on the Hegelian dialectic. Having read the work and attended the concomitant disputes, the critic Nikolai Strakhov wrote to Leo Tolstoy, not without relish, that Soloviev 'clearly refutes Hegel, while secretly following him.'[22]

In June 1875, Soloviev left Russia for London. The purpose of the trip was to 'study texts of Indian, gnostic and mediaeval philosophy' in the British Museum, for which purpose he received a stipend from

---

[17] PSS, III, p. 265.
[18] Ibid., I, pp. 37-152. This version includes the appendix, 'The Theory of Auguste Comte on the Three Phases in the Intellectual Development of Humanity.' The extensive notes to the work are found on pp. 264-329.
[19] Ibid., p. 39.
[20] Ibid., p. 113.
[21] Never used by Hegel himself and introduced into philosophical discourse by J. E. Erdmann in 1853 (in the third volume of his work *Versuch Einer Wissenschaftlichen Darstellung der Geschichte der Neuern Philosophie*), the term *panlogism* had by the late nineteenth century in Russia passed into regular usage as a descriptor, customarily negative, for the Hegelian system. Soloviev defines it as the idea that 'our rational thought creates from its very self, i.e. from itself as form, the entirety of its content.' William Desmond describes panlogism more as a philosophical approach, which sees 'the whole as the concretion of the logical idea as absolutely self-mediating thought.' W. Desmond, *Philosophy and its Others: Ways of Being and Mind*, New York, 1990, p. 220.
[22] PSS, III, p. 286.

Moscow University.²³ The period of study was fixed by the University at one year and three months. But Soloviev stayed in London less than three months before another enigmatic departure, this time to Cairo. In 'Three Meetings' (1898), he portrays his time in London as 'blessed days' during which, alone in the reading room, he read only those books 'about her' (i.e. Sophia) chosen for him by 'mysterious powers.'²⁴ It is not known exactly what Soloviev read during this time and, were it not for the account of a Russian acquaintance he made in London, Ivan Ianzhul, we would have next to nothing to go on.²⁵ It can be assumed that Soloviev carried through his intention of looking at general studies on Gnosis written before the discovery of Hippolytus, which present accounts of the various gnostic systems 'from a different and more philosophical perspective than is the case in Iranaeus or Epiphanius.'²⁶ But Ianzhul tells us more. According to him, he would often find Soloviev absorbed in a certain, strangely illustrated Kabbalistic book. The philosopher's face would reflect an internal struggle and when Ianzhul asked him why he spent so long reading the same book, Soloviev replied, 'It is very interesting; in every line of this book there is more life than in all of European scholarship.'²⁷ Strémooukhoff argues convincingly that this book was *Kabbala Denudata*, or *The Kabbala Unveiled*, written in 1677-84.²⁸ It consists of three books of the Zohar, the principal text of the Kabbala dating to the late thirteenth century, accompanied by glosses written by Knorr of Rosenroth inserted in square brackets between the lines of the original text. It is an immensely opaque work based on the esoteric interpretation of Jewish scripture through the numerical value of the

---

23   Ibid., p. 316.
24   Solov'ev, "Nepodvizhno," p. 120.
25   I. I. Ianzhul, 'Vospominaniia o perezhitom,' *Russkaia starina*, 3, 1910, pp. 477-500.
26   PSS, III, pp. 315-16.
27   Ianzhul, 'Vospominaniia o perezhitom,' pp. 481-82.
28   Christian Knorr von Rosenroth, *Kabbala Denudata*, ed. Samuel Liddell MacGregor Mathers, London, 1887. Originally published in Latin, the book was a good source on Kabbalistic knowledge, particularly as filtered through a Christian lens, for those without knowledge of Hebrew. It is cited by Soloviev in the 1880s as the main source of his knowledge of the Kabbala. Strémooukhoff, *Vladimir Solov'ev and His Messianic Work*, pp. 49, 343.

original Hebrew letters.²⁹ Soloviev will have been attracted not only by the philosophy of the Zohar, as will be discussed in due course, but also by the form in which he found it in *Kabbala Denudata*, which follows thinkers such as Pico della Mirandola in reinterpreting Neoplatonic and, in this case, Jewish thought along broadly Christian lines. The syncretic project implied in such a task would have made an immediate impression on Soloviev.

Paul Allen cites several other sources that Soloviev may have looked at during his time in the British Museum. These include the alchemical treatises of Solomon Trismogin³⁰ as well as works on American Shakerism.³¹ Whatever he actually read, it can be supposed that Soloviev was deeply immersed in works of a principally esoteric character, in which he found many resonances with the movement of his own thought.

In October 1875, Soloviev abandoned his studies at the British Museum and travelled to Cairo. The reasons for his sudden departure may not have been clear even to the philosopher himself. In the first dialogue of *La Sophia*, he writes: 'a confused dream led me to the banks of the Nile. Here, in the cradle of history, I wanted to find a thread that, through the ruins and graves of the past, would link the primordial life of mankind with its new life, which I anticipate.'³² How much surer is the summons given in 'Three Meetings,' written years after the fact, when the philosopher describes how, in that same reading room of the British Museum, Sophia had appeared to him for the first time since childhood: '«В Египте будь!» — внутри раздался голос.'³³

---

29 As in Greek, each letter in Hebrew is also a number. For an accessible account of the numerical methods employed in the Zohar, see Gershom Scholem, *Kabbalah*, Jerusalem, 1974.

30 Solomon Trismogin, *Splendor Solis: Alchemial Treatises of Solomon Trismogin*, London, 1920.

31 See especially Frederick Evans, *Autobiography of a Shaker, and Revelation of the Apocalypse with an Appendix*, New York, 1889. Ianzhul tells us that, in 1875, Soloviev subscribed a future only to religious communities in America such as the Shakers. See Ianzhul, 'Vospominaniia o perezhitom,' p. 479. Allen argues that Shakerism exerted a considerable influence on Soloviev. See Allen, *Vladimir Soloviev*, pp. 100-10.

32 PSS, III, p. 75.

33 '"Go to Egypt!" a voice resounded inside.' Solov'ev, "Nepodvizhno," p. 121.

The immediate fruit of his time in Egypt, apart from the enduring memory of his vision in the desert, became four fragments, written in 1876 — two monologues (*La Sophia*) and two dialogues (*Sophie*) — of a work Soloviev intended to become the basis of a new, 'universal religion' and the foundation of his future system.[34] The dialogues present a discussion between Sophia and *Philosophe* which at times reaches an intimacy and intensity utterly unknown in Soloviev's other philosophical works of the period. The style of both works is informal, their method untraditional, and their content wide-ranging. Soloviev employs a huge array of terminology taken from sources as diverse as gnosticism, mediaeval theology and German Idealism. The fragments, taken together, represent an audacious attempt to demonstrate the commensurability of the central terms and tenets of fundamentally different schools of thought.

Soloviev returned to Moscow in June 1876 to take up a lectureship at the University, a position he held for a little over six months before moving to St Petersburg. In a letter of late 1876 to his friend Dmitrii Tsertelev, the philosopher writes that he had decided 'to publish for the doctoral dissertation only the first, purely philosophical part of the system, the positive dialectics, expanding it accordingly.'[35] Up

---

[34] In a letter to his mother of March 1876, he describes the work as 'mystical-theosophical-philosophical-theurgic-political in content and dialogical in form.' See Solov'ev, *Pis'ma*, II, p. 23. To his father, he is more restrained, calling it 'a composition of small size but great significance, *Principes de la religion universelle*.' Ibid., p. 27. In reaction, perhaps, to his father's advice against publication, Soloviev writes in his next letter: 'it is essential that I publish it since it will be the foundation of all my future work and I cannot do anything without referring to it.' Ibid., p. 28. Following normal usage, *La Sophia* is hereafter used to refer to all fragments taken together while the context should make clear whether the monologues or dialogues are under consideration. In their textological analysis of these fragments, published an entire century after their composition, A. P. Kozyrev and N. V. Kotrelev maintain that the two monologues were written first. They also argue, convincingly, that these fragments can be considered together as one work and the dialogues, although intended as a development and refinement of ideas in the monologues, as another. This is further corroborated by the fact that Soloviev gave both monologues the title *La Sophia* whereas the dialogues bear the title *Sophie*. This latter, being the name of a concrete being as opposed to an impersonal force, 'underlines the personal, living, and mystical character of this principle.' PSS, III, pp. 320-27. Since both 'works' are unfinished, the attachment of one fragment to another does not construct a fully coherent text in either case.

[35] Solov'ev, *Pis'ma*, II, p. 240.

to this point, Soloviev had still been intending to submit a reworked and expanded version of *La Sophia* for his doctorate.³⁶ The importance of his decision to go forward with 'pure philosophy' should not be understated. In effect, he was excising a crucial component of his 'universal teaching,' at least until a more suitable time, and marketing the respectable philosopher over the ecstatic visionary.³⁷ For Soloviev, 'pure philosophy' did not necessarily mean restricting himself to a critical philosophy which stopped at the supposed limits of the knowable, but a grounding of the known—whether through mystical, logical, or empirical knowledge—in that most human of principles, reason. In accordance with this repositioning, we find that speculation on the existence of sundry metaphysical entities is arrested after *La Sophia* and replaced, in *Philosphical Principles of Integral Knowledge* and, yet more so, in *Critique of Abstract Principles*, with a metaphysics that searches for its basis in rational principles already present, to some degree, in human consciousness.

Philosphical Principles was serialized in *Zhurnal ministerstva narodnogo prosveshcheniia* in 1877. It is the first published statement of Soloviev's system and carries through much of the material from *La Sophia* in sanitized form. Far from giving up his aspiration to accommodate the fullness of his experience within the bounds of philosophy, Soloviev now began to dedicate himself more and more to the study of mystical writings.³⁸ In a letter of April 1877 to Countess S. A. Tolstaia, he writes:

> In the mystics are many confirmations of my own ideas, but no new light. Moreover, almost all of them are incredibly subjective by nature [...] As a result, only Paracelsus, Boehme and Swedenborg are real people, which leaves me with a rather open ballpark.³⁹

---

36 See Ibid., p. 233.
37 As seen from a draft structure of his 'Principles of the Universal Teaching,' 'Philosophical Principles' would have formed only the first part of his future work. The second and third parts were entitled 'Dogmas' and 'Morality' respectively. PSS, II, p. 175.
38 In a letter to Tsertelev of April 1877, he writes: 'I am living extremely humbly and solitarily; I read mystics in the library, write my dissertation, and see almost no one.' Solov'ev, *Pis'ma*, II, p. 236.
39 Ibid., p. 200.

In November 1877 the publication of *Philosphical Principles* was halted[40] and a new work, *Critique of Abstract Principles*, began to be published in the journal *Russkii vestnik*. So ended a period of remarkable creative energy and considerable vacillation, in which Soloviev's original syncretic idea, captured in the colourful and undisciplined prose of *La Sophia*, had been replaced by a broadly theoretical exposition of his system, in which his former ideas were contained as the unsaid content of a radically different form. In *Critique*, Soloviev had finally found a suitable work for his doctoral dissertation, which he defended on 6 April 1880.

THE MATERIAL WORLD

> For me, the conscious conviction that the present condition of humanity is *not as it should be* means *it should be changed*, transformed. I do not recognize the existing evil as eternal; I do not believe in the devil. In acknowledging the necessity of transformation, I commit my whole life and all my energies to actualizing that transformation. But the most important question is: where are the means?
>
> Letter to E. K. Romanova, 2 August 1873.[41]

From the conception of Soloviev's project in the heady days of his youth to his last years of frailty and uncertainty, the philosopher was quite literally fixated on the imperfection of the world as it stood and dedicated to its transformation. For him, the gap between *that which is* and *that which should be* did not indicate the presence, whether in human consciousness or a world of ideal-material duality, of two irreconcilably separate spheres of being, one of which must necessarily be extinguished to facilitate the coming-to-be of the other, but a moral imperative to act toward the sowing of the ideal in the real. He firmly believed in the perfectability of the created order, and of humanity

---

40   *Philosophical Principles of Integral Knowledge* remained unfinished.
41   Solov'ev, "Nepodvizhno," p. 173.

as both an individual and a collective organism—the church or Body of Christ.⁴² The nature of this perfection, its contours and character, did not fundamentally change for the duration of Soloviev's life. But the means of its realization underwent considerable alteration, often in unexpected directions. 'I know,' wrote Soloviev in 1873, 'that any transformation occurs from within, from the human heart and mind. People are led by their *convictions*, therefore one must act on their convictions; one must convince people of the truth.'⁴³

Soloviev's early philosophy was, however esoteric its provenance, an attempt to lead his reader to a recognition of the truth. This may be said of any system of philosophy. What marks out the Russian philosopher from, say, Kant or Hegel, is that the *knowledge* of truth attained by the human mind is insufficient to realize his goal, namely, the transformation of our lived reality. In itself, 'pure' thinking, however much informed by the ingenuities of the dialectic or other intellectual models, cannot lead to fundamental changes in human consciousness or the created order.⁴⁴ Through 'pure philosophy,' Soloviev was instead looking for a philosophical justification of an essentially non-philosophical activity, a form of being and acting in the world led by the heart and will rather than a thinking directed by the mind. In a reply to a journal review of *Critique* he writes:

> Whatever my prospects and tasks in the future, the published work has the most modest pretensions. It is a critical work of a preparatory nature, a sort of clearing of the intellectual ground for the foundations of a spiritual building of the future. To speak without metaphor, I wanted, starting from the principles present to consciousness, to bring the mind of the reader to the *limits* of that synthetic and all-embracing perspective which, in my opinion, comprises the truth and the salvation.⁴⁵

---

⁴² See Sutton, *The Religious Philosophy of Vladimir Solovyov*, pp. 51-54.
⁴³ From letter to E. K. Romanova, 2 August 1873. See Solov'ev, "Nepodvizhno," p. 174.
⁴⁴ Soloviev was familiar with Schelling's critique of Hegel from a similar perspective. See A. Bowie, *Schelling and Modern European Philosophy: an Introduction*, London and New York, 1993, p. 167. For Soloviev's early thoughts on Schelling, see PSS, I, pp. 63-64.
⁴⁵ PSS, III, p. 455.

Soloviev understands that his current project only has meaning insofar as it points beyond itself to a more complete perspective, a perspective which 'comprises the truth and the salvation.' Its contours can be mapped out by 'pure philosophy' but its actualization lies outside its remit. Yet the fact that his philosophy seeks to surpass itself in activity does not mean for Soloviev that it is somehow of less value than the activity it seeks to promote.[46] One of the unrealized projects of the period immediately after *Critique* was Soloviev's attempt to create a philosophy of science, which became the basis of a series of lectures the philosopher delivered to the Higher Women's Courses in St Petersburg in 1882.[47] In these lectures, and his written plans, he formulates a concept of 'science' as a synthesis of all human modes of knowledge that goes well beyond the narrow usage of the term in contemporary usage. 'The highest thing one can demand from science (*nauka*), its highest task,' he writes, 'is to explain to us what is, to show us what should be, and to teach us what we should do.'[48] Science, from this perspective, becomes the means not for the objective, dispassionate investigation of law-governed phenomena, but a way of knowing, whose purpose is to 'counteract [the] evil and meaninglessness [of the phenomenal world]; its service to meaning should be an *active* service. In the face of a lifeless nature and suffering humanity, the whole of science turns into a single, universal medicine.'[49]

---

[46] It is surely a mistake, therefore, to regard the apparently hierarchical tables found in *Philosophical Principles* as carrying value-judgments as to their contents. True, Soloviev does describe *mistika* (mystical experience) as the 'highest' art form, yet just as his core tripartite distinction between good, truth and beauty exists only as a unity, mirroring the trinitarian logic of the work as a whole, so the various forms of art and knowledge operate synthetically rather than dialectically. The picture is complicated by Soloviev's argument that different modes enjoy predominance in different historical epochs yet it should be remembered that history too, in Soloviev's conception, moves according to a similar triune logic far removed from the Hegelian dialectic.

[47] Fragments of these lectures under the heading 'Ob istinnoi nauke' are published in A. P. Kozyrev, '"Naukouchenie" Vladimir Solov'eva: k istorii neudavshegosia zamysla 1880-x godov,' in *Solov'ev i gnostiki*, Moscow, 2007, pp. 219-67 (pp. 239-67).

[48] Ibid., p. 222.

[49] Ibid., p. 245. It is not difficult to intuit the presence of Nikolai Fedorov in this passage, whose influence on Soloviev at this period was extremely significant. See pp. 91-92.

Soloviev defined the word 'scientific' as 'the opposite of unmediated (*neposredstvennyi*),'[50] a comment that strikes the reader as puzzling at first. But what perhaps he meant was this: true 'science' is always a response, filtered through the mind, to the direct experience of incommensurability between the real and the ideal, whereby such experience is mediated through the ingenuity of human intention. In arriving at conscious articulation, 'science' transforms the data of subjective experience (experiential, spiritual, or otherwise) into a mediated body of knowledge which acts on others through force of conviction. Despite the typically Solovievian pretensions of such a universal science, however, its construction could have meaning only in so far as it led humanity to the realization of its ideal task.

That beyond 'the limits of that synthetic and all-embracing perspective' lies a 'task,' and that a full and complete awareness of theoretical truth — the goal of the early period — draws in its wake the necessity of practical activity along broadly defined lines, is clear from Soloviev's *Critique*. Here he defines the goal of the historical process as 'the realization, or complete incarnation, of the divine principle, i.e. the joint spiritualization of matter and the materialization of the spirit, or the inner harmony and balance of both principles.'[51] In this process, the task of humanity is understood as the realization of 'his divine idea, i.e. All-Unity, or the absolute fullness of being, through the freedom of reason, in material nature,' which corresponds to the first part of the posited goal of history, namely 'the spiritualization of matter.' The human being is thus the mediator between the absolute realm of the spirit and the world of material form, sowing, or revealing, the former in the latter through the medium of reason.

It should be pointed out that some elements of Soloviev's thought on humanity and the material world undergo substantive changes in his early period, particularly those regarding the final determination of his teleology and the role allotted humanity within it. The focus on the conscious activity of humanity in *Critique* represents the most fundamental break with the earlier work. In *La Sophia*, Soloviev had

---

50 Ibid., p. 260.
51 Ibid., p. 162.

talked of the 'aim of the cosmic process,'[52] in which the human being remains a passive organ answering to a concrete part of the divine plan. The goal of this process is seen as 'the materialization of the divinity,' and posits the agent of action exclusively in the Godhead. In *Critique*, to the contrary, the human being appears as a conscious and active agent endowed with a concrete task, 'the spiritualization of matter,' which now appears beside 'the materialization of spirit' as its necessary correlative. This development goes hand in hand with a rethinking of the fate of matter in the soteriological process: whereas in *La Sophia* the end point of history would witness the destruction of matter and the recommunion of humanity with the spiritual realm, in *Critique* both humanity *and* matter become associated in a common movement toward transcendence and salvation. Despite its name, therefore, as well as Soloviev's protestations to the contrary, *Critique* marks the start of Soloviev's positive philosophy.[53]

This important development aside, however, Soloviev's metaphysics and gnoseology, the fields most extensively developed during this period, exhibit very little change, and by far the greater part of his ideas on humanity and the material world retain an unmistakeable unity of vision and purpose. The centrality of these questions in his philosophy is aptly demonstrated by the philosopher's continual attempts, through logic and speculation, to dispel the myth of the absolute incommensurability of spirit and matter which had been the starting point for much idealist and religious philosophy after Plato. For Soloviev, matter did not represent the mutability of lifeless agency but the final manifestation of the absolute, through which and in which the divine could be perceived and known.

---

[52] PSS, III, p. 135.
[53] Sergei Soloviev describes the philosopher as having had a 'negative attitude to factual reality' throughout the 1870s. 'At that time,' he writes, 'he considered the task of philosophy and theurgy to be the dematerialization of the material world, the restoration of the realm of pure spirits.' By contrast, according to the author, in the mid-1880s the 'goal of humanity' becomes 'the spiritualization of its corporeality and the triumph over death and decay.' S. M. Solov'ev, *Zhizn' i tvorcheskaia evoliutsiia*, pp. 85, 31. While agreeing with Soloviev's broad characterization of this development, its origin should rather be sought between the writing of *La Sophia* and *Critique*, i.e. between 1876 and 1878.

To lead the mind of the reader to such a conclusion, Soloviev employs various arguments. Importantly, he never resorts to a statement of the sufficiency of mystical intuition alone in grounding the possibility or actuality of divine immanence in the created order. 'The synthesis of the mystical and natural elements through the medium of reason needed by true knowledge,' he writes, 'is not a *given of consciousness*, but *a task for the mind*, for whose completion consciousness offers only fragmentary and partially enigmatic data.'[54]

The early Soloviev engages this task on several fronts. On the ontological plane, he attempts to resolve the question of what matter actually is, its nature and laws, and what there might be besides it. On the metaphysical plane, he argues for the absolute principle's reliance on matter for its own realization, or concrete manifestation. In his anthropology, he sketches a portrait of the human being as the mediator between the spiritual and material realms, and of Christ the God-man as the bringer to perfection of such mediation in his Incarnation and Resurrection. In all these spheres, the common feature is Soloviev's attempt to discover the locus of mediation between spirit and matter, and from there to work out its precise character and meaning for the created world.

I. THE MONAD

One of the most unusual constants in Soloviev's early work is his writing on the concept of the *monad*, introduced into philosophical discourse by Leibniz. The subject appears with much the same content, though radically different expression, in every major work of the period. In *Crisis of Western Philosophy*, Leibniz' teaching on the monad, replete with extensive quotes, is reproduced in Soloviev's rapid survey of the achievements and failures of the Western canon of thought. In *Critique*, Leibniz' name is not mentioned. Instead, Soloviev puts the concept of the monad to different use, seeing in it the logical conclusion of the atomic theories of contemporary science. Both works, however, arrive at

---

[54] PSS, III, pp. 309-10.

an association of the monad with the atom, and thus make an attempt to appropriate the terminology of the natural sciences.

Soloviev's use of contemporary scientific thought may in part be understood as an important component in his syncretic project of combining what he believed to be mutually exclusive spheres of knowledge and discourses in an integral whole. Such ideas could engage thinkers such as the positivists — for Soloviev the principal representatives of the 'crisis' in Western philosophy — on their own ground and, he hoped, serve as a crushing rebuke. But this was not merely a matter of demonstrating the vulnerability of all aspects of being, even the most basic, to the incursions of the philosophy of All-Unity. Philosophy for Soloviev was not a performance, however virtuosic, and his philosophical discourse not an end in itself but a process leading to genuine results with a concrete application. Beyond the ritual throwing-down of the gauntlet to incredulous positivism, he hoped to find some form of ontological proof for the presence of a spiritual element at the core of objective, material being. Through an exploration of what at that time was considered the most basic element of the physical world — the atom — he was attempting to find a 'scientific' basis for his intuition of divine immanence.[55] If he could demonstrate the simultaneous presence of both a spiritual and material element in the atom itself, he could convince his readership of the bridge between spirit and matter at the heart of reality. The material world, constituted of a multitude of atoms, could then be presented as a genuine spiritual-corporeal organism, and the necessity of including both moments, the spiritual *and* the material, in assessing the truth of any given phenomenon could be recognized.[56]

A large part of the story of Western philosophy, as portrayed by Soloviev in *Crisis*, is the story of the overcoming of the duality between

---

[55] Developments in the field of atomic science in the twentieth century may be seen to have undermined many of Soloviev's arguments. By 'atom,' however, Soloviev merely meant the most basic component of the physical world, that which is not itself made up of any other component parts.

[56] That Soloviev understood the world as an *organism* is already implied in his use of the concept *World Soul*, which attributes to the material body of the Earth the motivational and volitional activity — whether embodied in the will-to-life of single-cell organisms or the reflective capabilities of humanity — of a concrete person.

idea and matter, a duality entrenched by Descartes' rigid separation of *res extensa* and *res cogitans*.⁵⁷ It is in Spinoza that Soloviev finds the first steps toward reconciling the extremes of the Cartesian worldview and positing the mutual dependence of subject on object, body on soul. 'The soul (*dusha*) for Spinoza is merely the idea of the body, or the body in its ideal activity, just as the body is the soul as object, as formed idea. Thus there is no soul without body, but also no body without soul — all of corporeal nature, all individual things are animate.'⁵⁸ Having asserted the substantial identity of the soul and body, however, in Soloviev's view Spinoza fails to provide any real link between the two. Since the essence of corporeality consists, for Spinoza as much as for Descartes, exclusively in spatial extension, the unity of body and spirit remains wholly abstract, without any basis in reality. We are left with the immediate sense of our body and the object world but a purely notional appreciation of the soul. For between objects located in a particular portion of space and the non-spatial 'soul,' or essence, with which they are allegedly conjoined, there is as yet no vital link, no *real* principle whereby the non-corporeal posits itself as, or transforms itself into, a corporeal body.⁵⁹ Soloviev's 'concern for concreteness' is again presented in sharp relief. Spinoza's one substance remains for him wholly abstract since it provides no evidence to vouchsafe the consubstantiality of its two aspects.

Why was this link so important to Soloviev? Spinoza, after all, was just as convinced as he of the dual but non-duplicitous nature of God, or absolute reality, as *natura naturans* and *natura naturata*, two aspects of a single substance. But, unlike Soloviev, he insisted that there was absolutely no crossover between the two, and maintained a rigid separation between the realms of body and soul, co-existent but entirely divergent. Soloviev, on the contrary, was not only searching for an empirical proof of the indwelling of the soul in the body, the immanence of spirit in matter, but for a way of expressing that real

---

[57] See R. Descartes, *The Philosophical Writings of Descartes*, 3 vols, Cambridge, 1984-91, II, pp. 50-62.
[58] Ibid., p. 48.
[59] Ibid., p. 49.

interaction between them which he had allegedly experienced in his visions. The search for a way of conceiving how such radically different spheres could not only find a notional unity in a monistic metaphysics, as in Spinoza, but unite in their very interaction is in many ways the principal driving force of the philosophy of All-Unity. Soloviev's thought was always moving toward the discovery of a middle term that could link previously irreconcilable spheres. No aspect of being, physical or metaphysical, should be cut off from any other, but all should exist in reciprocity and relation.[60]

Where Spinoza fails for Soloviev, Leibniz's teaching on the monad picks up the pieces.[61] The shift in the understanding of corporeal substance effected by Leibniz was of vital importance to the early Soloviev, and is reflected in his choice of citations. 'The fundamental mistake of Descartes, according to Leibniz,' he writes, 'is the senseless identification of extension with corporeal substance resulting from his failure to understand the nature of substance (*substantsiia*) in general.'[62] The idea of *active force*, which Leibniz posited at the heart of his concept of substance, transformed the understanding of matter as something purely passive and began to unravel the myth of extended matter as object only and not subject. This idea, quotes Soloviev from Leibniz,

> differs from the pure potential of scholasticism in that this latter is only the imminent possibility of action, requiring an external stimulus to transition into action, while active force includes some sort of act, or entelechy, occupying the middle ground between the ability to act and the action itself [...] I claim that this active quality belongs to any

---

60 As a synonym for 'All-Unity,' Soloviev uses the term 'free communality' (*svobodnaia obshchinnost'*), which underlines the moment of reciprocity and relation. See PSS, III, p. 13.
61 According to Stuart Hampshire, the 'concepts of substance, individuality, causality, divine creation, soul, matter, activity, are all allotted different senses in Leibniz and in Spinoza.' See Stuart Hampshire, *Spinoza and Spinzoism*, Oxford, 2005, p. ix. That Soloviev should 'complete' Spinoza's intuition of the consubstantiality of body and soul with Leibniz's monadology is typical of his proclivity to measure markedly different bodies of thought by the same yardstick. By stressing certain ideas over others, even to the exclusion of some, he manages to paint a picture of uniform progression where to most there would appear only reaction and counter-reaction.
62 PSS, I, p. 49.

substance, that from here there always proceeds a certain action, and that, consequently, corporeal substance itself, just like spiritual substance, never stops acting.[63]

Soloviev's belief that the world represented a living organism pushed him toward a philosophy which at the very least would recognize matter's basic requirement to life. For him, the ramifications of Spinoza's insistence on the absolute non-coincidence of spirit and matter were a denial of the life he saw operating 'beneath the mask of impassionate matter.'[64] His organic vision of nature brought with it the recognition of a subjective side to the material world. In Leibniz' concept of the monad he wished to see the fundamental movers of nature, independent forces possessed of the subjective ability to will and represent.[65] It was this recognition of individual, subjective being at the heart of the objective world that allowed Soloviev to break down the stark divide separating subject and object, body and soul. In matter, following Leibniz' theory, there now moved a multiplicity of life-forces guided by an entelechy that could not be reduced to the mechanical laws of cause and effect. 'All that exists,' wrote Soloviev, 'is not only animate but also made up of souls.' The 'substance of the corporeal body is thus acknowledged as the non-corporeal monad,' the body's guiding principle or 'soul.' But what sort of being did these independent subjects, or monads, lay claim to? How did their activity manifest itself and what was the nature of their interaction with extended matter? In *Crisis*, Soloviev associates these monadic 'souls' with *atoms*, a line of enquiry more extensively developed in the chapter on 'Atomism' of his *Critique*.

The property common to all material things, Soloviev argues in *Critique*, again expanding on arguments he found in Leibniz, is impenetrability. Impenetrability is nothing but 'the disclosure of being-

---

[63] Ibid., pp. 49-50.
[64] 'И под личиной вещества бесстрастной/ Везде огонь божественный горит.' From 'Khot' my navek nezrimymi tsepiami' (1875). Solov'ev, "*Nepodvizhno*," p. 22.
[65] The word 'will' is used here with a caveat. In *Crisis*, Soloviev attributes to monads not *will* (*volia*) or *wanting* (*khotenie*), but desire, or striving (*stremlenie*). The word *stremlenie* is used by the philosopher to indicate movement which is not conscious but nevertheless goal-oriented. The prevalence of the term in Soloviev's philosophy owes much to Schelling and mystics such as Jacob Boehme.

in-itself,' meaning that each thing has its own existence and cannot be replaced or effaced by any other thing. It resists the action of that which is other to it. Impenetrability thus presupposes the existence of subject and object, or of two things which find themselves in relation to one another. Since, according to the principles of atomism, the material world is made up of a multiplicity of elementary things, or atoms, these latter must find themselves in a certain interrelationship with one another, each one experiencing the impenetrability of the others. But, since impenetrability as a property is only manifested in the resistance of an atom to another's activity, this latter activity must itself be posited as impenetrability's logical precondition. In other words, impenetrability, the sine qua non of matter, is only the result of a prior movement at the level of atomic life. Thus, each atom must direct itself toward the other; in Soloviev's words, it 'desires to fill the other's place.'

At this stage in the argument it seems a foreign element has entered the philosopher's discourse. While the reader may follow Soloviev's logic when it demands that each atom must direct itself toward each other as the precondition of impenetrability, this self-directing manifesting itself in the force of attraction, it in no way governs the inner *motivation* for this movement. Not only does Soloviev posit a conscious will as the basis for the activity of each atom, but he also defines this will as essentially egoistic — a will to conquer and destroy. This assumption is neither explained nor acknowledged.[66] Furthermore, having followed Leibniz in associating monads with *individual* forces, Soloviev departs significantly from the latter in one, essential respect: he wholly rejects, again without acknowledging the fact, Leibniz' denial of the possibility

---

66 In his equation of the monad with egoistic force, Soloviev departs not only from Leibniz put from his teacher Pamfil Iurkevich, in whom his appreciation of the former doubtless has its source. In his work 'Idea' of 1859, Iurkevich accepts the Leibnizian hypothesis of pre-established harmony. 'The individual activity of the monad,' he writes, 'is also an expression of the world's purposeful activity. The reconciliation of the general and the particular does not require the destruction of the individuality and particularity of separate creatures. Everything in the world partakes of the feeling [...] of independent life, yet this feeling is not *egoistic*, contrary to the common good of the world. Precisely here, in this feeling of individuality, lies the foundation for acting toward the common good.' P. D. Iurkevich, 'Ideia,' in *Filosofskie proizvedeniia*, ed. A. I. Abramov and I. V. Borisova, Moscow, 1990, pp. 9-68 (p. 44).

of intersubstantial (transeunt) causation.⁶⁷ By positing a motivational force on the part of the simple substances he calls monads, and further deriving the world of matter *qua* impenetrability from such a force, he attributes precisely that causal link between such entities that Leibniz dedicated so much energy to refuting.⁶⁸ This has led critic Sergei Polovinkin to number Soloviev amongst the proponents of a trend in Russian Neo-Leibnizianism committed to the 'opening up of monads,' arguing that the philosopher attempted to 'make monadology into a metaphysical basis for a particular kind of personalism.'⁶⁹ To argue that all created substances were individual-animate was one thing; to state that they were also efficient *causes*, in the philosophical sense, was a very different proposition. Just what kind of 'personhood' lurks behind each monad is revealed only in Soloviev's unpublished *La Sophia*, which we treat later in the chapter, while in the published works he endeavours to justify the positing of a personal, egoistic force from the nature of physical reality itself.

Just how far Soloviev moves in the direction of 'opening up monadology' becomes clear as his argument develops in *Critique*. Since none can actually fill another's place, each atom must, he argues, find

---

67   According to Leibniz, 'how any succession can follow from the nature of a thing [is] impossible if we assume that this nature is not individual.' Yet he also insists that 'anything which occurs in what is strictly a substance must be a case of action in the metaphysically rigorous sense of something which occurs in a substance spontaneously, arising out of its own depths.' Cited in M. E. Bobro, *Self and Substance in Leibniz*, Dordrecht, 2004, pp. 85, 86.

68   It should be noted that Leibniz' monadology becomes more involved on the subject of causation once complex monads arise through embodiment (see ibid., pp. 88-90) yet Soloviev's argument here is carried out entirely at the level of the disembodied monad. 'Each monad,' comments Bertrand Russell of Leibniz' monadology, 'is limited, not be something else, but by itself.' B. Russell, *A Critical Exposition of the Philosophy of Leibniz*, London, 2005, p. 171. Daniel Garber has argued convincingly that the conviction as to the impossibility of transeunt causality drops away from Leibniz' published work from the 1690s. 'Perhaps,' writes Garber, 'Leibniz realised that the argument simply didn't succeed in establishing the conclusion with respect to the activity of substance. Since God must sustain bodies for them to persist in their existence [...] placing all their properties in them doesn't at all settle the question of whether they are genuinely active or whether it is really God who is responsible for them doing what they do.' D. Garber, *Leibniz, Body, Substance, Monad*, Oxford and New York, 2009, p. 199.

69   S. M. Polovinkin, 'V. S. Solov'ev i russkoe neoleibnitsianstvo,' *Voprosy filosofii*, 2, 2002, pp. 90-96 (94-95).

itself in a certain equilibrium with all others, which acts as a common boundary to their interaction. This common boundary between many atoms forms a defined sphere of activity for each atom, as a result of which they take on spatial properties. 'Space, or extension,' he writes, 'is merely the result of the interaction of atoms, an expression of their equilibrium [...], the limit of their inner being-in-themselves and thus a definite form of their external being, that is, their being-for-another.' It follows that atoms cannot be defined as the last components of matter since 'matter is merely their product.' They can only be described as 'material' in their interaction with each other. In a purely material sense, therefore, an atom is a 'mathematical point' or a 'spatial zero.' But this definition is insufficient since 'however many zeros we took and however we combined them, we would get nothing but zero.' Since atoms, in themselves, are the cause of the activity which produces matter, Soloviev therefore argues that each atom must be defined as a force (*sila*) and 'the actual substantiality of atoms, being immaterial, should be dynamic.' In this way, atoms 'are understood not as components (passive elements) but as the active *producers* of the material world; they are immaterial, dynamic individuals, existing in themselves and acting from themselves as *living forces*, or *monads*.'[70]

This is by no means the conclusion on which the philosopher wishes to rest. Leaning heavily on the thought of other thinkers, particularly Leibniz, he has brought the reader to the limits of his ontological argument, and it is at these limits that he believes he has demonstrated that the material world is the product of immaterial, or spiritual, force. But, in so doing, he admits that he has deprived matter of any reality. Monads alone are given the category of true existence, but these are inaccessible to scientific experiment and become known only through speculation.

> These absolute centres of living force are thus not physical realities but metaphysical essences. Absolute reality, therefore, truly belongs to metaphysical essences, whereas physical reality is acknowledged as mere phenomenon, i.e. conditional being, or simply illusion.[71]

---

[70] PSS, III, pp. 207-10.
[71] Ibid., p. 211.

This is the reverse of what Soloviev had hoped to prove. To admit that the only reality immediately accessible to us—that of the material world—is mere illusion, and that reality belongs to immaterial essences utterly unknowable to our senses was for the philosopher tantamount to an admittance not just of human inability to know the truth, but of the powerlessness of truth itself. For Soloviev, 'the truth should be the truth of all, not its contradiction; truth should explain and not negate reality.'[72] The reduction of cognized reality to an illusion does nothing to explain the facts of our material reality, and Soloviev could not reconcile himself with it. In *Critique*, a metaphysical argument is not forthcoming; instead, Soloviev moves on to the gnoseological section of the work, in which he attempts to overcome the critical philosophy of Kant. His reader, meanwhile, is left to ponder the results of a 'logical' argument that appears, the more he wrestles with it, to blur the boundaries of 'pure philosophy' with an organic and personalistic appreciation of nature that, for the moment, dares not speak its name.

Soloviev's association of the monad with the atom will strike many as unfounded, even arbitrary. Leibniz himself had designed the concept of the monad—the '*true* atom of nature'—precisely to supersede the concept of the atom as understood by the atomists of his age.[73] There had, of course, been many advances in atomic science between the time of Leibniz and the time Soloviev was writing, and the latter is right to indicate the lack of consensus in atomic theories of the time.[74] The pioneering work of figures such as Ernest Rutherford lay in the future and there was room for considerable debate of both a scientific and philosophical nature. It appears, however, that Soloviev rather too easily aligns himself with a particular current of thought which tended to view atoms as *non-material* forces, zero points in whose interaction the derivation of matter should be sought.[75]

---

[72] Ibid., p. 205.
[73] See Daniel Garber, 'Leibniz, Gottfried Wilhelm,' *Routledge Encyclopedia of Philosophy* (1998) <http://www.rep.routledge.com/article/DA952SECT11> [accessed 12 January 2006]. Soloviev is wrong to attribute the identification of the monad with the atom to Leibniz. See PSS, III, pp. 207-08.
[74] Ibid., p. 208.
[75] In his thought on atomism, Soloviev drew particularly on the various theories presented in the work of G. T. Fechner, the founder of psychophysiology. See G. T. Fechner,

His position suffers even more from hindsight. From a contemporary perspective, the atom is yet more dissimilar to Leibniz's monad: science has disproved its absolute indivisibility and shown it to be a bona fide material entity. Moreover, unlike monads, of which no two can be the same, atoms can be separated into different types, but not unique individuals.

But if we consider what Soloviev meant by the word 'atom,' namely the fundamental building-block of the created world — the last possible constituent of matter which cannot be further broken down into other constituent parts[76] — we may avoid condemning his idea to the more outlandish excesses of nineteenth-century idealism. Through his pseudo-scientific constructs, Soloviev was trying to pinpoint the moment at which matter and spirit intersected and, as it were, ran into one another. Using a mixture of pure speculation, logic, and theoretical physics, he arrived at a threefold definition of this moment as the metaphysical *soul*, the physical *atom*, and, most importantly, the grey area between the two — the sphere of creation, the *monad*. In these three terms are expressed the spiritual, material, and spiritual-corporeal aspects respectively. The monad, as the third principle, is both soul and atom, the 'space' where, in unending cycles, spirit begets matter, and matter returns to spirit. This ambiguity was key to Soloviev's early philosophy and he exploits it as much as possible. As much as an objective investigation into philosophical truth, his thought was involved in the discovery of a discourse capable of containing such truth.[77] In terms such as the monad, the first *tertium quid* to appear in his discourse,[78] he finds a way of verbally expressing the unity of the

---

Über die physikalische und philosophische Atomenlehre. Zweite vermehrte Auflage, Leipzig, 1864. See also the editorial notes in PSS, III, p. 506.

[76] In this, he followed the meaning the Ancient Greeks gave to the word as 'a hypothetical body, so infinitely small as to be incapable of further division; and thus held to be one of the ultimate particles of matter.' See 'atom, *n*.1' in *OED*. Goethe, whom Soloviev followed in many areas also associated the atom, which he understood in the same way, with the monad. See James Boyd, *Notes to Goethe's Poems*, 2 vols, Oxford, 1944-49, II, pp. 137-43.

[77] On Soloviev's discourse as locus of ambiguity, see Edith Clowes insightful article: E. Clowes, 'The Limits of Discourse: Solov'ev's Language of Syzygy and the Project of Thinking Total-Unity,' *Slavic Review*, 55, 3, 1996, pp. 552-66.

[78] For the significance of Sophia as *tertium quid* in Soloviev's thought, see Kornblatt, *Wisdom Writings*, p. 27. For Soloviev's understanding of his own role in Russian society as

dual aspects that inhere in any given phenomenon. By hemming it in on either side with the terms soul and atom, as he does in *Crisis* and *La Sophia*, he makes present to the reader the constant movement between the two poles, which meet in the monad as their crossover point.[79] This is far from rigorous philosophy but it does tell us much about Soloviev's method and intentions at this early stage of his career.

In *Critique*, these groups of three terms, representing the two poles of any given reality and their point of intersection, are extensively developed, particularly in Soloviev's metaphysics. In this last and most sophisticated work of the period, the philosopher consistently refuses to limit the content of thought to a single concept, instead building up clusters of terms, each of which adds a new tone to the content it purports to carry. The use of the conjunction *or* between two nouns, for example, occurs here as a matter of course. This tendency of any concept to 'outgrow' itself adds a dynamism to the reality it is trying to express. A movement is intuited, which coaxes the reader into the fluid world of the philosophy of All-Unity, where nothing can stay as it is without passing into its opposite.[80]

The answer to the question 'What is?' proves for Soloviev to be rather a question of what is *becoming*. His vision of reality is underpinned by constant movement under the seeming immobility of matter. In his published works, particularly *Critique*, this movement becomes subsumed into the movement of his philosophy itself. The mental processes that Soloviev means to engender in his reader thus mirror his vision of the restlessness of reality. But philosophy, and the movement

---

tertium quid, and its comparison to Socrates, see A. L. Crone, *Eros and Creativity in Russian Religious Renewal: The Philosophers and the Freudians*, Leiden and Boston, 2010, p. 20.

[79] Jan Krasicki argues that in his concept of the 'atom-monad' Soloviev combines elements of Democritus' 'atom,' Plato's 'idea,' and Leibniz' 'monad.' Krasitskii, *Bog, chelovek i zlo*, p. 127.

[80] Soloviev illustrates his brand of dynamic ontology in *Critique* by quoting the following couplets from Goethe, whose influence looms large in this period: Nun Alles sich mit göttlichem Erkühnen/ Zu übertreffen strebt; Denn Alles muss in Nichts zerfallen/ Wenn es im Seyn beharren will (With godlike courage all things/ strive to surpass themselves; And into nothing everything must fall,/ If it in being would persist). PSS, III, p. 149.

it induces in its addressee, can only convince the reader of its vision over time, and thus lacks the immediacy of concrete reality, which presents a multiplicity of states in one moment.

In both *Crisis* and *Critique*, Soloviev brings us to a point at which the alleged authenticity of matter as something we see and experience is overturned and acknowledged as mere illusion, the result of the independent activity of metaphysical entities, or *monads*. However, this is not the end of the story.

> That which we took for objective reality as a given outside ourselves — the world of our experience — turns out to be merely a subjective phenomenon, or illusion, and that which was rejected as subjective fantasy — the results of our speculation — turns out to be the expression of the truly substantial [...] Since metaphysical essence, as such, only becomes known through pure speculation, this latter turns out to be the source of true knowledge, whereas real experience, as mere illusory perception, does not provide us with any true knowledge and can have only a conditional, subordinate meaning.[81]

At this point, the reader expects Soloviev to turn to an exposition of his metaphysics using 'pure speculation.' But this does not occur. Instead, in *Crisis* he begins his treatment of the critical philosophy of Kant, just as in *Critique* he moves to the gnoseological section of the work. We are thus faced with the strange circumstance that, with the exception of *La Sophia* and *Philosophical Principles*, both of which remained unpublished, Soloviev's metaphysics is mapped out only in the process of the exposition of his gnoseology, and lacks an independent platform.

II. THEOGONY

Although Soloviev incorporates Leibniz's teaching on the monad into his system, the philosopher cannot settle on it as an exhaustive account of reality. 'Expressing the moment of multiplicity and independence powerfully and entirely logically,' he argues, 'for the opposite moment

---

[81] Ibid., pp. 211, 212.

of shared essence and unity the Leibnizian philosophy offers only brilliant guesses and witty metaphors.'[82]

For Soloviev, Leibniz had demonstrated conclusively that reality, or substance, belongs to a multiplicity of subjective centres of individual force, which through their activity of representation 'produce' the material world (this second point being Soloviev's own, unacknowledged contribution to monadology). But the unity of the whole remained only an abstract construction, without a linking principle that could firmly anchor it in the reality of multiplicity. Soloviev, it will be remembered, had uncovered the same lacuna in the thought of Spinoza who, in stressing the moment of unity, had failed to provide any real explanation for the existence of 'the many.' 'In what, then,' Soloviev asks in *Crisis*, 'does the necessity of finite things consist? How does *number*, albeit infinite, appear in a unitary substance? Where has multiplicity come from?'[83] It is these questions Soloviev tries to solve with his metaphysics, most elaborately in *La Sophia* but most powerfully in *Philosophical Principles* and *Critique*. As he would later in *Justification of the Good*, where he attempts to draw the entire edifice of human ethics from the experiential givenness of three human feelings — shame, pity and reverence[84] — Soloviev starts his theogony not from the paucity of human understanding in the face of the divine abyss but from the fact of determinate being itself, and the central imperative to explain its source in the *nihil* of God.[85] His

---

[82] PSS, I, p. 51.
[83] Ibid., p. 49.
[84] See pp. 167-68.
[85] In his attempt to create a theogonical theology, Soloviev is very close to his major influences of this period: Boehme, Schelling and Hegel. See the interesting comments of Ray Hunt on the central concerns of theogonical theology, whose root question, he argues, bifurcates into both a metaphysical and ontological aspect: '"Why is there anything at all, why not rather nothing"? *And* "Why, given that there is something, does the *nihil* perdure"? [...] Central to the task of conceiving/envisioning the eternal self-generation of God the determinate Creator (and Redeemer) from the abysmal indeterminacies of Godhead [...] is the emergence of "being" and "nonbeing" (or nothingness), their relation, and the relation to Godhead and God. Without theogony, there is no full stop to the regressive question, "Why...?"' R. L. Hunt, 'God and Godhead,' in L. McCullough and B. Schroeder (eds), *Thinking Through the Death of God: A Critical Companion to Thomas J. J. Altizer*, Albany, NY, 2004, pp. 47-64 (p. 54).

theogony is thus intimately connected with his cosmogony: the God that 'emerges' theogonically must be the God who positions herself toward the world as its Creator.

The problematic question that arises at this point is whether Soloviev promotes what Kathryn Tanner has termed a 'contrastive' view of divine transcendence, an approach where the absolute is defined *positively* against that which it is *not*, its character thereby emerging in contrast to determinate being rather than as that which is eternally beyond the same.[86] It is well known that the objections of later representatives of the so-called Neo-Patristic Synthesis to Soloviev's understanding of 'creation' in large part derive from his perceived conflation of the divine and created realms.[87] While there are grounds for such conclusions, especially early on in his career, Soloviev's thought on the nature of the Godhead and its relation to the world is more complex that many of his critics leave room for. His cosmogony does not function as a mere appendage to his theogony, nor is his theogony a prequel to cosmogony. Rather, as we shall see, the emergence of God involves the cosmos, just as the emergence of cosmos involves God, the latter functioning not only as the 'unmoved mover' of classical theology, but essentially and dynamically. The difference between the theogonic and cosmogonic processes is therefore not one of essence, or degree, but of a certain kind of perspective: the material substratum of being as seen from God's perspective is not identical to its appearance from a creaturely

---

[86] See K. Tanner, *God and Creation in Christian Theology: Tyranny and Empowerment?*, Oxford, 1988, pp. 37-48. Whatever the case, Soloviev surely has little in common with apophatic theology here, whose goal in contrasting the absolute to determinate being is by its very nature *negative* rather than positive. Paul Gavrilyuk sums it up elegantly when comparing Soloviev, along with Bulgakov, to Dionysian Platonism. 'Where Dionysius speaks apophatically about the things revealed,' he writes, 'the Russian sophiologists presume to speak cataphatically about the things hidden.' See P. L. Gavrilyuk, 'The Reception of Dionysius in Twentieth-Century Eastern Orthodoxy,' in S. Coakley (ed), *Re-Thinking Dionysius the Areopagite*, Malden, MA, 2009, pp. 177-94 (p. 182).

[87] See, for example, Georges Florovsky's rebuke to sophiology: 'the Divine Idea of creation is not creation itself; it is not the substance of creation, it is not a bearer of the cosmic-process [...] not a process within the Divine Idea [...] but the appearance, formation, and the realization of another *substratum*, of a multiplicity of created subjects. [It] remains always outside the created world, transcending it.' G. Florovsky, *Creation and Redemption. The Collected Works*, vol. III, Belmont, MA, 1976, p. 46.

perspective. There is a fissure in the ontic relation between matter and God on one hand, and matter and the body of the world on the other.

Soloviev's conception of the absolute, the guarantor of unity, shares the same ontological dynamism that we found in his treatment of phenomenal reality. God is drawn into being by the force of her inner nature. That there is being at all and not nothing, Soloviev will argue, can be explained by the nature of the absolute principle itself, which he links so closely with the created order as to risk the charge of pantheism, an accusation he indeed faced during his lifetime. His metaphysics is thus intimately linked with his theogony, which he interpreted as the inner logic of the absolute metaphysical principle in its creative movement out from itself. Soloviev applies his particular brand of logic not only to the metaphysical principle itself, but to the whole realm of being and its relation to the absolute. That which is created by the absolute principle—the material world—is understood as present in its very nature in concealed form, and it is to the proof of such a proposition that Soloviev applies his principles of 'organic logic.' It may be argued that such logic contains within itself a contradiction: Soloviev here embarks on a journey from divine nothingness, coaxing out the determinations of the absolute through, to all appearances, a form of logical speculation. Yet the destination of this journey—the determinate being of our material world—is not only known upon departure but used from the very outset as the determinative final term in the purportedly self-governed movement of the absolute out of itself. This contradiction remains, yet it can be said that Soloviev's theogonic-cosmogonic conception is much less about the result of the journey than it is an explication of its intermediate stages as manifesting a relationship between the divine and creaturely. In other words, the question for Soloviev is not only *why* does matter exist, but also *how* the absolute relates to the material world.

In the first part of the second monologue of *La Sophia*, entitled 'On the Three Phases of the Absolute Principle and on the Three Divine Hypostases,' Soloviev uses dialectics to break down the contradictions inherent in any understanding of the absolute. The pre-eminent example of such an approach was, of course, Hegel, and Soloviev replicates many of the former's methods. Instead of Hegel's starting point of the

II. THEOGONY

opposition of being and nothing,[88] however, he chooses two aspects of the absolute principle, which are not deduced but taken as givens at the very beginning of his theogony, here called 'the universal teaching':

> The first principle of the universal teaching is the absolute principle of all that exists. As an absolute principle it exists in itself, independent of all that exists. As the principle of all that exists, it exists in each thing and, as a consequence, comes to be known.[89]

This first division in the nature of the absolute principle, which consists in the opposition of itself as wholly free of all being, merely to its immanence in matter, may appear an inexplicable starting point for many readers, formulated to legitimize Soloviev's intuition. But the philosopher does not regard the opposition of these two aspects as the illogical ground of an emergent logic, but as directly stemming from his understanding of truth (*istina*), which receives its fullest expression in the following passage from *Critique*:

> Truth is the all-one substance. We cannot think of truth in any other way; if we took away one of the three predicates [i.e. *vse*: 'all'; *edinoe*: 'one'; or *sushchee*: 'substance' — OS], we would destroy the concept of truth itself. Thus, in removing the predicate of substance, truth turns into an empty subjective thought which does not correspond to anything real; if truth is not substantial, it becomes fantasy and therefore ceases to be truth. In removing the predicate "one," truth loses its identity and, falling into internal contradiction, disintegrates. Finally, if we take away the predicate "all," we deprive truth of actual content: as exclusively one, deprived of all, it is a meagre principle indeed, from which nothing can be deduced or explained. For within the concept of truth is the requirement to deduce and explain everything from it: truth is the truth of *all*. If all were outside it, it would be nothing.[90]

For Soloviev, 'to be absolute' means to be the union of oneself and one's other while remaining identical to oneself. Thus the one, the subject or possessor of All-Unity, must encapsulate its other in order to have

---

[88] See G. W. F. Hegel, *The Encyclopaedia Logic*, Indianopolis, 1991, pp. 136-41.
[89] PSS, II, p. 44.
[90] Ibid., III, p. 267.

nothing alien to itself, while at the same time remaining separate and distinguishable from this other. Its other must be the all, since multiplicity and individuation cannot exist in what is unitary and simple. The *one* must contain the *all* in order to remain absolute, for if the all—the reality of which is immediately present to us in the material world—were to exist separately from the one, this latter would thereby lose its absolute status and fall into contradiction with itself.

The absolute principle, therefore, must be both wholly independent of being and at the same time must incorporate being into itself. It can be seen that these two poles are not at all dissimilar to Hegel's categories of being and nothing after all: the absolute principle as independent of all being, i.e. without predication, may be defined as nothing, while in its inherence in matter it may be understood to lay claim to a form of being. But 'being' here is understood by Soloviev not merely as a dialectical concept but concretely, as a form of the absolute's indwelling in the spatial and temporal conditions of our material world, not in a theoretical dimension produced by the mind. The absolute is, moreover, not equated with this being but rather exists in each thing 'as the *principle* of all that exists.' It is thus not being in the proper sense, nor is it nothing: rather, it is the foundation of all being, that from which being derives and by which it subsists. In the same way, 'nothing' is not entirely unmitigated, but can rather be described as the 'lack of being,' or the quality of being distinct from being.[91] Even in the holding of these two aspects of the absolute principle together, a certain movement is already intuited between the two: each of them requires the other in order to be fully itself. There is no synthetic resolution, as in the Hegelian dialectic, but rather an energetic exchange between the conceptual pair.

But Soloviev still needs to find a way to express the mediation between the two poles. He needs to find the point of intersection between the two—just as he had tried to do with the monad in the

---

[91] Despite the Hegelian character of much of Soloviev's thought of this period, the latter's point of departure here demonstrates the extent of the gap between the two. He is not, as Hegel, interested in producing truth in its entirety from the dialectical movement of the human mind/spirit but proceeds from a certain givenness, namely the givenness of material form in its multiplicity.

physical world—so that the movement between them can become a fruit of the mind, accessible to reason and understandable to his readers. How does the nothing, or lack of being, become the foundation of a wholly determinate being? The answer to this question, which lies in the reconciliation between the two aspects, is first approached by Soloviev through the concept of *materia prima*, or the 'potential of being,' which becomes the first moment in the theogonic process pursued in his early work.[92]

The term is most extensively developed in *Philosophical Principles*, in which Soloviev refines arguments which in *La Sophia* had been somewhat rushed and not entirely substantiated.[93] Here Soloviev talks of the two 'centres' of the absolute principle, defining them both as 'the potentiality of being,' but in different respects.[94] The first is 'positive potentiality, freedom from being, the suprasubstantial (*sverkhsushchee*),' while the second, *materia prima*, is the 'material centre, the necessity of attraction toward being, negative unmediated (*neposredstvennyi*) potentiality, i.e. a determined or felt absence or deprivation of real being.'[95] We have already noted how the concept of truth, which is identical to the concept of the absolute principle, needs to possess the predicates of substance, unity, and multiplicity in order to be itself. There is thus necessity involved in the very idea of the absolute. Only in its interaction with its other—multiplicity—can the absolute be truly free since, without it, it has nothing from which to manifest its essential freedom, and unity, in Soloviev's view, must be the coming together of a definite multiplicity. Thus, the absolute principle 'eternally finds in itself its opposite, since

---

[92] The term *materia prima* dates back to mediaeval scholasticism, and is not to be thought of as matter in the conventional sense. For this purpose, another term was employed by the scholastics, *materia secunda*, which Soloviev indeed uses, albeit sparingly. The term received significant elaboration in Leibniz, Paracelsus, Boehme and Schelling.

[93] For example, in *La Sophia* Soloviev associates *materia prima* with the concept of 'universal will' rather haphazardly, and fails to provide an adequate analysis of the first pole of the absolute as existing wholly independently of being.

[94] Soloviev takes the concept of 'two centres' (in German, *Zentren*) directly from Boehme. See, for example, Boehme, *The Signature of All Things*, p. 190: 'the will [...] is the eternal wisdom, wherein all things which were in this world were known in two centres, viz. according to the fire and light.'

[95] PSS, II, p. 266 (my emphases).

only by relating to this opposite can it become known to itself: they are perfect correlatives.'[96] The absolute principle can only be free in its eternal differentiation of itself from the necessity contained within it.[97] Since it cannot be conceived otherwise, there arises movement in the first centre, which, as it were, is the beginning of realized being. This 'attraction toward being,' a necessary pull toward concrete manifestation which arises from the first centre of the absolute, Soloviev described as a 'thirst' or 'desire' for being. 'The association of *materia prima* with the ground of being—designated by Soloviev as a primal 'thirst' or 'yearning'—corresponds almost exactly to Schelling's exposition in *Die Weltalter*, in which the potencies of eternal nature 'take root in their freedom and their independence as the foundation and, so to speak, prime matter of everything distinct from the divine subject, as the refuge and place to live [...] for creatures away from eternity, as what is eternally in the middle between God and created beings.'[98] *Materia prima* can thus be understood as opening up the primal possibility of a middle, the point of mediation between the Creator and the creature, or the matrix of all relation. This place of mediation Soloviev would ultimately come to call the 'world soul,' or Sophia.

A peculiar circumstance in Soloviev's thought at this juncture is that, in its purely logical development, *materia prima* emerges *after* and *as a result of* the opposition between the absolute in-itself and the absolute as inhering in matter. But in the theogonic process, which Soloviev is simultaneously expounding to his reader, *materia prima* appears as a result of the movement of the first pole of the

---

[96] PSS, III, pp. 265-66. Soloviev further argues that since 'the absolute cannot have anything outside, or alien to, itself, this is its own necessity, its essence [...] It is its necessity in the same sense as it is necessary for us to live, to feel, to love.'

[97] This concept of free will as conditioned by necessity, enshrined here in the primordial will of the absolute principle, remained with Soloviev throughout his life.

[98] F. W. J. Schelling, *The Ages of the World*, Albany, NY, 2000, p. 29. For Schelling, as for Soloviev, the positing of 'prime matter' (*materia prima*) is necessary in order to vouchsafe, firstly, the 'passive base' with respect to the spirit and, secondly, to guard against a view that holds the pure emanation of the creature from the Godhead, which would 'sublimate all of the freedom of creatures in relation to God.' Ibid., p. 30. It is interesting to note that, in his synopsis of *Weltalter*, Schelling calls *materia prima* 'spiritual-corporeal matter.' Ibid., p. xxxiv.

absolute out of itself toward concrete being. This multi-layering of method is not incidental to the philosopher's purpose. For Soloviev, the substantial and *materia prima*,[99] the first and second centres of the absolute, are 'perfect correlatives': the one cannot be thought without the other. The dual perspective that emerges through his exposition — the first pole having precedence theogonically from the perspective of the divine, and the second logically from the perspective of creaturely existence — allows him to avoid a hierarchical conception of the absolute principle, and to argue instead for the equality of the centres, each being 'the begetter and begotten of the other.'

> On the one hand, *materia prima* is only the necessary property of the free substantial and without it cannot be thought. On the other hand, the *prima materia* is its first substratum, its foundation (basis), without which it cannot become manifest or *be* as such.[100]

In this picture of two centres of the absolute, each reliant on the other in different respects, and thus constantly moving between one another, it is already possible to make out the beginnings of a perichoretic view of the hypostatic absolute. Since *materia prima* has no meaning when separated from the first centre of the absolute, to consider it on its own may be seen as an artificial construct of logic with no basis in absolute reality. Soloviev writes that in the case of the absolute principle:

> [...] there can be no process, no temporal sequence; and if we cannot immediately imagine in one form the entire fullness of the absolute as manifest in its idea, the total reality of their [the centres of the absolute — OS] eternal interaction, but have to expound this interaction in parts, breaking it down into separate determinations beginning with the most general and potential and ending with the most concrete and real, then this [...] depends solely on the discursive character of our dialectical thinking in time and in no way determines the reality of the absolute itself and its eternal idea. The various determinations

---

[99] In *Philosophical Principles*, the single word *sushchee* (see glossary) becomes expressive of the first pole of the absolute principle.
[100] PSS, II, p. 267.

that our dialectics uncover in the idea of the substantial actually do exist in it. They exist, though, not as we *think* them but immediately (*zaraz*), in one eternal living form, which we can only contemplate intellectually.[101]

Soloviev's understanding of the absolute as a living organism, 'one eternal living form,' is here forcefully presented. It is difficult for us to conceptualise such an organism since it is more complex than the most intricate organic structures of the physical world. Just as it would be hard for a blood cell in the human body to conceive of such a thing as a human, so we, who are wholly absorbed in the being of the absolute, find it difficult to imagine the reality of the total organism. But this in itself, argues Soloviev, is no sign that the absolute organism does not exist. Indeed, through the discursive powers of human reasoning, we can arrive at a determination of the elements in which its being consists. But the living knowledge of the whole will remain outside the grasp of reason, which moves itself in time in a succession of logical moments.

The word *idea*, which occurs in the passage cited above, is one of the most difficult in Soloviev's early thought. By it he seems to understand a number of things: at times it has the meaning of a concept with purely logical content, at others it is a concrete being. Even when the reader is able to distinguish the various applications to which Soloviev puts the word, however, she finds that even within a given context it is not used entirely consistently.

The idea emerges for the first time in the further movement of *materia prima*. We recall that, since *materia prima* is conjoined with the first centre of the absolute, there must be constant movement between the two, as there is between two elements of a single organism. But what is the character of this movement in the case of the absolute, i.e. where is it headed, what is the idea of its movement? In framing the question this way, it is taken for granted that the absolute operates according to a preordained plan of which it is the creator. In a similar way, Soloviev assumes that the absolute is endowed of a will, which is the first cause

---

[101] Ibid., p. 268.

of its movement toward being and therefore its first centre, or pole. Directing itself toward the second pole, *materia prima*, the will becomes manifest in this second centre of being as the 'idea.'[102]

A few words on what Soloviev means by 'will' are in order. In *La Sophia*, the attribution of will to the first pole is justified in two ways: firstly, through analogy to our human inner experience as it pertains to will; and secondly, by assuming that there is some sort of meaning, or idea, present in the reality of the absolute. We shall return to the second basis of Soloviev's argument in the next section. Let us turn for the moment to its first element.

'Our will, i.e. the ability to will,' writes Soloviev, 'remains exactly the same after every act of willing; we can desire to our heart's content for this can never exhaust our will.'[103] This simple statement allows him to describe the first centre of the absolute, which is wholly distinct from being, as 'universal will,' since, following the essential nature of our own will, it remains the potential of being while never becoming equated with being.[104]

---

[102] The problem with associating *materia prima* with the idea of God is that the former is, by its very definition, formless (as the void in the first chapter of Genesis) and incapable of manifesting an idea-form, in the Platonic sense, as such. Soloviev's solution resonates with that of Aquinas, who argued that 'of itself *materia prima* has neither being nor knowability. It is [potential being] and has [weakened existence]. But because God's causality extends as far as the *materia prima*, his knowledge must do so too [...] In the strict sense of *exemplar* there is no idea of *materia prima* in God since it is not [manifested in being] apart from form. In this sense there is an idea of matter only *in composite*. In the broad sense of *ratio* one can speak of an idea of *materia prima* in God.' V. Boland, *Ideas in God according to Saint Thomas Aquinas*, Leiden, 1996, pp. 228-29. It is this broad sense of *ratio*, as the idea of relation (otherness) per se, that Soloviev connects to *materia prima* and, through it, to the Logos.

[103] PSS, II, p. 47. Whether it is viable to draw the 'will' of the absolute principle from an analogy with human inner experience remains an open question. The same analogy with human experience is used in *Philosophical Principles* to substantiate the first centre's association with will. The philosopher Sergii Bulgakov could not accept this portion of Soloviev's argument. See Note 108 (below).

[104] Soloviev is again leaning on Schelling here. '[Actual] Being, presumed to be prior to cognition, is, however, not Being, though it is likewise not cognition: it is real self-positing, it is a primal and fundamental *willing*, which makes itself into something and is the ground of all ways of being.' F. W.J. Schelling, *Philosophical Investigations into the Essence of Human Freedom*, Albany, NY, 2006, pp. 50-51 [my italics].

But the first centre only becomes will in its interaction with *materia prima*, which as the thirst for being, or necessity of being, represents its negative correlative. Will is thus the very activity of the first pole toward the second pole, or centre. That is to say, will is only manifested as such with the appearance of *materia prima*, since without this latter there is as yet no object for the will to assert itself upon, no way of becoming known.

Soloviev at this stage introduces an equivalent term for *materia prima*, which, like the term 'the substantial' (*sushchee*), becomes an integral part of his vocabulary, namely, 'essence' (*sushchnost'*).[105] The essence, or *materia prima*, as we have noted, is only seen as such when viewed in itself as an isolated, or abstract moment. And yet, as deriving directly from the will of the substantial, it cannot exist by itself in actuality, for it is only a logical moment in the make-up of the absolute. Thus the will eternally finds itself in its essence, through which the former becomes known to itself.[106] But there is also movement within the essence, which, as it is defined by the will, is transformed into the *idea*. This idea, which arises from the essence's determination by the will, is further described by Soloviev as the 'carrier (*nositel'nitsa*) of [the substantial's] manifestation, [...] its eternal form.'[107]

At this stage it can be said that the absolute, which at its conception was understood as the pure potentiality of being, or 'positive nothing,'

---

[105] If the term *materia prima* expresses, through its very conjugation, a closer correlation with the world of *matter*, the term *sushchnost'* (see glossary) conveys a deeper link with *the substantial* (*sushchee*), with which it shares a common root. Soloviev is again building up terms to express the same thing, but with varying tonalities, designed to draw the mind of the reader into the fluidity of his vision of reality. Naturally, sometimes it has the effect of simple obfuscation.

[106] The movement and content of Soloviev's dialectics, on this point and many others, is remarkably similar to Jacob Boehme. See, for example, Jacob Boehme, *The Signature of All Things*, London, 1934, p. 14. 'In the nothing the will would not be manifest to itself, wherefore we know that the will seeks itself, and finds itself in itself, and its seeking is a desire, and its finding is the essence of the desire, wherein the will finds itself.'

[107] PSS, III, pp. 267-68. The word translated 'carrier'—*nositel'nitsa*—is a feminine noun formed by adding the suffix –*nitsa* to the masculine form, which Soloviev would be expected to use. That Soloviev introduces Sophia here almost through the back door is indicative of his early desire to withhold her from the pages of his published works.

II. THEOGONY

which Soloviev also designates by the Kabbalistic term *en-soph* (literally, 'No limit,' i.e. limitlessness),[108] has taken on form in the idea, which is

---

[108] Soloviev uses the term 'en-soph' to express the absolute transcendence of God from all being, while qualifying this transcendence by the further, analogous term *positive nothing*, which allows him to posit the 'nothing,' paradoxically, as the ground of all being. The Kabbala is full of statements of this fundamental paradox. See, e.g., Knorr von Rosenroth, *Kabbala Denudata*, p. 263. 'He hath been conformed so that He may sustain all things; yet is He not formed, seeing that He is not discovered.' Interestingly, the Kabbala associates the beginning of form in the absolute with the possibility of a relationship to a personal God whom one may address *Thou* or *Father* (in the following citation, the Hebrew is inserted alongside the English translation in Roman script):

> And since in Him beginning and end exist not, hence He is not called AThH, *Atah*, Thou; seeing that He is concealed and not revealed. But HVA, *Hoa*, He, is He called. But in that aspect wherein the beginning is found, the name AThH, *Atah*, Thou, hath place, and the name AB, *Ab*, Father.

See Ibid., p. 279. Boehme, too, follows the Kabbala in positing movement within the nothing. See, e.g., Boehme, *The Signature of All Things*, p. 17: 'no joy can arise in the still nothing; it must arise only through motion and elevation that the nothing finds itself.' Sergii Bulgakov, who developed many aspects of Soloviev's thought, argued that the philosopher did not place enough emphasis on the ineffability of God, the unknowable aspect of the absolute, and suffered from 'excessive rationalism in theology.' While acknowledging that 'a final resolution to the question as to whether *en-soph* expresses the transcendental essence of God or just a moment of his non-disclosure (*neraskrytost'*) in being is extremely difficult,' he argues that Soloviev did not do justice to the ambiguity of the term. 'Although he characterizes the transcendental absolute by the Kabbalistic concept *en-soph* (despite its problematic nature, Soloviev introduces the concept without any explanation), i.e. in the terminology of negative theology, he then rationally *deduces*, unlawfully and without any explanation of its application to the first hypostasis, its relationship to the world and, as a consequence, their mutual determination. Soloviev clearly confuses, or at the very least insufficiently distinguishes, God as the NOT-something of negative theology and God as disclosed in the world at the beginning of this disclosure.' For Bulgakov, Soloviev's explicit association of *en-soph* with the first person of the Trinity, the Father (see PSS, II, p. 284), is unjustifiable. See S. N. Bulgakov, *Svet nevechernii: Sozertsaniia i umozreniia*, Moscow, 1994, pp. 122, 129-30. While Bulgakov's objections are in some respects justified, it may be said that he himself does not differentiate between 'en' (negativity per se) and *en-soph* (the Limitless), the first and second 'veils' of the negative existence (neither, however, does Soloviev). See S. L. M. Mathers, 'Introduction,' in *Kabbala Denudata*, London, 1887, pp. 4-35 (p. 20). Scholem writes that 'in the self-limitation of the divine Being which, instead of acting outwardly in its initial act, turns inwards towards itself, Nothingness emerges. Here we have an act in which Nothingness is called forth.' Gershom Scholem, 'Schöpfung aus Nichts und Selbstverschränkung Gottes,' *Eranos Jahrbuch*, 25, 1956, 87-119 (p. 118).

a reflection, or a making-known, of its essential character. The content of the idea, despite having been deduced from *materia prima*, is now infinitely richer, or fuller, than this latter. *Materia prima*, or essence, can be considered as pure form, or empty space — it is only 'the principle of form,'[109] not a definite form itself. It corresponds to that first cosmic moment in the history of the universe when infinite space rose out of nothing, but before that space came to be filled.[110]

The idea, on the contrary, is the same space, but already filled by the substantial through its will. It is the moment in Genesis when God says 'Let there be light.' And there was light, not gradually or progressively, but immediately, as a bursting forth from the void.[111] Just as this 'light' in Genesis precedes the creation of the sun and the earth, so here the emergence of the idea does not denote the materialization of the physical world. But it does augur a revolution in the absolute principle itself. It is no coincidence that, in the logical section of *Philosophical Principles*, Soloviev only chooses to use the word 'God,' which he now introduces as a synonym for the substantial, after his deduction of the idea.[112] For it is only now, insofar as it has become manifest to itself in its idea, that the substantial can claim the predicate of being: it *is*.[113]

En-soph and the idea now become the first two hypostases of the absolute principle, and are held together in an ineluctable unity.

---

[109] PSS, II, p. 50.

[110] In the terms of the Kabbala, the constellation of nothing into infinite space is called the *tsim-tsum*. According to Robin Waterfield, *tsim-tsum* means 'concentration or contraction, and more specifically in Cabalistic terms it means withdrawal or making space within God. The first act of creation of *En-Sof*, the Primordial Being, is not an outward act but an inward one of withdrawal; in the divine breathing, inhale preceded exhale. Space was made for the subsequent emanation which gave rise to the manifest world.' Jacob Boehme, *Essential Readings*, ed. Robin Waterfield, Wellingborough, 1989, p. 38.

[111] Genesis 1. 3.

[112] PSS, II, p. 268.

[113] It should be noted that Soloviev at this stage of his argument in *Critique* begins to treat the terms 'essence,' which we had defined as the idea-in-itself, or the idea in its separation from the substantial, and 'idea,' which is both the substantial and essence in their interaction, as identical. For the sake of clarity, from hereon in I use the term 'idea-essence' to refer to the first concept, and retain the word 'idea' in the second sense.

Their hypostatization is explained by Soloviev as a result of their necessary self-positing of each other, according to which the will that arises from *en-soph* only finds itself, or is manifested as such, in the idea, just as the idea is found by the will and determines itself as having its source in the same. Thus, the idea wills through *en-soph*, just as *en-soph* perceives, or represents through the idea. Again, Soloviev is here deducing the personhood, or hypostatization, of the absolute principle after a direct analogy with the human person, whose 'modes of being'—designated by Soloviev as will, representation, and feeling—never exhaust the full content of its individuality. Just as the human being not only wills, but also represents and feels, so the absolute is not wholly determined by will, which arises from *en-soph* in its relation to the idea, but also represents through this latter. The absolute principle, however, still lacks the final aspect of personhood—feeling. Soloviev now, therefore, concentrates his efforts on the idea-essence, coaxing out of it the further movement by which the recognition of feeling within the absolute is effected. The necessity of such a development was attested to by mystical thinkers such as Jacob Boehme, whose thought is mirrored by Soloviev in many essential details:

> Seeing then this eternal good cannot be an insensible essence (for so it were not manifest to itself), it introduceth itself in itself into a lubet, to behold and see what itself is; in which lubet is the wisdom: and then the lubet, thus seeing what itself is, bringeth itself into a desire to find out and feel what itself is, viz. to a *sensible perceivance* of the smell and taste of the colours, powers and virtues.[114]

Note here Boehme's use of the verb 'to see'—for Soloviev 'to represent'—and the final point of manifestation in which the absolute 'feels what itself is.' Boehme goes even further than Soloviev in drawing the nature of the absolute from human experience, positing not only feeling in God, or the eternal good, but also smell and taste.

---

114 Jacob Boehme, *Mysterium Magnum, or an Exposition of the First Book of Moses Called Genesis*, trans. John Sparrow, 2 vols, London, 1965, p. 6. 'Lubet' is the rather peculiar translation for the German 'Lust.'

Chapter I. THE FIRST THINGS

Having asserted the consubstantiality and absolute unity of the first and second centres of the absolute, Soloviev now returns to look at the idea-essence, that is, the idea in its separation from the will arising from *en-soph*. This again is a return to the logical process of separating out the moments of the great organism and developing their further movement. What sort of being does the idea-essence lay claim to? Just as he had with the concept of will, Soloviev first resorts to human inner experience to draw an analogy with the idea and the character of its being:

> If, [...] when I think, my thinking as a determination of my own essence, or a certain mode of my subjective nature, is some sort of being, and if the content, or object, of my thinking — that about which I am thinking, or the objective reason that formally determines my thinking — is also called being, then it is obvious that here the word [being — OS] is used in two different senses.[115]

These two senses, which logic separates one from another, are in fact, Soloviev argues, one. 'I cannot,' he writes, 'be *in general*; I must have a particularly determined being, I must be thus or otherwise, this or that, I must have a certain nature.'[116] Since, then, a person cannot be in the abstract, but must of necessity be something, i.e. there must be some content to her being that distinguishes her from other beings, a relation appears between the subject of thinking and its object, or content. To take a simple example: a person, in a certain place, at a certain moment, is thinking about her partner who is at work. Her being, at that moment, is qualified by the content of her thinking. The same goes for the other two 'modes' of being, will and feeling. I cannot feel without feeling *something*. Here, then, number and multiplicity, the possibility of relating of one thing to another, subject to object, has appeared where previously there was only the one.

But these two senses of being do differ from one another in that, in the first, which Soloviev designates 'my thinking as a determination of my own essence,' the being is necessarily relational, i.e. it is a relation

---

[115] PSS, II, p. 269.
[116] Ibid., p. 271.

II. THEOGONY

to *something*. The 'objective reason,' or content, of that thinking, 'is,' however, in a different sense. In this concept of being, there is no longer relation but a definite something, which has become objectified. The relational being is defined as subjective being, and that to which it relates objective being.

Since, then, the *idea-essence* by its very nature, as seen in the analogy with human thinking, cannot remain purely abstract, it must will itself into being with necessity. This is as much as to say that the essence as thirst for being must of necessity be quenched: it must find an object for its thirst. In such a way, we finally arrive at objective being, which arises out of the necessity the idea-essence contains within itself.

It may be worthwhile at this point to summarize the main stages of this development. Initially, the first centre—positive nothing, or *en-soph*—constellated itself into a second centre—the idea-essence or *prima materia*. Then the will of the first centre moved for the first time in the *idea-essence*, which became the idea. Since the idea-essence could not remain as such purely *in abstracto*, it must necessarily will itself into being, thereby creating the world of material form.

The full movement of the absolute out of itself, and consequently the fullness of its manifestation, is complete. On the basis of this movement, Soloviev posits three logical moments involved in any process of self-manifestation:[117]

> [...] 1) the subject of the manifestation (*proiavliaiushcheesia*) in-itself, in which the manifestation is contained in a hidden, or potential, state; 2) the manifestation as such, i.e. the confirmation of itself in the other or on the other, the disclosure, determination, or expression of that which is manifested (*proiavliaemoe*), its word, or Logos; 3) the return of the subject of the manifestation to itself, or the self-discovery of the subject of the manifestation in the manifestation.[118]

The first two moments will be clear from the material we have covered thus far. The first is equivalent to the positive nothing, or *en-soph*, and

---

[117] 'Process' here is understood temporally only insofar as it is logical. As has been noted, there is no process in the absolute itself.
[118] PSS, II, p. 270.

the second to the *idea*, here called 'word, or Logos.'[119] The third moment, however, is introduced for the first time. What is the meaning of this 'return' in the case of the absolute substance?

The return of the subject of the manifestation represents the first centre's recognition of the material world as having its being from itself, and the return of itself to itself to confirm the fact. It is insofar as this return occurs — from the material world to *en-soph* — that God is said to 'feel.'[120] In the same way as an outstretched hand feels the contour of an object with which it comes into contact, so God 'reaches' the material world in her movement out from herself; the 'return' back to herself is experienced as feeling. It is with the introduction of this third element, therefore, that God can be said to be a 'suffering' (*stradatel'nyi*) God, since this aspect of her being is *passive*; she can merely feel herself as thus constituted in the same way as a human being passively experiences changes in her own body.[121]

Only now is Soloviev's theogony at its end. Only now does he decide to call each 'positive principle of the upper trinity' by what he tells his reader is their 'real name': *en-soph*; the Word, or Logos; and the Holy Spirit.[122] The philosopher has 'deduced' the Christian Godhead using a principally logical, or dialectical, approach.

And yet note that Soloviev only writes that the subject of the manifestation 'returns to itself'; it does not confirm itself in its manifestation but only 'finds itself' there in order to return to itself. It

---

[119] Ibid., pp. 270-71. Clearly influenced by Genesis 1.3, Soloviev defines the Logos as 'the beginning, or principle, of light, in which is revealed, or becomes visible [...] the whole content of the absolute.'

[120] Ibid., p. 273.

[121] Ibid, p. 281. The idea of a 'suffering' God was, of course, central to the Jewish prophets, whom in later life Soloviev came to admire so much. Consider, for example, the words of God in Isaiah 42.14: For a long time I have held my peace/ I have kept still and restrained myself;/ now I will cry out like a woman in labour,/ I will gasp and pant. Paul Gavrilyuk has shown in his survey of patristic thought that many early Fathers gave voice to the 'paradoxical statement that God suffered impassibly.' P. L. Gavrilyuk, *The Suffering of the Impassible God: the Dialectics of Patristic Thought*, Oxford, 2005, p. 7. The extension of a suffering God outside the bounds of the economy of the Son is deeply controversial but Soloviev's thought on this subject can only be judged in the light of the argument that follows.

[122] Ibid., p. 270.

leaves its other to dwell again in itself. Even in this logical discourse, the reader gets the sense of the material world falling away, left behind by an errant God. 'Thus we have three positive principles in the absolute substance as the first centre, three necessary kinds, or forms, of its manifestation.' Yet, Soloviev writes,

> besides this, there is a fourth, negative principle, or its [i.e. the first centre of the absolute—OS] other [...]; being, or nature, does not belong amongst the first principles because of its relative and derivative meaning.[123]

This is an unexpected turn of phrase. That the material world, the 'other' of the absolute, is 'derivative' we can understand, since it was derived from the first centre of the absolute. In the same way, insofar as it relies on the absolute for its determination, it is 'relative.' Insofar as it is relative and derivative—the other, or opposite, of the positive absolute—it could perhaps be described as 'negative.' That it must be logically posited as a fourth principle besides the three principles of the first centre is also clear: while the absolute must contain its other in order to be itself, the other must also have its being outside the absolute for the absolute to manifest itself as such. Just as the nothing becomes the 'principle of form,' so the absolute both moves in, and is wholly distinct from, its other. Despite the paradox involved in such a proposition, we can acknowledge its logical necessity. But through Soloviev's purportedly logical discourse the outlines of a new idea begin to show through. Why does the philosopher decide to allocate the other a 'meaning' (*znachenie*), a word which otherwise has no application in his logic? Is not the meaning of the other, in logical terms, purely to act as the final ground for the manifestation of the absolute, allowing it to return to itself and experience itself as form? It is here that the conditionality and relativity of the fourth principle—the other of the absolute—cease to be being the mere result of logical supposition and become functions of a more profound teleology.

---

[123] Ibid., p. 270.

III. COSMOGONY

> *Белую лилию с розой,*
> *С алою розой мы сочетаем.*
> *Тайной пророческой грезой*
> *Вечную истину мы обретаем.*[124]
>
> Early March, 1876

In the last section, we noted how the emergence of the *idea*, Logos, or the Word, from *en-soph*, the first centre of the absolute, heralded the advent of being. Through the Logos the absolute will becomes known to itself. We traced the end of the theogonic process to the return of God to herself through 'feeling' her own form, as the Holy Spirit. The step between the Logos and the final step of the absolute's self-discovery in form is thus the creation of the material world. In this way, the primordial will (i.e. the will before it finds itself) is seen as the creative agent of pure, empty space, or uncreated matter — the 'formless void' of Genesis, the nexus of being itself — whereas the creation of definite form, our material reality, can only occur through the Logos.[125] Thus far, we have viewed this creative process, which with the introduction of the *Logos* bifurcated into two separate strands — that of the first centre, or positive nothing, and that of the second, or being itself — only from the 'perspective' of the absolute principle. From this angle, the will of the absolute is seen as the sole mover of creation — firstly of being itself, and then, through the Logos, of the material world. But the Logos, as an active principle, must play a part in this process. Thus, although these two strands exist in perfect unity,[126] Soloviev's logic moves to detail each moment in its separation from the other. Instead of from within the absolute, therefore, we will now try to explicate this process from within being. Our attention thus turns from theogony to cosmogony.

---

[124] 'The white lily with the rose,/ with the red rose we marry./ Through mystery of prophetic dreaming/ Eternal Truth we obtain.' From first verse of 'Pesnia ofitov' (1876). Solov'ev, *"Nepodvizhno,"* p. 25.

[125] Note the similarity to the Logos theology of the Gospel of John: 'All things came into being through him, and without him not one thing came into being' (John 1.3).

[126] Note Christ's words in John 10.30: 'The Father and I are one.'

III. COSMOGONY

We have already noted that the idea, from the point of view of being, can be described as empty space, or pure form, *materia prima*. But this is only when it is taken by itself as separate from the first centre, or will. When the will moves in it, there is a qualitative leap in terms of being. How are we to characterize this being? Here relation appears, namely the relation of the absolute, or first centre, to itself through its idea.

In *Critique*, Soloviev defines 'absolute truth' not as 'relation or being, but as that which *is* in the relation: the substantial.'[127] From here, we can conclude that this form of the idea is the purest example of truth there is, since it is a relation in which the subject of the knowing coincides with its object. The Logos — the formed being, or image, of the first centre of the absolute, or God — can thus also be defined as truth, or the subject of truth,[128] which is as much as to say that God knows herself as truth: truth is the definition of her being, which she enjoys only through the Logos.[129]

The other of the first centre was defined as the idea, or the something — the concrete possibility of relation, and thus multiplicity, number, or form. In this way, in the idea the absolute is seen in the fullness of his manifestation, as having taken on form. This formed world is an ideal world, similar to the Platonic world of ideas, in which the content of the absolute is seen for the first time as the image of God. From the point of view of being, the theogony is here complete: God is. But is she yet the all-one substance, truth, or the 'one and all'?[130]

God indeed contains her other — multiplicity, or the many — in the ideal world formed through her second centre. The union of this multiplicity in the one leads to the emergence of truth as the being, or Logos, of God. 'In the truth, "the many" does not exist in its separation, as only many; here each is connected to all and, accordingly, the many exists only in the one as *all*.'[131] In other words, in the truth 'the many' is never unmitigated since it is eternally returned to oneness through

---

[127] PSS, III, p. 265.
[128] See John 14.6: 'I am the way, and the truth, and the life. No one comes to the Father except through me.'
[129] See PSS, III, pp. 274-283.
[130] See glossary for the definition of truth as 'the all-one substance.'
[131] PSS, III, p. 267.

the activity of the Holy Spirit. And yet 'the many' must exist: it must *be* in order for the fullness of the absolute to become manifest to itself in its interaction with being. If the many were not, then there would be no return of the absolute principle to itself, and thus no self-knowledge or self-manifestation.

In his unfinished article of 1877, 'Faith, Reason and Experience,' Soloviev portrays the same three-step process involved in any self-manifestation with which he had characterized his theogony,[132] but this time from the perspective of being. He starts with the moment in which all elements are held in perfect unity — the Logos — and describes its movement out of itself as the development of an 'organic whole':

> In the development of any organic whole we have three logically necessary moments. Firstly, the absolute conjunction of all elements, whose particularity lies only in possibility or potential. Secondly, the development of the power of each element through its striving toward exclusive and absolute self-assertion. And thirdly, and finally, the actual self-assertion of each element within the limits of its idea or function through the realization of a harmonious, constellated whole.[133]

The third moment will be the subject of our next section. The necessity of the second moment, which had no place in the absolute principle as such, lies in the coming-to-be of 'the other.' Since 'the many' must have independent being outside the unity of God, each component of this many must will itself into being as one exclusive centre, as a *non*-part of the absolute.

As a consequence, an anti-divine principle comes into being in the sphere of the Logos, described by Soloviev in *La Sophia* as 'the idea of a not-me (*non-moi*), or alien being.'

> The anti-divine principle by its nature cannot be limited by the ideal sphere; in its own nature it is manifested as the idea of an actual not-me, as a wanting, or striving, for being, as desire or concupiscence.[134]

---

[132] See above, p. 63.
[133] PSS, III, p. 376. The serialization of 'Faith, Reason and Experience' began in the journal *Grazhdanin* in 1877 but stopped for unknown reasons. See commentary in PSS, III, pp. 515-16.
[134] PSS, II, p. 108.

In accordance with the will of the absolute that the 'other' possess being for itself, the will of the Logos, which it receives from the first centre, can here be understood as giving sway to its anti-divine counterpart, *materia prima*, in that it allows this latter to assert itself as distinct from its will. The Logos is subjected to separation and atomization as it submits to the power of the anti-divine principle. In effect, what Soloviev is describing here is a metaphysics of kenosis realized through the Logos in eternity: a giving of Godself to the forces of death and separation. As a consequence, *materia prima* becomes an independent power, ungoverned by the will of the first centre. Unlike the divine will in the Logos, *materia prima* is not known to itself since it has no being when separated from its source. It can thus only manifest itself in a blind striving after existence. It is this unidirectional character of the principle which allows Soloviev to describe it as *concupiscence*,[135] an unambiguously self-centred lust to possess being for itself.[136]

---

[135] At this point, Soloviev appears to be combining Schellingian cosmology with classical Christian theology to produce something rather original. Soloviev's *materia prima*, as lack of being, may be compared to the scholastics' concept of sin as lack (*carentia*), which come into being after the Fall. This 'lack' manifests itself precisely as lust, or concupiscence, which becomes the material substratum for all sin. Augustine associates concupiscence with the 'perverse will,' which 'desires lower things in a depraved and disordered way [...] It turns away from the higher and to the inferior.' See W. Pannenberg, *Anthropology in Theological Perspective*, London, 2004, pp. 87-104 (p. 88). Soloviev, in attributing concupiscence to *materia prima*, posits the same egoistic force at the heart of the absolute that he sees in the activity of monads. What he is working toward, as we shall see in the next section, is the positing of a catastrophe, or premundane Fall, within the Godhead before the creation of the world.

[136] There are echoes here of Leibniz' interpretation of *materia prima* as the passive force of each monad, which he associates with finitude and qualifies as 'confused perception,' as well as with Boehm's 'Lust.' See Russell, *Critical Exposition*, p 169. Again, though, it is Schelling whom Soloviev follows most proximately. Yet we notice a crucial, though subtle, difference between the two. In *Die Weltalter*, Schelling writes that 'everyone recognizes that God would not be able to create beings outside of it itself from a blind necessity in God's nature, but rather with the highest voluntarism [...] That initial life of blind necessity could not be said to have being because it never actually attained continuance, Being,' but rather just remained in striving and desire for Being. Therefore it is 'engulfed since eternity by something higher and placed back into potentiality.' Schelling, *Ages of the World*, pp. 5, 48. This is what Schelling means when he writes that 'blind, necessary being' is 'debased to the All [...] in a moment that is eternally, always, and still happening (Ibid., p. 29).' In Soloviev's kenotic metaphysics, this 'debasement to the All' is reversed. Instead of multiplicity always and eternally finding

Since *materia prima* is the ideal world, albeit in its separation from the divine will, it can only use the elements of this world, which make up the constellation of the first centre, for its being. In its blind striving, therefore, the anti-divine principle 'possesses the ideas and gives them corporeal existence, separating them one from another.'[137] The material world, with its concretization of the principle of separation through temporal and spatial dislocation, thus emerges in Soloviev's cosmogony as an actualization of the ideal world of forms held in unity by the Logos.

The formation of God and, through God, of the material world is now complete. But the reader is still puzzled as to the point of all this. The little word that slipped into Soloviev's vocabulary in the formulation of the three logical moments of theogony — *meaning* — now battles for our attention. After this colossal effort of logical speculation, the most we can say about the result, apart from its intrinsic value for knowledge, is that God can do nothing other than be God, or 'God is as God does.' If this is our resting point, then Soloviev can wave goodbye to any pretensions he may have had to storm the abstract castles in the clouds built by systems such as Hegelianism. Yet Soloviev could never stay content with a purely logical conception of God and reality. Beneath his logical discourse moves an entire sea of subtext: the influence of other systems of thought, Christianity, and his own personal experience are all bound together in the 'rational' movement of his thought.

It is true that the philosopher's logic owes a great deal to the Hegelian dialectic, more perhaps than Soloviev is willing to admit. For Hegel, just as for Soloviev, the 'essence' of the absolute 'is just this, to be

---

itself as an integral part of the All through acknowledging its source in the latter, the All, in the person of the Logos, effaces *itself* in order to give free, independent being to *materia prima*. For this reason, it is impossible to agree with Krasicki, who writes that 'in Soloviev's cosmogony the derivation of the world is connected not with a positive but a negative act of God' (Krasitskii, p. 84). The renunciation of divine will effected through the Logos is precisely that positive act which allows the material world to be formed through negative opposition (spiritual-material; infinite-finite etc.) with the Godhead. What this also means is that evil, the anti-divine principle, becomes a real active force and cannot be thought merely as a deficiency, or lack, within being which is eternally overcome by the power of absolute self-determination.

[137] PSS, II, p. 110.

immediately one and selfsame in *otherness*, or in absolute difference.'[138] Hegel's system is similarly characterized by a restless search for absolute reality, which reveals itself in the inner dynamism of his thought, never resting on one-sided interpretations but subsuming, incorporating, and expanding. The absolute for both thinkers is thus 'essentially a result, [...] it is first at the end what it truly is; and [...] precisely in this consists its nature, viz. to be actual, subject, the becoming of itself.'[139] The character of the absolute — the 'all-one substance' in Soloviev and 'Geist' in Hegel — also has many parallels. Most importantly, they both view it as an *organism*, a living, or total, reality, which moves and is moved by the often contradictory determinations, or elements, of which it consists.[140] Since, for Hegel, 'the organism does not produce something but only preserves itself [...], what is produced, is as much already present as produced,'[141] it can be described as the great individual, bringing out of itself what existed before only in possibility, or potential:

> Individuality is precisely the actualizing of what exists only in principle, and the perversion ceases to be regarded as a perversion of the good, for it is in fact really the conversion of the good, as a mere End, into an actual existence: the movement of individuality is the reality of the universal.[142]

For Hegel and Soloviev, this organism, as both simple unity and realized multiplicity, combines the greatest possible individuality with the greatest possible universality, i.e. it is both as simple and as complex as possible.[143]

There is reason to believe that Soloviev misread Hegel on a number of important points and that his overwhelming negativity toward the German thinker in his early period may have been based on an in-

---

[138] G. W. F. Hegel, *Phenomenology of Spirit*, Oxford, 1977, p. 142.
[139] Cited in Robert Stern, *Routledge philosophy guidebook to Hegel and the phenomenology of spirit*, London, 2002, p. 59.
[140] Compare Hegel, *Phenomenology of Spirit*, p. 154.
[141] Ibid., p. 156.
[142] Cited in Stern, *Hegel and the phenomenology of spirit*, p. 123.
[143] See especially PSS, III, pp. 112-14, 172.

complete familiarity with the latter's system.¹⁴⁴ But the fundamental areas of disagreement between the two, especially as to the role of dialectics in their systems, cannot be explained away as having arisen from a simple misreading, or misapplication, as Soloviev was entirely conscious of his adaptation of the Hegelian dialectic for his own purposes.

In his *Logic*, Hegel had drawn the concept of *becoming* out of the initial opposition of being and nothing. As we have seen, Soloviev begins his 'organic logic' from a similar position — namely, the opposition of the absolute as wholly separate from the world and the absolute as the principle of all being: in other words, the absolute as nothing and the absolute as something. But, unlike Hegel's preliminary terms, Soloviev posits an actual being as determined by these, opposite terms.¹⁴⁵ For Soloviev, Hegel's logical concepts were 'predicates without subjects, relationships which lack that to which they relate.'¹⁴⁶ It was impossible, he asserted, to conceive of being without positing the subject, or possessor, of being. 'The absolute first principle cannot be defined as being; it is that which possesses being [...], a positive power over being, absolute freedom.' Pure being, for Hegel identical to pure thought, was thus for early Soloviev an entirely empty construct and Hegel's system merely the development of pure nothing, as pure concept, out of itself.¹⁴⁷

For Hegel, 'Reason is the certainty of being all *reality*.'¹⁴⁸ 'Reason' (*Vernunft*), a technical term which departs from both ordinary usage and its application in other systems of German Idealism, is in the Hegelian view the unity of subject and object, the removal of the overarching contradiction between the two, and the breakthrough to absolute reality. The point of divergence with Soloviev is that the very

---

¹⁴⁴ Typical of this negative attitude toward Hegel is Soloviev's early description of the former's system as 'the result of a colossal absurdity.' See Ibid., p. 254. Soloviev's article on Hegel for the Brockhaus-Efron encyclopaedia is evidence of the philosopher's more positive stance toward the German thinker later in life. See V. S. Solov'ev, *Sobranie sochinenii*, ed. E. L. Radlov and S. M. Solov'ev, 12 vols, Brussels, 1966-70, x, pp. 301-20.
¹⁴⁵ In the case of the absolute as purely transcendent, 'being' is not properly a term that can be applied.
¹⁴⁶ PSS, III, p. 299.
¹⁴⁷ Ibid., p. 254.
¹⁴⁸ Hegel, *Phenomenology of Spirit*, p. 142.

unity between subject and object is, in the movement of the Hegelian dialectic, itself objectified. This development posits, amongst other things, the ability of the subject of thinking to remove itself from the unity, as experienced, and regard it as merely thought. In this way, reason also becomes the unity of thought and being, and the removal of the contradiction between the two is actualized as being is resolved into thinking.[149]

Soloviev makes similarly lofty claims for reason (*razum*); for him, as for Hegel, it was 'the absolute form,' working from within human consciousness to break down the separateness and contradictions of being in its activity as 'the correlation of all in unity.'[150] But Soloviev argues, *pace* Hegel, that 'absolute form demands an absolute content, and the absolute nature of subjective consciousness must be filled with an absolute object.'[151] Reason is the moving power of the absolute, but it is not the absolute itself; it cannot move itself independently as it appears to in Hegel's system. Hegel's famous formulation 'all that is rational is real, and all that is real rational,' is thus reworked into Soloviev's assertion that 'we presuppose as necessary attributes of the truth absolute actuality (*bezuslovnaia real'nost'*) and absolute rationality (*bezuslovnaia razumnost'*).'[152] The real is not sublated into the rational, nor the rational into the real, but both moments are preserved as necessary for the fullness of truth. 'Reason in the truly substantial never exists in its separateness as empty form; being the principle of unity, it is always the unity of something, the unity of the many from which it makes all.'[153] The real and the rational combine in the organic life of the absolute substance.

In the last section of *Philosophical Principles*, titled 'Principles of Organic Logic: Relative Categories Determining the Idea as a Being,'[154]

---

[149] See the useful editorial notes in G. W. F. Hegel, *Hegel's Phenomenology of spirit: selections*, ed. Howard P. Kainz, University Park, PA, 1994, p. 89.
[150] PSS, III, p. 255.
[151] Ibid., pp. 150, 255.
[152] Ibid., p. 14.
[153] Ibid., p. 267.
[154] Soloviev is here not trying to argue for the identity of Idea and Being, á la Hegel, but to prove the existence of the Idea as a concrete being. It is undoubtedly the most complex of Soloviev's experiments in 'organic logic.' See PSS, II, pp. 283-90.

the word 'idea' is stretched even further to yield two forms — one with lower case and another, capitalized form. The latter — *Idea* — is understood by Soloviev as a hypostasis of the absolute substance. It is important to remember that at this stage in Soloviev's argument, his 'organic logic' is not only concerned with the determinations of the absolute principle itself, which were concluded with the trinity of *en-soph*, Logos and the Holy Spirit, but with the interaction of these three persons with their objectified other, which Soloviev designates the 'idea' (with a lower case).

> When we distinguish the categories, this is only in the Logos, consequently not absolutely [...] To know logically means to know in relation, i.e. relatively. Logos is relation, initially the relation of the suprasubstantial to itself as such, or its self-differentiation. But since the suprasubstantial is absolute, that is, since it is also *all*, the Logos is also the relation of the suprasubstantial to all and the all to the suprasubstantial. The first relation is the inner, or hidden, Logos (λόγος ἐνδιάθετος); the second is the revealed Logos (λόγος προφορικός); the third is the incarnate, or concrete, Logos (Christ).[155]

For Soloviev, there existed 'three worlds,' each of which corresponded to one of the hypostases of the divine trinity he deduced in his theogony. Though the three hypostases 'correspond,' they are not, however, identical to the three worlds: the divine hypostases — *en-soph*, Logos, and the Holy Spirit are only the *principles*, or beginning, of these worlds, not the worlds themselves. In *La Sophia*, these worlds are designated 'the world of pure spirits, the world of minds or ideas, and, finally, the world of souls.' In the previous section on theogony, we looked at the first world, 'the world of pure spirits,' which in the passage above is equivalent to 'the relation of the suprasubstantial to itself as such, or its self-differentiation.' The second world, 'the world of minds or ideas' has been the subject of this section on cosmogony, and is equivalent to 'the relation of the suprasubstantial to all.' It

---

[155] Ibid., p. 284. Soloviev borrows the Greek terms in parentheses — 'ideal Logos' and 'spoken Logos' respectively — from Philo of Alexandria. As Aleksei Kozyrev observes in his notes to *Philosophical Principles*, Philo's Logos is 'the link between an abstract substantial, as yet without designation, and the actuality of concrete being.' Ibid., pp. 380-81.

represents the ideal world formed by the self-manifestation of the first centre of the absolute through its eternal Word, or Logos. The third world is the final *result* of the cosmogonic process, 'the world of souls,' and is equivalent to 'the relation of all to the suprasubstantial.' It represents the multiplicity of actual, material being as held in, and defined by, the Logos as its principle. Soloviev writes that 'just as the principles of the three worlds are one,' as we noted in the theogonic section, 'so the worlds themselves are one.'[156] That is to say, the results of the theogonic and cosmogonic processes, which appear as 'processes' only in their logical elucidation, are to be considered parts of a simple unity, which is nothing other than the absolute substance. Thus the two worlds, which together make up the realm of being, and the one world of the absolute principle in-itself, or the first centre, exist in an ineluctable unity, or as an absolute organism.

In order for that unity to be actual, however, there needs to be an agent of unity, through whose activity the many is once more returned to the one and the one to the many. This agent for Soloviev is the Logos, which is described simply as 'relation.' It is the agent of All-Unity, the moving power of all being which relates each thing to every other, God to the world, and the world to God. But since the relation within each world to the remaining two worlds is of a different kind, so too does the Logos differ. In the world of the absolute in-itself, or the suprasubstantial as such, the Logos is hidden, or concealed. Here it is only the possibility of relation, pure potential, or the 'idea in potentiality (magic or Maya).'[157] In the ideal world, God becomes

---

[156] Ibid., p. 112. In *La Sophia*, the principles of these worlds are designated *Dukh* (Spirit), *Um* (Mind), and *Dusha* (Soul). Here these terms have an analogous meaning to the hypostases of *en-soph*, Logos, and the Holy Spirit in *Philosophical Principles*.

[157] Soloviev may have been influenced by the definition of the idea as 'magical being' in mystics such as John Pordage, whom he had discovered while writing *Philosophical Principles*. In a letter of April 1877, he writes to Countess Tolstaia that he had found 'three specialists on Sophia: Georg Gichtel. Gottfried Arnold, and John Pordage,' although his assessment of these writers is generally negative, describing them as 'overly subjective, and, so to say, drivelling (*sliuniavyi*) in character [...] The most interesting thing is that all three have had personal experience almost the same as mine, although in theosophy proper all three are rather weak; they follow Boehme but are lower than he. I think Sophia had to do with them more because of their innocence than anything else.' Solov'ev, *Pis'ma*, II, p. 200. For more on the terms Magia, Mag and

known to herself through the person of the Logos, who is thus now *revealed*. Here, the Logos corresponds to 'the other as pure idea, i.e. in intelligible reality.' Finally, the Logos in the third world is the incarnate, or concrete, Logos — Christ, whose 'concrete idea is Sophia.' No sooner is a definition for this last Logos given, however, than Soloviev adds a disclaimer, writing that 'the meaning of this third Logos and its corresponding idea can only be explicated later.'

In terms, then, of the Logos's manifestation, which is itself the *form* of the unity of the three worlds, the first moment is unknown and unknowable since the Logos is contained within it only in a *hidden* capacity in the 'higher, supraessential (*sverkhsushchestvennyi*) Trinity.' The second moment is the Logos itself as revealed or manifested. Because the Logos, as the Word of God, introduces being into the absolute for the first time, not in an actual sense but only ideally, Soloviev calls it 'the very act of its [i.e. the absolute — OS] manifestation.' This 'act' may be imagined as following a similar pattern to human volitional activity. First, an idea rises in human consciousness which seeks to determine her activity as regards her will. This is equivalent to the 'ideal' stage of the absolute's self-manifestation, and contains the essence of the act itself. Second, the idea is carried through in the concrete execution of the act. This third moment in Soloviev's schema is 'the concrete idea,' or simply *Idea*, which now becomes capitalized. This Idea 'corresponds to the third, inner phase' of the absolute principle as the Holy Spirit; it is the Logos 'as manifested in its other' or 'the absolute, manifested for itself.'

The suprasubstantial principle, which Soloviev calls 'the absolute proper,' meaning the absolute in-itself in unity with concrete being — the absolute substance — is 'absolute inner unity.' The Idea as the manifested absolute is therefore '*realized unity, i.e. unity in all*, or in multiplicity.'

> This all, this multiplicity, is already contained in potentiality in the absolute, which is one and all. In the Logos, this potential multiplicity

---

Magnus, which occur in Soloviev's rough drafts for *Philosophical Principles*, see the accompanying notes to the text: PSS, II, pp. 381-82.

III. COSMOGONY

transitions into the act; accordingly, in the Idea it should again be returned to unity as actual. In other words, the suprasubstantial as such is the fundamental, substantial unity of the many before its manifestation (or, more precisely, independently of its manifestation), the Idea is its actual unity as already manifested, and the Logos is the principle of its differentiation.[158]

The Logos as 'the principle of differentiation' makes known the elements of the hidden God by giving them form in being. It is thus 'the producing (differentiating, active) principle of being, or nature; it corresponds to [being, or nature] but is not identical with them.'[159] The Logos is now further defined as 'the deity in being, or nature, just as the Idea is the deity in essence, or object (reflection).'[160]

The absolute substance, like the absolute proper, can now be seen to be composed of three subjects, or hypostases—the absolute in-itself, Logos, and the Idea—which correspond to the three subjects of the absolute in-itself but now straddle the three worlds of transition between non-being and being, the created and uncreated worlds. This unity is manifested in actual multiplicity in the Idea, but in what manner?

Taking on yet another layer of complexity, Soloviev writes that unity in the Idea appears in a different mode for each subject. In the world of the absolute in-itself—i.e. the world of 'pure spirits' or the absolute as distinct from its manifestation—the unity of all subjects, which is the full manifestation of Soloviev's absolute substance, is manifested as will, and this will further defined as the 'good.' In the world of the Logos—i.e. the world of 'pure ideas' or the ideal world—the unity of all subjects is known as 'truth.' Finally, in the world of the Idea—i.e. the world of 'pure souls' or the absolute after

---

[158] PSS, II, p. 286.

[159] Compare this hypostatic understanding of the Logos to Soloviev's anti-Hegelian estimation of reason in 'Faith, Reason and Experience': 'In itself, reason does not have the productive power which, for instance, will or imagination (*fantaziia*) have.' PSS, III, pp. 367-68.

[160] The idea of reflection, as in a mirror, has been crucial to the articulation of mystical thought. For a discussion of Sophia as mirror, see my 'The Sophianic Task in the Work of Vladimir Solov'ëv,' *Journal of Eastern Christian Studies*, 59, 2008, 3-4, pp. 167-83 (pp. 170-71).

its manifestation, as realized unity — the unity of all subjects is directly present as 'beauty.'

> Perfect unity consists in this: that the very same thing, precisely the Idea, which is thought as truth, is at the same time willed and wanted as the *good*, while this selfsame thing, and not something else, is felt as *beauty*. These determinations are not separate essences but only three forms, or images, in which the same thing appears for the different subjects, precisely the Idea, in which, therefore, dwells the entire fullness of the Deity.[161]

This definition of 'perfect unity' is in fact the furthest that Soloviev's 'organic logic' can take him. The positing of a unity between the good, truth and beauty, given here as the truth of the mind, remains the principal formulation of the Philosophy of All-Unity, to which Soloviev will return in different and innovative ways.[162] He has no logical apparatus capable of answering in what exactly the good consists, or of drawing out the content of its idea, just as it cannot approach the meaning of beauty. 'A logically defined answer is possible only in the second of these three questions, for good and beauty as such, being the object of will and feeling, and not thinking, are not subject to logical thinking, which relates to the idea only as truth.'[163] Where his logic reaches its limit, a new form of thinking begins. His arrival at the perfection of the threefold unity could not in itself explain how the 'fourth world,' which we saw posited at the end of the theogonic section,[164] could impinge on this unity. It is in his treatment of this fourth world in the unpublished *La Sophia* that the question of the meaning behind his early philosophy is to be pursued.

---

[161] PSS, II, p. 287 (my emphases).
[162] The idea that good, truth and beauty have a single source is an idea that can be found as early as Plato, though it is perhaps more central to Soloviev's system than any other thinker before him. Fedor Golubinskii (1797-1854), whom Pavel Florenskii saw as the Russian originator of the concept of Sophia, had already associated the three 'ideas' with three human 'abilities of the soul' (*sposobnosti dushi*): '[When the human being] delves into itself, it finds the idea of the truth in the mind, the idea of beauty in feeling, and the idea of good in the will.' F. A. Golubinskii, 'Obshchee vvedenie v filosofiiu,' *Leksii po filosofii i umozritel'noi psikhologii*, St Petersburg, 2006, pp. 31-56 (p. 51).
[163] Ibid, p. 287.
[164] See above, pp. 64-65.

IV. THE FOURTH WORLD

> В сне земном мы тени, тени...
> Жизнь — игра теней,
> Ряд далеких отражений
> Вечно светлых дней. [165]
>
> 9 June 1875

In the second dialogue of *La Sophia*, which immediately succeeds Sophia's exposition of the 'mystery' of the three worlds — a mystery which in *Philosophical Principles*, far from being presented as mysterious, had been 'deducted' using dialectical logic — *Philosophe* voices his overriding sense of incompleteness to *Sophia*:

> You revealed to me the inner nature and mutual relations of the three worlds. I came to know them in their differentiation and in their perfect unity. I also discovered that these three divine worlds contain in themselves the principles of our world, the world in which I live, move and exist. It is clear to me, however, that this last world is not wholly contained in these first, that it is different from them and thus forms a fourth. Their essential character is opposite. In the first unity and divine spirituality prevail; they are nothing other than the realization of this unity and spirituality. In them, multiplicity and materiality are only the mediating instrument of this divine unity; they make up the kingdom of love and peace. In our world, everything is the other way round. here multiplicity, separation, hate, coarse materiality always occupy first place, whereas divine unity appears only as an arbitrary product. Where does this new world come from?[166]

We have already had cause to note that Soloviev's earliest and most fundamental conviction was in the *imperfection* of this world and its need of transformation. Here this conviction is expressed with an intensity of feeling unequalled in Soloviev's other works of this period, both published and unpublished. An ethical dimension has entered

---

[165] 'In the earthly dream we are shadows, shadows.../ Life is the play of shadows,/ A series of long reflections of/ Eternally bright days.' From first verse of 'V sne zemnom my teni, teni...' (1875), Solov'ev, "Nepodvizhno," p. 21.

[166] PSS, II, p. 116.

the equation besides the purely theoretical. Alongside the impersonal forces of impenetrability and attraction which Soloviev draws from matter in *Crisis* and *Critique*, a broader and more emotive picture is painted of our world as governed by hate and separation rather than love and peace.

At all stages of its development, from the deduction of the Holy Trinity and the triune Idea as good-truth-beauty to the use of the dialectical pattern thesis-antithesis-synthesis, Soloviev's thought moves in groups of three: its method is just as indebted to trinity as its result. The addition of a 'fourth substantial formative principle,' in *Philosophical Principles* designated — again (!) — the 'idea,' to the previous three principles upsets the unity and uniformity of Soloviev's system. How are we to explain its emergence and the existence of the world of which it is the cause outside the 'perfect unity' of the three worlds? Is not perfection undermined and unity destroyed?

In Soloviev's handling of the cosmogonic process, the idea becomes object to the same degree as the substantial becomes subject. In other words, as the idea gains actuality in material existence, or becomes Idea, *materia prima* is brought out of a state of indifferent potentiality, takes on definite form, and the substantial becomes the actual subject, or 'carrier,' of its now incarnate idea. 'In this sense the idea is last but, on the other hand, only the idea in its potential existence can define the activity of the substantial as will, representation and feeling.' Yet the logical discourse of *Philosophical Principles* lacks anything like a consistently stated historical dimension, and to the reader it appears that the 'emergence' of God and world occurs only for the mind, in a succession of logical moments, rather than having an objective basis. In a rare moment of inconsistency, however, Soloviev describes the cosmological process as 'the gradual actualization, or formation, of the idea and, corresponding to this, the gradual potentialization, or materialization, of the substantial.'[167] With the word 'gradual,' Soloviev has introduced a temporal dimension into his thinking, and it is the historical articulation the philosopher gives his idea, with its roots in *La Sophia*, that is to dominate the period from *Critique* onward.

---

[167] PSS, II, p. 281.

IV. THE FOURTH WORLD

La Sophia operates at a remove very far indeed from Soloviev's other works of the period. His argument is here thrust into a deeply mythologized account of reality, which for its explication borrows terms from profoundly dissimilar traditions of thought. The cosmogony described in the second dialogue replicates much of the material in *Philosophical Principles*, but develops it from a radically different perspective. Here the hypostatic Idea is fully associated with Sophia and the 'anti-divine principle' with Satan, also called the 'cosmic spirit,' 'spirit of the cosmos,' or 'the prince of this world,' in whom Soloviev incarnates the wilful force of egoism he sees inhering in every atom.[168] In *La Sophia*, the two realms — the perfect unity of the three worlds, and the fourth world — meet, intersect, and do battle with one another. Theogony, cosmogony, and ontology are indistinguishable and create one overarching metaphysics that relies on a combination of mystical experience, logic, and empirical observation. Sophia — the Idea — speaks and is spoken to; she is perceived by *Philosophe* and herself perceives. Atomic attraction, which in *Critique* is presented as a fact of the physical world to be built into a coherent argument, is here presented as the result of the intentional activity of Satan, who is associated with *materia prima*.

Sophia's reply to the question of *Philosophe* as to the derivation of the fourth world begins the movement:

> It is not a new world. It is nothing other than the third world, the world of souls and bodies (we saw, you recall, that the soul is inseparable from the body) distanced from the two other worlds, for it is directly linked with the intellectual, or ideal, world while being distanced from it.[169]

Soloviev's answer as to how the distance between the third and fourth worlds came about lies in the progressive manifestation of the all-one across the three worlds, and the relation between them, which we saw resulting in the trinity *en-soph*-Logos-Holy Spirit. In *La Sophia*, Soloviev uses the terms Spirit, Mind and Soul as the representatives of this trinity, the principal subjects in each of the three worlds

---

[168] Ibid., pp. 122-34.
[169] Ibid., p. 116.

respectively. The first movement of the Spirit out of itself forms the Mind. The Mind, as pure being or pure form, is not yet manifest to itself, however, and requires further manifestation in the Soul. The Soul, or the Idea, has only matter in the proper sense of the word to use for its manifestation. But matter itself is the result of the anti-divine force which had been unleashed in the sphere of pure being for the purposes of the final manifestation of the other.[170] The Logos sacrificed its own essential being, as conjoined with the first centre, in order to effect the coming-to-be of this other. It is therefore for the Soul, or Idea, alone that matter exists without mediation; in the realm of the Mind, or Logos, matter only exists as coupled with those ideas of which it represents the concrete form, just as Spirit can only feel matter as its actualized content through the agency of the Logos. The fact that matter, which as real multiplicity contains an anti-divine potential, is so *immediately* present to the Soul means that a certain degree of freedom enters her activity. She is faced with two possibilities: either she lets herself be determined by the Mind and the ideal world, which govern her, or she can strive to have being for her own and assert herself as an independent principle, thus creating her own world out of herself. As soon as this latter course is chosen, however, she ceases to be the unity of the three worlds, the concrete Idea and loses control over being.[171]

---

[170] See above, p. 68-69.

[171] In *La Sophia*, the Soul is associated with Sophia but not to the point of identity. Samuel Cioran believes them to be equivalent terms, however: Cioran, *Vladimir Solov'ev and the Knighthood of the Divine Sophia*, pp. 24-25. For an overview of the two terms in Soloviev's early thought, see W. E. Helleman, 'The World Soul and Sophia in the Early Work of Solov'ev,' in *Vladimir Solov'ev: Reconciler and Polemicist. Selected Papers of the International Solov'ev Conference held in Nijmegen, September 1998*, ed. Wil van den Bercken, Manon de Courten and Evert van der Zweerde, Leuven, 2000, pp. 163-84; D. A. Krylov, *Evkharisticheskaia chasha: Sofiinye nachala*, Moscow, 2006, pp. 196-203. The fall of the Soul as described by Soloviev corresponds with many accounts found in gnostic sources. Common to the majority of these belief systems was the idea that Sophia, the eighth and last aeon of the divine pleroma, or fullness, had fallen and thereby severed herself from the whole. According to Iranaeus, Sophia desired after the majesty of the father, to grasp it and make it her own. In Hippolytus' account, instead of remaining content with the reflected glory of her creator, Sophia tried to imitate him by creating out of herself all that exists. She did not reckon the distance between herself and the father, however, and created only that which was chaotic and formless, the opposite of the harmonious world of the aeons. It was from this void that

The Soul was only unity insofar as she was passively defined by the Spirit and Mind as an instrument of the all-one. The first result of her creation is Satan, who for Soloviev represents 'the Soul as the principle of separation, egoism, hate and enmity.'[172] Monads, or *souls*, which in *Critique* are seen as 'directing themselves toward each other' in a desire to 'fill the other's place,' are here described as 'atoms under the direction of Satan.' This latter is moved exclusively by the will to be the only centre to the exclusion of all else. His will is thus a centripetal force which would concentrate in a single point if not kept in check, and his activity is experienced throughout the physical world in the law of attraction. Were there not another agent who could repel the incursions of satanic attraction, all matter would be reduced to naught. In Soloviev's scheme, this role of inhibitor is fulfilled by the passive activity of the Demiurge who, as impenetrability, 'the principle of form, order, and relations,' resists the advances of the active Satan.[173]

La Sophia adds further speculation to the view of the monad as active *producer* of the material world advanced by Soloviev in his other works. Here he describes how each satanic centre, or monad, vies to replace the other but finds outside itself a multiplicity of impenetrable barriers. It is in this finding of otherness in sensible form that space and extension emerge under the banner of the Demiurge, the formal principle which relates each satanic centre to every other. Seeing that he is only able to operate from a multitude of centres thus constellated and that the reductive unity he yearns for cannot be immediately attained, Satan does battle with the Demiurge in time, which emerges as a result of the former's activity. Soloviev even goes so far as to split the phenomena of the physical world according to which of the two principles exercises dominion:

---

the material world had its source. See the editorial notes in PSS, II, pp. 343-44. For an in-depth study of the various gnostic systems in the writings of the heresiologists and the more recent discoveries at Nag Hammadi, see Kurt Rudolf, *Gnosis: the nature and the history of gnosticism*, San Francisco, 1983.

[172] PSS, II, p. 122.
[173] Ibid., p. 126. The role of Soloviev's demiurge is much like the role of the same figure in Plato's *Timaeus*, where it uses the ideal forms to create the lower material order and must bargain with necessity (in Soloviev: Satan, *materia prima*) in order so to do.

Monads in which Satan prevails, that is, monads in which desire, attraction, weight and inertia predominate and which exist only in-themselves—these are monads of which matter in the proper sense is consisted. They are Satan in concentrated and coagulated form, Satan materialized. Monads in which the Demiurge prevails, that is, [which exhibit] perception, centrifugal force and resistance, make up what is called the ether or imperceptible powers.[174]

All material objects, in this view, have a share in 'Satan materialized' since they have hardened themselves into definite form and, in so doing, created a boundary to the influence of the other. They are focused inward on themselves. But through the demiurgic powers of light, sound, or sensation—to name but a few—which give rise to perception, each object finds itself in a definite relation to all other objects, thus mitigating the extent of their isolation. On the ethical plane, the material world is governed by the force of *egoism*, the will to become the only centre of being, which finds its representative in Satan. The Demiurge rules over the formal principle of space, which separates each thing from another and constellates an entire, indestructible world outside each centre of satanic egoism.

The cosmic process, therefore, is viewed as a battle between Satan and the Demiurge, each vying for ascendancy. But since Satan, for Soloviev, is a principle of the Soul, and this latter the unity of actualized ideas contained within the absolute, he can only use the form of these definite ideas for his body, or matter. 'The material principle, blind desire, possesses the ideas and gives them corporeal existence, separating them from each other; but the divine will, following the unity of the Mind, gathers them together in actuality. This actual unity is called the *Soul*.'[175] The reader thus gains a rather confused picture

---

[174] Ibid., p. 128.
[175] Ibid., p. 110. Soloviev seems here to be mixing Gnostic cosmogonic myths involving the world soul and the principle of evil with Plato's account of the creation of the visible universe through the demiurge, who can only use the pattern of the world of Forms to guide him (*Timaeus*). The process of bridging these two worlds is, in Plato, realized by both the Demiurge and intelligent souls, these latter 'remembering' their link with the ideal world through an act of *anamnesis*, and in the majority of Gnostic systems by a withdrawal from evil, material form through a form of spiritual

of the activity and designation of the Soul: on the one hand, it is the source of the blind desire of satanic egoism that produces isolated material objects; on the other, it is the very unity of these objects as enacted through the divine will in the unity of the Mind (Logos). But it is precisely this radical equivocity of the Soul — at once the principle of disunity and the actuality of produced unity — which is the key component of Soloviev's sophiology. The material world is understood not, following Gnosticism, as a satanic creation of evil and darkness, but as the locus of a paradoxical relationship of identity in absolute otherness, a relationship, moreover, mediated in the 'Soul.' In this sense, matter itself — derived from the Logos *qua* relation yet allowed to manifest itself in otherness through the kenotic withdrawal of the same — becomes a cypher for a dual procession, simultaneously separated and bound up with this selfsame Logos. It is this aspect of Soloviev's thought that Hans Urs von Balthasar picks up on when writing about his cosmogony:

> [Soloviev] puts the [products of the world soul] under the irradiating activity of the divine creative Logos, but in such a way that in the inmost depths the mother and matrix of all forms shares in the successive acts of their information, since this matrix itself attains a deeper interiority in every one of its products and so acquires greater generative power. On its own, it is a 'barren womb,' but when it is fertilized by the Logos, it is no longer possible to say whether the forms generated are more the product of the Logos or more the product of the world-soul.[176]

Just as the Mind separates the principles inherent in the Spirit, Satan separates one from another in actual deed. In so doing, he acts according to the nature of his own desire but at the same time fulfils that part of the divine plan which demands not just ideal separation, formal multiplicity in potential alone, but real separation, multiplicity *in actu*. This act is not performable by God as such, since the principle of mutual

---

union with God attained through mystical knowledge (*gnosis*). Ultimately, Soloviev is after a union that is not interiorly realized in the soul, but externally in the material world.

176 H. U. Balthasar, *The Glory of the Lord: A Theological Aesthetics*, San Francisco, 1996, p. 313.

isolation is precisely that from which God must distinguish herself in order to become known. But it is in accordance with divine necessity. In Boehme's evocative phrase, evil — the principle of isolation — is the 'vital venom,'[177] the prerequisite to the manifestation and triumph of God on Earth.

In *Critique*, the 'other,' or 'idea,' of *Philosophical Principles* becomes identified with the second 'principle' of the all-one substance. In this second principle Soloviev posits

> the antithesis of the absolute (matter) and identity with it (idea); in fact, this second principle is not one nor the other, nor even both together. As opposed to the all-one *substance* (the first principle), it is the *becoming* all-one (*stanoviashcheesia vseedinoe*).[178]

The notion of process, intimated in *Philosophical Principles* by Soloviev's use of the word 'gradual,' is here made explicit. We recall that, for Soloviev, to be absolute means to be the union of oneself and one's other, the one and the many, the absolute and the conditional. But in *Critique* the philosopher sets himself a more searching question: 'In what respect is the absolute all and not-all?'[179] Since, as we have noted, the absolute cannot contain the principle of falsehood and separation within itself as an actual act (this 'act' in *La Sophia* is attributed to the activity of Satan), such an act must be realized outside it. But, writes Soloviev

> [The many] cannot have reality in itself, it cannot be absolutely independent of the absolute; the many — not all, i.e. the untrue (since truth is All-Unity) — cannot exist absolutely since that would be a contradiction. Consequently, if it must exist within an other, this other cannot be absolutely outside the absolute. It should be both within the absolute and, so as to contain in actuality the particular, or the untrue, it must be outside the absolute. Thus, alongside the absolute substance as such, which is all-one *actu*, we must posit another being (*sushchestvo*), which is also absolute but not identical with the absolute as such. [...] If to be the subject of absolute content in an eternal and indivisible act

---

[177] Boehme, *Mysterium Magnum*, p. 10.
[178] PSS, III, p. 282.
[179] Ibid., p. 283.

is the property of the one true being, or God, the other being must be the subject of the same content in a gradual process; if the first *is* all-one, the second *becomes* all-one. [...] This second all-one, or "second god," [...] has a divine element, All-Unity as its eternal potential, which gradually transitions into actuality; on the other hand, it has in itself that non-divine, particular, non-all, natural, or material element, by virtue of which it is *not* all-one, but only *becomes* so.[180]

At the end of his grand theogony-cosmogony, Soloviev seems to have arrived at the need to presuppose another absolute being *besides* God, a being who is not absolute in an eternal act but only becomes so in the course of time. This being, as well as the dynamics of the process of becoming, will be the subject of our next chapter.

Before moving on, however, it is pertinent to make a few final remarks on the nature of 'becoming' in Soloviev. To view the philosopher's theogony and cosmogony as the real 'processes' of creation is to make a profound category mistake. Soloviev, like Thomas Aquinas, argues that all that exists is radically contingent: it has no reason in and of itself for being. Our logical thought merely separates the various components of reality, which, as far as being is concerned, exist in an indivisible unity. The doctrine of creation, in the biblical account as well as in the gnostic sources with which he was familiar, is not, according to Soloviev, about an event but about a relationship with the One who grounds reality and gives it meaning.[181] His method of revealing the essence of this relationship involves a simultaneous exposition of the logical process, according to which the middle term is attained through the opposition of two opposing terms, and the theogonic-cosmogonic process, in which the first term begets the middle term (in the logical process, the agent of reconciliation), which in turn begets the last term.

---

[180] Ibid., p. 284. Basing himself on quotes such as this, Zen'kovskii argues that Soloviev's thought is characterized by an 'undeniable inner duplicity' and posits dualism at the heart of his system. See Zen'kovskii, 'Vladimir Solov'ev,' p. 31. Against such a view, it may be said that the full force of Soloviev's reasoning is reserved precisely to counter absolute dualism of any kind.

[181] The parallels with Aquinas' theology in this regard are striking. See PSS, III, pp. 43, 311. For Aquinas views on creation, see St Thomas Aquinas, *Aquinas on Creation*, trans. Steven E. Baldner and William E. Carroll, Toronto, 1997.

This creates room for a conception of God that is neither absolutely static nor wholly predictable in its movement. It also allows the philosopher to express not only the unity of the Christian Trinity but the co-equality of its three hypostases, whose relationship is neither hierarchical nor absolutely undifferentiated. Not only are the persons of the Trinity dependent on each other but every component of being, from the infinitesimally small 'atom' to the complex human organism, is radically contingent on every other. Nevertheless, Soloviev's notion of the 'second absolute' owes more to Plato and Schelling than it does to Christian tradition,[182] and raises significant difficulties from the perspective of the latter. He was to distance himself from it in his middle period, although he struggled to maintain his conviction in the involvement of the absolute in temporal process and history until the end of his life.

The temporal notion of process belongs only to the 'fourth world,' which Soloviev had deduced from a comparison of the previous three with the conditions of our material existence. This world is involved in a process of becoming absolute, of returning to the absolute from which it has its source. Whether the absolute substance would be enriched as a result of this return, as Frederick Copleston argues, or whether it would merely effect a 'restoration' to a 'previous' state of unity, is not immediately clear from Soloviev's early writings.[183] But the similarity between Soloviev's teaching on this fourth world and the ideas he had come across in the Kabbala and other mystical writings allows us some room to substantiate Copleston's theory.[184]

---

[182] See Copleston, 'V. S. Solov'ev,' p. 224.
[183] Ibid., p. 236.
[184] Many, if not all, of the elements that Soloviev drew from the Kabbala were those foregrounded in the work of the Christian Kabbalists. Not learning Hebrew until later, he would have been unable to familiarize himself with the original texts, as Konstantin Burmistrov has shown in his assiduous research on the subject. See K. Burmistrov, 'Vladimir Solov'ev i Kabbala,' *Issledovaniia po istorii russkoi mysli* (*Ezhegodnik*), Moscow, 1998, p. 7-104. Burmistrov's assertion, however, that in this period Soloviev would have had 'no idea what the authentic Kabbalistic tradition was all about' seems overstated. Although the Christian Kabbalists privileged certain strands over others, altering many in line with Christian revelation, works such as *Kabbala denudata* nevertheless made a core of Kabbalistic teaching available to Western readers.

IV. THE FOURTH WORLD

The Kabbala reproduces Soloviev's three worlds in many essential characteristics. Central to its teaching is that the trinity formed by these three worlds — in early Soloviev, *en-soph*-Logos-Holy Spirit — only 'finds its realization in the quaternary.'[185] This 'quaternary,' which lies beyond the first nine determinations of the table of emanations, or *sephirot*, to use the Kabbalistic term, differs from the previous three worlds consisting of three sephirot each in that it includes only one, *Shekhinah*, or *Malkhuth*, which is called the Divine Presence, God's dwelling in the world, and 'the end of thought.'[186] *Shekhinah* is a kind of channel through which the influences of the nine superior sephirot are transmitted and intermixed. It is said in this connection that 'Malkhuth is Kether [the first sephira, the Ancient of Ancients - OS] after another manner' since the fullness of God dwells in it.[187] This is related to the doctrine of correspondences which was so prominent in the works of mystics such as Paracelsus and is summed up in the Emerald Table of Hermes: 'whatever is below is like that which is above; and that which is above is like that which is below.'[188]

Shekhinah, which is absolute like *Kether* but not in the same way, is transposed into Soloviev's philosophical discourse as 'the second absolute,' 'All-Unity in a state of becoming.' In Soloviev's Satan we find the reverse-face of God, the principle of unity become the principle of mutual isolation and separation; in the Demiurge we see the malevolent counterpart of the Logos, the relating power of all *in* God become the

---

185 Mathers, 'Introduction,' p. 35. Strémooukhoff highlights the similarities between the two tables of nine determinations, or three trinities — Spirit-Soul-Matter (absolute); Will-Representation-Feeling (Logos); Good-Truth-Beauty (Idea) — which Soloviev formulates in *Philosophical Principles*, and the first nine determinations of the sephirotic scale of the Kabbala — Kether-Chochmah-Binah (*nephesh*); Hesed-Geburah-Tipheret (*ruash*); Netzah-Hod-Yesod (*neshamah*). Strémooukhoff, *Vladimir Solov'ev and His Messianic Work*, p. 350. For more on the sephirotic table and its place in the teaching of the Kabbala, see Scholem, *Kabbalah*, pp. 118-25. Burmistrov connects the idea of four worlds with Gnosticism rather than the Kabbala. Burmistrov, 'Vladimir Solov'ev i Kabbala,' pp. 24-25.
186 Ibid., p. 112.
187 Knorr von Rosenroth, *Kabbala Denudata*, p. 96. 'God attains His fullest personal disclosure precisely because of His manifestation in Malkuth, where He is called "I."' Burmistrov, 'Vladimir Solov'ev i Kabbala,' p. 86.
188 Trismogin, *Splendor Solis*, p. 101.

relating power of all *outside* God. In Soloviev, the 'after another manner' becomes a perverse parody of truth, the semblance or illusion of God. In the Soul the monadic legions of egoism and separation begin to lose their power over being, and gradually transition into actualized unity within a transfigured and transfiguring nature. Before this transition can begin to occur, however, the Soul must herself, just as her children Satan and the Demiurge, become incarnate in the material world: she must find a body for her manifestation.

Chapter II
HUMANITY

Soloviev would never again return to the sort of metaphysical speculation that had characterized the works of his early period. The process of the hypostatization of the absolute we find in *Philosophical Principles*, for example, while leaving a definite trace on the philosopher's evolution, finds only a distant echo in his later years. Whatever the merits of his early work, however, it should be recalled that the theoretical pursuit of 'first things' had never been conceived by Soloviev as a goal in itself but as a certain kind of mise-en-scène or preparatory act, a 'clearing of the intellectual ground for the foundations of a spiritual building of the future.' There is a pull toward the human that inheres in the nature of Soloviev's metaphysics, and which lends it a certain mobility somewhat at odds with an understanding of the field as the science of what is ultimate, or changeless. As he writes to his cousin at age eighteen, 'only human nature and life are worth studying in themselves.'[1] Already very early on in his career, the anthropological element is primary, with metaphysics prominent only insofar as it is related to human life.

The dynamism in Soloviev's conception of God derives from this inability to think the divine without the human, a coupling rendered conceptually by the philosopher's term *theanthropy*. In his lectures on the subject, *Lectures on Theanthropy* (1877-81), God, who for Soloviev was so emphatically 'not of the dead, but of the living,'[2] becomes the protagonist in the 'universal drama'[3] of world history that was to lead humanity to liberation from death and salvation. So sweeping is the historical scope of this work, so thoroughgoing its association of

---

[1] Solov'ev, "Nepodvizhno," p. 156.
[2] Mark 12.27; Matthew 22.32.
[3] S², II, p. 55.

the divine with the movement of humanity in time, that hereafter it becomes impossible to talk of Soloviev's conception of God without reference to her relationship to historical humanity, and to her saving acts in history whose culmination the philosopher saw in the Incarnation and Resurrection of Christ. 'It is not cosmocentrism nor anthropocentrism,' writes Vasilii Zen'kovskii, 'that define Soloviev's approach to all questions but historiocentrism. This is not to say that he transforms every problem into a historical survey of its various resolutions but that, for him, all "faces" of being reveal themselves in history, in the development of humanity.'[4]

That history occupies an important place in Soloviev's philosophy is not surprising, given that he was the son of one of Russia's most eminent historians. And yet, faced with the elevated claims he makes for humanity and its role in the realization of the Kingdom of God, as well as the frequent characterizations of Soloviev's thought as a variation on the theme of Gnostic anthropocentrism,[5] the locus, not of the human at the very centre of his philosophical schema, but of history is worth stressing. The human being, Soloviev asserts against Protagorus, is not the measure of all things. Although he claims that humanity is the potential 'form' for absolute content, Soloviev understands this potentiality not merely as innate to the human spirit, i.e. existing in an interior space and requiring merely the right attitude to become reality. Rather, this potential is itself historicized, and its gradual realization becomes not only a matter for human spiritual aspiration but a grandly conceived historical project which involves, in a way that may at times appear contradictory, not only humanity but the rest of the natural world. History becomes the arena in which authentic being is disclosed, and the place of meeting between humanity and the divine.

There is therefore a dynamism in Soloviev's understanding of what it means to be human, which allows him to move beyond the static view of Gnosticism or any number of philosophies before or contemporary

---

[4] V. V. Zen'kovskii, 'Russkie mysliteli i Evropa,' pp. 114-140 (p. 24).
[5] For two recent examples of this approach, see I. I. Evlampiev, *Istoriia russkoi metafiziki v XIX-XX vekakh. Russkaia filosofiia v poiskakh absoliuta*, 2 vols, St Petersburg, 2000, I, pp. 183-86; A. P. Kozyrev, *Solov'ev i gnostiki*.

with him.[6] The essence of humanity is here not fixed but entirely open in terms of its future. The human subject in Soloviev, unlike its Aristotelian counterpart which had enjoyed such decisive influence in the development of Western metaphysics, cannot be thought of apart from its context. Humanity is pre-eminently an historical being, and its being is defined and conditioned by this, its rootedness in time.

This understanding of humanity as ontologically embedded in history allows Soloviev to develop a projectional view of human nature with a strong orientation toward the future. Humanity is perpetually involved in the movement of becoming, with the conditions of its present forever ceding to the prerogatives of the future. His anthropology is thus geared toward determining the direction of humanity's movement in history and sketching the contours of a future, ideal humanity at the 'end' of time. From here stems the overwhelming emphasis throughout his thought on the *task* of humanity, the activity required of him if the goal of the historical process is to be fulfilled. It is tempting, therefore, to do as Tomáš Masaryk does and associate the 'second absolute' which we arrived at in the last chapter ('All-Unity in a state of becoming') directly with humanity.[7] But such a conclusion fails to understand the essence of Soloviev's theanthropy: what is becoming, in the historical sense, is not a something—be that humanity or any other natural phenomenon—but a *relationship*: namely, the interaction between the divine and human principles. For the same reason, it is impossible to speak of creation itself—the material world as a whole—as the subject of becoming in his thought. Yet in an inscrutable way, which Soloviev attempts to articulate in his thought on the body of Christ, All-Unity does indeed become *in* humanity (though not exclusively for it), in the process of which the material world too is drawn into its movement.

---

[6] Sergei Khoruzhii regards the inclusion of process and 'anthropological dynamics' into Soloviev's conception of human being as one of his principal contributions to world philosophy. Even in Hegel and Schelling, he argues, 'the dynamic elements in their picture of reality, spirit and reason, had to large extent become autonomized by isolating themselves from the human and removing themselves from anthropology.' S. Khoruzhii, 'Solov'ev i Nitsshe v krizise evropeiskogo cheloveka,' in *Opyty iz russkoi dukhovnoi traditsii*, Moscow, 2005, pp. 249-286 (p. 260).

[7] T. G. Masaryk, *Spirit of Russia: Studies in History, Literature and Philosophy*, 3 vols, London, 1955, II, p. 247.

I. ANTHROPOGENY AND HISTORY

Soloviev was amongst the first generation of thinkers to mature in the wake of the scientific, philosophical and religious implications of Charles Darwin's publication of *Origin of the Species* in 1859, which appeared in Russian translation five years later. The philosopher seems to have been aware of evolutionary theory from an early age and, especially in his later work, reveals not only a close understanding of Darwin's ideas but even a close affinity with them.[8] As with other scientific work he drew on, he sought not to undermine Darwinian evolutionary theory from the combative perspective of religionism but to incorporate it within a broader theoretical framework that did justice to his particular understanding of historical development as it pertained to both humanity and the natural world. That evolution was not only compatible with the biblical account of the creation of humanity, but that it was only the combination of the two that could offer a holistic picture of reality is a conviction which, in one form or another, pervades much of his thinking on the nature of history. In his influential work of 1895, *Justification of the Good*, he wrote:

> The order of the substantial is not the same as the order of the phenomenon. Higher, more positive and fuller forms and conditions of being exist (metaphysically) before those lower than they, although they appear or are disclosed after them. This does not negate evolution which, as fact, is impossible to negate [...] The conditions of the phenomenon derive from natural evolution, but that which is disclosed from God.[9]

The pre-existence of certain phenomena in history, Soloviev argued, does not mitigate against later evolutionary developments laying claim to a 'fuller form of being.' Applying this to the great challenge that Darwinian theory represented for the biblical belief of Soloviev's era — the postulation that the human species evolved from the primate

---

[8] Sergii Bulgakov writes that Soloviev was a 'passionate advocate of scientific evolutionism,' the difference between the philosopher and outright Darwinists being that, for the former, 'natural science offered [...] an answer not to scientific problems but to those of Naturphilosophie.' Bulgakov, 'Chto daet sovremennomu soznaniiu filosofiia Vl. Solov'eva,' p. 423.

[9] S¹, I, p. 273.

kingdom—it seems that such ideas were not only viewed by Soloviev as compatible with the biblical view of creation but as fundamentally enhancing human understanding of the same. The gradual emergence of humanity through natural selection (a process which is given a typically Solovievian reworking), he argued, in no way detracts from humanity's favoured status as made 'in the image of God.' If the human being really is the 'crown of creation' and the end of God's work, as it is traditionally presented in biblical thought, the fact that the natural world arrived at a creature such as man through its own processes demonstrates, for Soloviev, that the conglomerate of such processes amounts to more than science acknowledges as the merely 'natural.'

Soloviev's argument and method on the question of humanity and its place in history proceeded from a dual foundation. Firstly, he looked at *how* humanity came into being in the historical context of evolution. Secondly, he attempted an answer as to *what* the human being is, its essential characteristics and attributes. It is the combination of these two perspectives, and the proximity of the answers he finds to the *how* and the *what* of human existence, that create the unique dynamics of his thought and produce the same curious tension between cause and result that we saw at work in his organic logic. Unlike Darwin, who by and large restricted himself to the formulation of evolutionary laws within the context of their direct operation, viewing the results of evolution as governed by the adaptability of a given species according to the laws of natural selection, the existence of humanity according to Soloviev is not dependent on the past; rather, the past is dependent for its momentum on the fact of the human being. That is to say, there is a teleology in prehistory which has such a creature as humanity as its inevitable goal;[10] humanity is not the result of random mutations but, as Soloviev puts it in *Lectures*, 'the whole of nature aspired and gravitated toward the human being.'[11] The philosophical and theological question of the nature and vocation of human existence is thus itself historicized; its

---

[10] In his preparatory notes to *La Sophia*, Soloviev writes: 'the world process is absolutely necessary and goal-oriented. Chance and arbitrariness exist only in human ignorance.' Rossiiskii Gosudarstvennyi Arkhiv Liteteratury i Iskusstva (RGALI), f. 446, op. 1, d. 40, p. 22 of 31.

[11] S², II, p. 154. A similar idea has emerged in recent science-theology debate under the term the 'anthropic principle.'

evolution in time is understood as the result of a guiding force operating within history. An answer to the question of what humanity *is* becomes bound up with the question of *how* it came to be.

The 'cosmic mind' as the guiding force of prehistory with which, in *La Sophia*, the figure of the Demiurge had been associated remained Soloviev's preferred term for the agent of the historical process throughout his career.[12] But there was another term that was of equal, if not greater, importance. In his 'Lectures on the History of Philosophy' (1880-81), the philosopher connects this sense of an active force outside nature that directs and leads it with the gradual becoming of something within it, the object of transformation and evolution — the 'world soul.'

> Nature is not only a senseless, material *process* but carries in itself an ideal content. The natural process itself, objectively considered as the world process, involves the gradual realization of an eternal content, the gradual birth of a natural idea, the world soul.[13]

The peculiarity of Soloviev's historical construct lies not in his conviction that the history of the world represents a teleologically oriented process, here described as the gradual birth of 'the world soul,' for such had been the view of any number of religious thinkers from antiquity to the present. It is rather in his particular approach to the question of agency in the world process that the uniqueness of his perspective consists. This approach is characterized, like his methodology, by a duality according to which the guiding principle of history occupies a position at once removed from the world process and, at the same time, fully integrated within it. The world, in Soloviev's thought, is both moved and mover; the progression of historical stages is just as much the bursting forth of the otherworldly as the culmination of its own, natural processes. Evolution and revelation are thus cohorts in the realization of world meaning.[14] This combination of immanentalist

---

[12] See particularly Soloviev's 1889 article 'Beauty in Nature,' in which the 'cosmic mind' and 'creative principle' (*zizhditel'noe nachalo*) of nature are allocated a major role in the world process. V. S. Solov'ev, *Filosofiia iskusstva i literaturnaia kritika*, ed. R. Gal'tseva and I. Rodnianskaia, Moscow, 1991, pp. 52-56.

[13] V. S. Solov'ev, 'Lektsii po istorii filosofii,' *Voprosy filosofii*, 1989, 6, pp. 76-132 (p. 93).

[14] Konstantin Antonov notes in this connection an 'interesting aporia' in Soloviev's thought: 'on one hand, he is required to show that Christianity is the logically

and transcendentalist approaches is particularly evident in Soloviev's handling of the evolution of humanity.

Unlike those systems contemporaneous with him which, in the wake of geological evidence proving the earth was considerably older than the biblical literature supposed, had begun to view the border between history and prehistory as lying in that period when human civilizations first started documenting their existence through written records, Soloviev regards this border as the creation, or evolution, of humanity. When the first human being appeared on earth, there occurred, in his view, a monumental shift in the historical landscape; 'the cosmogonic process,' he writes, 'ends with the creation of the perfect organism — the human organism.'[15]

Soloviev presents the human being as the furthest point that organic life can reach by its own devices, that form beyond which it is impossible for it to progress. The creation of the world has reached its conclusion. That Soloviev regards the arrival of humanity on the world stage as the end point of cosmogony, in line with the so-called priestly account of creation found in Genesis 1 and yet sharply at odds with Darwinian theory, as well as modern geology and zoology, has several important implications for his system. Firstly, the creation of humanity, while located within the flow of time, becomes an unprecedented event in the evolutionary development of the world, after which can only come something entirely new, the beginning of a new process. Before the arrival of humanity, according to him, we can speak only of the cosmogonic process; after it, cosmogony gives way to history.

---

necessary culmination of the historical process and, on the other, to demonstrate its exclusivity as a 'new, unprecedented fact in the life of the world'. Countering the views of authors who believe Soloviev to have tied religious history too closely to natural causality, Antonov writes that the historical laws the philosopher outlines only 'fix the formal structure of the movement of this or that process while, like a mathematical equation, allowing him to replace the variable with the differing dynamic forces of these processes in different combinations. These forces do not obey a given law, but form it in their interaction. Likewise, the eschatological transition to the kingdom of the future age should be understood not as the result of the historical process [...] but its *causa finalis*.' K.M. Antonov, *Filosofiia religii v russkoi metafizike XIX — nachalo XX veka*, Moscow, 2009, pp. 117, 118.

[15] S^2, II, p. 138.

> When, after many millennia of elemental and cosmic battle, in which the meaning of the world was revealed merely as a deterministic force of external law, there appeared the first rational creature, this was a new revelation — the revelation of the meaning of the world as an idea, in consciousness.[16]

For Soloviev, the newness that humanity represents in the world is precisely its rationality, the faculty traditionally used to separate humanity from the animal and plant kingdoms. But the philosopher understands reason not so much according to its common usage as a faculty innate to human beings, nor as a static instrument used to join together judgements and arrive at conclusions, but as a potentiality as yet unrealized that contains the seeds of its future actualization. Reason for him is 'the pure form of All-Unity,'[17] the potential to contain within itself absolute content, or God. History begins only with the emergence of this reason in the world in the form of humanity.

Until the emergence of human consciousness, the guiding principle of being could only operate within nature as deterministic law. The great significance of human reason is that no longer does the teleological force of the world manifest itself for material objects as pure determinism. Instead, through human consciousness, it gains the potential of acting as the guiding principle of *inner* being, not only governing the external forms of the natural world but freeing the inner life of nature through humanity to participate in the realization of world meaning. After 'an external covering has been created in nature for the divine idea, there begins a new process in which this same idea is developed as the principle of inner All-Unity in the form of consciousness and free activity.'[18] Evolution is here not arrested but acquires an interior dimension. The subject of evolution, the world soul, has found the organic form in which it can operate from itself, not as the mere longing we had previously observed in Soloviev's *materia prima*, but as the incarnate principle of free and conscious humanity. The latter, far from being subject to cosmic or cosmogonic activity, 'now not only participates in the activity of cosmic principles, but is able to know the goal of such activity and therefore to

---

[16] Solov'ev, *Dukhovnye osnovy*, p. 87.
[17] S², II, p. 139.
[18] Ibid., p. 139.

work knowingly and freely toward its realization.'[19] Thus, 'the meaning of the historical process (in contrast to the cosmic) is that it is conducted with the ever growing participation of individual agents.'[20]

If this first aspect of Soloviev's anthropogeny has the effect of separating humanity from the created order, however, of seeing in its emergence an unprecedented act and a radical discontinuity from that which had come before, an equally strong second strand draws humanity once again toward nature and affirms it as an integral and inseparable part of the created world. This tendency is evident in Soloviev's middle period, and especially in the 'philosophy of biblical history' espoused in his monumental *History and Future of Theocracy* (1886). Here the tension between Soloviev's historical association of revelation and evolution is in clear view. If the creation of the human being can be understood as the end of cosmogony and the beginning of a new process, it should equally be seen as the cumulative outcome of the entire cosmogonic process — that for which all else was a preparation. There is thus a dual aspect to humanity in Soloviev's anthropological conception, a continuity and a discontinuity, an evolvedness and a fundamental newness. Seeing in Genesis 2.7[21] a representation of this dual nature, he writes:

> *God creates the human being from the ground.* Earthly nature is essential for it from the very beginning. It is not an accidental appendage but the constant foundation and matter of its life. Humanity is not immediately created from nothing. Being a creation of God as the active cause, it is alongside this a production of the earth as the material cause, and its essence in its dual composition can be called the earth of God (*Bogo-zemlia*). Humanity is thus, by his very origin, (genetically) linked with the material world.[22]

Both nature and God have an involvement in the phenomenon of humanity. Viewed from one perspective, God creates newness where before there had been only determinism, cause and effect. But from another perspective, nature fulfils her own vocation through

---

[19] FI, p. 73.
[20] S¹, I, p. 256.
[21] 'Then the Lord God formed man from the dust of the ground, and breathed into his nostrils the breath of life.'
[22] SS, IV, p. 339.

a kind of self-transcendence, by creating the conditions for another order of being apart from, but not over and against, the natural.

> In the human being, nature outgrows herself and transitions (in consciousness) into the realm of absolute being. Perceiving and carrying in its consciousness the eternal divine idea, while at the same time inextricably linked to the nature of the external world in its factual origin and existence, humanity is the natural mediator between God and the material world, the transmitter of the all-unifying divine principle to elemental multiplicity, the builder and organizer of the universe.[23]

In such a way, Soloviev derives the essence of humanity's activity from human nature, or the fact of human being, itself. That which humanity is — namely, the creation of God out of the earth — defines the nature of its activity. As its being is defined by its dual aspect as both product of nature and creation of God, so its entire life is bound up in the mediation of these two, both in the inner life of consciousness and in the external life of material reality. To know how humanity should act, therefore, it is necessary to know what it is. Ethics is dependent on ontology. Indeed, Soloviev's ethical system is merely an extension of his ontology, a formulation of moral imperatives based not on the quality of the action itself as, for example, in Kant, but on the central phenomenological fact of human nature.

For Soloviev, humanity is above all this middle term between God and creation, the 'transmitter' of the divine to the material world. It is 'God's deputy on earth, so that in a certain sense God herself rules her earthly creatures through humanity alone.'[24] But as this role in natural humanity only exists in potentiality — as an ideal given by reason — Soloviev's ontology becomes subsumed into history: what actually *is* turns out to be involved in a process of becoming. Here again we see the metaphysical, anthropological and cosmological dynamism that penetrates all of Soloviev's work. It is important to note, however, that, while in Soloviev's eschatology that which absolutely *is* only emerges in its fullness at the end of history, the preceding historical steps are not deprived of ontological status. Rather, these

---

[23] S², II, p. 140.
[24] SS, IV, p. 342.

preliminary stages gradually lose their onesidedness and exclusivity as they become reintegrated into the totality of their connections to the whole.[25] History does not undermine ontology by representing a series of illusory steps before the attainment of true being but, as a biologist reveals the ever-increasing complexity of interactions within a unitary organism, so history uncovers the layeredness of being, the interrelation of the parts of the one universe. We may prefer to say, therefore, that instead of that which *is* being subsumed into a process of becoming, in Soloviev's thought that which *is* becomes revealed as that which *relates*, and that which absolutely *is* is precisely the fullness of relation of everything to all, or All-Unity. The momentum of relation is the energy of history.

For history to reveal the interconnectedness of being in a series of progressive steps, or for it to strive toward the relatedness of all in all, this unity, argues Soloviev, has itself to exist prior to any given moment in historical time, for otherwise its teleological aspect, not having a goal before it, would be undermined. Before the human being, this unity could only operate on creation from without, as a blind striving for relation as such. The great significance of the phenomenon of reason, in Soloviev's view, is that this relatedness of all being now exists *ideally* within creation, in the consciousness of humanity.

For Soloviev, reason is the potential form for absolute content by virtue of the fact that it 'is a sort of correlation, namely the correlation of all in unity,'[26] the ability to contain within itself the totality of being in its interconnectedness. It is just this, though — an *ability* — since in itself 'it cannot have the creative force which belongs, for example, to will or fantasy.'[27] Reason in Soloviev's thought may thus be described as the very power of relation, or the form of relatedness itself. 'Reason is a kind of relation (ratio) between things that gives them a particular form. But relation presupposes relating parties, form presupposes

---

[25] 'The positive link of the progressive kingdoms [i.e. plant, animal, human etc. — OS] can be seen in the fact that each type (the later they occur, the fuller they become) embraces or includes in itself those lower than it, so that the world process is not only a process of development toward an eventual perfection but also a process in which the universe is *gathered together*' (my emphases). S¹, I, p. 275.
[26] PSS, III, p. 255.
[27] Ibid., p. 367.

content.'²⁸ In other words, the faculty of reason demands a definite content; it cannot produce its own world but must work with the elements of the world in order to have effect. It must be the relation of something existent to something else. And since, as we have seen, humanity is by its very nature the mediator between God and creation, reason becomes the most quintessentially human of all abilities, that in which these two are mediated. 'The human principle is reason (ratio), that is, the relation of the divine and the material.'²⁹

Already in Soloviev's conception of human nature, therefore, we have the seeds of human being's vocation: to use the relating power of reason to realize All-Unity, which exists in it as an ideal, in material reality. This ideal All-Unity, accessible to it through reason, is the trace of that radical discontinuity with the created order planted in humanity by God, and which Soloviev expresses by the biblical term 'the image of God.' The 'task' of humanity is to cultivate this image, or ideal, so that it may grow into its ultimate goal, rendered by Soloviev again in biblical terms as the 'likeness of God.'

> The likeness of God in humanity or, more precisely, the likeness of humanity to God, is the actual realization of that image of God in which the human being was created and which was placed in it at the beginning. This ideal image, which is the innermost essence of humanity, does not depend on its will. The actual realization of this image, or assimilation to God, however, occurs not without the will and activity of itself humanity.³⁰

Not only is history an outpouring of ontological reality through time, not only is the meaning of historical time the disclosure of this reality as relation, but humanity is called to be the agent of this process. It is to realise itself as 'the image of God,' to bring to fruition that which lies dormant within it as mere potential. In this way, Soloviev's ontology has as its direct result the formulation of the human being's ideal activity in the world, the task it must take on if it is to realise, and grow into, the fullness of its own, created being.

---

[28] S², II, p. 165.
[29] Ibid., p. 155.
[30] SS, IV, p. 341.

II. THE TASK AND THE KINGDOM OF GOD

The connection between thought and action, expressed in Eastern Orthodox theology and Marxist philosophy by the term *praxis*, is fundamental to an understanding of the Russian religious and philosophical tradition.[31] 'Theology without action,' wrote Maximus the Confessor, 'is the theology of demons.'[32] When, therefore, in 1881 after the death of Fedor Dostoevsky, Soloviev spoke at the graveside of his friend of a great 'panhuman task' that was to unite all nations and peoples, he was not setting out on a new path but positioning himself in a long line of saints, thinkers and writers in the Eastern and Russian tradition who had insisted on the practical application of doctrine and theology and the unity of thought and action in Christian faith.[33] Nor was this a diversion from his earlier, more unilaterally theoretical work, since the fixing and formulation of the 'first things' was always meant merely as a preparation for 'a spiritual building of the future,' as a *justification* of the task incumbent on humanity. To know what humanity should do, in Soloviev's view, one must know what it *is*, an answer to which question he sought in his early period.

On the face of things, as we have seen, this would seem to introduce a relatively straightforward dependency of ethics on ontology, at least as far as Soloviev's anthropological model is concerned. In human nature itself is the ground and condition for the task humanity is to realise. But as we have also argued, one of the peculiarities of Soloviev's thought lies in his conviction that the moment of being is revealed, in the life of humanity as well as in other spheres, in the process of becoming. Humanity's being is irrevocably connected to its historicity, its being in time. Viewed from this angle, action can be understood as

---

31 'All Russian religious philosophy,' writes Judith Kornblatt, 'insists on the role of action, a task or *zadacha* whose accomplishment will mean the reunion of God and creation.' J. D. Kornblatt, 'Russian Religious Thought and the Jewish Kabbala,' in *The Occult in Soviet and Russian Culture*, ed. B. G. Rosenthal, Ithaca, NY, 1997, pp. 75-95 (p. 86).
32 Cited in Timothy Ware, *The Orthodox Church*, Harmondsworth, 1972, p. 215.
33 Many examples could be cited here of this general approach. Suffice it to say that the two literary giants of Soloviev's era, Dostoevsky and Tolstoy, diametrically opposed in so many respects, come together precisely in their emphasis on praxis, the practice and practicability of the Christian faith.

the link between being and becoming of humanity, a sort of synthetic resolution of the two, for only in acting is the distance between them bridged. Through conscious acts, the human being reveals itself as the historical being *par excellence*, for action is the location of the present in the ever-moving area between a past of memory and the future of hope, a realization of the oneness of history through a conscious self-positioning toward its ideal future. Soloviev writes:

> The whole of history speaks of one thing and one thing alone: how collective humanity becomes better and bigger than its very self, how it outgrows its current present, moving it into the past while promoting to the present that which up to that very point had been something contradictory to reality, a dream, a subjective ideal, a utopia.[34]

This constant outgrowth of the present into the reality of a future imperative is the mark of the historical process, in which humanity incarnates the ideal in the real. Since the historical process is not only understood in Soloviev's work as a series of unrelated movements in time, each with its own goal and imperatives, but as a unitary and fundamentally logical process in which all ideals point toward a single destination, namely the Kingdom of God, human agency becomes the means of approaching the future consummation of all goals in an overarching narrative of fulfilment. To put it in theological terms, in conscious action humanity locates itself within salvation history.[35]

Soloviev's conception is here coloured by his belief that in such an orientation toward the final goal of the world and historical process, the gap between the individual human and collective humanity is overcome. In goal-oriented activity, the human being is not only the moving power of history, the sower of the future in the present, but also the unifier of his own, individual being with the rest of humankind through a commonality of direction. Just as Soloviev's

---

[34] S², II, pp. 613-14.
[35] Notions of healing and salvation are deeply rooted in all of Soloviev's works, and his philosophy in general has an overwhelmingly soteriological thrust. In *Spiritual Foundations of Life* (1882-84), the most theological of his works, he portrays the meaning of history as 'the restoration of all in its absolute wholeness, or universal healing.' Solov'ev, *Dukhovnye osnovy*, p. 100.

understanding of human nature was ultimately demonstrated to lie in relating—in an active and dynamic rather than static relation to being—so authentic human being, which for Soloviev is the collective life of humanity as a whole rather than the aggregate of its individual members, is revealed in human activity.[36] Historical humanity discovers its unity in action, not stasis.

It is telling, therefore, that unity of confession, in this case Christianity, was never the task uppermost in Soloviev's mind.[37] Instead, we find that unity is achieved not so much through a static state of being or belonging—be it personal conviction or confessional allegiance—but in the dynamism of the task itself. Human beings are not unified by membership in a group but by a shared vocation, a common task.

> This task, i.e. authentic Christianity, is panhuman not only in the sense that it should unite all peoples in *one faith*, but above all in the sense that it should unite and reconcile all human affairs into one universal, common task.[38]

Although Soloviev does not explicitly conduct his argument here in terms of communion, its ecclesiological implications are clear. 'Being church,' just as being human, does not involve uniformity of constitution or doctrine but a shared sense of mission. It demands, he writes, 'complete unity of resolution, not homogeneity of life nor exclusivity of aspiration.'[39]

---

[36] That such a unity between all members of humanity was possible, indeed more 'real' than its present condition of division, was an axiom of Soloviev's thought. It was from this perspective that he even went so far as to praise Auguste Comte's comparison of unified humanity to a great organism (Le Grand Être). See his article, 'The Idea of Humanity in the Thought of Auguste Comte,' in SS, IX, pp. 172-93. One may also mention the significant influence on him of the kabbalistic idea that God was constellated in human form (Adam Kadmon). Above all, however, it seems that the Pauline notion of the body of Christ remained central for him at least from his middle period onward.

[37] This should be kept in mind when considering Soloviev's ecumenical work on the unification of the churches. Inter-denominational union was for him not a goal in itself but the provision of a sound basis for the realization of the task.

[38] V. S. Solov'ev, *Literaturnaia kritika*, Moscow, 1990, p. 244.

[39] SS, IV, p. 599.

That Soloviev sees the task as synonymous with 'authentic Christianity' per se, rather than a particular aspect of Christian practice, gives us pause for thought. Unlike the task proposed by that other great Russian utopian, Nikolai Fedorov, which he straightforwardly described as 'the resurrection of the fathers' — the return to life of all those who have died — Soloviev's project from the outset displays an elusiveness that makes it difficult to arrive at any concrete articulation of its character.[40] Unlike Fedorov's project, what Soloviev is speaking of cannot be exhausted by a stipulation of any definite action or behaviour. The task he is advocating, and continues to advocate for the rest of his life, is more even than a complex of practices, rituals or activities. It is best described as a form of praxis, understood in the theological sense, a combination of reflection and action that assimilates the human nature of the doer into the energy of its intention. This energy is the movement of history itself, understood not as the succession of one moment by another in a series of infinite degree, but as the becoming of the fullness of being. Soloviev's task is thus the realization of the very historicity of humanity, the discovery and conscious application of the role humanity is to play in the soteriological drama as ordained by its creator God from the beginning of time. Humanity is called to tune its own, human history to the goal of history, to locate itself within the entirety of historical time by tying itself, and the world, to salvation history.

It follows from here that the nature of Soloviev's task is best approached through the goal it serves, since it has value only insofar as it looks beyond itself to the ideal future and locates itself within

---

[40] Despite this difference, there is clearly a great affinity between Soloviev's project and that of Fedorov. In 1881, Soloviev wrote to the latter: 'I accept your project *unconditionally* without the need for any further conversation.' In the same letter, Soloviev even proclaims Fedorov his 'teacher and spiritual father.' The great difference between the two philosophers, evident even in this first surviving letter, lies not so much in the formulation of the task itself as in the means required to achieve it. In a later, undated letter, Soloviev argues that 'the mere physical resurrection of the dead cannot be the goal in and of itself [...] Our task should have a religious not a scientific character.' Solov'ev, *Pis'ma*, II, pp. 345-47. Strémooukhoff argues that the decisive influence in Soloviev's emergence from what he regards as his early, predominantly theoretical period to the middle period with its emphasis on action belongs to Fedorov. See Strémooukhoff, *Vladimir Solov'ev and His Messianic Work*, pp. 135-36. See also S. Semenova, *Filosof budushchego veka: Nikolai Fedorov*, Moscow, 2004, pp. 115-25.

II. THE TASK AND THE KINGDOM OF GOD

a broader soteriological framework. This goal is associated throughout Soloviev's thought with the realization of the Kingdom of God which, in the face of all the formulations and reformulations we meet in his works, remains his dominant theological motif throughout.

> The inner possibility, the main condition for union with God, can be found [...] in the human being itself—the Kingdom of God is inside us. But this possibility should transition into action, humanity should manifest the Kingdom of God concealed within it [...] The Kingdom of God is taken by force, and those who persevere shall possess it. Without these efforts, the possibility will remain mere possibility, the promise of future bliss will be lost, and the embryo of true life will waste away and die. And so the Kingdom of God, perfect in the eternal divine idea ('in heaven') and potentially inhering in our nature, is also necessarily something enacted for us and through us. From this perspective, it is our work, the task of our activity.[41]

The 'inner possibility' of the Kingdom of God is that same image planted by God in humanity of which we spoke earlier. The human being is called to know this image through reason, to recognise it in itself, and to work toward its realization through the attainment of 'likeness' to God. In the biblical language of the Kingdom, Soloviev moves away from an argument in which the task of humanity is portrayed as self-enclosed, as a matter of *self*-realization alone and nothing besides. The task involves not only humanity's assimilation to God through the attainment of her likeness, but that of the whole created order. The particular challenge of Soloviev's thought in this area lies in understanding how the Kingdom of God can appear to us in two different ways: as the goal of humanity, and as the eternal possession of God, for whom it exists in the fullness of its absolute manifestation.[42] According to this view, if it is right to say that the image of God exists within humanity as a potentiality gradually actualized in history it is

---

[41] S², II, p. 309.
[42] 'For God and in God [...] the Kingdom of God is already created [...] the entire hierarchical construction of the universe in all its complex perfection, all the depths of true knowledge and the entire fullness of the living and sacramental interaction between God and creation, all this three-part whole exists as one perfect, concrete in all its parts, and immaculate organism of God's creation (*bogotvorenie*) or the body of God.' Solov'ev, *Dukhovnye osnovy*, pp. 110-11.

equally the case that its final, exterior manifestation already exists outside humanity, as perfected in God. Recalling the words of the Lord's Prayer, Soloviev writes:

> We do not say may your Kingdom be created but may your Kingdom come. Only something that already *is* may come. The Kingdom of God in itself already is, for everything is subject in its essence to God Almighty. But we should wish that the Kingdom of God was not only over everything, which it already is, but that God was all in all and that everything was one in Her.[43]

We are to speak, then, not of the creation of the Kingdom of God, for the Kingdom already *is*, but of humanity's involvement in an historical process in which the Kingdom 'comes.' In fact, for Soloviev it is not permissible to speak of the Kingdom as a created thing at all, whether by God or humanity, since it is 'not some object separate from other objects. It is their true constellation (*ustroenie*) in which nothing harms another and nothing is lost.'[44] The Kingdom is not objectified being but rather being that has transcended itself in relation, the relatedness of all in God. It is a form of being whose character is disclosed not primarily by its content, the multiplicity of its components, but by the way in which these components relate to one another. The task, therefore, is not 'to build and tear down,' nor to add to the content of being, but to break the isolation of being by relating all to God, by conforming our discontinuous present to the eternal continuous. To stress again: this relatedness of all in God already exists in and for the eternal God in all the complexity of its interaction between history and eternity, but it is necessary that it should exist in and for historical being itself. It is not enough for Soloviev that the Kingdom of God already extends over all things. The divine rule must operate *within* the inner life of all things, not only that of humanity; it must manifest itself from within the whole creation as the law of its own being in time. The transcendence of the Kingdom which rules over all things must become immanent in history.[45]

---

[43] Ibid., p. 37.

[44] The soteriological element is again to the fore here. Compare with John 6.39: 'And this is the will of him who sent me, that I should lose nothing of all that he has given me, but raise it up on the last day.'

[45] Ignacio Ellacuría has written in a similar vein of 'the unavoidable need to make the Kingdom's transcendence historical' in the context of his own liberation theology.

II. THE TASK AND THE KINGDOM OF GOD

Intimately connected to this gradual realization of the Kingdom within history, there is, as we have seen, another process in Soloviev's thought, in which the interiority of the Kingdom to humanity gradually acquires an externality in the space of creation. The realization of the Kingdom thus becomes a process conducted from two centres: one in which the transcendence of God manifests itself in history, or in which the God of eternity becomes the God of history; and the second in which the Kingdom inside humanity transforms both human nature and the material world. The first process, in which the transcendence of the Kingdom is historicized from the locus of the transcendent, and which is properly the activity of the divine, is denoted in Soloviev by the term 'materialization of spirit' (*materializatsiia dukha*). The second is connected with ctivity of human and expressed by the term 'spiritualization of matter' (*odukhotvorenie materii*). Together they express the totality of the divine-human (*bogochelovecheskii*) process which, while from the perspective of God is complete and perfected, from the perspective of historical humanity is expressed as a task, the object of its efforts.

Humanity is to actualize in history what, for God in eternity, is given. It should again be stressed that this cannot mean creation, or activity directed toward a definite object. Rather, Soloviev understands it as a conforming of the two Kingdoms, that within humanity and that which transcends it. 'There is the Kingdom of God *inside* us and the Kingdom outside us. The agreement (*sovpadenie*) of the one and the other, the complete dissolution (*rastvorenie*) of the inner Kingdom of God with the external Kingdom is the goal of our activity.'[46] Humanity is thus involved in a double process of correlation, the conscious bringing of its own nature into 'likeness' with God, and the externalizing of that likeness in the world around it. The realization of the Kingdom of God is not merely, therefore, the actualization of the innermost core of humanity, the image of God, but alongside this and just as strongly the extension of the rule of God, or theocracy, to all created being.[47]

See I. Ellacuría, 'Utopia and Prophecy in Latin America,' in *Mysterium liberationis: fundamental concepts of liberation theology*, ed. I. Ellacuría and J. Sobrino, New York, 1993, pp. 289-328 (p. 294).

46   SS, IV, p. 591.
47   'The Kingdom of God has not only an inner dimension in the spirit, but also an external dimension in power. It is a real theocracy.' S^2, I, p. 226.

The transformation of its own nature and the transformation of the world are the two complementary and mutually conditioning aspects of humanity's task, and the basis of Soloviev's soteriology.

> Humanity's cooperation with God in this task of universal healing should consist in the gradual, free and conscious transformation of carnal life within itself and outside itself into spiritual life: the materialization of spirit and the spiritualization of matter, the reunion of the two principles on whose division carnal life is based.[48]

Recalling Soloviev's formulation of the dual nature of humanity as 'the earth of God,' the indwelling of divine spirit in earthly matter, and the characterization of the human's vocation as the ideal correlation of these two, the task is understood to go beyond its merely ideal aspect (as realised within the interior space of human consciousness) and incorporate the external, natural world. This breaking out of human interiority itself requires a new revelation, and it is to this new revelation that we now shift our attention. Viewed from another angle, however, the unity of humanity and the natural world in the salvation history of the world is but an extension of Soloviev's view on the evolvedness of humanity, its continuation of the process initiated in prehistory rather than its radical intervention in the same. By virtue of humanity's continuity with the cosmic process, the same process that had begun with the creation of the world continues in humanity, itself a product of the earth. The spiritual dimension of its activity does not stand against the 'carnal' world of matter, but draws it into itself, transfiguring and spiritualizing it. In this sense, humanity is as much the bearer of the natural principle as it is the divine idea. Just as with the emergence of the human being the transcendence of the spirit was first embodied as potential in history, so through humanity's development in history the isolation, or non-transcendence, of the material principle it carries within itself is spiritualized and drawn into the realm of divine being. History is a continuation of cosmology.[49] It is Soloviev's insistence

---

[48] PSS, III, p. 162.

[49] Sutton points to Soloviev's conviction that the 'cosmic process itself is intimately connected with the historical process.' Sutton, *The Religious Philosophy of Vladimir Solovyov*, p. 67.

that 'there is no gulf between the real essence of spiritual and material nature, that the two are most intimately connected and constantly interact,'[50] that provides his anthropological vision with its dynamic structure and irreducibility to a single principle. In humanity matter and spirit meet, and in history the two are conformed to each other through its conscious activity. The material structure of the world, which in humanity transitions into potential likeness to the spirit of God, is itself brought into this movement, and participates in the liberation and healing from the isolation of carnal life which is gradually realized in history. Humanity and world in Soloviev's thought are thus geared toward a common goal — the realization of the Kingdom of God.

III. CHRIST THE GOD-MAN

Soloviev's *Lectures on Theanthropy* (1877-81) represent a watermark in his early work not so much because of the emphasis he places on the person of Jesus Christ — his entire metaphysics from the earlier work so coloured by Gnostic influences to his late *Short Story of the Antichrist* (1900) has a profound Christological basis — but because of its refocusing of Christology away from metaphysical speculation as to the second person's perichoretic function within the godhead toward the nature of Christ's activity in history. This is not to say that Soloviev was interested in the historical person of Jesus, for he seemed least of all concerned with this.[51] Rather, in *Lectures* and the works of biblical exegesis that follow it, Soloviev's central problematic becomes the historicization of the transcendent God, which finds its culmination in the Incarnation, and the articulation of humanity's ideal response to this prior action on the part of the divine. Christ in Soloviev's thought is important not in the precise character of his appearance in history, nor in what he taught during his life, but insofar as such

---

[50] PSS, III, pp. 157-58.
[51] Soloviev had nothing but contempt for the, at that time, new trend of historical criticism in biblical studies. 'We proclaim nothing but the authenticity of the biblical story in its general characteristics and in no way the pedantic precision of biblical chronology and statistics,' he wrote in *History and Future of Theocracy*. SS, IV, p. 422.

a phenomenon appeared at all, and its implications for humanity and world. The significance of Christianity lies not in its doctrine or its theology, which though important would make of the religion, if these were its only fundamental characteristics, an eclectic system alongside other systems, but in the person of Christ himself.

> Christianity has its own content, independent from all the elements of which it consists, and this content is solely and exclusively Christ. In Christianity as such we find Christ and only Christ. Here is a truth repeated many times but very poorly understood.[52]

Just as the emergence of the first human on the world stage was for Soloviev an event of unparalleled newness signifying the potential attainment of the absolute idea through reason, so too the Incarnation represents an act utterly unprecedented in history.

> When after many millennia of human history there appeared the first *spiritual* human, in whom the natural life of the flesh was not only illumined by the divine meaning of the life of the world but illumined by him as the spirit of love, this was a new revelation of that same meaning [to have become embodied in humanity as an idea] as a living personal power able to attract to itself and harness the living force of matter.[53]

Once again we notice the same combination of revelation and evolution, discontinuity and continuity, that we saw in Soloviev's treatment of the creation and evolution of the human being. In Jesus Christ, the 'first spiritual human,' creation steps into a new phase of its history; a newness is now present that is irreducible to the history of its appearance. And yet there is also an evolvedness in Christ, as there was in Soloviev's picture of humanity, not in the sense of creatureliness, for Soloviev's Christology never arrives at a direct association with the created order, but in the sense that the Incarnation for him represents the culmination and flowering of the entire historical drama up to that point. As he writes, 'the historical appearance of Christ [...] is indissolubly connected to the entire world process, and with the denial

---

[52] S², II, p. 105.
[53] Solov'ev, *Dukhovnye osnovy*, p. 87.

of this appearance the meaning and directionality of the universe are lost.'[54] As the new dimension of human consciousness arises from the unconscious attempts of nature to transcend itself, so the newness of Christ emerges from the self-transcending movement of humanity in history. 'The whole of nature aspired and gravitated toward the human; the whole of human history was directed toward the God-man.'[55] God in Christ is thus understood not as a *deus ex machina* intervening in history, but as intimately bound to the entirety of the historical life of his creation.

> It is not the transcendent God who becomes incarnate in Jesus, that is to say, that which is incarnated is not the absolute, self-enclosed fullness of being (which would be impossible). Rather, it is God the Word, a principle which manifests itself outwardly and is active on the periphery of being. Its personal incarnation in an individual human is only the last link in a long series of incarnations, both physical and historical. This appearance of God in human flesh is only the fullest, most perfect theophany in a series of other incomplete preparatory and transformative theophanies.[56]

We have discussed the emphasis Soloviev places on the historicization of the transcendent in a general salvific landscape that is directed toward the coming of the Kingdom of God. Here, though, it appears he is directing his reader away from an understanding of transcendence *qua* transcendence as the fundamental characteristic of the divine and toward a re-envisioning of the divine nature. While leaving a space, at least conceptually, for God's transcendence, he suggests that the fullness of the divine nature cannot be grasped in isolation, but only when manifested outwardly for the other. The Christian God is portrayed not primarily as the transcendent one become historical, nor even the historical one become transcendent, but eternally the union of the one and the other in and through Christ. God is intimately connected to her creation in a way that eludes a linear conception of her saving acts in

---

[54] S¹, I, p. 272. In his work, *Meaning of Love*, Soloviev even talks of a 'christogonic process.' See S², II, p. 500.
[55] S², II, p. 154.
[56] Ibid., p. 154.

history; she is eternally the 'beyond in the midst of life,' to use Dietrich Bonhoeffer's phrase.[57] *Life*, not transcendence, is the characteristic that defines God as such.

In Soloviev's preferred terms, the divine is not only involved in the materialization of spirit but equally in the spiritualization of matter; God operates not merely from within eternity but just as strongly from within history.[58] And it is precisely in the person of Christ, in whom 'the whole fullness of deity dwells bodily,'[59] that God forms a unity of these two distinct activities which, though separable by reason, are eternally one. Christ has 'from the centre of eternity become the centre of history'; the two are united, although not conflated, in the God-man. It is from this perspective that the enthusiastic advocate of the Russian sophiological tradition, John Milbank, comments that 'from eternity God has always been the God-Man and the Russians are right: the theanthropic exceeds even the theological.'[60]

---

[57] 'God's "beyond" is not the beyond of our cognitive faculties. The transcendence of epistemological theory has nothing to do with the transcendence of God. God is beyond in the midst of our life. The church stands not at the boundaries where human powers give out, but in the middle of the village.' D. Bonhoeffer, *Letters and Papers from Prison*, New York, 1971, p. 282. Bonhoeffer's reflections on the transcendence of God draw him very close to Soloviev. Like the latter, the German theologian suggests that we do ill to confuse the epistemic transcendence of the divine, God's inscrutability to our cognitive faculties, with God's actual self-transcendence to both history and world.

[58] 'Life in general,' wrote Soloviev, 'is the unification of the spiritual principle with matter, or nature, the incarnation of spirit, the spiritualization of matter.' The dual process through which spirit and matter unite, therefore, is the mark not just of God but of life itself. S², I, p. 80.

[59] Colossians 2.9.

[60] J. Milbank, 'Sophiology and Theurgy: the New Theological Horizon,' *The Centre of Theology and Philosophy: Online Papers*, University of Nottingham (2007), <http://www.theologyphilosophycentre.co.uk/papers/Milbank_SophiologyTheurgy.doc> [accessed 16 June 2008] (p. 54 of 64). Brandon Gallaher writes: 'God's being is always already enacted in Christ as the divine organism (Logos and Sophia) and therefore whatever exists in creation exists in and by Christ because it is a moment of the one divine Christoform action of God's eternal self-realization as Sophia.' B. Gallaher, 'The Christological Focus of Vladimir Solov'ev's Sophiology,' *Modern Theology*, 25, 4, 2009, pp. 617-46 (p. 628). We should also note the comments of Anthony Baker and Rocco Gangle (on Bulgakov, though just as applicable to Soloviev), which seem to sum up the essence of sophiology: 'the Christian God (in contrast to the Plotinian One) is, "prior" to any question of creation, always already a God in relation. The "absolute" is always already the "absolute-relative"; not simply internally relation*al* as Trinity, but also,

For Soloviev, indeed, theanthropy exceeds theology, and in the person of Jesus Christ, the God-man, we find the central interpretative paradigm of his philosophy of All-Unity and the active principle in his concept of *bogochelovechestvo*. In Christ, he sees not just the historical appearance of the eternal God of spirit but also the fulfilment of humanity. In the latter the ideal relatedness of all things was first attained as an idea in the relating power of reason. But 'that unity in which the universe is sustained and connected cannot remain merely an abstract idea. It is the living, personal power of God, and the all-unifying essence of this power is revealed to us in the theanthropic person of Christ.'[61] Human consciousness and its quintessential attribute, reason, represent the potential ability to grasp the interrelation of all in God, the power to grasp the interconnectedness of the universe. But this All-Unity, even when attained, remains and is destined to remain within the confines of human consciousness which, as form, may contain the fullness of the divine and material realms yet remains powerless to realise this fullness outwardly in the world around it. The interiority of the Kingdom to humanity cannot overcome its interiority by its own means. In this, then, is the purpose of the Incarnation in the Solovievian conception: for the divine to unite with humanity in such a way that its inner life no longer stands over and against the external life but is released, so that the image of God which grows within it may, in the words of another biblical passage, 'pour out on all flesh' and become incarnate in the material world.[62]

> The God-Man, or existent reason (Logos), not only understands the meaning of all in the abstract but realises it in reality [...] The highest task of humanity as such (pure humanity) and the purely human sphere of being is to gather the universe in the idea; the task of the God-man and the Kingdom of God is to gather the universe in reality.[63]

---

and by virtue of this, relat*ing* as a Godhead to an "imaginary" exteriority, to a beloved companion who springs from the love that is the intrinsic essence of God himself.' A. Baker and R. Gangle, 'Ecclesia: The Art of the Visual,' in C. Davis, J. Milbank and S. Žižek (eds), *Theology and the Political: The New Debate*, Durham and London, 2005, 267-80 (p. 273).

61 Solov'ev, *Dukhovnye osnovy*, p. 21.
62 Joel 2.29.
63 S¹, I, p. 275.

The ideal relatedness of all in God which for the first time in history acquired reality, at least potentially, in man's faculty of reason — the 'correlation of all in unity' — now finds itself 'existent' not only interiorly but outwardly, in concrete, material form. While Soloviev assigns the task of relating the fractured and fractious components of the universe together interiorly through reason to humanity, the particular mission of Christ, and the Kingdom he proclaimed is to do so in reality.[64] No longer is the divine contained within human consciousness alone, but in the first 'spiritual human,' Christ, it takes on flesh and is born in matter.

Alongside this, however, we must hold to the understanding that for Soloviev the Incarnation does not stand in opposition to the development of human consciousness or negate the previous development of the natural world. The Incarnation is viewed in his work both as God embarking on a new process within history, and as continuing the process that began with the creation of the world and continued through the emergence of the human organism. In line with Orthodox teaching, Soloviev sees the Incarnation as the adoption of the fullness of human life, not just its semblance. Christ is both man and God, and must himself experience the presence of the Kingdom as it is to God 'in heaven,' as well as its interiority to humanity 'on earth.' This demand carries with it certain ramifications. For God to experience the interiority of the Kingdom means for her to experience the split between inner and external life, to become located within a context in which the limits of consciousness are concretely felt.

> The divine principle here is not enclosed only by the confines of human consciousness, as it was in previous, incomplete theophanies, but itself takes on these confines. It is not that it has entered completely into these confines of natural consciousness, for this would be impossible, but that it feels these confines in actuality as its own at any given moment, and this self-limiting of God in Christ frees His humanity, allowing His natural will to surrender freely itself to the divine principle not as an external power (for such a self-renunciation would not be free) but as the inner good (*blago vnutrennee*), and thus to actually attain this good.[65]

---

[64] For Soloviev, 'the Gospel of Christ is the Gospel of the *Kingdom*. Christ begins his ministry with the good news about the *nearing* of the Kingdom, the nearing of something new, unprecedented.' SS, IV, p. 591.
[65] S², II, p. 157.

III. CHRIST THE GOD-MAN

It is Christ's self-experience of the interiority of the Kingdom, Soloviev is arguing, that makes room for his full humanity and thus freedom, for if the split between inner consciousness and external life were not concretely experienced, his humanity would be unable to freely conform itself to the Kingdom that lies outside, such a distinction no longer having a basis in reality. This conforming of inner consciousness to God's Kingdom is made perfect in Christ insofar as He is able to allow himself to be completely defined by the divine principle, bringing His humanity into full correlation with the presence of God within it since he is, in himself, the absolute union of the two. What is revealed in Christ is thus 'the infinitude of the human soul, able to fit within itself the entire infinitude of God.'[66] In Christ human nature for the first time transcends the limits of its finitude, the self-confined interiority of the Kingdom, and is shot through with divinity. The humanity of Christ is 'spiritualized' or divinized not despite his humanity but because of it.

Since the fullness of Christ's humanity meant for Soloviev that he had to enter fully into the human experience and to feel the 'confines' of human consciousness as his own while remaining fully God, this experience necessarily presupposes a process of becoming in time. If we are to speak of the Incarnation as the divine interceding in history through Christ, therefore, we must also speak of the *mission* of Christ. In his divine aspect, Christ is God incarnate but in his humanity he is necessarily involved in conforming this humanity to God. The Incarnation is consequently not the resting point for Soloviev's conception of the God-man, since to understand Christ solely from an incarnational perspective is to arrive at precisely the kind of static and unidimensional Christology he was trying to avoid. If Christ puts on humanity, he argues, he puts on temporality and becoming: not virtually or seemingly, but actually and concretely. Like humanity, then, Christ has a task to realise on earth, namely the conformation of his humanity to the divine. The culmination of this earthly mission for Soloviev is the Resurrection. Viewed from this perspective, the Christ-event, seen as a theanthropic whole, encompasses incarnation and resurrection, each effective toward a singular purpose.

---

[66] FI, p. 245.

> Only in the Incarnation and Resurrection of the God-man does natural being in the form of the human organism first fulfil its infinite ambition, gaining for itself the fullness and integrity of divine life [...] It is not in the death of the natural individual that the world's contradiction between the personal and the general is resolved but in its resurrection and eternal life. And this resolution is attained through the rational and free activity of the human will. The condition for resurrection is a personal feat (*podvig*), that act of the rational human will with which Christ renounced the law of sin and became obedient to the absolute will of God, making the principle of His humanity a channel for divine activity on the material world.[67]

Note here Soloviev's insistence on the participation of Christ's human will in the fulfilment of his earthly mission. Yet it is not that this will participates in the act of resurrection itself, but rather that it constitutes for Soloviev the '*condition* for resurrection,' becoming the ground, or channel, for the divinity that becomes manifest therein.

Running alongside this, and most striking of all, is the historical picture painted by the philosopher. In a few words, he summarizes the main points of our survey thus far. As nature outgrows, or self-transcends, itself in humanity, so humanity outgrows itself in Christ. Just as the natural world reaches its fullest development in human, the perfect natural organism, so humanity realises its fullest potential in the God-man, both the perfect natural and the perfect spiritual organism. Important here, to put it in spatial terms, is once more the locus of transcendence. That which is transcended is transcended not from a position outside itself but from within. Transcendence here is not the result of a transcendent subject acting from without on a non-transcendent object but a subjective process, a growing outwardly from a prior position of limitation. Thus Soloviev can write of 'natural being in the form of the human organism,' for humanity is both the bearer of nature per se and a nature transcendent, or the human principle as such. In a similar way, Christ is both the bearer of humanity and a humanity transcendent, a normative humanity and a spiritualized, or 'glorified,' humanity. As cosmology grows into anthropology, Soloviev's anthropology now grows into Christology.

---

[67] Solov'ev, *Dukhovnye osnovy*, pp. 97-98.

III. CHRIST THE GOD-MAN

Humanity does not negate the natural principle but realises it, bringing it to the goal of its strivings and adopting it within itself, transforming while preserving it in its integrity. Likewise, Christ takes humanity and bears it in himself, transfiguring but at the same time integrating and preserving it. In his transfiguration of human nature, both the human principle and the natural principle with which humanity is inextricably bound are brought into the movement of the God-man.

As we saw in the section on anthropology, Soloviev derives the task of humanity in the world from human nature itself: the dual nature of the human being as 'the earth of God,' both natural and divine, resulted in the formulation of task as the mediation of these two principles, the materialization of spirit and the spiritualization of matter. That which humanity *is*, namely the unity of matter and spirit, it is called to realise in itself and the world around it. This unity was further defined as the ideal interrelatedness of all in God, potential access to which was first achieved in the world through the emergence of human consciousness and its faculty of reason. Reason becomes the great relater, the ability to contain within itself the complex interrelatedness of being, and the task of humanity to use that reason to 'gather the universe' in its ideal dimension.

Yet the unique significance of the person of Christ in Soloviev's thought does not lie in his ability to use reason to relate the elements of the world together in the ideal space of human consciousness, but to do so in reality. Borrowing from and developing the Logos theology of John's Gospel, Soloviev uses the terms 'Word made flesh,' 'Meaning made flesh,' 'realized Logos' and 'existent reason'[68] to give voice to his conviction that in Christ that which exists interiorly to humanity as the potential of absolute content has become externalised in concrete, material form. That very relating power of reason, 'the correlation of all in unity,' the essential characteristic of the human being, itself speaks, moves and acts through the person of Jesus Christ.

The theologian Karl Rahner described Jesus Christ as 'a man in whom reality does not lag behind the demands of human nature.'[69] In Soloviev's thought, Christ is the perfect human precisely insofar

---

[68] S², II, p. 169; PSS, II, p. 281; S¹, I, p. 275.
[69] K. Rahner, *The Practice of Faith*, London, 1985, p. 8.

as there is no gap between his being and his nature, between what is demanded of him as fully human and what he fulfils in reality.[70] He is the ideal relatedness of spirit and matter in one body and one soul. And yet this does not mean that his humanity is conformed to God, the ideal, through divine fiat but rather, as Soloviev writes, through 'a personal feat,' 'an act of the rational human will.' He fulfils his mission through his humanity, not despite it.

Even so, Soloviev simultaneously asserts that the divine is only able to operate from within humanity in Christ insofar as His rational human consciousness is able to renounce itself freely and become obedient to the absolute will of God. Although rarely stated explicitly, the idea of *kenosis*, which in the Christological tradition dates back to the Pauline epistles and refers to Christ's 'self-emptying' both in the Incarnation and his earthly life, stands central to Soloviev's theology. Its further development lies in the philosopher's reworking of the concept of the 'body of Christ.'

IV. THE BODY OF CHRIST

Many of the most important concepts from the early part of Soloviev's middle period are taken from the Bible and early Christian thought, whether orthodox or heterodox, ranging from the 'image' and 'likeness' of God to the 'Kingdom of God' and the church. But there is one particular writer within that context whose mark is writ large over all of Soloviev's thought from *Lectures on Theanthropy* onwards, and that is the Apostle Paul. Other than the cases in which Soloviev explicitly points to Paul as the original source for the content of his thought,[71] the Christological language he employs is often directly taken from Paul's writings.[72] The most important of these borrowings is that most

---

[70] In the Confession of Chalcedon, this idea was expressed by the words 'in all things like unto us, without sin.'

[71] See, for example, S², I, p. 96.

[72] The singularity of much of Paul's language puts the question of the source of these borrowings beyond question. 'To clothe yourself with Christ' (Galatians 3.27), 'to grow into the full stature of Christ' (Ephesians 4.13), 'that Christ may be formed in all' (Galatians 4.19) are all Pauline idioms that occur practically word-for-word in Soloviev's discourse.

IV. THE BODY OF CHRIST

significant of Pauline concepts — the body of Christ.[73] Christ's body, in the sacramental life of the church and the growing body of collective humanity, becomes the new subject of history after the Incarnation, and it is in and through this body that salvation from death and decay is to occur.

Considering the centrality of Soloviev's Christology to his interpretative framework, it is tempting to conclude that an overarching Christocentrism characterizes his philosophy as a whole.[74] To arrive at such a conclusion, however, is to fail to recognize how far Soloviev actually moves *away* from a more traditional Christocentric model, in which the second person of the Trinity appropriates the distinctive character of the first and third persons and post-incarnational history is relegated to a mere afterthought in the life of the universe.[75] In contrast to such thinking, the Russian philosopher, while affirming the centrality of the Christ-event to the historical life of the world, argues that the death and resurrection of the God-man mark not the end point of salvation history but the beginning of a new process in which humanity is to be actively involved.[76]

> Christ came into the world not to enrich its life with a few new ceremonies but to save it. With His death and resurrection, He saved the world in principle, at its root, at its centre. The expansion of this salvation to the entire circle of human and earthly life, the realization of

---

[73] John Robinson writes that 'one could say without exaggeration that the concept of the body forms the keystone of Paul's theology [...] It is from the body of sin and death that we are delivered; it is through the body of Christ on the Cross that we are saved; it is into His body the Church that we are incorporated.' J. A. T. Robinson, *The Body: A Study in Pauline Theology*, London, 1966, p. 9.

[74] Paul Allen describes Soloviev's brand of mysticism, from which derives his philosophy, as 'Christocentric in the highest degree.' Allen, *Vladimir Soloviev*, p. 288.

[75] In contemporary Christian theology, Karl Barth's term 'christological concentration,' while intended to avoid a hierarchical understanding of the Trinity rather than advocate one, has led to some confusion. Amongst others, Jürgen Moltmann has been keen to avoid its Christocentric implications by developing a pneumatological theology of creation alongside other, more traditional Christological interpretations. See especially Jürgen Moltmann, *God in Creation: An Ecological Doctrine of Creation*, London, 1985.

[76] 'Soloviev,' writes Dmitrii Krylov, 'clearly proceeded from a trinitarian rather than Christocentric understanding of history'. Krylov, *Evkharisticheskaia chasha*, p. 177.

the principle of salvation in all of our reality: this He can do not alone, but only together with humanity itself, for no one can actually be saved by force or unwittingly.[77]

Despite this insistence on the non-finality of the Christ-event and the continuing presence and action of the divine Word in history, Soloviev is extremely careful not to cast doubt on the efficacy of the saving act of God through Christ. To understand his position more fully, it may be helpful to employ two terms recently advanced by the French theologian Jacques Dupuis. Dupuis writes of 'the qualitative plenitude' of God's revelation in Christ — its unsurpassable nature and significance for the world and humanity — while at the same time speaking of another, as-yet-unrealised fullness, which he describes as 'quantitative.' He argues that, qualitatively, the salvation that came through Christ cannot be surpassed by future revelation but represents soteriological consummation in its most intense and concentrated essence. The salvation whose inner core revealed itself in Christ, however, has not yet spread itself across all creation; its quantitative breadth awaits its full realization.[78]

Soloviev, like Dupuis, was faced with the problem of finding meaning in a post-incarnational world in which, despite the Incarnation, divine truth had not yet been realized in the whole of creation. The terms he uses to justify his conviction in the enduring meaning of history, affirming both the efficacy of the Christ-event in the context of salvation history yet at the same time its relativity to the historical present, share much with those of the French theologian. Soloviev writes that the God-man saved the world 'at its centre,' opposing this to a salvation that encompasses not only the centre but the 'periphery'

---

[77] S^2, II, p. 349. Comparing Solov'ievian 'messianism' with the 'accomplished messianism' of the Jewish historian Joseph Salvador, Strémooukhoff argues that the difference between the two lies precisely in the former's deferral of the fullness of salvation in Christ to a future time: 'the God-Man, it is true, has already been incarnate, but a universal and collective man-God must still be formed, a God-Manhood which will at the same time be the universal Church.' Strémooukhoff, *Vladimir Solov'ev and His Messianic Work*, p. 100.

[78] See especially J. Dupuis, 'The Truth will Make you Free,' *Louvain Studies*, 24, 1999, 3, pp. 211-63 (p. 235); *Toward a Christian Theology of Religious Pluralism*, Maryknoll, NY, 1997, pp. 296-97.

of being.⁷⁹ His soteriological conception is fundamentally synchronic as opposed to diachronic; salvation here is understood not so much according to a linear conception of time as the qualitative intensity of its historical manifestation. The soteriological contours of Soloviev's philosophy are thus plotted within a circle rather than along a line, with Christ as the centre in which all points cohere. But the very coherence of all points in him is precisely that which awaits realization: qualitatively, Christ was, is and will remain the centre of universal salvation; quantitatively this salvation must possess the entirety of being so that, in Soloviev's favoured words, God becomes 'all in all.'

> Although Christ irrevocably defeated evil at the genuine focus of the universe, i.e. in Himself, the overcoming of evil on the circumference of the world, i.e. in the collective whole of humanity, must be attained through the self-experience of humanity, for which a new process is required whereby the Christian world, baptized into Christ but not yet clothed in Him, is to develop anew.⁸⁰

This opposition between the ultimate defeat of evil in the person of Christ, the 'focus of the universe,' and its defeat at the 'circumference of the world' in collective humanity is central to Soloviev's envisioning of the task of humanity within a Christian context and is connected to his particular understanding of the nature of evil in the world. For him, evil, and its corollary suffering, lies in the will to self-affirmation to the exclusion of all else, in an egoistic impulse that governs human hearts and the elements of the natural world alike.⁸¹ In 'Lectures on the History of Philosophy,' he writes:

> 'This, i.e. particularity, which within the whole (in God) exists in positive unity with all, is the idea. For each separate creature, this idea is

---

79 As Ruth Coates has pointed out, the metaphor of the circle, and the relationship between centre and periphery, contains strong echoes of Neoplatonic thought, in particular Plotinus. See R. Coates, 'Mystical Union in the Philosophy of Vladimir Solovev,' in J. Andrew, D. Offord, R. Reid (eds), *Turgenev and Russian Culture: Essays to Honour Richard Peace*, Amsterdam, 2008, pp. 135-56 (p. 139).

80 S¹, I, p. 280.

81 'Evil is that concentrated state of will that affirms itself alone and negates every else. Suffering is the necessary reaction against this sort of will, a reaction to which the self-affirming creature yields involuntarily and inevitably and which it feels precisely as suffering.' S², II, p. 123.

> something exclusive, not encompassing but shutting out everything else. This external relationship of each to all makes up the order of material, peripheral being that exists in time and space.[82]

The 'peripherality' of material being here adduced by Soloviev lies in its non-centredness in God, according to which each particular ('this') finds itself in opposition to the whole rather than in the unity of the some. Soloviev here writes of particularity as 'the idea,' that form or principle in which God created the world. This idea exists in unity with all in God whereas on the circumference of being, or outside God, it persists in isolation. The concrete expression of this isolation is the very materiality of the world, centred in itself rather than God and closed to the influence of the other.[83] The significance of the Incarnation and Resurrection for Soloviev is that 'the contradiction between the personal and the general,' individual and universal, spirit and matter — the hitherto irreconcilable poles of universal life — are resolved in the person of Jesus Christ: the God 'in whom all things cohere' becomes a particular individual with a history in a concrete time and place. It is because Christ is incarnated in the particular as 'a living personal power' that he is not only the dwelling of the idea in matter, the assertion of the oneness of spirit and matter, but the active transformer of the material stratum of his own personality — his body — into a direct and immediate expression of his inner life which, rather than standing over and against other bodies, is open to the influence of the other.[84] The end point of this process is the Resurrection.

> The spiritual principle in its very victory over hostile nature must show its superiority, not destroying or devouring this vanquished nature but restoring it in a new, better form of being. Resurrection is the inner reconciliation of matter and spirit; nature here becomes one with spirit, its concrete articulation, its *spiritual body*.[85]

---

[82] Solov'ev, 'Lektsii po istorii filosofii,' p. 79.
[83] See the first chapter for a more detailed exposition of Soloviev's thought on matter and its derivation.
[84] We find very little by way of a direct characterization of the physical aspect of the Resurrection body in Soloviev's thought. It should be stressed, however, that his ideal is directed not toward physicality per se, but its relationship with the spirit.
[85] Solov'ev, *Dukhovnye osnovy*, p. 97.

IV. THE BODY OF CHRIST

The layering of agency involved in Soloviev's concept of theanthropy makes itself felt here once again. It is not only God who acts within nature but also nature which, in its search for transcendence, operates within God. And if the natural reaches the furthest point of its development in the human, then both aspects find their fulfilment in the God-man. The material world is not flung aside in Christ but risen up to new life, transfigured and glorified into the fullness of divine-human being. 'Jesus Christ, risen in the flesh,' writes Soloviev, 'showed that corporeal being is not excluded from the theanthropic union and that external and sensible materiality can and should become the actual weapon and visible reflection of divine power.'[86] In the risen body of Christ, material form is itself initiated into the historical movement of God's salvific plan for creation. If, before the Christ-event, the natural world had played a primarily static role, providing the material and backdrop for the action of God, it has now been put on an entirely new footing. Through the kenotic humanity of Christ in its act of putting itself 'in the proper relation of voluntary submission to, and agreement with, the divine principle, [humanity] again receives the meaning of a mediating, unifying principle between God and nature.'[87] In the Resurrection, through human agency, nature 'loses its material disconnectedness and weight, becoming the direct expression and weapon of the Divine spirit, the true spiritual body of the risen God-man.'[88] This resurrected matter, the body of Christ, now becomes the new subject of transformation; in the divinized humanity of Christ, the natural world is drawn into the logic of salvation history. In him it has shaken off its inertia, its self-centredness, and opened up to the ideal future of the Kingdom of God.

> Before Christianity the static foundation of life was human nature (the old Adam) and the divine the principle of change, movement, and progress. After Christianity, to the contrary, the divine itself, as already embodied,

---

[86] SS, IV, p. 189.

[87] S², II, p. 160. Gorodetzky writes: 'the cosmic and historic process of penetration of all by the divine element reveals itself as *self-denial*.' N. Gorodetzky, *The Humiliated Christ in Modern Russian Thought*, New York, 1938, p. 132.

[88] Solov'ev, *Dukhovnye osnovy*, pp. 96-97. Soloviev understands the Resurrection neither as solely a divine act, nor solely a human act, but the result of the perfect interaction between the two principles. It occurs 'through human agency' insofar as the kenotic movement is made on the part of the human being.

becomes the static foundation and the element of life for humanity. The unknown quantity now is humanity in its answer to this divine, a humanity able to unite with the divine by its own resources [...] As in the pre-Christian historical era the foundation, or material, was human nature, the active and formative principle divine reason [...] and the result the God-man, i.e. God become human, so in the process of Christianity the foundation, or material, is the divine nature (the Word made flesh, or the body of Christ, Sophia), the active and formative principle human reason, and the result the man-god, i.e. humanity become God.[89]

Recalling Soloviev's definition of the divine-human task as the joint 'materialization of spirit,' and 'the spiritualization of matter' — the first the activity of the divine and the second that of humanity — we see here that these two aspects now receive an historical articulation. The activity of the divine on and in the world, from the earliest theophanies in nature through the emergence of the image of God within human consciousness, reach their end in the Incarnation of the God-man. In this climactic event, the human principle, which ideally represents the full interrelatedness of matter and spirit, is brought to completeness in the resurrected body of Christ, and this 'new flesh, the spiritual body of the risen Christ, from now on becomes the divine substance (*substantsiia*) of humanity.'[90] God has attained her goal; from now on the divine becomes the cornerstone of human reality, the unchangeable. The materialization of spirit has reached its conclusion. Human nature itself, which before was but the material for the historical realization of divine nature, now moves into a new phase. The post-incarnational period is

---

[89] S², II, p. 169. Although stated in distinctively Solovievian terms, this passage concurs in all essential details with the doctrine of *theosis*, or deification, summed up in St Anathasius' words that God 'assumed humanity that we might become God.' Athanasius, *On the Incarnation*, Crestwood, NY, 1998, p. 93. In his reaction to Konstantin Leontiev's article 'Nashi novye khristiane. F. M. Dostoevskii i gr. Lev Tolstoi,' first published in the journal *Rus'* in 1883 ('Zametka v zashchitu Dostoevskogo ot obvineneniia v «novom» khristianstve') Soloviev quotes Athanasius' formulation, commenting that 'this belief is not heretical, but truly Christian, Orthodox and Russian (*otecheskaia*).' FI, p. 263. The opposition between the God-man and the man-God, understood in different terms, has a central place in the novels of Dostoevsky.

[90] RNB, f. 171, op. 22, d. 5. 'Zhiznennyi smysl khristianstva,' p. 10 of 13. See also Soloviev's words in *La Russie et l'église universelle*: 'before Jesus Christ, humanity, deprived of an actual centre, was only an organism in potentiality; in reality only separate organs, tribes, towns and nations held sway.' SS, XI, p. 313.

to be characterized by the spiritualization of matter, in which collective humanity transitions from a position of static materiality — the impenetrability of material form — to a dynamic and changing state whose condition and foundation becomes the newly constellated body of Christ, itself dynamically conceived and orientated.

An answer to the question as to how exactly the body of Christ represents this newly acquired dynamism is again to be sought in Soloviev's thought on the nature of material being. 'In the mechanical order,' he writes, 'the creature is not penetrable; in true being, however, it is open and penetrable.'[91] The character of material being is such that 'each [material object] becomes impenetrable and excludes the other.'[92] In this is the condition for the inertia of the material world; the exclusionary principle rooted in nature cannot grow into newness but only subsist in its isolation and self-centredness. The spiritualized body of the God-man is a new revelation in the natural order since it no longer obeys the laws of the mechanism, whose ineluctability finds its ultimate confirmation in the law of death and decay, but represents 'the first decisive victory over death'; the 'new flesh' of Christ, Soloviev writes, is a 'weapon' used for the direct expression of the spirit.[93] This instrumentalization of the corporeal body realized in Christ, its obedience to the spirit given at the core of his inner life, contrasts sharply with the law of material nature that the philosopher sees persisting in carnal reality.

> Flesh is being that is not in control of itself, being that is wholly directed outwards [...] It is being that dissolves in externality and ends with actual decomposition. In contrast, spirit is being that is governed by inner determinations, being that has entered into itself and possessed itself, that acts outwardly with its own power, not losing itself or disintegrating in the flesh.[94]

The material aspect of human life, argues Soloviev, is disordered and disunited. Far from our bodies being an expression of the inner life of the spirit, which by nature is eternal, they exhaust themselves 'in externality,' literally and physically separating us from our neighbours

---

[91] Solov'ev, 'Lektsii po istorii filosofii,' p. 78.
[92] Ibid., p. 77.
[93] SS, IV, p. 503.
[94] S², I, pp. 142-43.

and environment so that ultimately 'we are able to rid ourselves neither of corporeal death, nor of spiritual death.'[95] But in the ideal scheme of things, our bodies, Soloviev writes, should be the 'ultimate limit of the divine-human process as the pre-appointed dwelling-place of the Holy Spirit,'[96] not separating us from every other physical thing but enjoying communion in oneness with them. In the risen body of the God-man, a new kind of flesh, a new kind of matter — penetrable and dynamic — first gains a foothold in reality. The goal, however, is that the spirit of God be manifest in all, that all may be brought into the fullness of salvation in the risen Christ. 'Collective resurrection,' Soloviev writes, 'is the creation of the perfect form for everything that exists, the extreme expression and realization of the meaning and goodness of the universe and therefore the end and goal of history.'[97] The creation that he speaks of here is synonymous with the task of the spiritualization of matter, the bringing of the material world into absolute correlation with the spirit, which Soloviev calls upon humanity to fulfil. In the God-man Christ, this act was realized at the focus of the universe; humanity must expand this salvation to the periphery of being, by 'relating to all in His Spirit and, through this, [...] making it possible for His Spirit to become incarnate in all.'[98] But this new activity is only possible insofar as God has acted first in Christ. Before Christ, the human being could act within and on the world only within the limits of its material being, linking the disparate elements of being within consciousness but powerless to unite them in reality. In the resurrection of Christ, however, 'God discovers the actual power of Her infinitude and humanity expands its actuality to the infinite fullness of God.'[99] Humanity is henceforth able to relate the elements of the world not only in the ideal and interior space of reason but in the living spirit of 'existent reason.' By locating itself within Christ in the inner life of the now incarnate Word, humanity becomes one with him in his risen life and is conformed to his spiritual body. In this process, the interior

---

[95] Solov'ev, *Dukhovnye osnovy*, p. 23.
[96] S^2, I, p. 266.
[97] Ibid., p. 93.
[98] Ibid., p. 280.
[99] 'Zhiznennyi smysl khristianstva' (archive), p. 9 of 13.

life of the Kingdom, which had remained self-enclosed in human consciousness until the Resurrection, transitions into externality in the flesh, not to disappear and dissipate, but to transfigure and dwell therein. But the limit of our human bodies does not represent the final object of spiritualization. For Soloviev the spirit of Christ, or 'the grace of God' as he calls it here,[100] must become incarnate in all.

> If we become channels of the grace of God, then we should spread its action onto both our animal nature and the whole of our world, for one cannot place limits to divine-human power. As the incarnate God saves humanity, so humanity in union with God must save the whole of nature; for as humanity in the form of the Church is the living body of Christ, so the entire natural world must become the living body of a risen humanity. The whole creation must be redeemed and drawn into the freedom of the glory of the sons of God.[101]

Like all the key moments in Soloviev's philosophy of history, it is important not to misinterpret the 'transition' which occurs as a result of the Christ-event as the beginning of an utterly new process, or an absolute end to the previous development. The growth of the Kingdom inside humaniyty that had culminated in the Incarnation is not arrested but merely deprived of its finitude as it is drawn into the fullness of the infinite in the new, dynamic body of Christ. What Soloviev had referred to as humanity's task of 'gathering the universe in the idea,' its theoretical task, is not superseded by the practical task, newly potentialized in the Resurrection, of gathering the universe in reality. The feat of Christ was, in Soloviev's view, to reduce the limitedness of his humanity to such an absolute correlation with the spirit that his inner life no longer met with the confines of materiality but penetrated this matter with a life that was stronger than its death. Human nature was thereby released — or redeemed, in soteriological terms — to transcend the interiority of its ideal, the Kingdom of God. This inner life no longer stands against

---

[100] 'The action of the grace of God has always existed in the world. But from the time of the incarnation of Christ it entered into a visible and sensible form. In the Christian church the divine has not only an inner dimension, the imperceptible action of the spirit, but also some kind of actualized form or corporeality.' Solov'ev, *Dukhovnye osnovy*, p. 108.

[101] Ibid., p. 66.

material life, for the latter has been brought within the sphere of the former. In conforming the world to God interiorly, therefore, a humanity divinized in Christ *at one and the same time* conforms the world to God exteriorly. The theoretical and the practical have become one, and reason itself becomes not 'thought as perceptive but thought as creative.'[102] Fundamental to both sides of this activity, however, theory and practice, is the prior work of humanity in conforming *itself* to God.

> Our practical task is to make our material environment penetrable to our will, or obedient to us; our theoretical task is to make the same environment transparent for our mind, clear and understandable to us. Both of these represent the same task. But for the fulfilment of the task, before all else, we must ourselves become radiant (*svetlyi*) and penetrable for all.[103]

To really share in the life of Christ, the body of humanity must enter into the inner dynamism of the body of the risen God-man, whose 'holy corporeality' (*sviataia telesnost'*) is not a block to material form but a force for incorporation, making room for others within itself. The flesh of human beings should ultimately, in Soloviev's scheme, become like the flesh of Christ, penetrable and open to all. In this process, the disparate lives of human individuals, nations and cultures gradually join together as one body united in him whose dynamic materiality draws in the static, one-dimensional materiality of humanity, transfiguring and spiritualizing it. Soloviev describes this process of humanity's gradual incorporation into the body of Christ as 'theanthropy in a state of becoming (perfect)' (*bogochelovechestvo sovershaiushcheesia*),[104] which he goes on to equate with the church.

---

[102] PSS, III, p. 314.

[103] Solov'ev, *Dukhovnye osnovy*, p. 74. If the foundation for the practical task is the body of Christ, the foundation for the theoretical is 'the mind of Christ' (*um Khristov*). See S², II, p. 308.

[104] See Solov'ev, *Dukhovnye osnovy*, p. 108. This formulation marks a subtle reorientation of emphasis, although not of substance, from Soloviev's earlier philosophy in which, as we saw, he defines the subject of history, his so-called 'second absolute,' by the more professedly abstract phrase 'All-Unity in the state of becoming' (*vseedinstvo stanoviashcheesia*). This shift away from the condition, or goal, of life — i.e. unity — toward the constituents of that unity, God and humanity, signals the philosopher's turn toward the covenantal philosophy and theology of history he accomplishes in *History and Future of Theocracy*.

IV. THE BODY OF CHRIST

> The determinative form of humanity as it is reborn into the Kingdom of God is the church. The church relates to natural humanity as this latter relates to the rest of earthly nature. It is in the natural human being that the ideal of earthly nature is realized; and it is in the church that the ideal of humanity is realized.[105]

It is not my intention here to offer a full account of Soloviev's multi-faceted views on the nature and vocation of the Christian church. My goal is rather to explore his ecclesiology from the perspective of the historical task of humanity insofar as it is synonymous with the body of Christ. In *History and Future of Theocracy*, we find the following description of the threefold nature of the church, again couched in the biblical terminology to which Soloviev was increasingly turning during this middle period of his life:

> Firstly, the church should *exist* on a real foundation; secondly, it should *live* and develop; thirdly, it should become *perfect*. From the perspective of its real existence, the church is a *building* created by Christ, the City of God, the New Jerusalem [...] From the perspective of its life, the church is the living *body of Christ*. Finally, from the perspective of its perfection, the church is the immaculate *bride of Christ*.[106]

Soloviev goes on to draw God's relation to the church in accordance with these, its three aspects, writing: 'God lives *in* the church as His temple; *through* the church as His body; and *with* the church as His wife or bride.'[107] If the first aspect of the church relates to the fact of its institution by Christ, its beginning point, and the third to the end point of its historical development, the second may be understood as the bridge between the two, that principle in which the post-incarnational period approaches the eschaton. That Soloviev connects the body of Christ precisely with the *life* of the church is perhaps unsurprising, but its importance should be underlined nevertheless.[108] The body of

---

[105] SS, IV, p. 605.
[106] Ibid., p. 601.
[107] Ibid., p. 602.
[108] On the importance of 'life' (in Greek, *zoe*) in reference to Christ and the Church, particularly in the fourth Gospel, see 'The Concept of Life in the NT,' in *Theological Dictionary of the New Testament*, ed. G. Kittel and G. Friedrich, Grand Rapids MI, 1985, p. 294. On its development in Pauline thought, see R. Bultmann, *Theology of the New Testament*, 2 vols, London, 1965, I, p. 210.

Christ is the life of the church in history, the principle of movement between its present reality and its future state of perfection.[109] God acts through his body, the church, and it is in this body that created humanity discovers the beginnings of the new life it is called to realize.

This new life is not only a construct of the mind but is dependent on the 'real-mystical link with Christ as the principle of theanthropy' embodied in the church.[110] This link between Christ and humanity is sustained and supported in Soloviev's ecclesiology by many factors, ranging from apostolic succession to the profession of a shared creed, all of which have vital significance in his thought. But humanity can only actually *participate* 'in the theanthropic life through the communication of the holy sacraments as the beginnings of a new, spiritual corporeality and life of grace (Christ as life in us).'[111] Its sacramental life, and in particular the Eucharist, is thus envisioned as the very lifeblood of the church, the guarantor of its continuing vitality and efficacy. The sacraments are understood here as the bearers not of tradition, nor of right belief, but of the Christ-event itself, and the newness that thereby became incarnate in history. As Soloviev writes, 'in them are given the actual beginnings of the spiritual-corporeal interaction of God with humanity.'[112] They are the receipt of the given, the 'gift' of the body of Christ as already risen and glorified. The 'inner meaning and purpose [of the Eucharist] is the spiritualization of human sustenance (and, correspondingly, the whole corporeal structure of humanity) through its incorporation into the sphere of the spiritual corporeality of the God-man Christ.'[113] In a passage from the final part of *La Russie et l'église universelle*, Soloviev directs himself to those who officiate the gifts of God to the people — the priests of the church:

---

[109] 'Real ecclesial substance,' comments the liberation theologian Jon Sobrino in the same vein, 'is the realization of the true *body of Christ* in history.' J. Sobrino, 'Communion, Conflict and Ecclesial Solidarity,' in *Mysterium Liberationis: Fundamental Concepts of Liberation Theology*, ed. I. Ellacuria and J. Sobrino, Maryknoll NY, 1993, pp. 615-36 (p. 630).
[110] S², I, p. 159.
[111] Ibid., p. 159.
[112] Ibid., p. 123.
[113] Ibid., p. 123.

> As Christ is one in His hypostasis, infinitely diverse insofar as He contains within Himself and reveals the ideal cosmos, and trinitarian insofar as He unites the divine essence with the rational soul of humanity and with material corporeality [...] so in the holy sacraments Christ is the principle of life, all life, not just spiritual but corporeal, not just individual but social. You, the offerers of the sacrifice, you are they who are appointed to sow the mystical but real grain of theanthropic life in humanity, you are the sowers in our nature of a divinized matter, a heavenly corporeality. The beginning of this task, the first source of a life that is more than natural in the earthly body of humanity should be an absolute fact that exceeds human reason, a mystery. But every mystery needs revealing, and the mystical elements which, in the grace of the sacraments, make their home in human nature should through your service enter, grow and become manifest in visible existence, in the social life of humanity, transforming it more and more into the living body of Christ.[114]

Particularly clear here is the emphasis on what Soloviev calls the 'Trinitarian' aspect of Christ, the conjoining in his one person of the divine, human, and material natures. The life of Christ is thus the all-reconciling unity of a being that has outgrown itself to include the totality of life, both divine and material, individual and universal. Alongside this, however, the philosopher is at pains to emphasize, in a way that is often lacking in other areas of his work, the mystery both of the Christ-event and of the sacramental life of the church. The sacrament, the beginning of new life in creation given through Christ, is inaccessible to reason for it is precisely reason that is transcended, albeit by an initial act of the rational will, in the feat of the God-man.[115] Humanity cannot work its way to salvation by its own means but must find its centre in the 'absolute fact' of the Christ-event as the condition for its own dwelling in God. The incorporation of humanity within the church as the body of Christ can thus only occur insofar as there has already occurred the prior act of God in Christ who, 'having transformed His material (mechanical) body into a spiritual (dynamic) one [...] gives it as food to humanity.'[116] God makes herself available

---

[114] SS, II, p. 342.
[115] Here again, Paul's words may serve as an approximate expression for this fundamental paradox. As he writes in his letter to the Galatians, 'through the law I died to the law, so that I might live to God.' Gal 2:19.
[116] Solov'ev, *Dukhovnye osnovy*, p. 99.

to humanity in the sacrament as the possibility of a new life other than the natural life of death and decay.

In this way, Soloviev extends his kenotic understanding of Christ beyond the sacrifice of his own self on the cross and the consequent victory over death in the Resurrection to his enduring presence in the sacramental life of the church. This life is sustained through Christ's perpetual kenosis, understood here as the continuing openness and self-giving of his body to the historical life of the church.[117] Communion with this life through the sacrament, however, is not merely a matter of receiving. According to Soloviev, to receive this food as gifted by God, to participate in the actual life of the church as the body of Christ, requires not so much a determined resolution of the will but its own kenotic movement, the transference of will into a state of pure passivity.

> Before the sacrament, the human will completely renounces everything that belongs to it, remaining in perfect potentiality, or purity, and thus becoming able, as pure form, to receive a supra-human content. Through the sacraments, that unitary and holy essence which is the Church in-itself (Ding an sich, or the noumenon of the church, in philosophical terminology), unites or incorporates within itself the inner essence of the human and makes the life theanthropic.[118]

---

[117] There has been much debate in both unreformed and reformed churches surrounding the Council of Trent's affirmation that the 'sacrifice of the mass' represents a repetition of the sacrifice of Christ on Calvary, only after a different, unbloody fashion. For a description of the proceedings at Trent, see J. F. McHugh, 'The sacrifice of the mass at the Council of Trent,' in *Sacrifice and Redemption: Durham Essays in Theology*, ed. S. W. Sykes, Cambridge, 2007, pp. 157-81. For an analysis of the theological questions involved in the notion of sacramental sacrifice from a Catholic perspective, see M. McGuckian, 'The Sacramental Sacrifice,' in *The Holy Sacrifice Of The Mass: A Search For An Acceptable Notion Of Sacrifice*, Mundelein, IL, 2005, pp. 107-33. The idea of an eternal kenosis should not be equated with an eternal suffering of God. Hans Urs von Balthasar has written much more persuasively of this kenotic economy than Soloviev, but their thinking on the subject is essentially the same. Balthasar writes of 'God-given Being [which] is both fullness and poverty at the same time: fullness as Being without limit, poverty modelled ultimately on God Himself because He knows no holding on to Himself, poverty in the act of Being which is given out, which as gift delivers itself without defence.' Graham Ward cites this statement to conclude that the 'kenotic economy is an economy of life through death, eternal resurrection through eternal crucifixion, an eternal giving of thanks through an eternal brokenness.' See G. Ward, 'Death, Discourse and Resurrection,' in L. Gardner, D. Moss, B. Quash and G. Ward (eds), *Balthasar at the End of Modernity*, 1999, pp. 15-68 (p. 52).

[118] S^1, I, p. 513.

The Eucharist thus involves two distinct, though inseparable, elements: firstly, the kenotic offering of God's self in the body of her Son, and, secondly, the renunciation of self on the part of the individual communicator. In both, however, is the limited, individual humanity of each party overcome, not in a static and immobile glory, but in the 'theanthropic life' of Christ, the shared life of God and humanity. Soloviev's position on the Eucharistic sacrifice should not therefore be interpreted in terms of a repetition of the one sacrifice of Jesus Christ on the cross, as formulated by the Council of Trent, for his understanding of sacrifice is not restricted to a single event which is then carried through in a series of future re-enactments. It is not so much that he sees Christ's sacrifice as repeated in the sacrament but rather that sacrificiality — the law of self-giving — has itself become the life of the church with its centre in his risen body. The freedom which is opened up in the dynamic unity of the body of Christ, freedom from the finitude of human aspiration, is attained through the giving-away of self to the other.[119] The 'supra-human' is assimilated not through a pushing-through to the other side of humanity but by its reduction to 'pure form,' a state of pure passivity and potentiality.

This law of self-giving, founded in the human feat of Jesus Christ and continued in the sacramental life of the church, in Soloviev's conception becomes the law not only of the workings of God and humanity but also of nature; the economy of the Son is seen as the sacrament of a broader economy that embraces both human and material worlds. The goal of this broader economy is to bring the realized salvation in Christ to its very outermost point, or 'circumference' as Soloviev calls it. As collective humanity grows into the body of Christ, entering more fully into the law of his sacramental self-giving and allowing room for

---

[119] It is interesting in this connection to note the more general reflections of Jacques Derrida in his enquiry as to the essence of religion. 'However little may be known of religion *in the singular*, we do know that it is always a response and responsibility that is prescribed, not chosen freely in an act of pure and abstractly autonomous will. There is no doubt that it implies freedom, will and responsibility, but let us try to think this; will and freedom *without autonomy*. Whether it is a question of sacredness, sacrificiality or of faith, the other makes the law, the law is other: to give ourselves back, and up, to the other. To every other and the utterly other.' J. Derrida, 'Faith and Knowledge: The Two Sources of "Religion" at the Limits of Reason Alone,' in *Acts of Religion*, New York, 2002, pp. 40-101 (p. 71).

the other, in so doing it makes room and incorporates within itself the material world around it. Just as the penetrable materiality of the body of Christ allows all that is human to commune within it, becoming the vessel for collective humanity, so the actualized-in-Christ penetrability of this new human organism opens up to incorporate within itself the entire natural world. The human form, in the life of the church as the body of Christ, becomes the potential receptacle for the material multiplicity of the world: not just the gatherer of the universe in the idea but, in and through Christ, the gatherer of the universe in reality.

V. DEATH AND FLESH

One of the notable things about Soloviev's Christology of the early and middle periods is the lack of attention he pays to the concrete conditions of the death of Christ, to the despair and abandonment of the cross. There is no doubt that it is there, in the background, but the philosopher's mind always seemed to rush forward in anticipation to the moment of resolution, the glory of the Resurrection that lay beyond the cold tomb. Mochul'skii writes perceptively in this regard that 'redemption for Soloviev meant victory over the three temptations [...] The struggle at Gethsemane and Golgotha, the Saviour's actual acceptance and living through of the sins of the whole world, his death and victory over death [...] go almost unmentioned' until later in his life when his 'evolutionism is replaced by apocalyptic thinking.'[120] Yet a condemnation of the phenomenon of death, rooted in one of the three fundamental feelings we earlier associated with the philosopher — an abhorrence for decay — and the conviction that, as Paul writes, in Christ death has 'lost its sting'[121] are crucial to an understanding of his

---

[120] Mochul'skii, *Zhizn' i uchenie*, p. 102-03. Compare also Levitskii's comment that 'the image of the imperishable beauty of Sophia outweighed in [Soloviev] the image of the suffering Christ; the mystery of the resurrection sometimes pushed the mystery of Golgotha into the background.' S. Levitskii, 'Vl. Solov'ev i Dostoevskii,' *Novyi zhurnal*, 1955, 41, pp. 197-209 (p. 206). In his book on the role of evil in Soloviev's thought, Jan Krasicki uses such biographical details to present a profoundly exaggerated picture of the change that occurs in Soloviev's late period. See Krasitskii, *Bog, chelovek i zlo*.

[121] See 1 Corinthians 15.55-56.

position throughout. 'Without the power of good,' he writes, 'without the possibility of its final victory over everything up to and including the "final enemy"—death—life would be fruitless.'[122] The 'life' of Christ that Soloviev saw operating in the sacraments of the church as his body was a life that is not, nor can be, negated by death. Understood sacramentally, as the continuation of the work of Christ, the task of the spiritualization of matter is necessarily the transition of all that is natural into the realm of immortality.

> By the free and conscious activity of a resurrected-in-Christ humanity, the death-dealing tree of its old nature, whose root is sin, whose growth is illness and whose fruit is death, should be transformed into the eternal tree of new life which is rooted in love and brotherhood, grows by the cross of spiritual battle and reaps the fruit of universal resurrection.[123]

Despite this emphasis on the conscious eradication of death, however, Masing-Delic's conclusion that Soloviev's system amounts to a kind of 'immortalization programme,' needs to be significantly expanded if it is to be accepted. In a passage from one of his late *Sunday Letters* (1897-98), Soloviev writes:

> We die because our spiritual power, interiorly bound by sins and passions, proves insufficient to claim, incorporate and transform into itself our entire external, corporeal being; it falls away and *our natural immortality* (until the final resurrection, to which we can attain only through Christ) is only half-realized, only our inner dimension is eternal, only the fleshless spirit. Yet Christ was risen as one whole (*vsetselo*).[124]

In Soloviev's thought, death is not the default condition of human nature but a sort of intruder. The natural immortality of humanity is not in need of explanation, for it is bound up with the fact of being human. The enigma for the mind is rather the very fact that we die, that our eternal spirits are overtaken by what Soloviev considered the base laws

---

[122] S¹, I, p. 97.
[123] Solov'ev, 'Zhiznennyi smysl khristianstva,' p. 63-64.
[124] SS, x, p. 36 (my emphases).

of physical existence.[125] Humanity is not, in his view, *made* immortal, nor does it make itself immortal, but 'rediscovers' its immortality as rooted in the image of the eternal God.[126]

But what exactly did immortality mean for Soloviev? Following Paul and faithful to his own thinking, the philosopher could not rest on the immortality of the soul without the body: Christ was risen as one whole, body and soul. Yet there is a key difference between the approaches of Paul and Soloviev on the question of what is involved in the spiritualization of the body, and its immortalization in a new form. The two key concepts in Pauline anthropology are σάρξ (*sarx*) and σῶμα (*soma*), which in the majority of cases translate into English as 'flesh' and 'body' respectively. With the word 'flesh' (σάρξ) he designates 'the whole person, considered from the point of view of his external, physical existence' but, crucially for the present consideration, 'man in contrast with God,' the state of humanity's being in the natural world that separates it from God and every other thing around him. The flesh for Paul is thus the principle of individuation and to live 'according to the flesh' is to live in opposition to God and to be controlled by the powers of this world — sin and death.[127] While the 'body' (σῶμα) also means the external presence of the whole person and 'repeats all the emphases of σάρξ before it diverges from it,' it is also for Paul 'the carrier of the

---

[125] Far from softening in later life, Soloviev's viscerally negative assessment of the phenomenon of death only became more pronounced. In *Three Conversations*, he describes it through the mouth of his protagonist as 'the extreme evil.' In *Justification of the Good*, he writes of the 'very process of death as physical lawlessness, as the victory of the blind and soulless force of poisonous matter over a living, organized body in which a rational spirit had become incarnate.' S¹, II, p. 727; I, p. 324.

[126] There is a great deal of literature from the early Christian period on the question of natural immortality, which was often seen as the preserve of Greek philosophy rather than the Hebrew Bible. For a fine introduction to the problem, see R. Swinburne, 'Soul, nature and immortality of the,' *Routledge Encyclopaedia of Philosophy* (1998) <http://www.rep.routledge.com/article/K096SECT2> [accessed 10 June 2008]. While Soloviev was heavily influenced by Plato and Leibniz, both of whom regarded the soul as innately immortal, he seeks to correlate their views with Christian thought, positing the source of immortality both inside the soul and outside it, at its divine source.

[127] On an anthropological plane, Pauline 'flesh' is thus equivalent to the character of Soloviev's *materia prima*, or Satan, on the metaphysical plane. My argument here and in what follows is based on Robinson's insightful treatment of the Pauline concepts in *The Body*, pp. 17-33.

resurrection.' Thus, while 'σάρξ stands for man, in the solidarity of creation, in his distance from God, σῶμα stands for man, in the solidarity of creation, as made for God.'[128] In this way, the two terms carry much of the same meaning, and have to do with a human being's external or physical life not considered in itself but *in its relation* to God. When Paul speaks of 'putting off the body of flesh'[129] he is not therefore pointing to the stripping away of inherently evil matter but to a correction in the human's relationship to God. Flesh, or matter, is for Paul not evil in itself, as it was for the vast majority of Gnostic worldviews; it is the relationship of the human being to God through his body that is liable to be corrupted through sin, not the body in and of itself. [130]

Soloviev's position does not differ from Paul's in substance. For the Russian philosopher, the body is both the potential receptacle for the fullness of theanthropic being, when united with God, and the principle of self-centred isolation when blocked off to divine influence. The elements of σάρξ and σῶμα are both present as strongly as they are in Paul. But we find a subtle change of emphasis from the Pauline conception in Soloviev's treatment of the body of Christ, the process it inaugurates, and the transformation of the human personality involved. If the body itself as corporeal form is Paul's central idiom, for Soloviev it is rather the materiality of the body, that of which it consists — content, not form. It is not in our bodies that Soloviev posits the historical locus of transformation but our *flesh*. 'We know,' he writes in *Spiritual Foundations*, 'that our flesh (*plot'*) is the earth from which and on which should grow the tree of eternal life, that earth which God wishes to flourish and be fruitful.'[131] Such a statement

---

[128] Ibid., pp. 26-27, 31.
[129] Colossians 2.11.
[130] This understanding of Pauline 'flesh' had been evident before Soloviev in Russian biblical exegesis. See, for example, F. A. Golubinskii and D. G. Levitskii, *Premudrost' i blagost' Bozhiia v sud'bakh mira i cheloveka (o konechnykh prichinakh)*, St Petersburg, 1907 (first edition: 1853). '[By flesh] the Apostle understands not only the sensual side of human nature, but the whole person with its sensuality, its mind, the entirety of its sensual and spiritual urges, dispositions, contemplations and actions in their disobedience to the law of the spirit of God. Flesh means the same as the person of the soul (*dushevnyi chelovek*), i.e. sinful, opposed by the Apostle to the spiritual person, sanctified by the grace of the Spirit (p. 116).'
[131] Solov'ev, *Dukhovnye osnovy*, p. 40.

would have been impossible for Paul since for him flesh is precisely that part of human existence which must be 'stripped away' to incorporate humanity within God through the body of Christ. Soloviev's use of the word 'flesh' here is a conscious decision to diverge from biblical usage.[132] What Soloviev is suggesting is that it is the very exteriority of the human person to God — the 'body of sin' or the flesh (σάρξ) that for Paul must be stripped away — that is to become the carrier of the new life available to all through Christ. The 'matter' of the world whose primary characteristic is to exclude all others in its egoistic erecting of barriers for the other (as outlined in Chapter 1) is itself to become the foundation for the new movement in the body of Christ. The very principle of evil and sin — the energy of individuation and self-assertion — is incorporated within this body such that its fundamental character, though unchanged, serves a purpose other than separation and isolation.[133] In this sense, we find the same puzzling 'coincidence of sinlessness and sinfulness' in Soloviev's handling of the person of Christ that a recent commentator has read into the theology of Karl Barth.[134]

1883 saw the publication, in the journal *Pravoslavnoe obozrenie*, of Soloviev's 'The Lived Meaning of Christianity,' which he had written

---

[132] Soloviev was very clear on the meaning of the word 'flesh' in the biblical thought. In *Justification if the Good*, writes: 'Not in itself, but only in its deficient relation to spirit, is the material nature of humanity that which the Bible calls *flesh*.' S^1, I, p. 140.

[133] Note the following passage from *Lectures on Theanthropy*: 'the essence of good is given through the activity of the divine but the energy for its manifestation in humanity can only be the transformation of the subdued power of a self-assertive personal will, which has transitioned into a potential state. [The saint] has conquered the power of evil by subordinating it to its higher principle and it has become the *foundation and carrier of good*' (my emphases). S^2, II, pp. 150-51. It should be said that Paul can, in places, be seen as following an argument not dissimilar to that of Soloviev. See, especially, the paradoxical statement of 2 Cor. 5:21: 'For our sake he made him to be sin who knew no sin, so that in him we might become the righteousness of God.'

[134] In his engaging discussion of the theme, Paul Jones puts particular emphasis on the receptivity of Christ's flesh in Barth's handling: 'As the nails are forced into his receptive flesh, in the moment at which he 'welcomes' sin into his being, Christ has actually become the sin that God rejects (thus 2 Cor. 5:21) [...] This entails more than Christ 'taking the negativities of existence into unbroken unity with God' [as in Tillich]. It entails Christ being the person in whom the horror of sinful hostility against God is halted, cancelled and rendered quite impossible.' P. D. Jones, 'Barth and Anselm: God, Christ and the Atonement,' *International Journal of Systematic Theology*, 12, 2010, 3, pp. 257-82 (p. 278).

the previous year.¹³⁵ The article is a philosophical commentary on the Logos theology of the fourth Gospel, an interest in which Soloviev nurtured his entire life. 'The truth of Christianity,' Soloviev summed up his argument toward the end of the article, 'consists in the spiritualization and divinization of the flesh.'¹³⁶ While the substance of the body of Christ is entirely irrelevant for Paul, for Soloviev, to the contrary, it is the entire point.¹³⁷ The risen body of the God-man is significant not so much because it is a body, that is, a corporeal and corporate form for collective humanity, but insofar as it consists of a new spiritualized matter, a divinized flesh. Christ's mystical role in the church is understood by Soloviev in terms of the change which the Christ-event has wrought in matter itself. 'The word was made flesh and this new spiritualized and divinized flesh remains the divine substance of the Church.'¹³⁸ It is the very materiality of the body of Christ that is foregrounded, a new matter which does not obey the laws of the mechanism but 'opens up' to the other, including it within itself: a matter in which the kenotic law of self-giving has become the guiding principle of its being. Such a materiality is hard to conceive, indeed perhaps impossible, for no matter how hard Soloviev tries to express it, there remains an unknown and unspoken aspect to his thought on the body of Christ such that it never quite gels with the contradictory formulations and reformulations he uses to define it. Important to remember, though, is that, as with all 'new' developments in Soloviev's

---

135 A further, drafted version of this article exists in the archives, with several fascinating passages that were left out of the final edit (see, for example, Chapter II, note 88). See Rossiiskaia natsional'naia biblioteka (RNB), f. 171, op. 22, d. 5. 'Zhiznennyi smysl khristianstva.' The article was reworked into the first chapter of the second part of *Spiritual Foundations of Life* (1882-84), with the omission of several more passages and the insertion of additional material. A seeming misprint in the original publication (1872 instead of 1882) has led several authors to claim this piece as Soloviev's earliest work, a claim that has been largely discounted on the weight of the evidence. For more details, see Kozyrev, *Solov'ev i gnostiki*, p. 237.

136 Solov'ev, 'Zhiznennyi smysl khristianstva,' p. 60.

137 Robinson points out that for Paul 'neither [σάρξ nor σῶμα] is to be defined in terms of the stuff of which it is composed [...] [σῶμα] fulfils its essence by being utterly subject to Spirit, not by being either material or immaterial [...] Creation transfigured at the *Parousia* may or may not be physical—its substance is quite irrelevant.' Robinson, *The Body*, p. 32.

138 Solov'ev, *Dukhovnye osnovy*, p. 124.

philosophy of history, the new matter of the body of Christ does not negate the matter of the world but realizes those initial strivings for self-transcendence that had resulted in the emergence of the human being and, eventually, in the Incarnation. The historical process in Soloviev is to be thought of as a synchronic whole: its first stage moves from the circumference of the circle to its centre — the Christ-event — and the second from this centre toward a repossession of the circumference. In contrast with the first stage of history, in which humanity is necessarily defined by the limits of its natural being, the divinized matter of the body of Christ has now been gifted to humanity so that, in the body of Christ, whose seeds are present in the sacramental life of the church, humanity may extend this spiritualized matter to the entire created order. It is for this reason that Soloviev treats the terms 'spiritualization' (*odukhotvorenie*) and 'humanization' (*ochelovechenie*) as synonymous.[139] The spiritualization of matter cannot take place without its humanization, for in the theanthropic life of the God-man humanity has been brought within the realm of the spirit. The divine and the human are one in the spiritualized corporeality of Christ. To speak about 'spiritualization' is thus to speak of 'humanization,' both of which are perfected in the God-man. In the final stage of history, the salvation that came through Christ is to be channelled, as it was in his person, through humanity, so that the material world becomes the substance and expression of the body of collective humanity.

---

[139] 'The fate of humanity, our rising above our animal nature,' writes Soloviev in his essay on the poetry of Aleksei Tolstoi, 'mainly depends on the humanization and spiritualization of these fundamental facts of life, on their rebirth from the blind instincts of nature into the conscious principles of worthy existence.' FI, pp. 496-97.

Chapter III
PROPHECY

The ideal of prophecy resonates across Soloviev's life and oeuvre. From early on, he understood his vocation in prophetic terms, and consciously sought to position himself in a line of prophets from both the Russian literary and Judeo-Christian traditions. In what follows, we look first at the middle period of Soloviev's life, during which his prophetic activism within Russian society reached its peak, seeking to uncover his motivations and the ideas that lay behind his activity. It was during this period that Soloviev's engagement with the Jewish question in Russia claimed a great part of his energies, and he became increasingly absorbed in the model and message of the Hebrew Prophets. The study of the prophecy of the past, as well as what he saw as the corruption of the powers of the present, led him ever more to reflect on the question of prophetic authenticity, both in relation to his own life and to that of historical humanity. These reflections were to burst into life in his late depiction of the Antichrist, on whose provenance the second section of this chapter focuses. After a discussion of what the 'apocalyptic turn' might have meant for Soloviev's vision of ideal human activity in the world, the last section explores his theoretical work on the nature of prophetic consciousness, and its centrality to the dynamics of the spiritualization of matter.

I. SOLOVIEV AS PROPHET, 1881-1897

There are a number of key events in Soloviev's biography that stand out both in terms of their character, and the consequences they wrought in his life. Such an event was his speech in the hall of the Credit Society, St Petersburg, on 28 March 1881. Two weeks earlier Tsar Alexander

Chapter III. PROPHECY

II had been assassinated, and Soloviev spoke on the day the case over the accused was to end, with the almost inevitable verdict of the death penalty. It was the second in a two-part lecture, the first given on 26 March, under the general title 'A Critique of Modern Education and the Crisis of the World Process.'[1] The two talks were intended as a response and development of a speech given by the Slavophile Ivan Aksakov some days earlier bewailing the idea of revolution as a Western innovation, and calling for a newly energized relationship between tsar and people. In the event, it went well beyond the relatively uncontroversial and quiescent ideas of Slavophilism into direct and dangerous provocation. Near the end of the speech, in a passage that is now one of the most famous of his pronouncements, Soloviev said:

> The present moment presents state power with a hitherto unprecedented opportunity to prove in deed its pretensions to be the supreme leader of the people [...] The Tsar can forgive them and, if he really feels his connection to the people, he should forgive them. The Russian people does not recognize two truths. If it accepts the truth of God as the truth, then it has no other, and the truth of God says: 'Do not kill' [...] The cold murder of an unarmed human being is repellent to the soul of the people. The great moment of [...] self-denial has arrived. Let the Tsar and Autocrat of Russia announce in deed that he is first of all a Christian, and as the leader of a Christian people he should, he must, be a Christian.
>
> The decision does not depend on us; it is not we who are called to judge [...], but if state power turns away from the Christian principle and steps onto the path of bloodshed, we will leave it, abandon it: we will renounce it.[2]

The consequences of the speech are well-known: Soloviev was denied the right to give public lectures for a time, and from then onward the net of censorship was to close in ever tighter around his publishing career

---

[1] Accounts of the lecture were distributed widely amongst the Russian intelligentsia in St Petersburg and Moscow. Writing later, in 1897, Soloviev refers to the 'apocryphal copies of the speech' and the 'fantastical rumours' that had spread abroad about it. S², II, p. 630. Whatever the case, the latter part of the speech, corroborated by multiple witnesses, is that which directly concerns us here. It is included as an appendix to the fourth volume of Soloviev's letters: Solov'ev, Pis'ma, IV, pp. 243-52. See also Strémooukhoff, *Vladimir Solov'ev and His Messianic Work*, p. 357.

[2] Solov'ev, Pis'ma, IV, p. 246.

in Russia. He only avoided harsher measures, including exile and hard labour, thanks to the personal intervention of Mikhail Loris-Melikov, Minister of Domestic Affairs, who pointed out to Tsar Alexander III several mitigating circumstances, such as his friendship with members of the Tsar's inner circle, his ascetic lifestyle, and the good name of his father.[3] Despite Soloviev's conviction that he was arguing firmly within Slavophile principles — marked by their uniquely high estimation of the Russian people and character — the Slavophile camp itself reacted with outrage.[4] In a moment, Soloviev had lost the majority of his intellectual sympathizers and companions.[5]

How did Soloviev come to give such a speech in the first place? First, let us note the defining characteristics of the speech in question, and the ideas that lie behind it. Central to its logic is the philosopher's belief in his right to speak for the Russian people. He, not anyone else, was entitled to give voice to the deepest yearnings of the people. He it was who was destined to represent this people before the eyes of the tsar, he who knew them most intimately. But it is not only the people for whom Soloviev claims to be speaking. Despite his statement that 'it is not for us to judge,' repeated a day later in evidence given to Nikolai Baranov, the St Petersburg governor,[6] the judgement he offers to the powers that be is much more than that of an individual person: it is the very judgement of God.

Abraham Heschel notes that prophecy is not so much 'the application of timeless standards to particular human situations' but 'an interpretation of a particular moment in history, a divine understanding of a human situation.' He thus describes prophecy as

---

[3] P. Shchegolev, ed., 'Sobytie 1-ogo marta i Vladimir Solov'ev: Novye dokumenty,' in *Byloe*, 1918, 4-5, pp. 330-36 (p. 334).

[4] See Aksakov's explosive reaction in *Pis'ma russkikh pisatelei k A. S. Suvorinu*, ed. D. I. Abramovich, Leningrad, 1927, p. 13.

[5] Shortly after the speech, Nikolai Liubimov wrote to Soloviev that 'Mikhail Nikiforovich [Katkov], who has always had such a love for you, is profoundly distressed and told me with tears in his eyes that your speech was an insult to the feelings of the people, a presumptuous challenge to the whole of society.' S², II, p. 630.

[6] 'Novye dokumenty,' p. 333. In his written evidence, as well as his letter to Tsar Alexander III, Soloviev seeks to bring his argument back onto more abstract grounds, to a discussion of the practice of authentic Christian values per se.

'exegesis of existence from a divine perspective.'[7] Soloviev's speech was not a speech 'against capital punishment,' as his nephew Sergei termed it;[8] it was a speech against the execution of two women and four men by the Russian state with Tsar Alexander III at its head. In this, its historical specificity, was its whole scandal. Had Soloviev spoken merely about the incompatibility of the death penalty with Christian values, his speech may have caused a degree of controversy but nothing like the storm that it did. His characterization of the historical moment may appear overstated: the political situation upon the death of Alexander II was unsettled yet relatively stable compared to later years. But the point is that his speech was made — or at the very least was so constructed[9] — precisely 'from a divine perspective' or, as Walter Brueggemmann has put it, 'from the perspective of the passion of God,'[10] which is enflamed and concerned by every infringement against divine justice.

From this reputed perspective of God, Soloviev presumes to announce to the supreme power of the state those actions which most fully correspond to the divine will. He then goes on to paint a picture of the potential consequences should the Russian leadership choose its own path over and against the ways of God: rebellion and revolt on the part of the people. Soloviev's words, much like those of Dostoevsky in his novel *Demons*, can very easily be interpreted as a prediction of the revolutions of the early twentieth century in Russia. But it is important to note that it is the exhortative rather than the predictive element of prophecy which is primary here. The future is disclosed 'in order to illumine what is involved in the present,'[11] not the other way round.

---

[7] A. Heschel, *The Prophets*, New York, 2001, p. xxvii.
[8] S. M. Solov'ev, *Zhizn' i tvorcheskaia evoliutsiia*, p. 165.
[9] Writing in 1897, Soloviev emphasizes the primacy of inspiration over calculation in the speech. It was 'not, properly speaking, a lecture but an improvised speech — without any notes, or even a drafted outline,' he writes. S², II, p. 630. It may be that he had not intended to speak on the subject at all, in line with a promise to steer clear of anything to do with the assassination he had given to Baranov the week before.
[10] W. Brueggemmann, *The Prophetic Imagination*, Minneapolis, 2001, p. 45.
[11] Heschel, *The Prophets*, p. 15. Soloviev makes this clear when he writes that 'everything I have said about the great mission of my homeland is not foreseeing (prediction) but preaching (predication). I do not *foresee events* which should happen but advocate for those actions which need to be fulfilled.' S², II, p. 268.

The difference is a crucial one, and fundamental to an understanding of prophecy in the Judeo-Christian context. Soloviev's goal was not, as many at the time interpreted it, to foment civil disobedience and even revolution, but to hold before state power a vision of a future in which God's prerogatives for the present are not actualized.[12]

On the other hand, Soloviev's self-identification with the potential voice of future dissent ('we will abandon it; we will renounce it!') is remarkable. The '*my*' (we) here is an attempt to represent not only those gathered in the hall but the entire Russian people. If we can legitimately speak, therefore, of the philosopher-prophet's claim to 'immersion in the mind of God,' we must at the same time speak of his equally strong claim to immersion in the soul of the people. This dual location of the prophet — both within God and within the soul of the people — has the effect of hemming in state power from both sides, above and below. The prophet becomes both the voice of the ruled and that of the principle of true rulership.

Although preceding events gave some idea of the philosopher's movement towards a prophetic mission, the boldness and audacity of the 1881 speech clearly heralds its arrival. Pamela Davidson describes it as 'very much in the prophetic tradition, [...] marking Soloviev's transition from private mystic and academic philosopher into the role of public preacher.'[13] But if the speech is the beginning of a specifically conceived prophetic vocation, it simultaneously marks the beginning of its demise. In the wake of the response to the speech, as well as his retreat from public life, which was only to increase in later life, Soloviev moved ever further from the belief that he was the mouthpiece of the people. In a 'note to Russian readers,' written some time in the late

---

[12] In a line from the poem 'Privet ministram,' omitted from every edition of Soloviev's poetry until 1974, Soloviev presents the reader with a yet more startling image: Тут сюда-туда вы кинетесь/ Либералами прикинетесь,/ Вверх ногами опрокинетесь,/ Подожмете хвост./ Но дела все ваши взвешены,/ Да и сами вы повешены, — / Вот конец и прост! 'Around and around you go/ Pretending to be liberals/ Head over heels you turn/ With your tail between your legs./ But all your affairs are well-weighed/ You yourselves are likewise hanged,/ And that's the end of that!' From 'Privet ministram' (1891). V. S. Solov'ev, *Stikhotvoreniia i shutochnye p'esy*, p. 151.

[13] Pamela Davidson, 'Vladimir Solov'ev and the Ideal of Prophecy,' *The Slavonic and East European Review*, 78, 2000, 4, pp. 643-70 (p. 651).

1880s and included in *La Russie et l'église universelle*, Soloviev refers to his former practice of publishing articles in Slavophile journals without an indication of their authorship. His sense of disappointment is raw and palpable:

> I did not put my name under the article in question ['Gosudarstvennaia filosofiia v programme Ministerstva Narodnogo Prosvescheniia,' *Rus'*, Sep 1885] since I assumed that I was merely expressing the feelings of the whole of Russian society. This was an illusion, and I can now proclaim my exclusive right to the role of *vox clamantis in deserto*.[14]

It is important to remember that what changed between the early and latter parts of the 1880s was not Soloviev's belief in the mission of the Russian people, nor his assessment of how ready they were to accept that mission. Even in his manifestly Slavophile 1877 speech 'Three Forces,' while propounding Russia as the 'third force' destined to unite the peoples of East and West, Soloviev readily admits that 'in Russian society there exists almost no consciousness of this higher task.'[15] In contrast to some of the more entrenched forms of Slavophilism, the philosopher had never presented Russia or the Russian people as ideal *in their actual being*; rather, they bore a principle that was necessary for the realization of ideal content, a principle that may just as well be realized as not.[16] What did change, however, was Soloviev's

---

[14] SS, XI, p. 210. However, as Davidson points out, Soloviev's willingness to adopt the 'self-conscious stance of the lone individual, working towards the distant goal of transforming society in the light of Christian truth' had been evident even earlier, particularly in the correspondence with Romanova. In 1873 he had written to the latter: 'I will not live to see the living fruit of my future work. I foresee nothing good for myself. The best I can hope for is to be taken for a madman.' Davidson, 'Ideal of Prophecy,' p. 646; Solov'ev, "Nepodvizhno," p. 177. The suggestion, therefore—which in Soloviev studies is often taken almost as a given—that the philosopher only discovered a sense of pessimism in the realizability of his project in later years should be rejected as not conforming to the facts. In an 1887 letter to Bishop Strossmayer, Soloviev writes: 'I am not so mad as to await the immediate realization of our aspirations; "to kindle the flame in the bosom of the bride of Christ" is my only wish.' Solov'ev, *Pis'ma, i*, p. 182.

[15] S², I, p. 30.

[16] This point, however, can be overstated. Kotrelev has noted that even 'Three Forces' is not so much an attempt to establish the exclusive significance of the Russian people as a 'call to the goal-oriented manifestation of a providential design in both the individual and the people.' Ibid., p. 645.

understanding of the locus of truth and, with it, his understanding of the locus of the prophet as truth-speaker.

Important to an appreciation of the 1881 speech from this perspective is the Slavophile idea of 'catholic consciousness' (*sobornoe soznanie*) found in the work of Aleksei Khomiakov, and later developed by many Russian thinkers, Soloviev amongst them. Standing against all forms of individualism, the idea of *sobornost'* and its correlative catholic consciousness affirms, according to Nikolai Berdiaev, that 'universal truth is revealed to universal consciousness alone,'[17] and that this universal consciousness is attained through a togetherness, a solidarity amongst knowing subjects, not so much in deed or in intention, but in the structure of consciousness that underlies it. Soloviev's 1881 speech seems to have proceeded from such a position.

With the disillusionment that followed in the wake of the speech, however, came a significant repositioning in his gnoseology, which we may characterize as a move away from catholic (*sobornyi*) to prophetic consciousness. No longer is the moment of unity between knower and collective consciousness stressed but, to the contrary, Soloviev now points to the likelihood of a radical discontinuity between prophet and the environment in which he or she is set. In an extended footnote to his 1886 poem, 'Prorok budushchego,' the philosopher describes the prophet of the future as one 'in whom the contradiction with the social environment that surrounds him reaches absolute incommensurability.'[18] With the full recognition of this incommensurability, the prophet's role as exposer of falsehood and sin comes to the fore. The prophet is still very much 'with' God, but no longer can he said to be 'with' the people in the same way that he was before.[19]

---

[17] N. A. Berdiaev, *Filosofiia svobody — Istoki i smysl russkogo kommunizma*, Moscow, 1997, p. 26.

[18] Solov'ev, "Nepodvizhno," p. 45.

[19] Berdaiev tries to accommodate the prophetic vocation, as developed and practised by Soloviev, within the framework of catholic consciousness. 'In his utmost depth,' he wrote, 'the prophet dwells in the Church and *sobornost'*. But he is an organ of creative development within the Church and therefore undergoes a severance with the stagnant forms of collective church life. He is directed to the as yet unknown future.' N. A. Berdaiev, 'Osnovnaia ideia Vl. Solov'eva,' in *Sobranie sochinenii*, 5 vols, Paris, 1983-97, III, pp. 205-13 (p. 209).

This is not to say that the change in Soloviev's understanding of prophetic activity, as well as the grounding of the same in his theoretical and literary work, took him away from a universalistic perspective toward one qualified by individualism. Indeed the very opposite is true: it is precisely at this stage of his career (i.e. following his forced retirement from his academic position) that, as he writes in an 'autobiographical note' of 1887, he began to concentrate his efforts on 'religious issues relating to the unification of the churches, and the reconciliation of Christianity with Judaism.'[20] It is therefore extremely striking that, at the very moment that Soloviev's belief in the actuality or desirability of universal, or catholic, consciousness begins to fall away, he moves toward a uniquely impassioned, and largely fruitless, advocacy for the catholicity of the Christian church and, more widely, for the unity of all peoples. The sobriquets given Soloviev by two commentators, Veniamin Novikov and Egbert Munzer — 'prophet of universalism' and 'prophet of Russian-Western Unity' respectively[21] — thus contain an aporia, for, while the prophet in Soloviev's thought of the mid-1880s onward is understood as standing over and against the people and society, the manifested aim of prophetic activity is, quite the reverse, to unite and reconcile. The problem, which will be approached in due course, is not so much in resolving any inherent contradiction as in understanding how prophetic consciousness in Soloviev's handling can, without necessarily undermining the bounds of individual existence, attain universality. In other words, the question surrounds the exact relation between the individual and the universal, microcosm and macrocosm.

As his feeling for the disconnect between his ideals and the reality of the social situation grew, so Soloviev's language and discourse underwent a change from what we might describe as temporally neutral and abstract to historico-specific and personal. If earlier his

---

[20] RGALI, f. 446, op. 1, d. 24. 'Avtobiograficheskaia zametka,' p. 1.
[21] V. Novik, 'Vladimir Solov'ev: Sotsial'noe izmerenie dukhovnosti,' in *Biblioteka "Vekhi,"* <http://www.vehi.net/soloviev/novik.html> [accessed 3 June 2008]; Egbert Munzer, 'Solovyev and the Meaning of History,' *The Review of Politics*, 11, 1949, 3, pp. 281-93. The chapter is taken from Munzer's unpublished work *Vladimir Solovyev: The Prophet of Western-Russian Unity*.

purpose was to expose false modes of thinking, or to point out the negative aspects of various –*isms*, in the *publitsistika*, poetry, and even theoretical works of his middle period he is concerned above all with the historical moment, and with the people and situations blocking the way to what he preached as the true path. As he had done in the 1881 speech, except now directing himself not only to those in power but to all without exception, he puts before his addressee the necessity of making a definite moral choice for good and evil in the here-and-now to avoid potential catastrophe and moral decrepitude in the future. 'Which East do you want to be,' he asks the Russian people at the end of the poem 1890 poem 'Ex Oriente Lux,' 'the East of Xerxes or of Christ?'[22]

Soloviev's prophetic pathos can be found at its most intense in those works that directly approached the question of reconciliation: *The Jews and the Christian Question* (1884) and *La Russie et l'église universelle* (1888). Consider, for example, the following passage from the former:

> Let the age-old myth that fuels and is fuelled by unlawful hostility [between Christians and fellow Christians, and Christians and Jews - OS] be renounced and melt away! May a new flame burn in the frigid heart of the bride of Christ! May all those barriers that separate that which is created for the unification of the universe be shattered and overthrown in the dust![23]

The concern with the removal of barriers and obstacles to the future development of the world and humankind is one of the defining characteristics of Soloviev's prophetic activity. His efforts on the reconciliation of the churches, of Christians with Jews, of nation with nation, were all geared toward the larger goal of the liberation of human personality, through the elimination of those factors that held it in continuing slavery, for the purposes of realizing its God-given task: final liberation from the ultimate enemy—death. The goal of absolute freedom, freedom from 'bondage to decay,' lay through the future commonality of purpose which Soloviev believed the unification of the separate parts of collective humanity would bring. From this perspective,

---

[22] Solov'ev, "Nepodvizhno," p. 58.
[23] S², I, p. 253.

the reconciliation of the churches, so prominent in Soloviev's middle period, should be understood as a means for the realization of his ideal rather than the ideal itself.

In Soloviev's understanding of his own vocation, central place belonged to two areas, in whose light most of his work was pursued, namely philosophy and prophecy. The prophet, for Soloviev, was first of all the 'free initiator of progressive movement in society.'[24] It is the freedom of the prophet's activity that allows him to live in a space unfettered by the realities of the present, and 'reveal the principle for the realization of humanity's ideal future.'[25] In this, the goal of prophecy coincides with that of Soloviev's philosophy, which had as its goal the preparation of society for the acceptance and application of the 'task,' the spiritualization of matter. Yet it was precisely these two vocations that he was least able to practise in the conditions of late nineteenth-century Russia. Driven forcibly from an environment in which he had been able to form his ideas in close contact with colleagues, increasingly isolated both professionally and intellectually, beset at almost every turn by the vicissitudes of censorship and unable to speak freely in a public forum, Soloviev's passionate sense of his own calling was matched by an equally strong force that seemed determined to extinguish it. 'It would be better,' he wrote to Tsar Alexander III in 1890 in a desperate attempt to turn the censor's attention away from his work, 'for me to be completely deprived of freedom than to have the partial freedom I now enjoy.'[26]

---

[24] Ibid., II, p. 243.

[25] Ibid., p. 242. Soloviev emphasizes that he understands the prophet 'not in the sense of a foreseer but in the sense of a free, inspired preacher.' S^2, I, p. 315. In *History and Future of Theocracy*, the prophet is described as he 'who is led by the freedom of individual initiative.' S^2, I, p. 231.

[26] S^2, II, p. 284. Given the difficulty Soloviev experienced in asserting his influence in Russian public life, the significance of the journal *Vestnik Evropy*, and the courage of its principal editor Mikhail Stasiulevich in giving him a platform to publish both his poetry and prose through the 1880s and into the 1890s, should not be underestimated. Without the journal, whose general ethos actually had very little in common with Soloviev, it is very likely that he would only have been able to publish abroad, and would thus have been denied the audience to whom the greater part of his writing was addressed. On the divergence between Soloviev's political views and those of *Vestnik Evropy*, see B. Mezhuev, 'Vl. S. Solov'ev i peterburgskoe obshchestvo 1890-x godov:

Whereas the Soloviev of *Critique of Abstract Principles* had reserved his most outspoken criticism for the forces of 'abstract clericalism' and 'false spiritualism,' in the middle period the full weight of the philosopher-prophet's ire became refocused, often issuing in written and spoken proclamations of fitful anger directed against specific individuals. It is to this time that Soloviev's obsession with counterfeits, which was ultimately to culminate in his portrayal of the Antichrist, began to take on definite shape.[27] As if in reaction to his previous undiscerning accommodation of slavophilic romanticism, he became ever more vocal in exposing what he saw as the incipient evil lurking behind the seemingly respectable exteriors of Russia's homegrown philosophies, ideologies and worldviews. In a trend that continued up to his death, Soloviev came to intuit everywhere the semblance of good: the ability of evil to clothe itself in a convincing but ultimately barren guise.

In his 1884 article 'The Slavic Question,' referring to his threefold foundation of theocratic society based on the figures of high priest, king and prophet, Soloviev wrote that the principle of prophecy is 'not as defined in its essence' and thus 'able to go much further in its abuses than the first two principles.'[28] By this he seems to mean that there is something dangerous about the freedom enjoyed by the prophet, its openness to the future and lack of determination on past tradition. For this reason, the question of discernment—where the criterion for prophetic authenticity should be sought—becomes a predominant motif in Soloviev's middle to late periods.

The prophet, in Soloviev's view, differs from figures such as witches or wizards in that the latter 'remain that which they were—witches and wizards, i.e. people more knowledgeable and powerful than others,

---

k predystorii imperskogo liberalizma,' in *Russkii arkhipelag* <http://www.archipelag.ru/geopolitics/nasledie/anthropology/12> [accessed 10 July 2008]; F. Nethercott, *Russian Legal Culture Before and After Communism: Criminal justice, politics and the public sphere*, London and New York, 2007, pp. 69-70. See also D. V. Silakova, '«Nesladnykh virshei polk za polkom nam shlet Vladimir Solov'ev»: Poeziia Vladimira Solov'eva v zhurnale "Vestnik Evropy",' *Aktsenty*, 2004, 1-2, pp. 50-54.

27 See especially *On Counterfeits* (1891) in S², II, pp. 305-16.

28 S², I, p. 317. The article, originally published in the journal *Izvestiia Slavianskogo obshchestva*, was later incorporated into the first issue of *The National Question in Russia* (1891).

but use that knowledge and power for self-serving means, without any relation to moral goals and laws.'²⁹ Prophets are servants of God rather than themselves; without the moral transformation of the individual in the light of the Gospel, therefore, true prophecy cannot exist.³⁰ 'False prophecy,' to the contrary, 'wishes to renew and correct the work of Christ instead of correcting itself and others according to the will and commandments of Christ.'³¹

The bitterly personal nature of some of Soloviev's poetry, often published in *Vestnik Evropy* with ellipses to disguise its intended addressee, as well as some of his correspondence, derives from his increasingly strong view of Russian society as governed by the domination of form over an often void inner content. Instead of the underpinnings of true theocracy, he saw around him a 'pseudo-theocracy,' ruled over by the 'triumvirate of the false churchman Pobedonostsev, false statesman Tolstoi, and false prophet Katkov.'³² Mikhail Katkov, editor of the conservative journal *Moskovskie vedomosti* and perhaps the most influential Slavophile writer of the era, was often the target for Solovievian satire. But it is the philosopher's correspondence with Aleksandr Kireev (1833-1910), by the latter's own admission one of the 'Last Mohicans of Slavophilism,' that leaves the most indelible impression on the reader's mind.³³ The tone of the letters is reminiscent of the exchanges between Jeremiah and the false prophet Hannaniah, and leaves one in no doubt that what was at stake was the mantle of true prophecy. Throughout the letters, Soloviev distinguishes his own model of public prophecy from that of

---

29 From the article 'Primitive Paganism and its Dead Remnants (1890).' SS, VI, p. 224.
30 See P. Davidson, 'The Moral Dimension of the Prophetic Ideal: Pushkin and His Readers,' *Slavic Review*, 61, 2002, 3, pp. 490-518 (pp. 23-26).
31 SS, IV, p. 619.
32 Solov'ev, *Pis'ma*, IV, p. 30. Soloviev is referring to Konstantin Pobedonostsev (1827-1907), the Ober-Procurator of the Holy Synod under Alexander III; Dmitrii Tolstoi (1823-89), Pobedonostev's predecessor in the position and Interior Minister during the 1880s; and Mikhail Katkov (1818-87).
33 The letters were published with helpful commentary by Aleksandr Nosov. V. S. Solov'ev, 'Pis'ma A. A. Kireevu,' *Simvol*, 1992, 27, pp. 191-254 (p. 217). For more on the precise details of their dispute, see Pauline Schrooyen, 'The Resolution of the "Great Controversy": The Debate between Vladimir Solov'ëv and Aleksandr Kireev on the Question of Church (Re)Union (1883-1897),' *Journal of Eastern Christian Studies*, 57, 2005, 1-2, pp. 67-90.

his enemy in a number of ways. Firstly, he points to the imperative of arguing from the consciousness of one's own sinfulness rather than any natural superiority, in this case in church relations between East and West. Secondly, though, and perhaps at odds with this emphasis on the deficiency of sinful humanity, Soloviev adopts a rhetorical style in which the full measure of his indignation for Kireev and his like is expressed in a profusion of mockery and cruel slights. The brute force of Soloviev's language, which is utterly merciless in the pursuit of its prey, is the most striking thing about the letters. Subtlety of argument is discarded along with any vestige of manners or elegance of prose. The adoption of the perspective of an angry, wounded advocate of the ways of God against the corruption of his age, seen at its height in the letters to Kireev but also finding a place in the passionate rhetoric of the works of the middle period, brings Soloviev very close, both in style and substance, to the Hebrew Prophets, whom he studied assiduously during this time.[34]

In 1881, the philosopher met Faivel' Gets (1850-1931), Jewish scholar and author of a series of works on the Jewish question in Russia. Over the next four years, under the guidance of Gets and others, Soloviev engaged in intensive study of Jewish history, the Hebrew Bible, and the Talmud. Partly influenced by his earlier reading of kabbalistic texts as well as an increasing fascination with early Jewish modes of interaction with the divine, Soloviev began to learn biblical Hebrew and, by the late 1880s, had acquired a good reading knowledge of the language.[35] He gave a series of well-received lectures on the Prophets, the notes from which have not survived, to the Society for the Spread of Enlightenment among Jews in Russia, into which he was welcomed as an honorary member.[36] The Prophets also feature heavily in major

---

[34] Francis Poulin has argued, on the basis of Soloviev's *La Russie et l'église universelle*, that the philosopher's ideal of the prophet owes more to the Pauline writings and early Slavophilism than it does to the Hebrew scriptures. See F. Poulin, 'Vladimir Solov'ev's *Rossiia i vselenskaia tserkov'*, Early Slavophilism's Pneumatic Spirit, and the Pauline Prophet,' *Russian Review*, 52, 1993, 4, pp. 528-39.

[35] See Solov'ev, *Pis'ma*, II, pp. 140, 144.

[36] Allen, *Vladimir Soloviev*, p. 220; Walter G. Moss, 'Vladimir Soloviev and the Jews in Russia,' *Russian Review*, 29, 1970, 2, pp. 181-91 (p. 185).

sections of his published work of the middle period, as well as numerous poems. Accompanying this renewed interest in the many dimensions of the Jewish question came a changing emphasis in his thought on the role of Judaism in universal history. In the early work *Lectures on Theanthropy*, Soloviev had written of the 'Old Testament God' as a 'pure I, separated from all content: I am because I am, and nothing more.'[37] He further argues that, since the 'will of an absolute I, free from any content, idea or nature, is pure arbitrariness (*proizvol*),' the only relation to such a God on the part of the 'human individual is *the law*.'[38] This conventionally Christian perspective, according to which the God of the New Testament fulfils the God of the Jews, and a free relationship of love replaces the role of the law in human-divine interaction, persists in Soloviev's thought during the early part of the 1880s.

In *The Jews and the Christian Question*, a passionate outcry against the oppression and persecution of Jews in Russia published in 1884, Soloviev writes in the spirit of reconciliation that 'we are separated from Jews because we are not yet fully Christians, and they from us because they are not yet fully Jews. For the fullness of Christianity embraces Judaism as well, and the fullness of Judaism is Christianity.'[39] Yet despite the intertestamental thrust of Soloviev's argument, it is clear that he regards the two faith traditions in a definite relationship of hierarchy: Christianity includes Judaism as an integral part of its own nature, whereas Judaism is a less developed form of Christianity whose nature impels it to grow into the completeness of its essential

---

[37] S², II, p. 71. Soloviev here quotes the words of God to Moses: 'I am who I am' (Exodus 3.14). His changing exegesis on the verse is telling. In *Lectures*, Soloviev justifies his translation of the Hebrew verb *ehyeh*, which has a future connotation despite Hebrew's lack of tense, with the present tense 'I am' (rather than the 'I shall be' preferred by many contemporary scholars) by commenting that it fits better with the conception of God found elsewhere in the Old Testament. S², II, pp. 67-68. Several years later, however, in *History and Future of Theocracy*, the same verse is translated as 'I am the one who is to come' (*ia esm' griadushchii*), which more ably renders the procedural sense of the imperfective aspect and corresponds to the all-pervasive dynamism of Soloviev's mature philosophy. Interesting too is the philosopher's unusual translation of the first commandment (Exodus 20.2) as 'I am your God, who is to come' rather than the standard 'I am the Lord your God.' SS, IV, p. 500.

[38] S², II, p. 71.

[39] Ibid., I, p. 210.

being.[40] However, while Soloviev sustains his negative assessment of Jewish law throughout *Lectures*, the seeds of a more nuanced approach are evident even there. Consider, for example, the following passage:

> Old Testament revelation [...] contains in itself an acknowledgement that the religion of law is not the normative, true religion but only a necessary transition to another, non-external relationship or link with the divine principle. This acknowledgement is expressed by the prophets, and the truth of Old Testament biblical religion consists in the fact that it is not only the religion of the law but the religion of the prophets as well.[41]

It appears that Soloviev's study of the Prophets compelled him to do more justice to the non-monolithic character of Judaism; Jewish religion was not only a matter of the law, but equally of prophecy. As a consequence, Soloviev's writing gradually developed a more complex understanding of the relationship between Judaism and Christianity, which extended even as far as a positive reassessment of the role of the law in Jewish faith.[42] The organic logic that had characterized his early theoretical philosophy was now brought to bear on his philosophy of history, and the approach to emerge was qualified by an emphasis on the equality of historical moments as seen from the perspective of divine revelation. History is no longer viewed as a series of intractable

---

[40] Despite this somewhat negative assessment, the radical nature of Soloviev's thought on the proximity between Judaism and Christianity, articulated in a Russian context of routinely aggressive anti-semitism, should not be understated. Soloviev's public expressions of support for the Jewish people and religion, as well as his philosophy and poetry, had a large influence on many Jewish thinkers and poets. See U. Fuzailov, 'Sofiia i talmud: Vladimir Solov'ev v evreiskom kontekste,' *Lekhaim*, 1.189 (2008) <http://www.lechaim.ru/ARHIV/189/paz.htm> [accessed 10 July 2008]; H. Bar-Yosef, 'Sophiology and the Concept of Femininity in Russian Symbolism and in Modern Hebrew Poetry,' *Journal of Modern Jewish Studies*, 2, 2003, 1, pp. 59-78.

[41] S^2, II, p. 72.

[42] The first signs of this new approach we find in Soloviev's 1886 article 'The Talmud and Recent Polemical Literature about it in Austria and Germany.' Kotrelev writes of this period that, 'occupied with studies of the Talmud, Soloviev somewhat shifted his emphases in his interpretation of Jewish ethics. The fundamental difference between Judaism and Christianity he came to see not so much at the moral as the philosophical-metaphysical level.' Ibid., I, p. 665.

events but as a single whole. 'One can only compare Judaism,' Soloviev wrote in the 1886 'The Talmud and Recent Polemical Literature about it in Austria and Germany,' 'with the rest of humanity to which it is related, as the trunk to the branches.'[43] This language of organicism, when applied to the Judeo-Christian tradition, moves away from the more explicitly supersecessionist approach we find in *Lectures*, and is expressive of Soloviev's newly calibrated view of history, with its firm roots in biblical theology.[44]

Soloviev's late article 'When did the Hebrew Prophets Live?' (1896) is not, as the title may suggest, an excursion into the area of biblical historical criticism. Indeed, the philosopher was little concerned with establishing the precise date of given prophetic statements and oracles. Instead, the title may be read as an open question to which there can be no definite answer, for in Soloviev's view the message and witness of the prophets were not historically determined: they lived on as speakers of truth regardless of the era in which they lived. The significance of the Hebrew prophets for the mature Soloviev cannot be exhausted by their prophesying of the Incarnation, nor even by their typological prefiguration of Christ, but by the very fact of prophetic consciousness itself. To put it in terms of history and time, the prophets were not, in his view, moved by the presentness of the future but by the futurity of the present. They lived the life of the future in the present, not the other way round. Prophetic consciousness for him involved a particular locatedness of the human subject within history that undermined the apparent irrevocability of the loss of the past to an ever-moving present, and the distance of the future in the face of an infinite series of historical moments. It was this fundamental change in the operation of time, realized in prophetic consciousness, that allowed Soloviev to construct an organic philosophy of history in the Judeo-Christian context in the works of his middle period.

---

[43] SS, VI, p. 18.

[44] A similar, organic discourse pervades *History and Future of Theocracy*. Note, for example, the following passage: 'If their [the Jewish people's - OS] ideal fulfilment is in Christ, then in them is His actual beginning; if Christ is the fruit, then they are the root of the tree of life: neither the first without the second nor the second without the first can exist or be understood.' Ibid., IV, p. 583.

II. SOLOVIEV, AUTHENTICITY AND THE ANTICHRIST

It is a peculiar fact of Soloviev studies that much of the criticism that surrounds his work ultimately derives from an assessment of whether or not it proceeds from a true foundation. In particular, the character of Soloviev's inspiration has governed the assessments of two thinkers from the Russian Orthodox tradition who have proved enormously influential in defining the nature of the philosopher's legacy: Georges Florovsky and Sergei Khoruzhii. As Florovsky writes, 'Soloviev must be judged not only on the basis of his philosophy but also on the merits of his religious life.'[45] At the very beginning of his philosophical path, Soloviev had written of 'mystical impulses, which make [the human being] either a divine or a demonic being,'[46] early on recognizing that a claim to spiritual insight or experience is no vouchsafe for authenticity. Which side of the divide the philosopher falls on is clear for Florovsky, who had once been his enthusiastic proponent, as we can see from the heading of a chapter from his major work: 'The Seductive Path of Vladimir Soloviev.'[47] For Florovsky, Soloviev philosophized from a position outside the church, trusting his own mind and natural resources over and against tradition and Orthodox practice. He had not only been tempted by the devil, but had fallen into seduction (*prelest'*) and his philosophy as a whole is characterized by 'demonism.' The distance between Soloviev and true Orthodoxy is articulated in even more categorical tones by Khoruzhii, though very much in the spirit of Florovsky:

> His sophianic visions; his mediumistic writing; his way of life, which for all its asceticism lacked structure and discipline; his chaotically impaired physical nature, which created a dangerous defencelessness; his susceptibility to 'seduction' (*prelest'*) — in all of this, and much else besides, it is impossible not to see a divergence with both the spirit and the letter of Orthodox asceticism.[48]

---

45 G. Florovsky, *Ways of Russian Theology*, Vaduz, 1987, II, p. 251.
46 PSS, III, p. 149.
47 Florovsky, *Ways of Russian Theology*, II, pp. 243-51.
48 S. Khoruzhii, 'V. Solov'ev i mistiko-asketicheskaia traditsiia Pravoslaviia,' in *O starom i novom*, St Petersburg, 2000, pp. 182-206 (p. 203).

The ideal of prophecy in Soloviev as a Christian model for human action, marked as it was by ambiguity and inner division, became associated with this alleged imbalance in his religious experience, and was thus largely abandoned after his death. True, the Symbolist poets valued this element in Soloviev's thought, developing it in new and daring ways, but their reading of the philosopher was hardly impartial, and their experiments were as far from the Solovievian spirit as they were from Eastern Orthodoxy.[49]

Against Soloviev's ideal of the prophet, Florovsky and Khoruzhii contrapose that of the *podvizhnik*, the ascetic hero battling with her inner life in order to transform both herself and world.[50] In so doing they follow a long line of Orthodox thinkers before and after Soloviev who have understood human action in the world along similar lines.[51] When Soloviev's most notable continuator, Sergii Bulgakov, wrote a piece entitled 'Heroism and the Spiritual Struggle (*podvizhnichestvo*)' for the *Vekhi* series of essays in 1909, it may be argued that he was self-consciously steering himself away from his predecessor's ideal of the prophet, and aligning himself with this tradition.[52] Soloviev's ideal

---

[49] Florovsky writes that 'the development of Solovievian themes by Blok and others serves as an immanent critique (and exposure) of his experiment, and calls into question all "religion of romanticism," religious estheticism, or esthetic religion.' Florovsky, *Ways of Russian Theology*, II, p. 251. Even accepting Florovsky's negative opinion of Russian Symbolism, one might justifiably cite one of Soloviev's favourite sayings: abusus non tollit usum (abuse is not an argument against proper use).

[50] The word *podvizhnik* is very much associated with the Eastern monastic tradition, although it can refer to those living in the world. There is little doubt that Khoruzhii is right in saying that Soloviev did not do sufficient justice to Eastern monasticism, particularly Hesychasm, although it should be noted that the philosopher's relationship to contemplative Christianity underwent significant changes in the last decade of his life. Khoruzhii, 'V. Solov'ev i mistiko-asketicheskaia traditsiia Pravoslaviia,' p. 197. The word *podvig* (heroic deed) occurs on many occasions in Soloviev's work in the context of ideal human activity, and there is no suggestion that he saw it at odds with the ideal of prophecy.

[51] Outside Orthodoxy, a similar conception can be noted in the advocacy of the 'heroic humanism' of the saint by the Christian philosopher Jacques Maritain, who has been as influential in the Catholic context as Florovsky in the Orthodox. See J. M. Maritain, *True Humanism*, London, 1941.

[52] See, however, Bulgakov's late essay *The Spirit of Prophecy* (1939), where he writes of prophecy as an 'act of religious life, a *personal* meeting with God, which does, may and ought to take place in the life of *everyone*, according to one's measure and capacity.'

of prophecy has thus received very little elaboration from the angle of Christian philosophy and theology, receiving only in places the light reflected from studies of other aspects of his legacy.

One of the most outspoken critiques of Soloviev's development of the prophetic ideal was philosopher Lev Shestov's article *Speculation and Apocalypse* (1927-28).[53] The core of Shestov's argument revolved around the absolute distinction which he drew, and maintained throughout his work, between the philosophical and the prophetic.[54] For him, the very idea that prophetic inspiration and rational thought lead to a similar result was anathema. 'The Jewish prophets,' he wrote, 'were prophets precisely because their inspiration carried them into a sphere unassailable to enquiry of whatever kind.'[55] Shestov thus cast doubt both on the prophetic ideal promoted in Soloviev's work and on the very possibility of reconciling his philosophical mind with prophetic activity. As Davidson has demonstrated, there is certainly a case to be answered here. The element of compulsion present in the election of the Hebrew prophets, for example, is almost entirely absent in Soloviev, who writes that he 'decided' to follow the prophetic vocation.[56] But Shestov's somewhat doctrinaire refusal to allocate any role to the agency of reason in biblical prophecy, and his judgement that Soloviev's thought on this theme promotes an 'autocracy of reason'[57] seems neither balanced nor fair.

For Shestov, an absolute chasm divides Athens and Jerusalem, with the paths of classical philosophy and Hebrew prophecy ever divergent on opposite sides. Yet it is ironic that the prophetic ideal he seems to hold in *Umozrenie* owes less to the Bible than it does to Plato who, in the dialogue *Timaeus*, depicts 'prophetic insight' as coming upon human beings when 'reason and sense are asleep.'[58] Soloviev's claim, and his

---

S. N. Bulgakov, *Towards a Russian Political Theology*, ed. R. Williams, Edinburgh, 1999, pp. 271, 287.

[53] L. Shestov, 'Umozrenie i Apokalipsis,' in *Vladimir Solov'ev: Pro et Contra*, II, pp. 467-530.
[54] The distinction is more fully developed in L. Shestov, *Afiny i Ierusalim*, Paris, 1951.
[55] Shestov, 'Umozrenie i Apokalipsis,' p. 492.
[56] Davidson, 'Ideal of Prophecy,' p. 654.
[57] Shestov, 'Umozrenie i Apokalipsis,' p. 487.
[58] *The Dialogues of Plato*, ed. B. Jowett, Oxford, 1953, III, p. 658.

disagreement with Shestov, is not so much that 'revelation coincides with natural thinking, prophetic inspiration with Hellenic gnosis,'[59] but that there exists one God and one truth, approachable, although not necessarily fully attainable, by the modes of philosophical enquiry and prophetic inspiration alike. Moreover, Hebrew prophecy differs from ecstatic states known throughout the ancient world in that the individuality of the prophet is not suppressed but rather exalted. In the biblical prophets, 'there is no striving to be one with God, no *unio mystica*, no indwelling of God within the spirit of the prophet through rapture, trances, or even spiritual contemplation.' Instead, the prophet's 'individuality is maintained and the divine message is accented by his own tones.'[60] As Abraham Heschel has written, 'prophetic illumination seems to take place in the full light of the mind, in the very centre of consciousness.'[61] While highlighting the complexity and variety of prophetic experience, Gerhard von Rad seeks to emphasize precisely its sobriety, commenting that in the majority of those cases in which prophets claim to speak the word of God 'no kind of change came over their ordinary consciousness,' indicating that 'revelation was a mental process.'[62] Despite this relatively unsensational means of revelation, however, von Rad comments that the prophets nevertheless had the sense of an 'event' having taken place. In other words, they did not merely 'think' their way to God but rather the processes of natural thought were in the prophetic experience somehow consonant with the 'coming' of the word of God.[63] The reception of the word was thus both an active process, in the sense of attained through human faculties, and a passive one, in the sense of given from without.

---

[59] Shestov, 'Umozrenie Apokalipsis,' p. 496. In *History and Future of Theocracy*, Soloviev speaks of Hebrew prophecy and Hellenistic philosophy as 'phenomena at once entirely unalike and entirely close to one another.' SS, IV, p. 412.

[60] W.S. Waltzburger, 'Prophets and Prophecy,' in *Encyclopaedia Judaica*, 16 vols, 1973, XIII, pp. 1150-1182 (p. 1151). The contrast drawn between ecstasy and prophecy that is a feature of much recent biblical scholarship was largely a response to the conflation of the two in the work of Gustav Hölscher. See G. Hölscher, *Die Profeten*, Leipzig, 1914. Lindblom, however, continues to view ecstatic states as structurally analogous to prophetic states. See J. Lindblom, *Prophecy in Ancient Israel*, Oxford, 1962, pp. 1-46.

[61] Heschel, *The Prophets*, p. 459.

[62] G. von Rad, *Old Testament Theology*, 2 vols, London, 1979, II, p. 67.

[63] Ibid., p. 68.

Biblical prophecy, peculiarly, is depicted not as the attainment of a particular state of consciousness, be it ecstatic or otherwise, but a sense of calling. The prophet 'is not a person who has had an experience, but one who has a task, and the marks of whose existence are the consistency and wholeheartedness in the dedication to it.'[64] As Walter Moberly writes, the prophet's 'consciousness is indeed altered, but not through transitory or induced states of "exaltation" but through appropriation of God's will in such a way that one's vision of the world and of life within it, and one's conduct correspondingly, is transformed.'[65] 'The prophet,' writes another author about the Hebrew tradition, 'is not necessarily someone who can "tell the future" as it will be. Instead, the prophet has a vision of the future as it should be, and as it might be, if the people align their behaviour with the ethical precepts of the covenant.'[66] Prophecy, then, is not itself authenticated by irregular, or even regular, sorties into the divine presence but by the application of the vision, or message, there received to the concrete conditions of mundane existence, both in the prophet's own life and in the life of society around him. Following the Gospel dictum of knowing a tree by its fruits, Moberly therefore suggests that the true criterion for prophecy lies not so much in the source of inspiration, which is to all extents and purposes closed to rational enquiry, but by the 'prophet's lifestyle and message, whose moral character are open to scrutiny in the present.'[67]

Be Soloviev's moral characteristics as they may, the problematics of the moral standing of the prophet figure are provocatively explored

---

[64] Heschel, *The Prophets*, pp. 459-60.
[65] W. Moberly, *Prophecy and discernment*, Cambridge, 2006, p. 81.
[66] S. Schwartz, *Judaism and Justice: the Jewish Passion to Repair the World*, Woodstock VT, 2006, p. 51. Despite the paucity of the interpretation of prophecy as prediction, it persists in readings of Soloviev which look to *Short Story of the Antichrist* for fulfilled warnings such as the formation of the European Union, and so on. As regards the imaginative landscape of the story, as Viacheslav Serbinenko writes, during this time 'futurological aims did not have a decisive meaning' for Soloviev, and faithfulness to the concrete details of the tale was not his principal agenda. See V. V. Serbinenko, 'Spor ob antikhriste: Vl. Solov'ev i G. Fedotov,' in *Russkaia filosofiia: kurs lektsii*, pp. 220-32 (p. 221).
[67] Moberly, *Prophecy and discernment*, p. 81.

in the person of the Antichrist in his *Short Story*, who, he writes, exhibited 'the highest manifestations of abstinence, selflessness and active charity.'⁶⁸ The Antichrist is further portrayed as 'not only a philanthropist, but a philozoist. He himself was a vegetarian, forbade vivisection, and established strict surveillance over abattoirs; societies for the protection of animals were encouraged by him in every possible way.'⁶⁹ It is as if Soloviev were implanting each one of his reputed personal virtues and ethical norms into a setting where they become nothing but window dressing, artificial apparatus supporting the barren heart beneath.⁷⁰

It would be wrong, however, to read into these statements a rejection of those ways of ethical living that Soloviev had practised throughout his life, and which there is no reason to suspect he discarded in his last years. There is nothing to suggest that the Russian philosopher's apocalyptic turn was accompanied by a Nietzschean rejection of moralism. Instead, reading *Short Story* as the final fruit of Soloviev's protracted battle with counterfeit good — that is, as a continuation of his previous work rather than a departure from it — allows us room to bring some of our comments on prophetic authenticity under the spotlight offered by the intensity of these later years. Having read the work to the audience gathered at the packed Hall of the City Duma in St Petersburg on 26 February 1900, Soloviev added the following interpretation to the words he had spoken:

> Such is the impending and inevitable dénouement of world history. We shall not see it, but events of the not-too-distant future throw their prophetic shadow, and in our lifetimes more clearly and undeniably than ever do counterfeit good, fraudulent truth and fake beauty rise before our eyes. All the elements of the great deception are already before

---

68 S¹, II, p. 740.
69 Ibid., pp. 746-47.
70 On Soloviev's 'limitless generosity,' which was said to contain elements of the naïveté of the holy fool, and which often left him wholly unprotected against the elements, resulting in the inability to feed himself and even illness, see Trubetskoi, *Mirosozertsanie*, p. 26. On his vegetarianism, see Nosov's note in '«Nasha liubov' nuzhna Rossii...»: Perepiska E. N. Trubetskogo i M. K. Morozovoi,' *Novyi mir*, 1993, 9, pp. 172-229 (p. 229).

us, and our immediate descendants will see how all these things shall interweave and come together in one living and individual phenomenon, in Christ turned inside out (*Khristos naiznanku*), the Antichrist. The most profound meaning of world history is the fact that in this final historical phenomenon of the evil principle there shall be such a great deal of good. It is required that the prince of this world be allowed to show himself toward the end from the best angle, to become freely adorned in every semblance of good. Only when he has exhausted everything that can be said in his favour, when all that was decent about him falls away, and, finally unmasked, he openly appears in his own form of evil, lies and monstrosity — only then can he in truth be condemned and of necessity perish.[71]

What Soloviev wished to underline in his portrait of the Antichrist was above all the proximity it evinces between good and evil. His 'Christ turned inside out' was not the feral and immoral beast of popular imagination but the consummate imitator, to the untrained eye as spotless in virtue and in deed as the incarnate God.[72] In a revealing article, Grigorii Fedotov sketched the essential details of two traditions present in church teaching on the Antichrist, the first of which, dating back to Irenaeus, represents the enemy of God as evil to the core, both inwardly and outwardly, while the second, with its origins in the work of Hippolytus, follows the model of an evil which seeks to disguise itself by dressing in the raiment of good.[73] While comparing the portrait of the Antichrist found in *Short Story* to the latter, Fedotov nevertheless points to an essential difference between Soloviev's creation and those known to church tradition.[74] While Soloviev follows his predecessors in

---

[71] Nikolai Kotrelev, 'Eskhatologiia u Vladimira Solov'eva («k istorii Trekh razgovorov»),' in *Eskhatologicheskii sbornik*, St Petersburg, 2006, pp. 238-57 (p. 253).

[72] Vasilii Rozanov, present at the reading, later explained his falling off his chair due to drowsiness by the fact that Soloviev's Antichrist was boring and 'imitated Christ too much.' See V. A. Fateev, *S russkoi bezdnoi v dushe: zhizneopisanie Vasiliia Rozanova*, St Petersburg, 2002, p. 262.

[73] G. P. Fedotov, 'Ob antikhristovom dobre,' in *Litso Rossii: Sbornik statei (1918-1931)*, Paris, 1967, pp. 31-48 (pp. 35-38). Note also Paul's comment that 'even Satan disguises himself as an angel of light' in 2 Cor 11.14.

[74] The potential sources of Soloviev's Antichrist are numerous, of which the biblical model and Nietzsche's *Übermensch*, to whom many commentators have pointed, are but two. Although Soloviev writes that 'it is impossible to show the portrait of the Antichrist'

depicting the Antichrist as outwardly virtuous, he adds to his portrait, crucially, the moment of self-deception.⁷⁵ Thus, the Antichrist does not clothe himself in Christian virtue in a ploy to deceive the world, but is himself deceived into believing in the authenticity of such virtue. Soloviev makes this clear when he writes:

> His clear mind always validated the truth of those things in which it was proper to believe: good, God, the Messiah. He *believed* in this, but loved himself alone. He believed in God, but in the depth of his soul he involuntarily and inexplicably preferred himself to Her. He believed in the Good, but the all-seeing eye of eternity knew that this person would bow before an evil power just as soon as it had prevailed upon him, not by a trick of emotions or base passions, nor even by the high lure of power, but by limitless self-love alone.⁷⁶

In a strange reversal of Mephistopheles' claim in Goethe's *Faust* to be 'part of that Power which would do evil constantly, and constantly does good,'⁷⁷ Soloviev's Antichrist is portrayed as genuinely striving for good

---

and 'in church literature we find only his passport with some general and particular characteristics,' he nevertheless believes his version is founded on 'Holy Scripture, church tradition and common sense.' S¹, II, pp. 734-35. On the basis of a forgotten review article Soloviev wrote on German historian Johannes Janssen's *Geschichte des deutschen Volkes seit dem Ausgang des Mittelalters* in 1885 in *Pravoslavnoe obozrenie*, Kotrelev highlights the clear similarity between the German mystery play Soloviev describes in the article and the plot of *Short Story*.' See Kotrelev, 'Eskhatologiia,' pp. 244-50. Here too Soloviev gives a psychological foundation for his understanding of the nature of evil and its tendency to disguise itself. 'As a consequence of the indestructible theomorphism (*bogopodobie*) of human nature,' he writes, 'evil in and of itself has for us no charm. From here stems the ever-present need for forces hostile to humanity to decorate evil in falsehood and take on all kinds of deceptive forms and masks.' V. S. Solov'ev, 'Reformatsiia v Germanii po noveishemu issledovaniiu,' *Pravoslavnoe obozrenie*, August, 1885, pp. 698-742 (p. 698). Soloviev's Antichrist should be seen as his own creation, in which elements of biblical and church tradition, autobiography, rival philosophies and ideologies, and much else all find a place.

⁷⁵ Fedotov, 'Ob antikhristovom dobre,' pp. 32-33. Fedotov goes on to argue that, since this 'falsification of the good' has no roots in the Christian tradition, it is alien to the Christian ideal and thus antithetical to Soloviev's project. Strémooukhoff believes Fedotov to have overstated the case, arguing instead that Soloviev's Antichrist willingly partakes in deception. See Strémooukhoff, *Vladimir Solov'ev and His Messianic Work*, pp. 328-30.

⁷⁶ S¹, II, p. 740.

⁷⁷ Goethe, *Faust: Part One*, Oxford, 1998, p. 42.

yet working only evil.⁷⁸ So when, freshly inspired by his meeting with what we may assume is the devil, he pens his seminal work 'The Open Path to Universal Peace and Prosperity,'⁷⁹ we are not to read these words as hollow promises intended to coddle and deceive but rather as goals to which he authentically aspires. Nor is it necessary to conclude, along with commentators who wish to interpret the story as symptomatic of Soloviev's alleged disillusionment in his previously held ideals, that there is something fundamentally anti-Christian, or evil, in the goal of universal peace and prosperity itself (leaving aside, for the moment, the question of what kind of peace and prosperity are here at stake). While the nature of the Antichrist's mission becomes more explicit as the story progresses and the full extent of his lust for earthly power gradually revealed, at this stage there is little *outwardly* to distinguish him from a great benefactor of humanity, for which indeed he is taken. And yet how great is the inner divergence from that ideal: as Soloviev writes, 'he loved himself alone.' This self-love, rooted in the 'depth of his soul,' rather than — even despite — any calculation or will, is the force that colours his activity and adds its mark to everything he does.⁸⁰

The criterion for prophetic authenticity, which in Soloviev's work is inextricably bound to the authenticity of the Good, resides not in the practice of human will, whose real motives may be hidden from it, but in that of love. Primacy belongs not to the former but the

---

78   In the 1885 review article cited in note 74 above, Soloviev offers the French Revolution and German Reformation as two examples of the ability of evil to deceive not only others but also itself. 'The work of destruction and murder,' he wrote, 'was veiled with the most elevated ideas: a return to the pure Gospel teaching (in the Reformation); the restoration of human and citizen rights, and the spread of liberty, equality and fraternity (in the French Revolution). This deceptive appearance, these elevated words not only attracted the crowd but enticed the instigators and leaders of the movement as well.' Solov'ev, 'Reformatsiia,' p. 698.

79   S¹, II, pp. 742-43.

80   Nel Grillaert has noted that 'what distinguishes the superman-Antichrist from other "godless" *personae* in 19th century Russian literature, is that this character does not put forward any philosophical reasoning to renounce God and Christian principles: the only reason why the superman cannot submit to God and Christ is his self-love [...] the Antichrist is egoism incarnate, his apparent benevolence is nothing more than extreme pride and lust for power.' Nel Grillaert, 'A Short Story about the Übermensch: Vladimir Solov'ëv's Interpretation of and Response to Nietzsche's Übermensch,' *Studies in East European Thought*, 55, 2003, 2, pp. 157-184 (p. 172).

latter. The difference between Christ and the Antichrist[81] is found in the radical divergence in the nature of their love. The activity, or 'task,' of both issues from this love, which is the active force in the movement toward the future; the Antichrist is a false prophet not primarily because of his goals or motives, which are governed by the will, but because his love is entirely directed toward himself. It is on this point that Soloviev's project differs most substantially from other utopian philosophies of the time, most notably those deriving from the thought of Karl Marx. As Jacques Maritain has noted, 'Marx believed *in practice* in free will, i.e. in the will's mastery of its own motives, by which it dominates inwardly the whole conditioning of its acts.'[82] Through portraying the Antichrist as an aspiring worker of good, whose 'clear mind' and 'superhuman' will are not sufficient to save him from the gravest self-deception, Soloviev wishes to relate to his reader his conviction in the non-mastery of the will over its own motives. Neither the will nor the representation of the mind are, in Soloviev's view, fully capable of exercising authority over the inward 'conditioning,' as Maritain puts it, of its activity.

Fedotov claims that, when creating his Antichrist, Soloviev 'was pursuing the aim of exposing the idea of a non-church-centred morality in the teaching and life of Leo Tolstoy.'[83] While it is true that there are many places in *Three Conversations* that seem to have been written expressly to challenge Tolstoyan ethics with its insistence on non-resistance to evil, these considerations play at best a peripheral role in *Short Story*. Instead, it appears more plausible to suggest, as does Kotrelev in his notes to Soloviev's 1899 article 'The Idea of the Superman,' that the principal intellectual target of the philosopher's story is the *bête noire* of his later years, Friedrich Nietzsche.[84]

---

[81] Soloviev's thought on Christ as Prophet follows in the next section. Although the philosopher describes the figure of Apollonius, rather than the Antichrist, as 'the false prophet and thaumaturge,' drawing a parallel with the second beast mentioned in Revelation 13.11-15 (S¹, II, p. 641), there is no reason to dissociate the Antichrist himself, as 'false messiah,' from the conception of false prophecy.
[82] Maritain, *True Humanism*, pp. 122-23.
[83] Fedotov, 'Ob antikhristovom dobre,' p. 39.
[84] S², II, p. 706. The literature on the topic of Soloviev and Nietzsche is substantial. For two introductions to the theme, see Ludolf Müller, 'Nietzsche und Solovjev,'

Apart from the numerous works of the 1890s that directly polemicize with Nietzsche, the connection is made even more likely by the fact that the word Soloviev uses to refer to the Antichrist, who is only recognized and named as such at the very end of the story by the Elder Ioann,[85] is 'superman,' or 'Übermensch' (*sverkhchelovek*). In his article on Lermontov, Soloviev writes that the essence of Nietzscheanism, with which he charges the poet, is 'the appropriation to oneself *in advance* of some kind of exclusive superhuman significance — oneself as individual ego, or Ego & Co — and the demand that this appropriated, but in no way justified, greatness be recognized by others and become the norm of activity.'[86]

The peculiarity of Soloviev's repudiation of such egocentrism is that it is based not on ethics but on a metaphysics of love. The philosopher turned away from his early partiality for Schopenhauer, who in his thought on the primacy of the will and 'will to life' laid much of the groundwork for Nietzsche's reformulation of the same to 'will to power,' not only because of his revulsion for the moral content of Nietzsche's teaching but because of a shift in his ontology. If earlier he had followed Boehme and Schelling in positing a primordial will as the beginning of the theogonic and cosmogonic process,[87] contrasting the expansive, self-giving will of God to the restrictive, self-perpetuating will of Satan,[88] he now appears to distance himself from a primarily

---

Zeitschrift für philosophische Forschung, 1, 1947, 4, pp. 499-520; N.V. Motroshilova, 'Vl. Solov'ev o F. Nitsshe: Poisk novykh filosofskikh paradigm,' in *Fridrikh Nitsshe i filosofiia v Rossii: sbornik statei*, ed., St Petersburg, 1999, pp. 46-57.

[85] S¹, II, pp. 754-55.
[86] FI, pp. 379-80.
[87] Soloviev's divergence from Schelling on this point is especially revealing since many commentators continue to see no difference between the two thinkers in this area. Piama Gaidenko's assertion that Soloviev shared Schelling's conviction that 'will was the defining principle of being' must be modified to allow for the fact that, while the former uses the Schellingian terminology of wanting (*khotenie*), attraction (*vlechenie*), and striving (*stremlenie*) to denote some kind of primal ground of being, he associates these not with will but rather with sensation and feeling. See P. Gaidenko, 'Gnosticheskie motivy v ucheniiakh Shellinga i Vl. Solov'eva,' in I. Surat (ed), *Vittorio: mezhdunarodnyi nauchnyi sbornik, posviashchennyi 75-letiiu Vittorio Strady*, Moscow, 2005, pp. 68-93 (p. 68).
[88] See pp. 81–84.

voluntaristic understanding of agency in the world.[89] The existentialist voluntarism of Nietzsche, which viewed the 'will to power' as the reality underlying all being,[90] is mistaken, in Soloviev's view, since it confuses what is secondary for what is primary. The will to power, portrayed so forcibly in Soloviev's Antichrist, is merely a corollary of self-love. Thus, the ideal of human liberation through will to power is a myth, for it fails to recognize how this will — freed from the reputedly senseless dichotomy of good and evil — is itself conditioned by the self-love in which it resides.[91] The solution for Soloviev is not, as Michael Stoeber

---

[89] Such a development has seeds very early on in Soloviev's writing career. In *Crisis*, comments Evlampiev, Soloviev criticizes Schopenhauer for the fact that, 'having correctly defined the direction of enquiries into the absolute, he proceeds to reduce the intuition of the absolute to the will, i.e. to reduce the entire integrity of inner experience to one of its aspects. It is precisely this that explains his rather unexpected appeal to the philosophy of Eduard von Hartmann as the "highest" attainment of all European philosophy.' I. I. Evlampiev, 'Shopengauer i "Kritika otvlechennych nachal" v filosofii Vl. Solov'eva,' in *Issledovaniia po istorii russkoi mysli: Ezhegodnik*, M. A. Kolerov and N. S. Plotnikov (eds), Moscow, 2004/05, pp. 45-70 (p. 56).

[90] It is debatable whether Nietzsche meant to give the concept 'will to power' (*Wille zur Macht*) any overarching, metaphysical significance, or whether it was merely one of the ways he suggested for interpreting human reality. For an overview of the significance of the phrase in his work, see L. L. Williams, 'Will to Power in Nietzsche's Published Works and the Nachlass,' *Journal of the History of Ideas*, 57, 1996, 3, pp. 447-63. In any event, our argument rests on the understanding that 'will to power' designates a basic expansion of the concept of will per se, that is, will as the active component in human agency. Heidegger writes: 'in the name "will to power" the word "power" connotes nothing less than the essence of the way the will wills itself inasmuch as it is a commanding.' M. Heidegger, 'The Word of Nietzsche: "God is Dead",' in *The Question Concerning Technology and Other Essays*, New York, 1977, pp. 53-112 (p. 77).

[91] This may go some way to explaining Soloviev's peculiar resolution of one of philosophy's most insistent questions: the problem of the freedom of the will. In an 1894 letter to Sergei Trubetskoi, he wrote that 'in choosing the Good, the will is a pure nothing, absolute passivity, or Theotokos (*Bogoroditsa*). Will, or freedom, appears only in the choice of evil, since for this choice, as opposed to the former, there is absolutely no foundation.' 'K istorii odnoi druzhby. V. S. Solov'ev i S. N. Trubetskoi. Novye materialy,' *De visu*, 3, 1993, p. 13. In *Justification of the Good*, while leaving room for the possibility of an irrevocable choice of evil over good, Soloviev seems to suggest that finding a creature that would consciously act in such a way is, if not impossible, then at least highly improbable. 'Such a lack of receptivity to the perfectly known good would be something absolutely irrational, and only such an irrational act satisfies the precise concept of absolute freedom of will.' Here, though, the question again is not in the first place whether absolute freedom of choice over good or evil exists but what is meant by the 'good.' Moral philosophy is thus 'presupposed by the metaphysical question of the freedom of the will, and in no way depends on it.' S¹, I, pp. 118-19.

has interpreted the distinction between Dostoevsky and Nietzsche, the substitution of will to power with 'will to love,'[92] but rather the rejection of will as the true ground of human agency and its replacement by love itself as ontological principle, acting for good or ill dependent upon its character. Whereas 'both Nietzsche and Dostoevsky begin with the same ontological premise of a fundamental will as the dynamic source of substantive existence,'[93] Soloviev posits a similar dynamism in love.

What precisely Soloviev means by 'love,' and how human agency can be understood apart from the primacy of the will, will be taken up in the following section. The point to emphasize here is that the human will, and the motives and acts that flow therefrom, are an insufficient guide to the authenticity of the actor, particularly when that agency, as does prophecy, involves a claim to speak for God. Although the words and deeds of the true or false prophet are perfectly capable in and of themselves of exposing the character of the love from which such words proceed — as is the case with the later years of the rule of the Antichrist in *Short Story* — it is equally likely that, in times less concentrated than the end times depicted in the story, a prophetic witness that does not, so to speak, practise its word to the furthest limits of its application will leave a final objective judgment as to its nature impossible.[94] In his own critique of Nietzscheanism, 'Idea of the

---

[92] 'For Dostoevsky,' writes Stoeber, 'the appropriate teleology is not will to power but will to love.' M. Stoeber, 'Dostoevsky's Devil: The Will to Power,' *Journal of Religion*, 74, 1994, 1, pp. 26-44 (p. 42).

[93] Ibid., p. 42. Despite this difference, Stoeber's fascinating treatment of the parallels between the Nietzschean ideal of will to power and the character of the devil in *Brothers Karamazov* reveals significant similarities between Dostoevsky's approach to Nietzsche and that of Soloviev.

[94] There is, of course, a wealth of positive evaluations of Soloviev's character. Of interest here though are the negative assessments of two religious thinkers who were to come to prominence after his death. Far from connecting the authenticity of prophecy to the authenticity of love, Vasilii Rozanov writes about Soloviev's 'prophetic gift,' which he does not doubt, as a 'misfortune [...] which separated him from the crowd as an enigmatic figure who stood all alone. In his relationships with people there is an arrogance and coldness. Despite his kindness, which was almost affected, in every little note he penned it was evident in three or so lines that he loved no one and that people weighed heavily on him.' V. V. Rozanov, 'Avtoportret Vl. S. Solov'eva,' in *Okolo narodnoi dushi: Stat'i 1906-08 gg.*, Moscow, 2003, pp. 392-99 (p. 398). Berdiaev, too, sees fit to comment on the character of Soloviev's love: 'Soloviev was an extraordinarily good person, and extremely compassionate [...] But it was an almost indifferent goodness;

Superman,' Soloviev offered his readers his own means for discerning activity that proceeds from an authentic foundation from its opposite. 'Here,' he wrote, 'is the real criterion for an evaluation of all works and phenomena in this world: how far do each of them correspond to those conditions essential for the rebirth of the mortal and suffering human being into an immortal and blessed superhuman.'[95] It is no accident that this statement echoes that part of Nietzsche's thought that Soloviev deemed to be truly authentic, namely the idea that humanity should strive toward its own self-transcendence: the human should become superhuman. Yet notice Soloviev's careful use of words: he talks not of a superhuman effort of will but of the 'conditions' in which the human condition is transcended. It is our argument in what follows that these conditions are for Soloviev synonymous with the structure of prophetic consciousness that he describes in his philosophy, particularly of the middle period, but which permeates his entire oeuvre.

III. THE APOCALYPTIC TURN, 1897-1900

The isolation that Soloviev felt intellectually and existentially during the period of his fiercest disputes with state power and entrenched cultural forces transitioned in the mid-1890s into direct, physical isolation. In his new residence at the edge of Lake Saimaa in Finland, whose influence on the philosopher is clear through the many poems dedicated to it, the fury of the years of public prophecy subsides and is replaced by something approaching calm.[96] The move appears to

---

there was little warmth it, little personal engagement. This was connected with Soloviev's type of eroticism, with his Platonism.' N. A. Berdiaev, 'Vladimir Solov'ev i my,' *Sovremennye zapiski*, 1937, 63, pp. 368-73 (p. 369).

[95] S², II, p. 618.

[96] Hamutal Bar-Yosef describes the Lake Saimaa of Soloviev's poetry as a 'symbol of Sophia sleeping, wrapped in peace, pure and enlightening, seen only by the poet's inner eye.' Bar-Yosef, 'Sophiology and the Concept of Femininity in Russian Symbolism and in Modern Hebrew Poetry,' p. 67. Mints believes that Soloviev's Saimaa and Imatra poems are characterized more than any others by a 'belief in the "earthly"' as opposed to the early poems where the tones of an 'ascetic renunciation of life' were more audible. Mints, 'Vladimir Solov'ev — poet,' p. 26.

have been largely dictated by health considerations and the persistent advice of his doctor, and it seems that Soloviev thrived in his new location, at least as far as we can tell from his letters and the balance of the poetry. Although he was to resume his life of wandering, Soloviev's direct interaction with society continued to wane toward the turn of the century. As his work refocused away from the political scene to the level of the individual, he turned his attention more and more to those intellectual and creative figures who had influenced his own development. Something had changed, and it is the nature of that change that has determined much of the writing on Soloviev's legacy.

Evgenii Trubetskoi's *The Worldview of Vladimir Soloviev*, the earliest major work to tackle not only the content of Soloviev's work but to attempt to sketch its general trajectory, proved hugely influential in its interpretation of his last years. It appears that part of the *raison d'être* of Trubetskoi's work was to take the ambiguity which surrounded Soloviev's own relation to his theocracy and develop it to the point where it became indistinguishable from the outright negation of the same.[97] In so doing, the position that Soloviev was portrayed as having adopted in his last years would fall in line with Trubetskoi's own conviction in the absolute unrealizability of the Kingdom of God on earth. This position was taken as almost a given by the thinkers who made up the 'Vladimir Soloviev Religious-Philosophical Society,' founded by Trubetskoi and Morozova in 1905 to continue the interpretation and development of Soloviev's work.[98] Thus, Berdiaev spoke for many when he wrote that the 'theocratic system is undoubtedly the weakest part of Soloviev's religious philosophy, which he himself destroyed near the end of his life. The collapse of

---

[97] Writing of the theocratic ideal set out in *History and Future of Theocracy* and *La Russie et l'église universelle* in a letter to his beloved Margarita Morozova, Trubetskoi writes that while 'Soloviev did not quite renounce it, he did abandon this dream at the end of his life ("*Three Conversations*"). It is now necessary that this theocracy definitively become an "Überwundener Standpunkt" [an obsolete, superseded position].' 'Nasha liubov',' p. 183.

[98] On the remarkable success of the Society in its early years, see I. I. Ivanova, 'Rol' obshchestvennykh organizatsii filosofov v obespechenii ikh vliianiia na obshchestvo,' in *Vyzovy sovremennosti i otvetstvennost' filosofa: materialy «Kruglogo stola», posviashchennogo vsemirnomu Dniu filosofii*, ed. I. I. Ivanova, Biskek, 2003, pp. 32-38 (pp. 36-37).

the theocratic utopia is perhaps the most significant event in the intellectual and spiritual life of Vladimir Soloviev.'[99] Since for Soloviev, as will be discussed shortly, prophecy is both 'the root and the crown' of 'theocratic organization,'[100] such a collapse would have meant the essential disappearance of the prophetic model as a norm for individual activity. Further, it would mean the discarding of any emphasis on Christian politics, or a Christianized political order.[101]

It is not at all clear, however, that Soloviev lost his belief in the theocratic ideal, nor indeed in the ideal of the universal church. One of the only sources we possess where the philosopher himself describes the change between his middle and late periods appears in his 1899 introduction to the Platonic dialogues.

> With the growth of life experience and *without any change in the essence of my convictions*, I came to grow ever more doubtful of the utility and realizability of those external plans to which were dedicated my so-called 'best years.'[102]

Soloviev did not renounce his previous work, nor did he set off in a fundamentally new direction. He writes here merely of the 'utility and realizability' of his previous 'external plans'—the means of realizing his ideal—without commenting on its goal: namely, the realization of the Kingdom of God. Other than the fact that Soloviev continued to hold his *History and Future of Theocracy* in the highest regard at least until the mid-1890s,[103] a number of further considerations make the notion that he gave up on any external realization of his ideal—that

---

[99] Berdiaev, 'Vladimir Solov'ev i my,' p. 370.
[100] SS, IV, p. 504.
[101] Trubetskoi thus portrays Soloviev as withdrawing into the inner world of the spirit and abandoning all projects connected to political or societal transformation. 'What a lesson there is in the fact that Soloviev's *external* plans collapsed! In religious creativity we [i.e. Russia—OS] can attain great things; in politics we shall be glad for the merely tolerable.' 'Nasha liubov',' p. 188.
[102] SS, XII, p. 360 (my emphases).
[103] Even in July 1894, after the publication of the majority of his works and immediately before beginning to publish chapters from what would become *Justification of the Good*, Soloviev described *History and Future of Theocracy* as his 'major work.' S², II, p. 546.

All-Unity should be realized on earth as a real theocracy in all aspects of human life—highly dubious.[104] The reimmersion in the flow of life at an individual level with which we characterized the period of the mid-1890s coincided with an increased attention toward a figure whose influence on Soloviev had always been great namely Plato.[105] As is the case with his articles on Pushkin of the same time, Soloviev was interested above all in the consonance between the work of both men—the 'pure poetry' of Pushkin, and the idealist philosophy of Plato—and their lives; that is, the extent to which the ideal which shone through their work became incarnate in their persons. Soloviev is rather condemnatory of Pushkin from this perspective, and his treatment of Plato serves as the more instructive, and subtle, example.

In *Justification of the Good*, the philosopher had been concerned with illustrating the irreconcilable dualism of Platonism, arguing that Plato found 'authentic satisfaction [...] in the contemplation of the eternal, intelligible truth of all' to the detriment of 'striving to realize or incarnate the truth in his environment.'[106] As Soloviev's reading of Plato progressed, however, continuing through his translation of the dialogues up to his death, a subtle change in emphasis resulted. The 1898 *The Life Drama of Plato*, as the name suggests, focuses on the influence the philosopher's life had on the course of his work. The last line of the introduction reads very much like advice thrown down to any potential future investigator of Soloviev's own work and life: 'Plato himself as the protagonist of his life's drama—here is the true principle of the unity of Plato's work.'[107] It is Soloviev's interpretation of that drama, which he summarizes at the end of the work, that interests us here:

---

[104] Judith Kornblatt is one of few to go against the grain in arguing that the philosopher's 'writings on beauty, art, and love that dominate the 1890s, as well as his own poetry, show that Solovyov did not so much abandon his hope for a future society based on universalist Christian ideals as seek out new ways to express his vision.' Kornblatt, *Introduction*, p. 21.

[105] For an introduction to the theme, see A. G. Tikholaz, 'Platon v filosofii vseedinstva Vladimira Solov'eva,' in *Platon i platonizm v russkoi religioznoi filosofii vtoroi poloviny XIX—nachala XX vekov*, Kiev, 2003, pp. 149-200.

[106] S¹, I, p. 321.

[107] Ibid., 585.

The death of Socrates with all its dramatism; the fateful question: is it worth living when truth in its best incarnation is lawfully put to death; the decision: the meaning of life is in another, ideal world, whereas this world is the kingdom of evil and deception; the appearance of sacred Eros, casting a bridge between the two worlds and setting the task of their full unification — the salvation of the higher world, its rebirth; the powerless rejection of the task; its substitution with another — transformation, the redemption of society by wise political directives through the agency of an obedient tyrant.[108]

Soloviev's description of what he sees as the tragic epilogue to Plato's life in the last few lines relate to the writing of the latter's last dialogue, *The Laws*, for which he does not hide his contempt, describing it as not just the 'forgetting, but the direct renunciation of Socrates and of philosophy itself.'[109] Whereas, in *Justification of the Good*, he had criticized Plato for remaining too aloof from earthly reality,[110] his charge in *Life Drama* is rather the reverse: instead of the transfiguration of the earthly realm through that which is from above, Plato is here understood to have erred by falling back on the mere transformation of society from its own resources, a society fatefully and irrevocably disconnected from any higher reality; instead of being too disinterested in politics, Plato is accused of being consumed by it. Moreover, the reason he gives for the tragic degeneration of Plato's work at the end of his life is the philosopher's own inability to play through the drama of his own life to the end. 'Since the true and profound redemption and full relief that come through the *regeneration* (*pererozhdenie*) of human nature proved too much for him, he adopts a more superficial though more accessible task — the *transformation* of social relations.'[111] The deradicalization of ideal human activity by the substitution of transformation for rebirth as the goal of both personal and social life — such is the core of Soloviev's accusation against Plato, and, as the philosopher looked back on the

---

[108] Ibid., p. 624.
[109] Ibid., p. 623.
[110] 'It is clear that the political task enjoys no inner connection with the main interest of the philosopher, and that in essence he cares not how people organize themselves on earth, where truth does not and will not live.' Ibid., I, p. 321.
[111] Ibid., II, pp. 620-21. See also SS, XII, pp. 394-95.

years of his middle period, it is almost certain there is a reproach meant for himself here too.[112]

In late 1898, on the fiftieth anniversary of the death of Vissarion Belinskii, Soloviev gave a talk on his esteemed predecessor at the Philosophical Society, founded in St Petersburg a year earlier on the philosopher's initiative. The text has not survived but, alongside a relatively detailed account of Soloviev's main points published the following day in the newspaper *Novoe vremia*,[113] we have the testimony of literary critic Natal'ia Maksheeva, who was in attendance. Having reproached Belinskii for not having developed his philosophical ideas, founded in a profound humanism, to the level of conscious faith, Soloviev went on to a make a sort of public admonition before his audience. In Maksheeva's words:

> He reproached himself for the fact that in former years, engaged with the still irresolvable question of the unification of churches, he lost sight of those everyday concerns of modernity which Belinskii had served [...] 'Mea culpa, mea maxima culpa!' he exclaimed [...] He ended his talk by directing himself to Russian society with the wish that it should not rest on its indifference to religion. 'God grant,' he said, 'that the time will come when true belief in the living God will overshadow (*osenit'*) and spiritualize even our native land.'[114]

---

[112] The theme of rebirth, associated in the Gospel of John with the conversation between Jesus and Nicodemus (John 3.1-10), was not new ground for Soloviev. Very much in the spirit of Christian Platonism, he wrote in *Lectures* that 'the inner acceptance of Christ, i.e. the new spiritual human, consists in spiritual rebirth, in that birth from above or from the spirit which is mentioned in the conversation with Nicodemus. This is when the human being, recognizing the inauthenticity of carnal, material life, feels in itself the positive source of another, authentic life (independent both of the flesh and the human mind) — the law given in the revelation of Christ — and, accepting this new life revealed by Christ as the absolute imperative, the good and the truth, voluntarily submits its carnal and human life to it, uniting interiorly with Christ as the progenitor of this new spiritual life, the head of the new spiritual kingdom.' S^2, II, p. 162. In a short, undated article in the archives titled 'Our Nicodemuses,' Soloviev writes of the many people in contemporary Russia who, like the biblical character, believe such rebirth to be impossible. RNB. f. 718, op. 2, d. 9. Published as Vl. Solov'ev, 'Nashi Nikodimy,' in Z. G. Mints, 'Iz istorii polemiki vokrug L'va Tolstogo (L. Tolstoi i Vl. Solov'ev),' *Uchenye zapiski Tartuskogo gosudarstvennogo universiteta*, 184, 9, 1966, pp. 89-110 (pp. 109-10).

[113] 'V filosofskom obshchestve,' *Novoe vremia*, 13 Oct 1898, no. 8126, p. 3.

[114] N. A. Maksheeva, 'Vospominaniia o Vl. S. Solov'eve,' in *Vl. Solov'ev: Pro et Contra*, I, pp. 360-72 (p. 371).

The quiet sadness of these last words, in which can be heard echoes of the poetry of Fedor Tiutchev, differs much from the sharp rebukes the philosopher had levelled at his foes some years previously. Gone are the inspired calls for cosmic justice, gone the idea of a grandiose synthesis between East and West with the Pope and Tsar as its spiritual and temporal powers. While Soloviev's insistence on directing himself to society remained unchanged, his words here are softer, less accusatory: they demand not submission to God's law but rather seek to articulate a shared hope, and a shared mission. In such words can perhaps be detected the beginnings of a return of the *vox clamantis in deserto* to the bosom of the people, a departure from a position of opposition to one of sympathy largely determined by a sense of failure in the application of his own prophetic vocation.

Soloviev did not renounce his hope for a unified church, nor for a just and Christianized political order, nor for the realization of the Kingdom on earth. But he did come to see how all these ideals, when separated from the constant need for repentance and regeneration, and from those commonplace injustices that so moved Belinskii in the society around him, can become surrogates for a lack of concern at a concrete level, a deficit of love for the neighbour. Soloviev's philosophy had always recognized that the most general love does not exclude but magnifies, exalts and intensifies the particular, but it seems that it was precisely here that he believed himself to have fallen short.

The repentance that followed such consciousness was worked through not only interiorly, away from public eyes, but on the pages of *Short Story*. Vladimir Bibikhin has written that 'in his Antichrist Soloviev purifies himself of his impulses as activist and organizer, just as Dostoevsky wrestles with himself in the form of the Inquisitor. Indeed, Soloviev built projects of universal unity with the gesture of a super-gifted superman.'[115] The portrayal of so many of Soloviev's own traits and ideals in the figure of the Antichrist, all peppered with a healthy dose of his particular brand of humour, was not, in this understanding,

---

[115] V. V. Bibikhin, 'Dve legendy, odno videnie: inkvizitor i antikhrist,' *Iskusstvo kino*, 1994, 4, pp. 6-11 (p. 10).

evidence of their wholesale rejection; rather, it may be thought of as a way for a very public prophet publicly to repent.

There was at the heart of the Philosophy of All-Unity a grand pretension, which stemmed inherently from the very task it sought to accomplish, and from which its creator could not remain immune. Soloviev had been involved in trying to build a philosophical system that would reconcile all truths within itself, negating none yet revealing their limitations when severed from the greater truth that is the whole. The nature of this project took it beyond the bounds of philosophical or intellectual enquiry, driving ever on to reveal the workings of the good, truth, and beauty in history, and finally determining the character of ideal human activity in the world. Yet the source of this grandiose synthesis, despite its universal reach, remained nowhere other than in the sophisticated mind of Soloviev himself. As the philosopher looked back on his earlier life, it is as though he came to suspect that the fruit of his mind — All-Unity — had itself usurped the place of God; and, particularly during the middle period characterized by such frenetic activity for political, social and ecclesial reconciliation, that he had been relying for his ideal's realization on the sheer force of his will alone.[116]

In portraying the late turn in Soloviev's worldview principally from an interior perspective, we are not trying to claim that exterior motives did not play their part. Soloviev's feeling that the drama of world history had come to an end, his forebodings about so-called 'Panmongolism,' and the inroads Nietzscheanism was making in Europe have all been well documented. But there exists a fundamental consonance between Soloviev's consciousness of the potential evil lying at the root of his philosophy, the individual evil that becomes incarnate in the figure of the Antichrist, and the social evil depicted in *Short Story*. The

---

[116] It should be stressed that sufficient protection against such temptation had always been present in Soloviev's kenotic Christology. But it seems that he only felt the full measure of its implications in his last two years. He ends *The Life Drama of Plato* with the following moral, which, like much else in this significant work, he no doubt held to be equally applicable in relation to himself: 'The weakness and fall of the "divine" Plato are significant insofar as they underscore and explain man's impossibility to realize its purpose, i.e. to become a real superman by the power of the mind, genius and moral will alone; they explain the need for the real, living God-man.' S^1, II, p. 625.

philosopher William Desmond has explored many of these aspects with a depth and clarity that is hard to surpass. Countering a conception of what he calls 'divine holism,' which he believes Soloviev to have renounced in *Short Story*, he argues that late in life the philosopher sensed the danger that in his project 'the ultimate transcendence of God might be so radically immanentized in the worldly "All-Unity" that the putative ecumenical community becomes but the *seeming* of the most exalted: a community that *poses* as the highest, but its posing is imposture, and hence this highest risks really being the lowest, that is, an idol.'[117] The 'god of the whole,' which for Desmond represents precisely this temptation, here becomes 'incarnate in the projected ideals of certain forms of worldly community itself, forms that in mimicking religious community threaten its corruption.'[118] He goes on to define the Antichristic community as follows:

> It is the *production of the counterfeits of God and the usurpation of reconciliation* in the form of communities that have all the appearance of being ultimate and unsurpassable. Think here of how there is nothing beyond that is envisaged by the last Emperor of the world in Solov'ev's story of the anti-Christ. There seems nothing beyond this *nec plus ultra* of spiritual-worldly power. Those who will not bow to this last Emperor do so in the name of a Christ beyond this *nec plus ultra*. Their faith is in a God beyond this power claiming "nothing beyond."[119]

The Antichrist, in Desmond's view, is the absolute representative of a society that has lost the discourse, and with it the reality, of transcendence; that is, of a society that has become wholly grounded in itself. As the grounding voice of such a community, he is not the great deceiver who tricks humanity into accepting dross disguised as gold but the actual guarantor of such an order. For him, and for his followers, there really is *nothing beyond*. His word — his logos — is entirely sufficient for the satisfaction of itself and its task: it affords what it promises. As Bibikhin writes:

---

[117] Desmond, 'God Beyond the Whole,' p. 180.
[118] Ibid., p. 180.
[119] Ibid., p. 183.

Soloviev's Antichrist speaks to a monstrous degree; he is chiefly one who speaks. To such a degree, in fact, that if he had not yet said something, he could say it better than anyone and in a way that pleases all. When, weary from the supra-effort of universal reconciliation, he asks the three new apostles to tell him what they want from him, he is sincerely ready to give them whatever they choose and is absolutely certain that he can please everyone. In the sphere of the human word there are no formulae that can trouble the Antichrist. For him there is nothing that is impossible, except the acceptance of the Son of God, that is, the Infant, the one who does not speak or who is deprived of the word, or who in any event does not speak in a humanly ordered way.[120]

The true God that emerges from Soloviev's depiction of the Antichrist is still one God but, in the words of Desmond, 'this One is not the "All-Unity" of the becoming of immanence toward its own self-completion. It is God beyond the whole, as always qualitatively other to finite entities, even while being with them in the most intimate of communities, even in the undergoing of death itself.'[121] The philosophy of All-Unity, or rather the philosopher himself as its creative source, Soloviev came to believe, had not allowed room for that which it posited above all else: the continual fecundity of the divine principle as the gathering power of unity, whose nature is such that, in uniting the multiplicity of phenomenal reality, it is not determined by such content but remains the ever-flowing source of life, eternally beyond even the most all-embracing structure, or structures, of being. Paradoxically, humanity's usurpation of the divine function — the focusing of reality in its transcendent ground — leads to the loss of the very ground it tries to assert. Thus, while the true self-transcendence of the material order, which had reached its climax in the Incarnation, is realised 'from within,' the conscious self-transcending impulse of humanity now seeks to realize itself, not through that interiority which is other to itself, but through the self-owned *power from within*. Human thoughts

---

[120] Bibikhin, 'Dve legendy,' p. 9. Krasicki writes that 'in the cacophany of "voices" which make up the speech of the Antichrist, one can make out the "voices" of different religious prophets, reformers, and philosophers, but one single "voice" is missing: the "voice" of silence, or the voice of "Christ Himself."' Krasicki, *Bog, chelovek i zlo*, p. 353.
[121] Desmond, 'God Beyond the Whole,' p. 189.

become God's thoughts,[122] and the beyond that seeks to operate from this 'within' becomes imprisoned by the shell of the human *ratio*, newly divested of its kenotic otherness; the divine logos that wishes to eternally renew the interior life of humanity and, through it, the world is co-opted into the service of its opposite: slavery and absolute monism.[123]

Soloviev's fear that the all-too-human drive for All-Unity, far from opening a space for the unimpeded operation of the divine economy, might itself supplant the action of God in the world led him in his later years, not to rethink the nature or implications of his project, but to assume a reoriented form of personal prophecy that, unlike the self-possession that characterized the prophetism of the early years, was to consume his entire being. Whereas the philosopher had once 'decided' to follow the prophetic vocation, now a clear element of compulsion is introduced alongside the retention of a generally philosophical approach to revelation. At the same time, discussion around conformity to ideals, or absolute norms, diminishes, to be replaced by the increasing role of two factors in human life which, while implicitly recognized in Soloviev's early gnoseology as having fundamental importance, now lay claim to that significance in the philosopher's life itself: feeling and imagination. The change is brought out well in an alternative draft for the introduction to *Three Conversations*. Here Soloviev writes:

> The writing of this book was inspired by 'the shadows of future events.' These shadows have made themselves known to me many times, and I have never had any reason to doubt them. But the last time, about two years ago, they lay on my soul with particular force, persistence and unassailability. I not only realized with my mind, but felt with my whole being that the 'present form of this world is passing away.' This feeling took possession of me and gave rise to a number of ideas, which I there and then decided to express and convey to others.[124]

---

[122] 'For my thoughts are not your thoughts, nor are your ways my ways, says the Lord.' Isaiah 55.8.

[123] See also W. Desmond, 'Religious Imagination and the Counterfeit Doubles of God,' in *Is There a Sabbath for Thought? Between Religion and Philosophy*, New York, 2005, pp. 134-66.

[124] Cited in Kotrelev, 'Eskhatologiia,' p. 255. In the published version of *Three Conversations*, these sentences conveying the circumstances leading up to the work's composition were contracted to the following statement: 'About two years ago a particular change

While the philosopher continues, in contrast to the Hebrew prophets, to have a measure of choice as to whether to relate the revelation received to others,[125] it is clear that by his repeated reference to 'feeling,' as well as its juxtaposition with the workings of the mind, Soloviev intended to indicate a shift in his understanding of the prophetic sensibility. The essence of this shift resides not so much in the foregrounding of feeling as a particular mode of human being-in-the-world over, though not against, the will and representation, for such an emphasis had been present since at least as early as *Critique of Abstract Principles*. Rather, it is possible to conceive these last years, instead of a rejection of the previous work, the final outcome of the battle between feeling and reason whose mark as was writ large on Soloviev's written work, public pronouncements and life. By this 'battle,' we mean the prophetic exercise of the transference of the vision of God, received in his sophianic experience and spilling over into the search for a cosmic justice, into his philosophy, and the conditions and contingencies of everyday existence.

Toward the end, Soloviev appears to have grown wary of the singular poise of his philosophical prose, in which many have posited an excessive schematism, and whose lofty goal had been to raise the 'faith of our fathers to a new level of rational consciousness.' In *The Great Schism and Christian Politics*, he had described the task of the church as 'first, to affirm the truth of theanthropy as a dogma of *faith* (confess it); second, to justify it for *consciousness* and; third, to realize it in practical *life*.'[126] This schema, in which the primary data of faith is 'elevated' to the level of rational consciousness, ultimately transitioning into real presence, now comes increasingly under threat. The grand dialectic whereby the 'absolute realizes good through truth in beauty'[127] undergoes a kind of reversal. That which is transitory, fleeting, and elusive — beauty, feeling,

---

in my nervous disposition (*dushevnoe nastroenie*), which there is no need to go into here, aroused in me the strong and persistent desire to cover in a clear and accessible way those principal questions about evil which should affect everyone.' S¹, II, p. 636.

125 Compare, for example, Jeremiah: 'If I say, "I will not mention him, or speak any more in his name," then within me there is something like a burning fire shut up in my bones; I am weary with holding it in, and I cannot.' Jeremiah 20.9.
126 S², I, p. 88.
127 *PSS*, II, p. 281; S², II, p. 104.

passion — claims the position which Soloviev had always granted it, but whose true efficacy had been restricted by the bonds of the dialectic. What his thought had posited as the final stage — the realization of the Kingdom of God, the spiritualization of the material world — proves to be the very beginning; the quickening power of faith becomes both first and last word. A large part of Soloviev's apocalypticism is nothing other than the full realization of this reversal. The God of faith is not enlarged by human consciousness but herself animates consciousness, realizing herself through the assent of the whole human person to her vivifying power. There is a givenness, present in the very reception of the divine gift of life, that precedes any attempted actualization. From here derives Soloviev's late fascination, not so much with the ideas of those thinkers who had accompanied him on his intellectual journey, but with the extent to which their ideas witness to the One who is beyond the idea, and by whom consciousness is gifted. The drama of the thinker's life as lived in the light of this One now becomes his guiding concern. There occurs a reorientation from an interest in the *ethos* of a given body of thought — its ideals, suppositions, dialectic, all that is fixed and eternal — to a preoccupation with the *pathos* in which such thought was pursued — the task the thinker sets herself, the relation of the ideal to his or her life, and so on. This is certainly the case with Plato, but we find the most fascinating example of it in Soloviev's speech on Belinskii, whose understanding of pathos, it seems, was fully shared by the philosopher. In the words of the author who related the content of the speech in *Novoe vremia*:

> In himself Belinskii did not contribute anything to philosophy and in this case the only ground for philosophy, as Mr Soloviev put it, consists in the *pathos of his life*: that which animated him and by which he lived. The speaker tried in his lecture to characterize and give reasons for the constant nervous turmoil in which Belinskii always lived. He was a 'man of desires,' uncommonly sensitive, more impressionable than perceptive, he knew no impassive value judgments; he would either be in raptures over something, or else castigate himself for such imprudence [...] He related to his own views at times with merciless severity, cursing himself and calling them loathsome. This self-castigation, which many took for a change in his convictions, was nothing other than a profound understanding of his tasks, impossible to reconcile with half-truths, the continual battle of

feeling with rationality [...] He waged his battle from the perspective of the moral principle, but at the same time with the consciousness of his national duty, with a burning love for the fatherland.[128]

As in his treatment of Plato, many elements of Soloviev's own development enter his reading of Belinskii. As if to forestall critics who would come to see in his later years a comprehensive break with the past, Soloviev points to the 'battle between feeling and rationality' as productive of that creative tension which never allowed Belinskii to rest secure on any given idea, or worldview. Behind the seemingly chaotic substitution of views and opinions Soloviev sees a restless thirst for justice, founded on love. By emphasizing this non-finality of Belinskian pathos, its inexhaustible desire for the greatest good, Soloviev is able to articulate a mode of human being whose inner dignity consisted precisely in its consonance with the transcendent realm; just as the God whose presence 'beyond the whole,' to borrow once more Desmond's phrase, made itself increasingly known during his late period, so the openness of pathos secured an attitude that was neither lacking momentum nor entirely prescriptive. The 'task' remains but, in the context of pathos, acquires an immediacy that takes it beyond goal-oriented activity along conventional lines. It is such immediacy, with reference to poetic creation, that Belinskii associates with the pathos of being-in-love in his work *The Works of Alexander Pushkin* (1843):

> In pathos the poet is in love with the idea as a beautiful, living creature; he is passionately suffused with it, and he contemplates it not with reason or the intellect, not with feeling and not with any one ability of the soul, but with the entire fullness and integrity of his moral being. The idea appears in his work not as an abstract idea, not as a dead form, but as a living creation in which the living beauty of the form witnesses

---

[128] 'V filosofskom obshchestve,' p. 3. We know just how important Belinskii's 'pathos' was to Soloviev since the newspaper originally misquoted the philosopher as having, bizarrely, talked about the 'satin of Belinskii's life' (*atlas dushevnoi zhizni*). The next day Soloviev wrote to its editor, Aleksei Suvorin, that this 'curious mistake' caused him to experience 'a profound, though short-lived, despair' since he had really spoken of the 'pathos of life (one of Belinskii's favourite expressions).' Solov'ev, *Pis'ma*, IV, p. 251.

> to the presence in it of a divine idea [...] Ideas derive from reason; but it is not reason that creates and gives birth to what is living, but love. The difference between an abstract and a poetic idea is therefore clear: the first is a fruit of the mind, the second the fruit of love, as passion [...] Pathos turns the simple intellectual attainment of the idea into love for the idea, full of energy and passionate desire [...] All the poet's works should be marked with a unitary pathos. And it is this pathos, suffused in the entirety of the creative activity of the poet, that is the key to his personality and poetry.[129]

Many of these ideas have parallels in Soloviev's writings, but what we wish to emphasize here is Belinskii's promotion of pathos — the quality of being-in-love with the idea — as the criterion for an assessment of the poet's personality and work. It is this same criterion that Soloviev uses in his assessment of Belinskii. The difference between the two consists in the fact that, by his application of pathos, Soloviev means to assess not Belinskii the poet but Belinskii the *prophet*, calling him 'the man of desires' (*muzh zhelanii*) — the epithet that God uses to address the prophet Daniel.[130] There is, Soloviev is asserting, something about this continual desiring, this location of the individual within the energy of pathos, that is genuinely prophetic. It is telling that the majority of English translations render Daniel's epithet as 'greatly beloved,' highlighting the tension between the passive and active meanings in the original Hebrew; the energy and desire of pathos derive precisely from the love of which it partakes. To love is not simply to act; it is to allow that love, as primary ontological principle, to possess one's entire being. The dwelling in love already contains the

---

[129] V. G. Belinskii, *Sochineniia Aleksandra Pushkina*, Moscow, 1995, pp. 231-32, 234.

[130] Daniel 9.23; 10.11,19. The Prophet Daniel had a unique significance in Soloviev's eschatology of the late period. In the programme of the speech he was to give on the end of universal history in February 1900, circulated beforehand, we find the following point for discussion: 'The goal of the historical process, or the end of universal history is the principal defining concept for a philosophy of history. This concept is found only in positive religions, and the only fully developed foundation for a philosophy of history is biblical-Christian revelation, especially that contained in two sacred books: the Prophet Daniel and the Apocalypse of John the Divine.' Kotrelev, 'Eskhatologiia,' p. 251. In *Justification of the Good*, Soloviev calls the Book of Daniel 'the first philosophy of history in the world.' S¹, I, p. 363.

reality of its practice.[131] Such, then, is the nature of authentic prophecy in Soloviev's handling. In the economy of love, the prophet is neither wholly autonomous nor heteronomous but theonomous: possessed of the love of God yet intimately and individually loved in his turn.[132]

---

[131] In a sermon given in 1685, the English churchman Thomas Ken commented on the two, mutually conditioning aspects of the phrase, the active love and the being-beloved. 'If then you would learn Daniel's secret, that powerful inflammative and preservative of love, which Daniel had, and which made him, according to the text, understood in a passive sense, a man greatly beloved: take the very same expression in an active sense, and then you have it; he did greatly love, and therefore he was greatly beloved: that was all the court-cunning, all the philtre that Daniel had. It is love that most naturally attracts love; and from this love he is called, "a man of desires"; of desires for the glory of God, and for the welfare of King and people; still I am short: he was a man full of desires; so full that he was made up of desires, he was all desires; for so the original emphatically styles him, "thou art desires" (Dan. IX. 23).' Cited in J. Hoyles, *The Edges of Augustinianism: the Aesthetics of Spirituality in Thomas Ken, John Byrom and William Law*, The Hague, 1972, p. 53. In an 1851 sermon, one of the most notable Russian theologians of the nineteenth century, Metropolitan Filaret of Moscow, explained Daniel's epithet 'man of desires' as meaning a 'man who lives and breathes desires extended to God, a perfect man of prayer.' See Filaret, 'Beseda po osviashchenii khrama Sviatago Blagovernago Velikago Kniazia Aleksandra Nevskago, pri dome Kommercheskoi Akademii,' in *Sochineniia Filareta Mitropolita Moskovskago i Kolomenskago: slova i rechi*, ed. A. I. Mamontova, 5 vols, Moscow, 1873-85, v, pp. 136-40 (p. 138). The connection between desire and prayer was present, too, outside the Orthodox context. Semen Gamaleia (1743-1822), an early popularizer of Boehme, writes that 'in the secret ears of God it is not our words that make a voice, but our desire [...] Your desire is already your prayer, and constant desire is prayer of the mind [*umozritel'naia molitva*, the highest form of prayer in certain strands of Hesychasm — OS].' S. N. Gameleia, *Pis'ma*, Moscow, 4 vols, 1856-60, ii, p. 56. Gameleia may here be quoting, or paraphrasing, Augustine. 'Every desire within us that calls to God already constitutes a prayer. If you would never cease to pray never cease to long after it. The continuance of thy longing is the continuance of thy prayer.' Augustine, 'Psalm XXXVIII,' in *Expositions of the Book of Psalms*, London, 1848, pp. 68-94 (p. 82). One might also point to the interesting resonance of the term with Louis Claude Saint-Martin's 'man of desire,' which he associated with true 'intelligence' and which James Billington sees as the key component in the self-definition of the early Russian *intelligentsiia*. See J. Billington, *The Icon and the Axe: An Interpretive History of Russian Culture*, New York, 1970, pp. 255-57. Soloviev knew the works of Saint-Martin well, although he regarded him as secondary in theosophic talent to Boehme.

[132] The concept of 'theonomy' was introduced by theologian Paul Tillich. For a discussion of the applicability of the term to Soloviev's thought, see Valliere, 'Vladimir Solov'ev (1853-1900): Commentary,' p. 52. Anna Lisa Crone uses the Russian legend of the Firebird, in which the 'personae are doubled' and the beloved is 'pursuer and the benefactor and beneficiary' of the Firebird's magic powers, to demonstrate the mutuality of love. Crone, *Eros and Creativity*, p. 44. The dual activity of love as both

Chapter III. PROPHECY

The last years of Soloviev's life represent a radicalization both of his practice of the prophetic vocation and of his prophetic agenda. The public reading of *Short Story* was consciously intended to initiate its listeners into the pathos of the end.[133] It adopted a different mode of presentation that rested not on bringing his readers or listeners to a consciousness of ideals, or ethical norms, but on the incorporation of both audience and ideal into an imaginative landscape in which the imperative to be authentically human became a matter of life or death.[134] The work is not a measure of his disappointment in his former ideals but, as Sergei Trubetskoi wrote shortly after Soloviev's death, the final act in his life's drama from which he 'emerged victor both as a philosopher and as a Christian, preserving his ideals, believing in their ultimate triumph in their most apparent defeat.'[135] Indeed, what

---

bearer of ideal content and that which is borne carries the imprint of Soloviev's Sophia who, as Kornblatt has written, 'is both the message *and* bearer of the message or, in the imagery from Proverbs, both the house builder and the house itself.' See Kornblatt, *Introduction*, p. 90. Kornblatt intuits a similar dynamic in Soloviev's portrayal of Socrates' dæmon: 'like light, the demon that motivates Socrates is both object and agent, transformer and transformed.' J. D. Kornblatt, 'The Transfiguration of Plato in the Erotic Philosophy of Vladimir Solov'ev,' *Religion and Literature*, 24, 2, 1992, pp. 35-50 (p. 40). We also find a similar idea in the journals of Søren Kierkegaard: 'we generally think of the recipient as inactive and of the object to be revealed as conveying itself to him. But this is how it is: the recipient is the lover, and then the loved one is revealed to him, for he himself is transformed in the likeness of the loved one. Becoming what one understands is the only thorough way to understand, and one understands only according to what one oneself becomes.' S. Kierkegaard, *Papers and Journals: A Selection*, London, 1996, p. 343.

[133] 'The *Short Story* [...] is not a "photograph" of the future, but precisely a cautionary *parable* about the power of the forces of evil in the present and future.' Rashkovskii, 'Bibleiskii realizm,' p. 442.

[134] A similar contrast between ethos and pathos is evident in classical rhetorics. 'A mimetic poet, as well as a prose orator, has a choice of two, contrasted, modes of presentation. Either he can appeal to his audience to view his figures in an "ethical" way, as characterized agents, whose moral or personal qualities are presented for calm and rational assessment. Or he can aim at a more intuitive response, inducing his audience to share his figures' emotions, or to respond to the pathos of their situation, with very limited critical or ethical detachment.' C. Gill, 'The Ēthos/Pathos Distinction in Rhetorical and Literary Criticism,' *The Classical Quarterly*, 34, 1984, 1, pp. 149-166 (pp. 165-66).

[135] S. N. Trubetskoi, 'Predislovie,' in *SS*, XII, pp. 496-99 (p. 498). Janko Lavrin, too, sees not pessimism in Soloviev's final years but rather the reverse. 'By trying to explain the character and even the sequence of Plato's works by means of the inner drama of

comes through most strongly in *Short Story* is the nearness of triumph in seeming defeat, the proximity of God in the face of absolute distance. By fully inhabiting the pathos of the end, Soloviev was able to articulate a situation in which the living God would not only be recognized as the truth and the good by the mind and will, but *felt* immediately and passionately as that, and that alone, which is able to overcome the desolation of the reign of the Antichrist. The eschatological hope, which he believed to have been muffled by an excess of formulae and ethical supplication, is here felt at its most intense.[136]

Sergei Trubetskoi called the drama of Soloviev's life 'the drama of idealism.'[137] Through the changing emphases of his oeuvre, the task of realizing the ideal in the real — the spiritualization of matter — remained the constant background of his endeavour, both in terms of its justification and actualization. The pathos that energized him should be applied not only to the last two years of his life, important though they are, but to its entirety. Similarly, the prophetism of his life and work is not restricted to one period but exists wherever the 'task,' in all its multiple formulations, is paramount. But it was only in the year he died that, animated by the pathos of the end, he was able, in the introduction to his recitation of *Short Story*, to stand before an audience and publicly lay claim to prophetic insight:

> This story in its particulars was created by my imagination. Yet everything important in it, if indeed the fruit of imagination, is in any event that of one higher and mightier than my own — that imagination which not only visualizes but itself creates universal history.[138]

Essentially, *Short Story of the Antichrist* may be described as a story about a false prophet set within the putative context of an authentic

---

Plato's disappointment [...] he incidentally clarified and overcame his own pessimistic leanings. Instead of accepting the one-sided dualism of Plato, he thus made a final attempt to bridge it.' J. Lavrin, 'Note on Solovyev,' in V. Solovyev, *Plato*, London, 1935, pp. 1-21 (p. 20).

[136] Evgenii Rashkovskii argues that Soloviev's is an eschatology 'not of fear but rather an eschatology of hope'. Rashkovskii, *Smysli v istorii*, p. 207.
[137] Trubetskoi, 'Predislovie,' p. 497.
[138] Kotrelev, 'Eskhatologiia,' p. 252.

prophetic pronouncement whose goal is to engender precisely that kind of prophetic pathos whose reality is denied, or suppressed, by the events therein portrayed. Its complexity derives in no small part from the peculiarity of Soloviev's assumed position: as prophet, led by God; as philosopher, forever searching for the criterion for the authenticity of such 'leading.'

IV. PROPHECY AND THE THREEFOLD OFFICE

As an Orthodox Christian, Soloviev's public advocacy for the primacy of Rome and its representative the Pope could not fail to arouse the curiosity, praise and condemnation of his contemporaries and future biographers. Viewed alongside his vision of a united front between the Pope and the Russian tsar laid out in *La Russie et l'église universelle* (1888),[139] the picture becomes so beguiling that it is difficult to get beyond the simple fact of its articulation. As a consequence, the role of prophecy in Soloviev's theocratic ideal has been pushed to the margins, outpunched, so to speak, by the proposed alliance of the Russian monarchy and the Holy See.[140] Yet not only is it doubtful that his disillusionment in the practicability of such an alliance was accompanied by a similar disillusionment in prophecy, it is also clear that within the threefold construction of theocracy the pre-eminent role belonged not to the high priest or king but to the prophet, and that this is where he wished the attention of his readers to be directed.

---

[139] See especially SS, XI, pp. 327-44.

[140] Another possible reason that prophecy is often given scant coverage in Soloviev's theocracy is the desire to see in the Russian philosopher an heir to the Byzantine tradition and its model of power which, as Sutton has noted, is qualified by 'dyarchy' and the reciprocity of high priest and king. J. Sutton, 'The Centenary of the Death of Vladimir Solov'ëv,' *Studies in East European Thought*, 52, 2000, pp. 309-26 (p. 310). Walicki, while acknowledging the mediating role of the prophet between high priest and king, nevertheless, in our view, overemphasizes the importance of the latter two roles, leading to the dubious parallel he draws between Soloviev's theocracy and the imperial projects of Constantine the Great, Charlemagne and Dante. See Walicki, 'Solov'ëv's Theocratic Utopia and Two Romantic Poets: Fëdor Tjutčev and Adam Mickiewicz,' in *Vladimir Solov'ëv: Reconciler and Polemicist*, pp. 473-484.

For Soloviev, theocracy was a 'spiritual structure' whose goal was the 'preparation of humanity for the Kingdom of God, the perfection of the theanthropic union.'[141] 'The essence of theocracy is the free interaction between God and humanity.'[142] In this sense, theocracy was not a utopia in the sense of a perfected social order but a structure intended to ensure the optimum conditions for the realization of the Kingdom of God. Or, viewed in its negative agenda, theocracy is the removal of those barriers which impede the rule of God in human society, thus guaranteeing the freedom of divine-human interaction. In other words, theocracy for Soloviev had an instrumental function; it was not intended to substitute for the eschatological Kingdom of God but rather to 'prepare' for its coming. If it is permissible to use the term 'utopia' for Soloviev's understanding of the Kingdom of God, therefore, theocracy is to be thought of as the pathway to utopia rather than the final state itself.[143] The picture, however, is more complex than this suggests, for Soloviev obviously regarded some elements of his theocracy not only as means but as goals in themselves. 'The Kingdom of God is not only interior, in the spirit, but external, in power: it is a real *theocracy*.'[144] Theocracy is not only the clearing of the way for the rule of God, but the due inauguration of that rule. In order to understand Soloviev's position, therefore, one must separate what is merely instrumental from what is abiding and constitutive.

Soloviev's theocratic project was an attempt to translate the 'national theocracy' of the Jews outlined in *History and Future of Theocracy* (1886)

---

[141] SS, XI, pp. 77, 78.

[142] Ibid., IV, p. 470.

[143] 'Theocracy does not designate the unilateral control and power of the Church over all other institutions and communities. Rather, for Solovyov, theocracy represents the expression of this solidarity in the political, social, economic and cultural sphere, i.e. the connecting of all the institutions and practices of society to the loving wisdom of God, as mediated in and through the Church [...] Such a hierarchy is not a mask for a totalitarian theocracy but instead the dynamic expression of relationality based on the principle of relative autonomy and relative dependence — an imperfect mirroring of the absolute independence of the three divine persons.' A. Pabst, 'Wisdom and the Art of Politics,' in A. Pabst and C. Schneider (eds), *Encounter Between Eastern Orthodoxy and Radical Orthodoxy: Transfiguring the World Through the Word*, Farnham, Surrey, 2009, pp. 109-40 (p. 136).

[144] S^2, I, p. 226.

into a 'universal theocracy' of the Christian era. This objective is pursued in two distinct ways. On one hand, Soloviev transplants his theocratic ideal from Jewish to Christian soil by way of a simple extension of the range of influence of each major theocratic type: instead of the Levitical High Priest, a universal vicariate; instead of the Davidic King, a universal monarchy; instead of prophets of the God of Israel, prophets of the God of all nations. On the other hand, this universalization of scope is accompanied by a universalization of the theocratic offices themselves so that the roles of high priest, king, and prophet are presented as the province not only of selected individuals but that of all people. In this way, not only is society called to enact the tripartite division of power but the individual too is to incarnate in herself the virtues of the kingly, priestly and prophetic types. Moreover, it is the individual realization of the ideal (more precisely, its individual realization within the context of the church as the united body of humanity) that has precedence over the social in the light of the eschaton and the Kingdom of God. As Soloviev writes, 'all true believers will be prophets of God at the end of time at the appearance of the triumphant church, when all will also be kings and priests';[145] to this end the 'separation of the priesthood and monarchy as particular external institutions is only a necessary temporal means.'[146] All three offices are ultimately to be fulfilled by the individual although, as this quote makes clear, the priest and king as 'external,' social types will cease to have effect.[147]

The basis of Soloviev's argument was the biblical idea that Jesus Christ had reconciled the three theocratic offices in his person as the perfect high priest, king and prophet. As these three were anointed with the one unction for the service of God in ancient Israel, so Christ as the anointed one (messiah) integrated the roles of each within himself. Although the doctrine of the threefold office of Christ is present in the New Testament and patristic writings, it was not until

---

[145] Ibid., p. 239.
[146] SS, IV, p. 549.
[147] Seen in this light, Florovsky's opinion that Soloviev 'preached a certain eternal union of the Roman pontiff and the Russian Tsar—a union of the highest bearers of the two greatest gifts: Tsardom and Priesthood'—seems to miss the point entirely. See G. Florovsky, *Ways of Russian Theology*, Belmont, II, p. 90.

IV. PROPHECY AND THE THREEFOLD OFFICE

it was adopted by the Reformers, most notably John Calvin, that it received systematic exposition.[148] For Calvin, the role of prophet was equated with that of teacher, the supplier of sound doctrine necessary for salvation. Since Christ had brought to earth the Gospel, whose truth could not be augmented or ameliorated, he was therefore the last prophet: 'the perfect doctrine he has brought has made an end of all prophecies.'[149] Although they gave a role to interpreters of doctrine, what the Reformers were objecting to in the established church was the exclusive application of the kingly and priestly functions of the threefold office to members of the clergy as separate from the laity. Leaning on New Testament texts such as the first letter of Peter in which the faithful are described as a 'royal priesthood' and the Letter to the Hebrews with its emphasis on Christ the great High Priest, the weight of their message fell on the individual believer's adoption of the priestly function of Christ through the personal offering of 'spiritual sacrifices acceptable to God.'[150] Thus developed Martin Luther's 'priesthood of all believers,' one of the lightning rods of Protestantism. Apart from their extension of the threefold office to all Christians, however, which was in any case more a change in practice than in doctrine, the Reformed tradition did not fundamentally depart from the interpretation of the office in the early church. They continued, as did their forebears, to regard each office as working toward a different purpose according to its nature: the prophet as teacher and guide, the king as the ruler and commander of the new humanity, the priest as the offerer of sacrifice. Moreover, it was the latter, priestly function, understood as the conformation of the self to the spirit of Christ through imitation of his sacrificial self-giving, that was primary and on which the other two functions depended.

---

[148] Robert Sherman writes that 'while the notion of the threefold office was by no means restricted to the theological reflection of Calvin or the Reformed tradition [...] it is fair to say that [it] became a characteristically Reformed way of unpacking theologically the various works of the one Mediator, Christ, and this was due to Calvin's lead.' R. L. Sherman, *King, Priest and Prophet*, New York, 2004, p. 66. In a questionnaire, Soloviev described John Calvin as his 'least appealing historical figure.' See N. Kotrelev, 'Blagonamerennost' ne spasaet cheloveka,' p. 73.

[149] Cited in Sherman, *King, Priest and Prophet*, p. 66.

[150] 1 Peter 2.5-8.

Chapter III. PROPHECY

Soloviev's approach departs substantially from both reformed and non-reformed traditions. The most important innovation he introduces is the incorporation of the threefold office within a dialectical framework. As he writes in *History and Future of Theocracy*:

> If theocracy is the combination of the divine and human principles (in the practical life of humanity), then the full organization of theocracy is determined by a threefold activity: 1) the activity of the governing divine principle, in relation to which the human plays an entirely subordinate and passive role (the priestly office, representing the divine element in theocracy); 2) the activity of the free human principle (represented in theocracy by the civil, state or worldly power; and 3) the *synthetic (theanthropic) activity of both these principles*, interiorly united between themselves (in free social power, which in theocracy belongs to the [...] prophets) [...] The first represents the aim of God (the priesthood), the second human freedom (worldly power), and the third the inner combination of the one and the other (prophecy). Due to the theanthropic character of theocracy, this third (prophetic) power should in the given sense be acknowledged as the most perfect and fullest expression of the theanthropic union, the real weapon of the God who is to come.[151]

This understanding of prophecy as the dialectical synthesis of the priestly and kingly functions allows Soloviev to interpret the New Testament ideal of a 'royal priesthood' not as a call to the adoption of priestly, or even kingly, virtues on the part of the believer but as the combination of both in prophetic activity. Instead of Luther's priesthood of all believers, Soloviev advocates a prophethood of all believers. Further, in stressing the active-passive antithesis in the first dialectical pair, the philosopher suggests it is this fundamental distinction that is overcome in the prophetic synthesis. Prophecy from this perspective becomes a kind of active passivity, or passive activity, a point we shall return to later. Also to be noted is Soloviev's emphasis on the interiority of the synthetic resolution of the priestly and kingly offices in prophecy. 'The prophetic vocation,' he writes in *La Russie et l'église universelle*, 'is characterized by exclusively interior and purely spiritual conditions.'[152] However, the question of how exactly Solovievian prophecy might function in both

---

[151] SS, IV, pp. 502, 503.
[152] Ibid., XI, p. 344.

IV. PROPHECY AND THE THREEFOLD OFFICE

the social life of theocracy and the individual life of the believer is never wholly elucidated, and there remains much that is unsaid in this area. On one hand, concrete prophetic activity is seen as conditional on the fulfilment of the priestly and kingly offices, as Soloviev's treatment of the saving act of Christ illustrates:

> Only on condition of the passive sacrifice of atonement together with the active feat (*podvig*) of salvation can the fullness of spiritual-corporeal *interaction* and *mutuality* of the divine and human principles be achieved; only the redeemer and saviour of humanity can become for it the mediator and transmitter of the life-giving Spirit of God. In other words, only the one true High Priest and King can be the one true Prophet.[153]

On the other hand, Soloviev's historical survey of theocracy does not present prophecy as emerging from the offices of priest and king. Rather the reverse: in the figure of Moses, whom the philosopher describes as the 'creator of national theocracy' and the 'greatest of the prophets,'[154] Soloviev already posits the 'fullness of theanthopric autarchy (*edinovlastie*),' that is, the threefold office in its undivided manifestation. The dyarchy of priest and king are not historically antecedent to their combination in the role of the prophet; instead, the prophetic consummation of triune power already existed at the very beginning of the theocratic path in the personality of Moses. The three offices that were separated after Moses are thus returned to unity in the person of Christ, who reinstitutes what once was lost. There is, therefore, something both culminal and primary about biblical prophecy in Soloviev's handling: it is, he writes, 'both the root and crown of theocratic organization: in one sense it is the first and absolute power, in another sense merely the third power, conditional on the other two.'[155]

The loss of the primary prophetic consciousness from Moses onward is mirrored on an individual scale in Soloviev's application of the threefold office to the fall of collective humanity. In breaking what he calls the 'messianic law,' which consists in 'submitting to God and

---

[153] Ibid., IV, p. 590.
[154] Ibid., p. 423; XI, p. 326.
[155] SS, IV, p. 504.

subjecting nature to oneself in order to save it,' humanity 'preferred to attain the goal directly, on its own, breaking the order laid down by divine reason.'

> It wanted to unite with lower nature arbitrarily, by the power of its own desire, supposing in this way to procure absolute kingly power, an unlimited autocracy (*samoderzhavie*) equal to God's. It did not want to submit its kingly power to its priesthood and thus became unable to satisfy its true aspirations, to carry out its prophetic vocation.[156]

The distinction between what we have translated as 'autarchy' (*edinovlastie*) and 'autocracy' (*samoderzhavie*) that Soloviev draws here is fundamental to an understanding of his conception of prophecy. Much like his earlier application of the dialectical method to 'abstract principles,' the prophetic resolution of the threefold office is not the 'overcoming' or subsuming (the Hegelian *Aufhebung*) of the foundational dialectical pair of priest and king, but their actual union. The 'royal priesthood' is attained not through the practising of that human freedom which inheres in the kingly office but through the submission of the same to the priestly office, that is, sacrificial self-giving. In this offering up of purely human freedom, the human being discovers that true, theanthropic freedom which is the mark of the prophet. 'Real freedom,' writes Soloviev in *Justification of the Good*, 'humanity must itself earn through an inner feat (*vnutrennii podvig*).'

Although this kind of freedom had, from as early as the writing of *Spiritual Foundations of Life* (1882-84), been seen by Soloviev as the defining attribute of prophecy, it never receives systematic exposition in his work. On the social plane, he believed it to be manifest in the fact that prophets of all times and all ages, and — Soloviev is keen to point out — not only in the Judeo-Christian tradition, are characterized precisely by a lack of definite characteristics: they are of all ages and genders, all classes and castes, all nations and traditions. They are not restricted in their thinking and activity by tradition and doctrine, and need no authorization from other human beings. Their prophetic

---

[156] Ibid., p. 311. See Chapter 1, note 171 for parallels with the fall of Sophia.

vocation is a 'direct personal gift'[157] ordained by none and authenticated by none other than God. In the Christian context, therefore, anyone 'who does not resist divine grace but aids its activity through their freedom [...] by the law and mercy of God can lay claim to supreme power as equals of the Pope and emperor.'[158] While emphasizing the democratic nature of prophecy, however, Soloviev does not view its practice as belonging to human beings by right, without any need for the prior movement of self-transformation; the infusion of divine grace received through prophetic freedom is conditional upon that 'inner feat' which allows such free activity to emerge. Soloviev's concept of prophecy is thus marked by a fundamental tension: the condition for its free activity is a kind of passivity. On the one hand, there is the immediacy of the prophetic gift, which can only be received; on the other, a necessity to earn that gift which seems to undercut its character as freely given.[159]

Soloviev never talks about a 'prophetic task' but it is clear that for him the kind of freedom that derives from prophecy has an agency in the world in which it finds itself, and works toward a specific purpose. At the social level, such freedom allows its bearers to hold before the established power of church and state an uncompromised vision of the ideal future, the Kingdom of God, for which the two offices were created and from which they came. 'The heralds,' Soloviev writes, 'of ideal perfection cannot make up a definite institution which, of necessity being imperfect, would contradict their message and take away all its meaning.'[160] Issuing from a place of freedom, their message,

---

[157] Solov'ev, *Dukhovnye osnovy*, p. 618.
[158] SS, XI, pp. 343-44.
[159] The exclusive emphasis on the giftedness of prophecy Soloviev regards to be the principal error of the reformed tradition. 'The essence of Protestantism,' he writes 'consists in the misuse of the third principle of Christian theocracy — the principle of prophecy, or the freedom of the individual spirit in the work of religion. Its *misuse* is observed in the fact that, firstly, the principle of prophecy, i.e. the freedom of individual inspiration, is acknowledged not in third place, i.e. under the condition of faithfulness to the two other principles of theocracy [...] but as the first and, in essence, only principle of the Kingdom of God [...] Priesthood is confused with prophecy, this latter being acknowledged not as a particular vocation or *duty of certain people* called by God, but as the natural *right of everyone*.' S², I, p. 238.
[160] Ibid., II, p. 587.

like the prophetic synthesis of the priestly and kingly offices itself, is directed not toward incremental change in institutional frameworks or the will and agency of those in authority, but 'to the inner world, to the conscience, exclusively to the feeling of the Divine immanent to humanity.'[161] By this the philosopher means to say that prophecy is not intended to remould existing conditions but to awaken in the other two offices their inner rootedness in the ideal which the prophet announces, namely the 'ideal of divinized humanity as the highest goal of their dual activity.'[162]

But the prophet's significance is not exhausted by the message he or she proclaims. Prophecy in Soloviev is not primarily about proclaiming the ideal but living it: prophets should 'show a given society its ideal in such a light as they are able to achieve it, and themselves realize it.'[163] 'Prophets are principally bearers of theanthropic consciousness and representatives of the most profound moral union of the *whole* person and world with God—a union for whose sake the priesthood and monarchy exist.'[164] It is the very fact of prophetic consciousness that reveals the prophet's full significance, and from which the ability to prophesy derives. This consciousness makes it possible 'to predict future events not only in words but also in deed, partially anticipating conditions and relations which do not belong to the contemporary state of humanity.'[165] Prophets, according to this view, are the bearers of the eschaton, the final coming of the Kingdom of God, in the interior dimension of consciousness. They are eschatological actors in the present life of humanity. In the integrity of their inner lives they live, as was earlier remarked in reference to the Hebrew Prophets, the life of the future in the present.

These considerations apply as much to the prophets of Jewish 'national theocracy' as they do to prophets of Soloviev's universal, Christian theocracy. While the philosopher in various places broaches the question of how the practice and function of prophecy changes

---

[161] Ibid., p. 271.
[162] Ibid., p. 271.
[163] SS, XI, p. 316.
[164] Ibid., IV, p. 549.
[165] Ibid., XI, p. 317.

IV. PROPHECY AND THE THREEFOLD OFFICE

in a post-incarnational context, an adequate answer is never wholly elucidated. Indeed on this issue, and the related question of the distinction between the social and eschatological roles of prophecy, there is a lack of clarity that speaks of a larger tension at the root of the Philosophy of All-Unity. We have seen how Soloviev attempts to reconcile a conviction in the fullness of salvation in Jesus Christ with the idea of the continuing economy of the Word in history. In many respects, his idea of prophetic consciousness was intended to create a conceptual space in which it became possible, in philosophical terms, to retain a degree of moral autonomy and purpose for human beings in a world in which salvation had already, in some respect, 'come.' Yet the Hebrew prophet, like the Christian, according to Soloviev, already contained within himself in consciousness the 'ideal of divinized humanity' that was realized in Christ; not only this, the social order of the Jews too reflected the union of the threefold office once held by Moses and regained by Christ.[166] The change that is enacted by the Christ-event, therefore, is not in the nature of prophetic consciousness, which Soloviev believed from the earliest times of covenantal history to have evinced a messianic and Christological tendency, but rather in the power of that consciousness to effect substantive change — change, that is, not only in the consciousness of individual, human actors but in the external world around that consciousness. Through the Resurrection and Ascension of Christ, the agency of God is able to operate not only from above but from within the created order. There is no longer just an interaction between the divine and the human, but a union in which a new, theanthropic power is born.

> By the appearance of the God-man *autarchy* is restored in heaven and on earth. The difference between the earthly and the heavenly worlds is preserved but henceforth there is no absolute separation or contradiction between them; for power belongs to one and the goal of heavenly and earthly being is one and the same: the complete and final victory of

---

[166] 'The Sons of Israel never forgot that society is the body of the perfect human being and that this latter is necessarily tripartite: the priest of the Almighty, the king of the earth, and the prophet of theanthropic union. This unique people anticipated and prepared for the coming of the God-man not only in the visions of its prophets but also in their social order, in the very fact of threefold theocracy.' Ibid., p. 327.

this all-one, heavenly-earthly, theanthropic power—a victory, in which power itself is abolished *as power* and fully appears as the manifest and living truth.[167]

This autarchy, the restoration of the threefold office in one divine-human person, in Soloviev's view puts an end, or the beginning of an end, not to the law of the Jews but to the laws of material nature itself, and their corollaries death and decay. Instead of a multitude of individual centres operating from themselves and dissipating their energy in a fruitless drive for self-affirmation, there is now one centre in the transfigured flesh of the God-man. The material world is not yet spiritualized, but its powers of individuation as the 'other' of the all-one God are transferred from the service of atomization to that of unity. The earthly has become the heavenly, not in substance but in essence, and the power in both harnessed toward a singular goal. Understood as an extension of Soloviev's Christology, prophecy is both the public remembrance in word and deed of the divinized humanity of the God-man, and the continuation of the task of spiritualization that was enacted in him. Prophetic consciousness is the incorporation within the prophetic spirit of Christ. In this way, prophecy becomes the final step in the path of *imitatio Christi*.

> [Jesus Christ] showed himself to be an absolutely pure and holy High Priest and offerer of sacrifice in bringing his humanity to his heavenly Father as a burnt offering; the true king of the world and material nature, rescuing it from the law of death by his resurrection and winning it for eternal life; and, finally, the perfect prophet, showing people in his ascension to heaven the absolute goal of their existence and giving them, by the descent of the Holy Spirit and foundation of the Church, the necessary powers and means to attain this goal.[168]

Beyond reference to the descent of the Holy Spirit, and the foundation of the Church as the Body of Christ, Soloviev says very little about these 'powers' that Christ gave to people. What he does do, however, is offer his readers in *La Russie et l'église universelle* a vision of a social

---

[167] SS, IV, p. 622.
[168] Ibid., XI, p. 327.

IV. PROPHECY AND THE THREEFOLD OFFICE

order founded on the threefold office of Christ differing little from that which had animated Jewish theocracy.

> Christ did not unite the divine and human in His individual person so that they may remain separated in His social body. Priest, King and Prophet, He gave Christian society its absolute form in the threefold monarchy. Founding the Church in His priesthood, sanctifying the state by His kingly power, He cared too for their unity and harmonious development, leaving the world the free and living action of His prophetic spirit.[169]

Here the Holy Spirit is instrumentalized as the reconciler of two external and temporal offices, and prophecy, which Soloviev had described as the 'root and crown' of theocracy, divested of much of its meaning and essential freedom. The idea of prophetic consciousness as a goal in itself is no longer visible. Yet as Soloviev's apocalyptic presentiments began to push out the idea of the gradual realization of the Kingdom of God in history, the philosopher began to distance himself from those external organs which had separated humanity from the immediacy of the Kingdom. Even earlier than this, his departure from an emphasis on the transformation of church-state relations may very well have derived from a growing unease with forms of external power connected to his fear of the counterfeit. But at its core the apocalypticism of the late years represented the logical conclusion of Soloviev's Christology, the final limit of articulation beyond which it could go no further. It was only natural that prophecy too, as eschatologically-oriented living, should undergo a transformation from the remembrance of things past in the face of the powers of the present to the practice of present power in the light of the eschatological future. The prophet as individual ideal rather than the office of prophecy now comes to the fore. Rather than the purpose of prophecy (socially, the unifying and correcting force of the Priest and King; at the level of consciousness, the union of the priestly and kingly functions in the individual), it is now the character of that freedom which is given in prophetic consciousness itself, unconnected to the role allocated it, that animates the philosopher's

---

[169] Ibid., p. 340.

work.[170] The pursuit of this theme passes from Soloviev's ecumenical and religious-historical work to his critical essays on thinkers and artists of the past and present, and especially to his aesthetics, where the concept of *theurgy* claims the ground vacated by theocracy.

In 1897, Soloviev wrote about the mid-1880s as having been a time when he had 'felt great enthusiasm for the theocratic idea *in its ecclesial form*.'[171] The statement gives us a glimpse into what the 'collapse of theocracy' which accompanied his later years, proclaimed by many after him but never by the philosopher himself, might have meant. What ceased to concern him was not the idea of theocracy per se but its direct application from the Jewish context to the structure and functioning of the Christian church. God's rule over all things is not denied, nor is the capacity of that rule to be channelled through humanity in the temporal order, but the eschatological implications of his Christology, his fears about counterfeit good, and continued reflection on the freedom of prophetic activity moved Soloviev ever further from seeking his ideal in concrete human institutions and authorities. While the social realization of theocracy in particular organs of power disappeared from the philosopher's agenda in later years, Soloviev continued to maintain a conviction in the potency of the theocratic ideal for the life of humanity, a potency seen in its most concentrated form in prophecy.

---

[170] Maritain's later vision of a new humanism shares a similar reorientation away from the roles practised in a Christian socio-temporal order to the freedom possessed by creation as gift from God. 'The guiding star in the supernatural world of this new humanism, the idea at its heart,' he wrote, 'will not be that of God's *holy empire* over all things, but rather that of the *holy freedom* of the creature whom grace unites to God.' Maritain, *True Humanism*, p. 156.

[171] S², II, p. 631 (my emphases).

— Excursus —

THE PRIMACY OF THE THIRD:
Soul, Feeling and Reverence

The use of the threefold dialectic in thought was not only characteristic of Soloviev's ideal of prophecy. It permeates his entire oeuvre, even in those places where it may not be at first evident. It is the basis for his metaphysics, his ethics, his gnoseology and his aesthetics, where patterns of three often inhere in larger tripartite structures, which in turn open onto yet larger superstructures. Even in those places where the reader may at first discern a duality, such as the distinctions Soloviev borrows from ancient philosophy — spirit and matter, body and soul, heaven and earth, divine and human — there is always a third term which relates the moment of unity: spiritualized matter, theanthropy, the Kingdom of God.

Although the model was present in Soloviev's philosophy from an early stage, it is not easily discernable in his Master's dissertation, *Crisis of Western Philosophy* (1874) where, despite the fact that his goal had been to reveal the limitations in the recent systems of Schopenhauer and von Hartmann, he nonetheless followed the former in interpreting cognition as involving two modes — will and representation — understood as the two key ingredients of the human self.[1] By the writing of *Philosophical Principles* (1877), however, another mode was added to these two, that of feeling (*chuvstvo*), and each mode combined with a 'hypostasis' and an 'idea,' set out schematically in a series of tables, such as the draft below:

---

[1] While Schopenhauer does not ignore the emotional aspect of human existence, he views it merely as a component of volitional activity. His 'will' is thus a 'covering term for the entire affective and volitional side of the self.' G. Zöller, 'Schopenhauer on the Self,' in *Cambridge Companion to Schopenhauer*, Cambridge, 1999, pp. 18-43 (p. 23).

— Excursus —

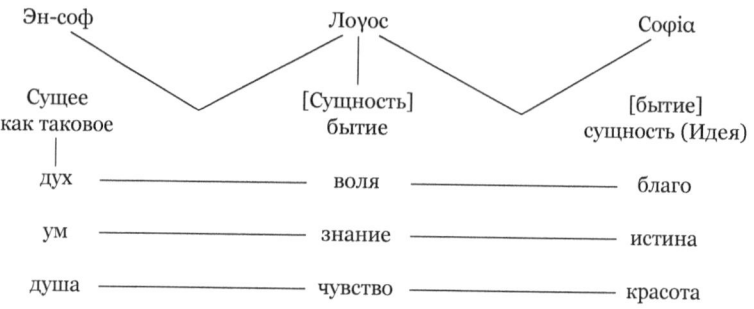

Figure 1[2]

Soloviev's association of the newly introduced mode of being—feeling—with the soul strikes one as particularly interesting in the context of Christian thought which had always, like Platonism before it, been keen to separate the soul from the taint of sentience and the particular. Augustine, for example, described the soul as 'a special substance, endowed with reason, adapted to rule the body.'[3] Far from being the master of the body, whether through will or reason, Soloviev conceived of the soul as that part of the human being which first steps into contact with the external world around it through sensation. The soul is thus a sentient being in the first place, whose nature it is to extend toward the other, to bridge the divide between self and not-self, inner consciousness and the material world.[4]

---

2   PSS, II, p. 381.

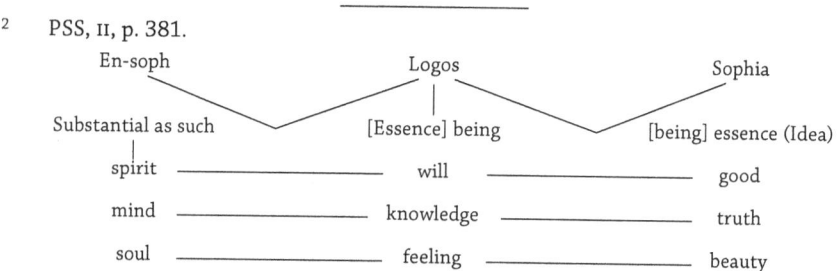

3   Augustine, *The Greatness of the Soul; The Teacher*, ed. J. Colleran, New York, 1949, p. 40. In the late eighteenth century, representatives of the Pietist movement attempted to introduce a corrective into the perceived intellectualism of Christian theology by arguing for the significance of feeling in Christian life. The movement was to play a major role in the emergence of German Romanticism.

4   This is not to say that Soloviev believed that the soul *only* felt for he talks elsewhere of the 'rational soul' (*razumnaia dusha*), but that it is in feeling or sensing that its most characteristic, essential activity consists. Charles Kahn has noted a similar emphasis

In the Soloviev archive in Moscow, there is a file labelled 'Articles on Questions of Religion, Morality and Philosophy: Odd Pages.' Scattered amongst these pages are several interesting passages relating to the body-soul distinction and feeling as a mode of subjective being. Their technical language, with Hegelian turns of phrase vying for space amongst interjections of automatic writing, dates them to the mid-1870s, around the time of the writing of *Philosophical Principles*. The following excerpt is taken from the first of these pages:

> We have, firstly, inner, psychical, subjective being, in which the existent is given to itself, or is for itself; this inner being in its simplest passive form is *sensation* (*oshchushchenie*), in its simplest distinctive form it appears as effort (*usilie*). The existent, insofar as it reveals itself in this inner form of being—the existent as sensing and striving—we call the soul or the psychical being. Secondly, we have external being, physical, objective, which comprises the object of sensation and effort, that which the soul senses as other, different from itself and that which it moves through its effort; this external, sensed and moved we call the body, in which the existent is given to the other, exists for the other [...] Sensation is nothing other than the coincidence or identity of psychical and corporeal being.[5]

Behind such formulations can be traced the influence of a thinker rarely mentioned in connection with Soloviev, but whom the latter respected and admired, namely the French metaphysician Maine de Biran (1766-1824). While emphasizing that the primary source and starting point for all philosophy is the reception of sense data,[6] Biran

---

on sensation in Aristotle's *De Anima*, although his argument relates to the 'fullness of treatment' Aristotle gives sensation over other faculties of the soul rather than sensation's potential superiority as its most essential activity. See C. H. Kahn, 'Sensation and Consciousness in Aristotle's Psychology,' in *Articles on Aristotle. Vol. IV Psychology and Aesthetics*, London, 2003, pp. 1-31 (pp. 5-6). It is very likely that Soloviev's association of the soul with feeling derived from his knowledge of the biblical corpus, and especially the work done by his teacher, Pamfil Iurkevich, on the heart as the seat of the soul in the Jewish and Christian scriptures. See P. D. Iurkevich, 'Serdtse i ego znachenie v dukhovnoi zhizni cheloveka po ucheniiu slova Bozhiia,' in *Filosofskie proizvedeniia*, pp. 69-103.

5   RGALI, f. 446, op. 1, d. 17. 'Stat'i po voprosam religii, morali, filosofii. Razroznennye listy,' p. 1 of 137.
6   Note, for example, the following statement from Biran: 'The faculty of receiving impressions is the first and the most general of all those which are manifested in the organic living being. It embraces them all: we cannot conceive any of them as existing before it or without it, nor any which is not more or less closely dependent on it.' M. de Biran, *The Influence of Habit on the Faculty of Thinking*, Westport, CT, 1970, p. 53.

nevertheless moved away from the sensualism of his predecessor Condillac by positing an autonomous sphere of activity in the human subject capable of rising above the immediate influence of sensation, and making free choices as regards the data therein received, a capability he called 'effort.'[7] For Biran, it was the inward awareness of this act of effort, combined with the meeting of resistance in that which is other to it, that guaranteed the unity and identity of the human subject. Soloviev believed Biran to have erred in two crucial, interrelated areas: firstly, in the 'identification of effort with the will,' and secondly, in the 'substitution of the entire concept of causality for one of its parts — the concept of active, directly efficient or immediate cause.'[8] Accordingly, while retaining Biran's terms of effort and resistance, Soloviev substantially modifies his theory of cognition. Instead of conflating it with 'will,' Soloviev conceives of 'effort' as that primary disposition toward being given in the striving (*stremlenie*) and wanting (*khotenie*) of the soul toward that which is other than it.[9] Since 'effort does not occur without resistance,'[10] prior to an awareness of either half of the conceptual pair is the state of sensation itself, in which

---

[7] Soloviev wrote a major entry on Maine de Biran for the Brockhaus-Efron Encyclopaedia, in which he compliments the French philosopher for having 'emphasized against the school of Condillac the significance of inner experience and the active side of psychical phenomena and insisted on the spiritual-corporeal character of the human being against one-sided Cartesian spiritualism.' SS, x, p. 429.

[8] Ibid., pp. 428-29.

[9] In his 'Svoboda voli i prichinnost'' (published posthumously), an 1892 response to the philosophy of his childhood friend Lev Lopatin, Soloviev directly associates wanting (*khotenie*) with sensation (*oshchushchenie*), not only in the cases where this seems evident (the statement 'I want to eat' really means, according to Soloviev, 'I sense hunger') but also with so-called 'deliberate decisions.' In the case of the latter, argues Soloviev, we cannot talk of a qualitatively new content arising out of an act of decision but only of the 'realization of what came before.' This 'before' represents a complex web of conscious and unconscious thoughts which affect the resulting action later manifested by their bearer. If this is called 'will,' writes Soloviev, then 'will is a thought that possesses enough energy to conform to its inner content and direct our external actions in a positive or negative sense.' In this sense, 'will' is merely the consequence of thought-sensations which arise on the basis of our psychical nature and cannot be considered an autonomous source of agency. 'Will expresses only a presupposed or actual reaction of the subject to an objective content given it in sensations, feelings and thoughts. In no sense is it the production of such a content from itself.' See V. S. Solov'ev, 'Freedom of Will and Causality,' in *Mysl' i slovo*, 2, 1918-21, pp. 169-85 (pp. 176-77).

[10] SS, x, p. 428.

the consciousness of a sensing and striving from inner experience is combined with the awareness, gained through resistance, of a world existing outside this consciousness. Sensation is therefore understood neither as a subjective act (as in Biran or Fichte), nor as the imposition of sensory data upon a passive subject (as in empiricism), but as the immediate givenness of the link between body and soul, inner and outer experience, psychical and corporeal life. This is why Soloviev describes it as the 'coincidence of psychical and corporeal being.' As such, it is not willed but directly *felt* by the soul. This granted, however, Soloviev quite clearly wishes to retain Biran's concept of effort as indicative of a certain agency belonging to the soul, and involved in the feeling of sensation not yet raised to the level of rational consciousness.

In a passage from the same archival file, possibly belonging to a later date, Soloviev writes about the nature of the three hypostases in the context of his spirit-matter distinction:

> 1) Real spirit, 2) mind 3) soul. In the soul the divine principle unites with matter in actuality [...] In the first hypostasis spirit and matter are *substantia* and *accidens*, in the second *causa* and *effectus*, and in the third they interact. Spiritual body, ideal body, real body. The kingdom or organism of spirits, the organism of minds, the organism of souls. The goal is real unity, the realization of God [...]
>
> Everything depends on the third, in it everything holds together. In the soul is the possibility of the living God. The power of the spirit is will (freedom), the power of the mind imagination, the power of the soul wanting and action.[11]

The emphatic claim that 'in the soul is the possibility of the living God' summarizes Soloviev's understanding of the soul as the meeting-place between the divine principle ('spirit') and its other ('matter'). Rather than existing in a relationship of substance to accident or cause to effect, spirit and matter in the soul are given in their interaction as mutually conditioning and conditioned. The soul, as the third hypostasis, thus represents the culmination of the process of real unity, the spiritualization of matter; in it 'everything holds together.' Insofar as it lays claim to a form of sentient being, the soul is the final point of

---

11   'Razroznennye listy,' p. 118 of 137.

the movement of the spirit toward actuality, which finds only an ideal resolution in the mind.[12] In this sense it is the 'realization' of the divine itself, the place of the closest and most intimate bond between God and the creature, and that on which God's Kingdom is founded.[13]

Soloviev first tried to articulate the nature of the 'action' of the feeling soul in his treatment of cognition in *Critique*. Here he again begins with the givenness of the link between subject and object in sensation but moves far beyond it to the positing of a series of similar links at the intelligible and supra-rational levels:

> The external activity of the object on our sensuality arouses a corresponding interaction between our mind and the idea of the object, translating the form of the object into our actual consciousness and connecting our given sensations with it. The chaos of external impressions and sensations is organized by our mind through their attribution to that form, or idea, of the object which exists in our spirit independently of sensations and thoughts, but which in them attains material reality and visibility for our actual natural consciousness. This idea, concealed from our outer eye in the invisible (unconscious) depth of the spirit, is translated by our mind, aroused by external impressions, from this depth onto the surface of everyday consciousness. This fleshless form is then incarnated in that material environment which consists of immediate states of our sensuality.[14]

---

[12] Soloviev's sources of inspiration for the essentially anti-Platonic idea that a sentient being has a greater claim to perfection than a purely ideal being are various. Other than the obvious importance of biblical thought and his own visionary experience, one may cite the following four as having had a decisive influence on the philosopher: a) the Kabbala, particularly the concept of *Shekhinah* (see p. 89); b) Duns Scotus, whose argument that 'the more perfect the form, the more real (actual) it is, and the more actual it is, the more strongly it takes root in matter and the more firmly it unites matter with itself' is cited approvingly by Soloviev in his encyclopaedia entry on the scholastic thinker (SS, X, p. 332); c) Christian mysticism and alchemy. Jacob Boehme, whom Soloviev read assiduously in his early years, had justified the introduction of feeling into the realm of the absolute by arguing that 'eternal good cannot be an insensible essence (for so it were not manifest to itself).' Boehme, *Mysterium Magnum*, p. 6; and lastly, d) Hegelianism whose essential characteristic Soloviev defined as 'the demand that the idea justify its authenticity by realizing itself in reality' (SS, X, p. 319).

[13] That God can be understood to 'feel,' not only in the sense of the inner life of the divine but in actual sensation, is made explicit by Soloviev in *Critique*. See PSS, III, p. 273.

[14] Ibid., pp. 301-02.

Soloviev's argument here is arcane and somewhat difficult to follow, but his main point seems to be that there is more to sensory immediacy than may at first appear to be the case. The participation of the human being in the act of cognition is not reducible to a simple reception of sense data but, to the contrary, involves a series of related activities whereby perceptive experience is facilitated. Receiving its initial impetus from primary sensory data, the mind communes with the 'idea' of the object present in the 'spirit,' before finally sowing the ideal form of the object in the immediacy of sensory perception. In accordance with such a scheme, he goes on to formulate yet another threefold definition:

> The actual cognition of the object (objective cognition) is defined, firstly, as *faith* in the absolute existence of the object; secondly, as the intellectual contemplation, or *imagination*, of its essence, or idea; and, finally, as the *creative* incarnation, or realization, of this idea in real sensations, or empirical data, of our natural, sensual consciousness.[15]

These three activities—faith, imagination and creativity—closely follow Soloviev's respective treatment of the will (spirit), representation (mind) and feeling (soul), and are best understood as the embodied activity of each. In other words, the aspect under which spirit manifests its will in lived experience is faith, the mind its representation—imagination, and the soul its feeling—creativity. Their operation cannot be said to occur in time, and all three have effect before any actual experience as such has taken place. As Soloviev writes: 'the all-one existent is known before sensory experience and rational thought in the threefold act of faith, imagination and creativity, which is presupposed by any actual cognition.'[16] The threefold act is thus not initiated by sensation but precedes it.

As the first component in cognition, faith (*vera*) should not be confused with sense-certainty or trust. From a philosophical perspective, faith for Soloviev was an 'expression in consciousness of the preconscious link of subject and object.' This expression exists in its most essential form in faith in the existence of the material world

---

[15] Ibid., p. 305. Konstantin Mochul'skii has described this theory as a sort of 'inverted Platonism.' Konstantin Mochul'skii, *Vladimir Solov'ev. Zhizn' i uchenie*, Paris, 1936, p. 116.
[16] PSS, III, p. 14.

since 'this faith merely reflects in our consciousness that primary, simple, and insuperable fact that we, i. e. a given subject, are part of a common being (*obshchee bytie*), a member of the universal whole.'[17] This is as much as to say that faith is the ground in which consciousness discovers that it is already, prior to the moment of thinking and concrete perception, involved in a being that exceeds its awareness of the same, and in which the subject as individual is always an abstraction from the greater fabric of the whole. That faith is understood as an activity of the will can be understood in two ways. Firstly, in the theological sense that Augustine had in mind when he wrote that *Nemo credit nisi volens* ('no one believes unless he is willing,' trans.); not that this means that one takes a conscious decision to believe but, as Pamfil Iurkevich interpreted the phrase, that the 'will is *directly* defined by the attractions and requirements of the heart or, as philosophers express it, by its strivings to absolute good.'[18] Secondly, faith is directly related in Soloviev's handling to that moment of kenotic self-giving that we earlier observed as the cornerstone of his Christology, and specifically in the priestly function of the threefold office.

In the very last pages of his late *Theoretical Philosophy* (1897-99), Soloviev proposes three 'certainties' (*dostovernosti*) as the basis for philosophy—the certainty of 'subjective states of consciousness as such'; the certainty of a 'general, logical *form* as such'; and the certainty of the 'philosophical intention to know the truth itself.' On this latter, which includes the former two moments, he writes the following:

> Philosophical intention, in its subjective certainty, unites to the logical meaning of its object (the concept of the truth, or absolute, itself) that resolution, or act, of the will in its giving away of itself to its object, which is the real principle of movement, and which transforms thought into the becoming ratio of truth (*stanoviashchiisia razum istiny*).[19]

This resolution of will, which Soloviev here associates with the 'philosophical intention to know the truth,' matches the definition

---

[17] *Filosofskii slovar' Vladimira Solov'eva*, Rostov-na-Donu, 1997, p. 25. From Soloviev's encyclopaedic article 'vera' (Faith), which did not feature in the 1966-70 collected works.
[18] Iurkevich, 'Serdtse i ego znachenie,' p. 94.
[19] S², I, pp. 829-30.

of faith he gave in the earlier *Lectures* as 'an act of spirit reaching beyond the limits of our reality,' and finds a particular resonance in the following passage from *History and Future of Theocracy*:

> In faith the human spirit steps beyond the limits of given, individual reality, and affirms the existence of such objects that *do not necessitate his recognition*: he freely recognizes them. Faith is a feat of the spirit (*podvig dukha*) which reveals things not seen (*oblichaiushchii veshchi nevidimye*[20]). The believing spirit does not lie passively in wait for the influence of the external object but goes bravely out to meet it; it does not slavishly follow phenomena but anticipates them: it is free and self-moving (*samodeiatelen*).[21]

Maine de Biran's mistake, in Soloviev's estimation, had been to confuse the essential freedom belonging to the spirit with the freedom of will alleged to belong to the subject of sensory perception, that is, the soul. The causality of phenomenal existence can indeed be traced through the human will, asserts Soloviev, but not in the direct sense that Biran claimed. Instead, by positing faith as the actual ground of cognition, Soloviev's theory achieves a displacement of the cognitive centre from individual subject to the spirit, which becomes the active component in cognition. This displacement, however, is nothing other than the freedom of recognition deriving from the subject's initial involvement in being as universal whole. Faith is the first step of cognition since in it the subject is already given over to the other as the structural prius of knowledge; it is the witness of that 'inner unity with the object by whose power [the subject] is in the object and the object in it (its absolute being = absolute being of the object).'[22] The 'recognition' of the other is 'free' precisely because it involves no concrete will or representation but is instead a 'resolution' to dwell, and assent to participation, within the immediacy of the being of the universal whole. From this angle, we can perhaps understand Soloviev's puzzling assertion, again used to counter Biran, that 'will is primarily, or in its highest expression, precisely that which attains its goal without any actual efforts whatsoever.' Freedom

---

20   See Hebrews 11.1.
21   SS, IV, p. 436.
22   PSS, III, p. 303.

is not an attribute or a predicate of the will but its most essential and integral nature; it is not *of* the will, it *is* the will. To speak in theological terms, the perfect will — that of God — is that whose efficacy is postulated on no resistance at all — manifested most essentially in the freedom of the spirit — and which penetrates all things to the degree that all things open themselves to it. In the movement of the will's self-giving through faith, this freedom of the spirit is appropriated, or inhabited, by the human subject. Thus, in positing faith as the first, metaphysical condition of cognition, Soloviev is claiming that there is a kenotic aspect to basic, sensory experience itself, a locatedness of the pre-conscious subject in being that is already trans-subjective.

Soloviev's faculty of imagination, or 'intellectual contemplation,' is extensively developed neither in *Critique* nor elsewhere, but is clearly a borrowing from Schelling's theory of cognition, with Platonic notions of the immutability of the eternal Forms also playing a role.[23] It is, however, in the link between imagination and the next stage, namely 'creativity,' that Soloviev's distinctive approach emerges. In *Critique* he writes little about this stage, describing it as 'psychical' or 'universal' creativity, and only at the very end of the work broaching the subject of 'the task of art,' or 'free theurgy.' He does, however, develop this strand of thought further in the appendix to the work, and especially in the numerous articles on the creative process, art and individual artists that continued to demand his attention up to his death.

The link between artistic creativity and the final stage of the threefold act — 'the *creative* incarnation, or realization, of the idea in real sensations' — is brought out in Soloviev's 1890 article 'The General Meaning of Art,' which he ends by defining art (*khudozhestvo*) as the 'realm of the incarnation of ideas as opposed to their initial conception and growth.'[24] In his article on the poet Aleksei Tolstoi, Soloviev makes the similar claim that the 'inspired artist, incarnating his contemplations in sensible forms, is the connecting link or mediator between the world of eternal ideas or first principles and the world

---

[23] Soloviev's thoughts on Schelling's 'intellectual contemplation' (*intellektuelle Anschauung*) appear in their fullest form in his encyclopaedia entry on Hegel. See SS, X, pp. 308-10.
[24] FI, p. 89.

of material phenomena.'25 The artist is thus involved not only in the production of art, but in the initial reception of that 'idea' which he is called to incarnate in word or image. In relation to poetry, to which Soloviev dedicated the majority of his writings on this subject,26 the following passage from his 1899 article 'The Meaning of Poetry in the Poems of Pushkin' makes this especially clear:

> The poet is not free (*volen*) in his creativity [...] The genuine freedom (*svoboda*) of creativity has as its preliminary condition passivity, a pure potentiality of mind and will. Freedom here belongs above all to those poetic forms, thoughts and sounds which themselves freely enter a soul ready to meet and receive them.27

Unlike philosophical or scientific formulae, according to Soloviev, 'artistic ideas and forms are not complex products of observation and reflection but appear to the intellectual gaze immediately in their inner integrity (the artist *sees* them, as Goethe and Hoffmann observed).'28 They arise and are sustained in neither the will nor the mind but in the soul. Commenting on the creative process depicted in certain poems of Pushkin, the philosopher writes of 'the dying of nature, the dying of corporeal life in the poet, and the awakening in him of poetry not as the activity of the mind but as the dispositions of a soul seized by lyrical agitation and striving to pour forth in free manifestation — free, i.e. not invented or composed.'29

The phrase 'creative feeling' (*tvorcheskoe chuvstvo*) appears for the first time in the appendix to *Critique*, 'On the Law of Historical Development.' In a note to his readers Soloviev explains that '"creative feeling" may seem a contradiction but it is clear that human being as

---

25   Ibid., pp. 492-93.
26   Although Soloviev had early on conceived of poetry as the most 'spiritual' of the arts, in his 1890 article 'On Lyrical Poetry,' he placed lyrical poetry in second place after music as the 'most direct revelation of the human soul.' By 1898, however, Soloviev had come to regard poetry as the 'highest art form,' which 'in its own way contains elements of all the other arts.' PSS, III, p. 337; FI, pp. 399, 533.
27   FI, p. 328.
28   S², II, p. 64. Soloviev corroborates his view that *Woe from Wit* is Griboedov's only significant work by the fact that 'he saw it in a dream before writing it.' FI, p. 87.
29   FI, pp. 327-28.

a finite creature cannot be an absolute creator, that is, create out of itself. Therefore its creativity necessarily presupposes the reception of higher creative powers in feeling.'[30] Contradiction or no, we are again faced with the typically Solovievian combination of passive and active elements in his portrayal of human agency; not only is passivity here the condition for activity, but both exist, as was the case in prophecy, in one integral act—'creative feeling.' A revealing passage from the philosopher's treatment of Pushkin's mission poem 'Prorok' (Prophet) further explores the efficacy of feeling in artistic endeavour:

> Genius does not furnish the poet with new feelings; it only strengthens previous feelings, raising them to a higher level, making the poet spiritually more perceptive and sensitive. And what does he perceive with this new sensitivity? Again nothing out of the ordinary; his heightened, regenerated (*pererozhdennye*) feelings do not help him to make up what does not exist, to invent something new, but only help him better to see and hear what is [...] Everything that already exists and is known to everyone stands before the spiritual perception of the poet, not in the way it is known but in the eternal power of its form, pierced through with light, down to the last speck of dust.[31]

Artistic creativity in Soloviev's handling does not involve innovation and novelty but rather an intensification of those 'dispositions of the soul,' experienced through feelings which unite the artist to her environment. The difference between the poetic vision and everyday perception is therefore not one of essence but of quality: the eye of the artist sees and feels the same things as does the prosaicist but the former's 'spiritual perception' is exceptional insofar as it pierces the merely phenomenal to sow in the object the ideal form available to her through contemplation and inspiration. This sense of exceeding the phenomenal to capture that aspect of the object which endures despite the ravages of time was for Soloviev the essence of lyricism.

---

[30] PSS, III, p. 337. Such feeling, as the prius of philosophical enquiry in the interpretation of the Romantics, was one of Hegel's principal targets for critique. The latter rejected the view that the 'Absolute is not supposed to be comprehended, it is to be felt and intuited; not the Notion of the Absolute, but the feeling and intuition of it, must govern what is said.' Hegel, *Phenomenology of Spirit*, p. 4.

[31] FI, p. 346.

> In order to capture and forever fix a single phenomenon in its ideal being, it is necessary to concentrate all the powers of the soul on it and in so doing to feel in it the concentrated powers of being; one must recognize its absolute value, see in it not just some thing, but the focus of everything, a sole specimen of the absolute.[32]

In these words we see the reflection of Soloviev's conception of faith as the self-giving to the other as the condition of all authentic cognition. But there is much more here besides; the cognitive leap of faith, the giving of self to other, is fleshed out by the assertion that true poetic vision is to be had through feeling in the other the 'concentrated powers of being,' a feeling-*in* that goes far beyond, for example, Schopenhauerian compassion as a feeling-*with*, which, though it claims 'immediate participation' in the suffering of another, nonetheless remains the exclusive movement of the I.[33] These two things — a concentration of the soul toward the object, and the feeling of that very power of concentration, or intensity, of being within the object — allow the artist, in Soloviev's scheme, to create out of the transitory things of this world a form that is enduring and eternal.

But such art as existed in the world contemporary with him represented Soloviev's ideal not on its own merit but only insofar as it pointed the way to a greater ideal that was still to come. Already in 1881, in his work *Spiritual Foundations of Life*, we find the mission statement for a new 'religious art' of the future, to which the philosopher gave the name 'theurgy,' and which was to occupy him for the rest of his life:

> The new religion cannot be only passive God-worship (θεοσέβεια) [...] but should become active God-action (θεουργία), i.e. the joint action of God and humanity for the re-creation of this latter from a carnal or natural state to spiritual and divine. This is not creation from nothing, but the transformation (*pretvorenie*) or transubstantiation (*presushchestvlenie*) of matter into spirit, carnal into divine life.[34]

---

[32] Ibid., p. 407.
[33] See A. Schopenhauer, *On the Basis of Morality*, Providence, RI, 1995, p. 144.
[34] Solov'ev, *Dukhovnye osnovy*, p. 98. θεοσέβεια (*teosebeia*) is a Hellenistic term occurring only once in the New Testament (1 Tim 2.10), which Augustine understood as synonymous with *pietas* and the 'worship of God.' See Augustine of Hippo, *The*

By the time Soloviev came to give his three speeches in memory of Dostoevsky, the notion that art was something more than depiction or social commentary, and that the art of the future would merge with religion as had its ancient ancestor, except this time in a conscious bond, had become firmly rooted in his thought. In the first speech, we find the following words:

> To depict does not yet mean to transform, and to expose is not yet to mend. Pure art raised humanity above the earth, and carried it to Olympic heights; the new art returns to the earth with love and compassion, not to be plunged into the darkness and evil of earthly life, since for this no art is needed, but to heal and renew this life. For this, one must be connected and close to the earth, and show love and compassion toward it, yet something more is also needed. For mighty action upon the earth, to convert and re-create it, one must attract and apply to the earth *unearthly powers*. Art, which has isolated and separated itself from religion, should enter into a new free union with it. Artists and poets should once more become priests (*zhretsy*) and prophets, but in another, more important and elevated sense: not only will the religious idea possess them, but they themselves will possess it, and consciously direct its earthly incarnations.³⁵

Enchiridion on Faith, Hope and Love, Washington, DC, 1996, p. 2. θεουργία (*teurgia*) is a term originating in the Chaldean Oracles written in the second century of the Common Era, which Soloviev may have read during his time at the British Library in London. Although the philosopher opposes theurgy to worship as 'active' to 'passive,' the Oracles rest instead on the opposition of theurgy and magic, the latter active and the former passive. As Ruth Majercik notes, 'theurgy emphasizes a passive attitude towards the gods (with the gods taking the initiative), whereas magic involves coercing or forcing the gods against their will [...] If magic is to be defined essentially as coercion, then theurgy can no longer be confused with magic, as both its intent (the salvation of the soul) and effect (a passive relation with the gods) are counter to magical practice as it is commonly understood.' R. Majercik, 'Introduction,' in *The Chaldean oracles: text, translation, and commentary*, Leiden, 1989, pp. 1-46 (p. 23).

35   FI, p. 231. Soloviev was clearly aware that the advocacy of an art form that did not yet exist might cause confusion amongst his readers. In his 1889 article 'Beauty in Nature,' to which stands the epigraph, modified from Dostoevsky's *Idiot*, '*красота спасаем мир*' (beauty *is* saving the world; the original statement, made by Prince Myshkin, is in the future tense — '*красота спасем мир*,' beauty *will* save the world), Soloviev writes that 'it would be a clear mistake to consider the methods and limits of artistic activity that exist today as final and absolutely compulsory [...] Even admitting that beauty is immutable, the volume and power of its realization in the form of a beautiful (*prekrasnyi*) reality has a multitude of stages, and there is no reason for the thinking spirit to come to a definitive rest on that stage we have managed

A little further on in the same speech, Soloviev states that there are as yet no representatives of this new art, yet in Dostoevsky it had found one of its most significant 'forerunners.'[36] The new art would not only be an expansion of the creative work of artists such as Dostoevsky, however; it would be the ultimate realization of the original strivings of nature itself, a new form of prophetic activity that would transfigure the world. As Soloviev writes, the 'aesthetic link between art and nature [...] consists not in repetition, but in the continuation of that artistic work which was begun by nature—in the future and fuller resolution of the same aesthetic task.'[37] Not only does the new art return to the earth with the goal of transfiguring it; it also continues that task begun at Creation, and of which the emergence of humanity and the God-man represented progressive stages. 'The task, unaccomplished by means of physical life, should be accomplished by means of human creativity.'[38] Despite Soloviev's reference to the application of 'unearthly powers' to earthly reality, therefore, the very attainment of such powers is to be understood as the ultimate realization of the strivings of the world order toward self-transcendence. It is thus possible to consider Soloviev's theurgy in the context of human artistic endeavour and natural beauty—as the final, conscious stage in an integral schema of universal creativity—and to make conclusions about its nature deriving from an aesthetics rooted in both.

Soloviev's mention of 'pure art' in his first Dostoevsky speech, and the distinction he draws between it and the engaged character of the new art, prefigures his later description of Pushkin as a 'pure poet.'[39] Soloviev's negative assessment of such 'pure art' is evident both in the Dostoevsky speeches, and *Lectures on Theanthropy*. In the latter, echoing his comments on pure art he describes Plato's ideal of human activity as one in which the human being 'constantly *dies* to practical life, i.e. abides in a state of pure contemplation of eternal ideas, excluding

---

to attain at the present historical moment, even though this moment has already lasted millennia.' FI, p. 32.
36 Ibid., p. 232.
37 Ibid., p. 74.
38 Ibid., p. 82.
39 Ibid., p. 348.

any active striving, any actual will.'⁴⁰ It is this utter removal of art, as such, from the vain world of human affairs that the early Soloviev saw as typical of the approaches of both 'pure philosophy' and 'pure art': the discarding of the real in favour of the ideal. Just as his attitude to the idealism of Plato underwent a subtle change, though, so did his understanding of 'pure art.' Emphasis shifted away from the products of creativity to the artist as creator. Accordingly, Soloviev re-evaluated the merits of pure art, and particularly the pure poetry of Pushkin, coming to see in it art's very essence. Poetry, wrote Soloviev, should 'serve the work of truth and good on earth, but only in its own way, by its beauty alone and nothing else.'⁴¹ While such was the demand for art, however, there appeared a different, radical demand for the artist herself.

In a late review article on Aleksei Tolstoi, Soloviev writes that Tolstoi, 'as poet, proved that one can serve pure art without separating it from the moral meaning of life, that this art should be pure from anything base and false but in no way from ideal content and practical meaning.'⁴² It was this separation of the poetic art from the realm of morality that the philosopher judged to be one of the major flaws of Pushkin, and which explains much of the negativity Soloviev read into Pushkin's character and biography.⁴³ But it is in his article on the poet Fedor Tiutchev that Soloviev's view on the importance of the inner life of the artist comes across most clearly, and which puts into perspective much of his negative coverage of Pushkin. Having talked about the 'consonance' of Tiutchev's inspiration with the 'life of nature,' his 'perfect reproduction of physical phenomena as conditions and activities of the living soul,' Soloviev goes on to comment:

> The advantage of Tiutchev over many [poets and artists] consists in the fact that he fully and consciously *believed* in that which he felt — he accepted and understood the living beauty he sensed not as his fantasy

---

[40] S², II, p. 69.
[41] FI, p. 321.
[42] Ibid., p. 505.
[43] See especially Soloviev's 1897 article 'Pushkin's Fate,' which provoked outrage amongst Russian literary circles at the time. FI, pp. 271-300. See, for example, V. V. Rozanov, 'Khristianstvo passivno ili aktivno?' in *Religiia. Filosofiia. Kul'tura*, Moscow, 1992, pp. 143-53.

but as *truth* [...] In Tiutchev [...], the dearest and most important thing is that he not only *felt* but *thought* as a poet [...] The conviction in the authenticity of the poetic vision of nature, and the integrity of his work that derives from it, the harmony between thought and feeling, inspiration and consciousness, place Tiutchev above even such a significant poet-thinker as Schiller.[44]

It is not difficult to spot Soloviev's threefold act of cognition — faith, imagination, creative incarnation — at the root of his argument in this passage. Tiutchev is esteemed not only for the intensity of his poetic vision, his lyrical feeling, but for his belief in the objective veracity of such feeling, and the sympathy he achieved between feeling and thought. Such poetic consciousness he places in opposition to those 'devotees of beauty who do not believe in their work,'[45] amongst whom he numbers the early Symbolists and, most controversially, Pushkin.[46] Soloviev's critique of the former, however, should not be confused with that of the latter. Whereas he viewed the Symbolists simply as bad poets,[47] there is no doubting his unparalleled estimation of Pushkin. Indeed, in all of Soloviev's late writings on Pushkin one intuits a deep sense of disappointment flowing not from his inadequate appreciation but precisely the extraordinary value he gave to Pushkin's poetry. Pushkin and Plato, the two obsessions of his late period, were tragic figures for Soloviev not because the body of work they left was somehow deficient, but because the ideal present in their work remained merely that — ideal — without producing qualitative changes in lived reality. In Pushkin's case, not only had he, according to Soloviev, felt more purely

---

44 FI, pp. 466, 468, 473.
45 Ibid., p. 471.
46 Commenting on Pushkin's poem 'Ia pomniu chudnoe mgnoven'e' (1825), Soloviev wrote that 'at the moment of creativity Pushkin actually experienced what is conveyed in these lines; he really saw the genius of pure beauty, he really felt in himself the rebirth of the deity. But this ideal reality existed for him only at the moment of creativity. Returning to life, *he immediately stopped believing* in the illumination he had experienced, he immediately acknowledged in it only a trick of the imagination — an ennobling trick (*nas vozvyshaiushchii obman*) yes, but a trick all the same, and nothing more' (my emphases). FI, p. 279.
47 See Soloviev's 1894 article, complete with pastiches, 'Russian Symbolists.' Ibid., pp. 506-17.

that anyone before or after the living form of beauty but, in his poem 'Prorok,' he had attained 'that height, in that most refined and rarefied atmosphere of thought, where the essence of the poetic vocation draws near and merges with the purest essence of the prophetic vocation.'[48] Yet he had not realized his prophetic vocation, leaving instead to future generations merely the remembrance in poetic form of the mission he received at the height of inspiration, a mission which in Soloviev's view had not transitioned into reality. For all its apparent peculiarity, Soloviev's argument should be understood as revolving around the audacious claim that, had Pushkin truly lived out his vocation, he could have changed the world in its very essence: the poet could have become the first theurgist.

Still, the art of today held great significance for Soloviev in that it 'anticipates, allows one to feel in advance the otherworldly reality that is to come and thus serves as a connecting link between the beauty of nature and the beauty of the future life.' In this context, the philosopher makes explicit the unity of art and prophecy, describing true art as 'inspired prophecy,' and a work of art as 'any perceptible depiction of any object or phenomenon from the perspective of its final state, or in the light of the future world.'[49] Yet this stage of the 'aesthetic task' was only the first in a threefold movement toward the 'beauty of the future age,' which Soloviev defines in 'The General Meaning of Art' as:

> 1) the direct objectification of those deepest inner attributes and qualities of the living idea, which cannot be expressed by nature; 2) the spiritualization of natural beauty and, through this, 3) the immortalization of its individual phenomena.

The art of today could only fulfil the first of these requirements, and neither the poem nor any other art form was to be the core model for Soloviev's new religious art. Instead of 'catching flashes of eternal beauty in our current reality and continuing them further,' the new art was to have as its object the entirety of the material world and its aim the

---

[48] Ibid., p. 353.
[49] Ibid., p. 83.

spiritualization and immortalization of each of its sundry phenomena. This art would not be involved in the production or communication of the ideal but in its incarnation in the real. For this creativity, everything depended on the soul and its mode of feeling. Through the intensity of feeling in the other 'the concentrated powers of being,' the religious artist would turn the sensual part of his being into the transformative focus of new life.

> A strong sensuality is the material of genius. As mechanical motion turns into warmth, and warmth into light, so the spiritual energy of creativity in its actual manifestation (in the order of time or process) is the transformation of the lowest energies of the sensual soul.[50]

Yet, just as Soloviev had characterized prophecy as that principle most open to misuse because of its essential freedom, so feeling and sensuality are prone to turn away from their vocation as agents of the spirit.

> Instead of serving as the buttress and weapon for the activity of the soul, instead of incarnating in the sensual realm the content of good and truth, giving it the form of beauty, our sensual soul gives itself to the blind and boundless striving of carnal life, which has no aim but only one external end — in death and decay. [51]

Such, for Soloviev, was the law not of the sinful few but of fallen humanity as a whole. If the act of cognition was predicated on the threefold, metaphysical and pre-conscious movement of faith, imagination and creative incarnation, the soul could and did lay claim to the final stage of cognition as uniquely its own, separate from faith and imagination, precisely because in the temporal order sensuality and sensation appeared not as the last but as the very first, primary data of consciousness given in the immediacy of lived experience. The goal now, according to Soloviev, was to step into a new, conscious faith that would inform feeling since, as he writes in *Meaning of Love*, it is 'only through consistent acts of conscious faith that we enter into a real

---

[50] Ibid., p. 276.
[51] Solov'ev, *Dukhovnye osnovy*, p. 67.

correlation with the realm of the truly existent and, through this, into a true correlation with our "other".[52] It is here that faith as a conscious act becomes synonymous in Soloviev's thought with faith in God. 'I am able to recognize the absolute significance of a given individual, or believe in her (without which true love is impossible), only by affirming her in God and, accordingly, believing in God herself as well as my own self as having in God the focus and root of my being.'[53] What we had described as the leap of faith allowing the 'feeling in the other' as the basis of real cognition, when transitioned into conscious belief, becomes the discovery that the feeling of unity between subject and object, self and other, given in sensation has its source in God as their shared transcendental ground, from where derives the striving through imagination and feeling to make of such sensation an enduring rather than a transitory presence. Such a condition becomes not only a feeling in the other but a feeling in God as the ground of the other. As such, it has much in common with Abraham Heschel's concept of 'prophetic sympathy,' which he describes as

> a feeling which feels the feeling to which it reacts—the opposite of emotional solitariness. In prophetic sympathy man is open to the presence and emotion of the transcendent Subject [...] Sympathy, which takes place for the sake of the divine will, and in which a divine concern becomes a human passion, is fulfilment of transcendence.[54]

Heschel goes on to differentiate sympathy from the imitation of God insofar as the former involves assimilation into the immediate, emotional life of what he calls the 'divine pathos.'

> Sympathy, whose object is an inner spiritual reality, is a disposition of the soul. The prototype of *imitatio* is an unchanging model; a constant traditional knowledge of it indicates a ready path to be followed. Pathos, on the other hand, is ever changing, according to the circumstances of the given situation. The content of sympathy is not fixed by any predetermination. What is abiding in it is simply the orientation toward

---

[52] S¹, II, p. 537.
[53] Ibid., p. 532.
[54] Heschel, *The Prophets*, p. 396.

the living reality of God [...] In sympathy, divine pathos is actually experienced in the moment of crisis; in *imitatio*, the fixed pattern is transmitted.⁵⁵

It was through such feeling in God or, to take it in its passive expression, participation in the divine pathos, that Soloviev's theurgy was to operate. Through such participation, human beings would become co-creators with the divine, 'channels of the grace of God'⁵⁶ onto the created order. To repeat, for Soloviev this was not a matter of absolute creation since the grace of God was not subject to change in itself, but of an increasing correlation with the kenotic life of God given in grace: the human being, he wrote, 'should only open a free path for grace, remove those obstacles which separate us and our world from the existent good.'

The significance of feeling as a mode of approaching, knowing or experiencing the divine permeates the pages of Soloviev's magnum opus, *Justification of the Good*. As a treatise in ethics, the work departs quite substantially in approach, though not in substance, from his earlier practical ethics in *Spiritual Foundations of Life*. Soloviev begins the latter by outlining three anthropological strategies as the 'principles' of ethical living:

> The task of religion is to repair our unnatural life. For we live irreligiously, inhumanely, in slavery to lower nature. We rebel against God, we alienate ourselves from our neighbours, we submit to the flesh. But for true life, that which should be, exactly the opposite is required: voluntary submission to God, solidarity with one another and rulership over nature [...] The principle of voluntary submission or concord with God is prayer, the principle of solidarity amongst people is charity, the principle of rulership over nature is liberation from its power through abstinence from the basest desires and passions.⁵⁷

This threefold relation of the ethical subject to that which is higher than it (God), that which is equal with it (other humans) and that which is below it (nature), is retained in *Justification of the Good* yet

---

55 Ibid., pp. 412, 413.
56 Solov'ev, *Dukhovnye osnovy*, p. 66.
57 Solov'ev, *Dukhovnye osnovy*, p. 19.

with a significant modification. In *Spiritual Foundations of Life*, moral value is posited in the externality of the act; prayer, charity and abstinence are understood as containing in themselves the power of unity between humanity and God, humans and fellow humans, and humans and nature respectively. In *Justification of the Good*, Soloviev argues for something more primary than the act, building his argument instead on three 'feelings,' innate to the human subject, which contain in embryonic form the entire content of ethical norms and behaviour, namely shame, pity and reverence:

> The fundamental feelings of *shame, pity* and *reverence* exhaust the realm of humanity's possible moral relations to that which is below it, that which is equal to it and that which is higher than it. *Rulership* over material sensuality, *solidarity* with living creatures and inner, voluntary *submission* to the suprahuman principle — these are the eternal, unshakeable foundations of the moral life of humanity [...] All other phenomena of moral life, all so-called virtues, can be understood as modifications of these three foundations or as the result of the interaction between them and the intellectual aspect of the human being.[58]

The same relation of the human being to the three spheres — below, equal to, and above — persists, yet here unity is achieved through the experiential immediacy of these three feelings occuring at a pre-conscious level.[59] Abstinence, charity and prayer are but the transition of the discovery of such unity into conscious acts. Particularly interesting is Soloviev's treatment of reverence (*blagogovenie*), which he also calls 'piety' (*blagochestie*) or 'religious feeling,' and which 'constitutes in humanity the moral foundation of religion and the religious order of life.'[60] At one level, reverence as it appears in his ethical framework

---

[58] S¹, I, p. 130.
[59] This is the essence of what Edward Swiderski has called Soloviev's 'virtue epistemology.' There is, Soloviev asserted, a pull toward the good in the primary data of consciousness itself, a fundamental interconnection between epistemic and moral truth. In this light, Swiderski reads the late *Theoretical Philosophy* as an 'attempt to demonstrate that if we are properly attuned to the intrinsic union of our moral and cognitive states, we are able to experience, and can bring to insight, an innate attraction to the Good.' E. Swiderski, 'Vladimir Solov'ëv's "Virtue Epistemology",' *Studies in East European Thought*, 53, 1999, pp. 199–218 (p. 205).
[60] S¹, I, p. 129.

is really a rather simple thing: the 'feeling of recognition toward something higher than us, and on which we depend.'[61] We might define it simply as a primary sense, or intuition, of God as that superior being on whom all other being, including that of the cognitive subject, is sustained. But there is much more to reverence than may at first appear to be the case.

As the third component in another of Soloviev's all-pervasive threefold conceptual clusters, it is no surprise to find that it stands in a definite relation to its two preceding terms. Yet this relation is more complex than Soloviev's fundamental trichotomy of will-representation-feeling since all three terms in question are said to be feelings. In this sense, they differ not in their 'mode of being,' which for all three is 'feeling,' but in the content revealed in that feeling.

The content, or object, of shame, according to Soloviev, is that 'realm of our material being which, although enjoying a direct relation to the spirit by dint of its capacity to arouse (affect) the latter interiorly, does not however serve as the expression and weapon of spiritual life. On the contrary, through shame the process of purely animal life strives to draw the human spirit into its sphere, to subordinate or absorb it.'[62] Through abstinence, which stems from the conscious decision to act on the feeling of shame as recognition of the non-identity of the human with the animal, the human being raises itself above mere instinct, refusing to be only an animal. This is why Soloviev describes shame as the 'purely human' root of morality, 'in essence alien to the animal world.'[63] But such a removal from the sphere of base instinct is not the end of the moral path. For once the human has attained a degree of autonomy from nature, the feeling of pity brings another truth to bear; its content is not humanity's elevated status vis-à-vis nature but the solidarity of all living creatures.

> If the feeling of shame separates humanity from the rest of nature and opposes it to other animals, the feeling of pity, to the contrary, connects him with the whole living world, and this in a dual sense: firstly, since it

---

[61] Ibid., p. 184.
[62] S¹, I, pp. 138-39.
[63] Ibid., p. 133.

[i. e. shame] belongs to humanity *together* with all other living creatures and, secondly, because all living creatures should become the *objects* of this feeling for humanity.[64]

Unlike Soloviev's previous work, in which the task of humanity was derived from an absolute perspective, that is to say, from human nature in its double constitution as both divine and natural ('the Earth of God'), in *Justification of the Good* the task emerges from an experiential base—the primary data of consciousness.[65] Thus, from the dual influence of the feelings of shame and pity arises the awareness that their content contains a task that needs to be realized:

> Humanity is ashamed of the carnal path because it is the path of fragmentation, the *dissipation* of life's powers that leads to death and decay. If it is really ashamed of this, if he feels this as that which should not be, then this means it should take the opposite path of wholeness and concentration leading to immortality and sempiternity (*netlenie*). If, further, it really pities all that are similar to himself, the *goal* of this path is to achieve immortality and sempiternity *for all*.[66]

Notice here the stress on the actuality, and intensity, of the emotion (if humanty *really* feels), and the connection between the magnification of this intensity and the necessity of a transition into action. Yet the intensity of purely human feeling is not, by itself, enough to attain Soloviev's outlandish goal of 'immortality for all,' for he admits that such a goal must forever remain beyond purely human agency. At this stage, though, the philosopher asks: is humanity 'really separated by some sort of impenetrable wall from that which is higher than it?'[67] The answer he

---

[64] Ibid., p. 153. The significance of pity as an emotion which, as shared, draws human beings into correlation with other animals is a measure of the difference between Soloviev and thinkers of the Western canon. Rei Terada notes, citing Derrida's argument in *On Grammatology*, that 'while Rousseau grants pity to "all living beings," animal pity is too visceral to be a meaningful emotion; for Rousseau as for Hegel, "animality has no history because feeling and understanding are, at root, functions of passivity".' R. Terada, *Feeling in theory: emotion after the "death of the subject,"* Cambridge MA, 2001, p. 35.

[65] This tendency had, however, been present in a less sustained form in *Critique*, where for example Soloviev writes that the 'sensations themselves [...] are attracted to that ideal form' that the human subject places upon them in the act of cognition. PSS, III, p. 302.

[66] S¹, I, p. 235.

[67] Ibid., p. 236.

gives is, of course, negative, yet his approach in *Justification of the Good* is remarkable precisely because the justification he offers for such an answer is not metaphysical, flowing from the principle of theanthropy as the union of divine and human elements, but experiential: in the feeling of reverence is the direct experience of the transcendence of the human being in God.

> In the two moral areas identified by shame and pity, the good is already perceived as the truth and realizes itself in actuality, but only imperfectly. In the third area of moral relations defined by religious feeling, or reverence, the true object of this feeling makes itself known as the highest or perfect good, not only in the process of realization, but absolutely and completely realized—the eternal existent (*vechno-sushchee*).
>
> The inner foundation of religion does not consist only in the consciousness of our dependence on an immeasurably superior power to us; in its pure form the religious condition ultimately boils down to the joyful *sensation* that there *is* a being infinitely better than we ourselves, and that our life and fate, as well as all that exists, depends precisely on it—not on some kind of senseless fate, but on the real and perfect Good, which is one and contains all within itself.[68]

That 'the reality of God is not a conclusion from religious feeling (*oshchushchenie*) but the content of that feeling—that which is itself felt,'[69] had in a way always been the fundamental supposition of Soloviev's philosophy, behind which rested the experience of a religious visionary seeking conscious expression. Yet it was not until the philosopher's late years that the full measure of this supposition made itself felt. It is stated with particular force in his 1897 article on Spinoza, 'The Conception of God,' where Soloviev stresses that 'in contrast with theoretical discussions on religious subjects, in any actual religion the deity, i.e. the highest object of reverence or religious feeling, is directly recognized as given in experience.'[70]

The discovery of reverence as a way of expressing the givenness of religious feeling in *Justification of the Good* is of vital importance in

---

[68] Ibid., p. 248.
[69] Ibid., p. 251.
[70] SS, IX, p. 15.

appreciating the late turn in Soloviev's work.[71] In it he finds a feeling in which there is already a merging of epistemic and moral elements, preconscious and conscious; reverence is understood as the experience of being sustained by something superior which itself is a kind of gratitude, a conscious thankfulness inhering in the very nature of things. As such, it precedes even faith as Soloviev's first component of cognition. Understood as givenness, or gift, reverence is thus a core ontological principle, and its conscious fostering by humanity the correlation of itself not only with God but with the whole creation. Seen, furthermore, as the continuation of that 'aesthetic task' begun in nature, reverence is the joining with the whole of the created order in offering praise to its Creator.[72]

As far as human beings are concerned, reverence is at once the pure acceptance of gift, as ontological foundation, and its conscious cultivation and realization. In other words, reverence too contains a task. In a passage that illustrates both Soloviev's continuing preference for a modified Hegelian discourse and the extent of his departure from Hegel himself, he writes:

> Grounded religious feeling demands from us not the negation and abolition of the world but only that we do not take the world as the absolutely independent principle of our life. Being in the world, we should not only ourselves become not of the world, but in this aspect should also act on the world in such a way that it too may cease to be of itself and become more and more of God.
>
> The essence of piety at the highest stage of universal consciousness consists in recognizing absolute worth in God alone, and only in connection with Her evaluating everything else as having a potentially absolute value, not in and of itself, but in and of God. *Everything becomes worthy by establishing its positive correlation with the One who is worthy.*[73]

---

[71] Reverence is mentioned in *Spiritual Foundations of Life* but has a mainly negative connotation as an inferior mode of feeling that leads to contemplative, rather than active, asceticism. See Solov'ev, *Dukhovnye osnovy*, p. 57.

[72] The idea that nature offers praise and thanksgiving to its Creator is particularly strong in the prophetic and Wisdom traditions, especially the Psalms. See, for example, Psalm 96 or Isaiah 55.12. See also T. E. Freitheim, 'Nature's Praise of God in the Psalms,' *Ex Auditu*, 1987, 3, pp. 16-30.

[73] S^1, I, p. 507.

In such a way, reverence, here called piety, becomes the lived realization, through feeling, of God's superiority to any concrete definition or framework, whether that be the dialectical movement of the human spirit or the historical unfolding of the cosmic process. In this sense it is a living in mystery much like the reverence that William Desmond sees as characteristic of a past era, and which he describes as 'a certain porosity to the elusive mystery of things, and most especially the enigma of human being, and the *nec plus ultra* of mystery, God.'[74] The development of reverence in *Justification of the Good* thus prefigures the emergence of the apocalyptic turn in Soloviev's last years, when God, as portrayed in *Short Story*, would break in on history as the one who is eternally beyond the process of becoming.

Reverence was not for Soloviev merely an intuition of the divine but the real experience of, and participation in, God, as had through feeling. Unlike the reverence of the ancients, whose conscious element was swallowed up in the deity and had thus remained passive, pseudo-magical knowledge of the divine, the new reverence was to be defined by an active relation of the individual to the object of its feeling—God. The subjective, interior state involved in the feeling of reverence, through the conscious attention of the individual, transitions into a free love for its object, which in its turn partakes of love, and gives of its own. It is with this sense of a journey embarked upon by the individual on the basis of the primary fact of reverence that Soloviev sums up the essence of his message in *Justification of the Good*.

> To condense the whole content [of *Justification of the Good*] to one sentence, we find that the perfect Good is ultimately defined as the inseparable organization of triune love. Having perceived its object as infinite perfection, the feeling of reverence, or piety, at first through a timid and involuntary, then a free filial submission to the higher principle, turns into pure, all-embracing and limitless love for it,

---

74 W. Desmond, *Is there a sabbath for thought?* New York, 2005, p. 4. 'Does what we call the desire to know, in its different forms,' Desmond asks in another article, 'have its roots in a more primal ontological reverence: a reverence not fixed on, confined to the determinate intelligibility of what is, but in attunement to the good of being, the glory of creation, the gift of the "to be"?' W. Desmond, 'On the Betrayals of Reverence,' in *Is there a sabbath for thought?* New York, 2005, pp. 262-88 (p. 268).

predicated solely on the recognition of its absolute nature — *amor ascendens*. But, conforming itself to its all-embracing subject, this love embraces in God everything else as well, first of all those who can, with us, equally participate in it, i. e. human beings; here our physical, then our moral-political pity, toward people becomes spiritual love for them, or *equalization (uravnenie) in love*. But the divine love assimilated by humanity, as all-embracing, cannot stop even here; becoming *amor descendens*, it acts on material nature too, to bring it into the fullness of absolute good, as the living throne of divine glory.[75]

This 'filial love,' likely deriving from the Pauline notion of adoption by God,[76] was also referred to in *La Russie et l'église universelle* in Soloviev's discussion of natural sonhood as analogous to growing into a maturity of relation to God. There the philosopher writes of the relation of son to father as, first, one of dependence like that of a small child; secondly, obedience like that of a youth; and thirdly, 'filial respect, the free feeling of reverence and mutual friendship' as a mature human would feel.[77] In a similar way, the freedom of mature reverence toward God possesses the soul to such a degree that the interiority of its feeling for itself becomes the dwelling in a love that exceeds the merely subjective[78] and embraces not only the sphere of other conscious creatures but the entire material order. The spiritualization of matter, then, becomes the work of a triune love, realized by a conscious humanity centred in God, or God as divinized humanity, and as final stage *amor descendens*.

---

[75] S¹, I, pp. 547-47. These three types of love are given further definition by Soloviev in his encyclopaedia entry 'Love': 1) love which gives more than it receives, or *descending love* (amor descendens), 2) love which receives more than it gives, or ascending love (amor ascendens), 3) love in which both parties are equal (amor aequalis). SS, X, p. 236.
[76] See Romans 8.23; Gal 4.5.
[77] SS, XI, p. 331.
[78] 'Love is that force which leads us interiorly out of the bounds of our given consciousness, unites us in an unbreakable bond with All and, making us real sons of God, makes us participants in the fullness of His essential Wisdom and sharers in His spirit.' Ibid., p. 346.

Chapter IV
THE LAST THINGS

The last period of Soloviev's life was one of both remarkable intensity and remarkable variety. Many of the themes that the philosopher had developed in his early and middle periods are approached with a renewed vigour and focus; previously diverging directions in thought are integrated, and new ones discovered in their interaction. In *The Life Drama of Plato* (1898) and his work on the Platonic dialogues, Soloviev brings to consummate expression his relation to one of the two great influences in his philosophical development; and, in *Theoretical Philosophy* (1897-99), he articulates the fruit of lifelong reflection on the other — Hegel. All of this receives peculiar illumination, not the shadow of eclipse, in the context of the pathos of the end in which *Three Conversations* and *Short Story of the Antichrist* (1900) are written. Far from breaking with his previous output, the works of the period from 1897 to his death in 1900 represent an intensification of the foundational impulse with which his philosophy began — the intuition of the unity of the spiritual and material realms — as well as a strengthening of the desire to externalize that intuition in immortal form.

Soloviev's brand of religious philosophy had always exhibited a strongly eschatological thrust: the first principles of being and creation had place only insofar as they lead to knowledge of how to act in relation to what *is*; when what *is* proved to be involved in a dynamic process of becoming, such action became the correlation of the individual with the being that would become incarnate at 'the end.' In this last period, however, the philosopher's embracing of the pathos of the end results in a subtle shift in his understanding both of the linearity of the historical process and of the correlation between the individual and universal components of the task of the spiritualization of matter.¹ The core of this change rests in his eschatology, and is best explored through an investigation of two phenomena which in one way or another exerted a definitive influence on the course of Soloviev's life and work: love and beauty.

LOVE

There can be little doubt that Soloviev's thought on love is the most controversial aspect of his legacy. In the early, unpublished *La Sophia*, in mediumistic script, we find a statement which, though more explicit than anything in the published work, finds echoes right up to his mature period. 'God loves everything, nature,' he wrote, 'with a direct and real love, as a man loves a woman with whom he is in love, since the relationship is the same: nature is the other half of God himself. Thus, the universal love of God is identical to natural or sexual love.'² On the basis of this and many analogous proclamations, Sergii Bulgakov, though mitigating his charge by claiming that it sits poorly with Soloviev's theology as a whole, talked of the philosopher's 'sexualization of the Eternal Feminine' and the 'fateful incursion of carnal sensuality into the spiritual realm.'³

While Soloviev clearly perceived and did his best to remain faithful to the 'subtle but precise line separating corporeal beauty from carnal' in his ideal of 'spiritual corporeality,'⁴ it seemed to most that this line

---

1. If this development can be understood as a transition from what biblical scholars call 'prophetic eschatology,' the optimistic view according to which God will restore the Earth through historical processes, to 'apocalyptic eschatology,' the pessimistic perspective whereby the future 'breaks in on' the present, it is only with significant reservations. The principal characteristics of apocalyptic, which David Aune defines as the 'temporal dualism of the two ages' and the 'radical discontinuity between this age and the next, coupled with pessimism regarding the existing order and otherworldly hope directed toward the future order,' can only be attributed to Soloviev based on a grave misunderstanding of his later work. See D. Aune, 'Apocalyptic,' in *Westminster Dictionary of New Testament and Early Christian Literature*, Louisville KY, and London, 2003, pp. 46-50 (p. 48).
2. PSS, II, p. 69.
3. S. N. Bulgakov, 'Muzhskoe i zhenskoe v Bozhestve,' in S. N. Bulgakov, *Religioznyi-filosofskii put'*, ed. A. P. Kozyrev, Moscow, 2003, pp. 343-65 (p. 357).
4. FI, p. 84.

was so elusive as to be practically indiscernible. The philosopher, who believed himself to have outdone Plato in safeguarding the crown of the celestial Aphrodite Uranios from the vulgar Aphrodite Pandemus,[5] and who reproached Pushkin for allowing his 'genius of pure beauty' to become the Whore of Babylon,[6] could not protect himself or his legacy from similar accusations in his direction. We are not so much concerned, however, with how far his divine Sophia avoids the tarnish of carnal sensuality, as with the problem that arises from his resolution of the role of humanity in the eschatological task of the spiritualization of matter, the final union of the heavenly and the earthly. This problem, to state it in its simplest terms, consists in the fact that both the disunity of spirit and matter that characterizes the fallen world and humanity and their ultimate reunification and restoration in the Kingdom of God are conditional on a kind of sensual desire, each differing according to its goal. Desire is the reason for the split, desire the ground for their reunification. Describing the results of the Fall, Soloviev writes:

> The kingdom of death is established; heaven and earth are separated by the human's desire immediately and materially to possess earthly reality, finite existence; humanity desired to experience and savour everything in external feeling. It desired to unite its heavenly spirit with the dust of the earth in an external and superficial bond. But such a bond cannot last, and necessarily leads to death.[7]

Soloviev's argument here is in no way unique to him. It resonates with many Gnostic sources, as well as the work of various Christian mystics, which posited primordial desire on the part of the World Soul as the cause of the Fall. But it is in the means the philosopher promotes as effecting the eradication of death, which consists in a kind of non-

---

[5] S¹, II, p. 534; PSS, II, pp. 209-10, 369. The myth of the two Aphrodites, one base and one exalted, is found in Pausanius' speech in Plato's *Symposium*. See Plato, *Symposium*, ed. C. Gill, London, 1999, pp. 12-13.

[6] FI, pp. 277-78. Soloviev makes much of the fact that, in an 1826 letter to Aleksei Vul'f, Pushkin described Anna Kern, once the inspiration for his most elevated poetry, as the 'Whore of Babylon.' A. S. Pushkin, *Pis'ma*, ed. B. L. Modzalevskii, 3 vols, Moscow, 1989, II, p. 10.

[7] SS, XI, p. 347.

continuous analogue of the very erotic desire that led to the Fall, that his approach diverges from both. In his middle period, the erotic thematic is largely concealed so that, while love had been consistently presented as the eschatological means of the reunification of spirit and matter from early on, its precise determinations were not immediately evident in Soloviev's published work until much later. In the following passage from *La Russie et l'église universelle*, for example, Soloviev gives his reader a reasonable idea of his eschatological goal but speaks in very general terms about the nature of the love by which it is achieved:

> To gain victory over death, humanity should join itself with all, not superficially in its sensuality, but in the absolute centre which is God. The universal human is reunited by Divine love, which not only elevates humanity to God but, identifying itself interiorly with God, gives it the possibility to embrace in Her all that is, i.e. uniting itself with the whole creation in an indissoluble and eternal bond. This love brings down the grace of God onto earthly nature and celebrates victory not only over moral evil, but over its physical consquences — illness and death — as well. The work of this love is the final Resurrection [...] The circle of universal life closes with the resurrection of flesh, the reunification of humanity in its wholeness, the final incarnation of Divine Wisdom.[8]

Much of what Soloviev writes here will be familiar based on our previous exposition. We have followed how the philosopher conceived the prophetic displacement of the centre of human being to God through feeling, a movement that we further traced through reverence to *amor ascendens*, a desire for God as the absolute source of all being. In this section, it is the nature of this final, descending love — the bringing down of the grace of God onto all creation — that concerns us; that is, love as the eschatological principle whose 'work' Soloviev posits as the 'final Resurrection.'

Christian thought has traditionally conceived of the movement of love as founded on a duality, the ascending love of humanity to God and the descending love of God to humanity, which encounter each other most completely in the Incarnation, which is thus their realized union.[9]

---

[8] Ibid., pp. 347-38.
[9] See P. Evdokimov, *The Sacrament of Love: The Nuptial Mystery in the Light of the Orthodox Tradition*, Crestwood NY, 1985, p. 79.

Amor ascendens, which rises from lower to higher as a kind of reverential desire, was associated with *eros* — a worldly, creaturely love which seeks its own fulfilment — and *amor descendens*, the gracious love of the Creator God that gives without thought of gain, with *agape*.[10] As a consequence, while the initial ascent of the individual believer into the realm of divinity may have been predicated on the winged flight of Eros, upon reaching its destination erotic love was of necessity purified of all that was fleeting, particular, self-deriving, and drawn into the self-giving, sacrificial movement of agapeic love. The Christian scriptural canon itself has no place whatsoever for the Hellenistic concept of *eros*, which occurs nowhere in the Greek New Testament or the Septuagint translation of the Hebrew Bible, nor does it feature in any substantial way in the writings of the early Church Fathers.[11] Twentieth-century theology, particularly in the reformed tradition, has largely cemented the antithesis between *eros* and *agape*, resulting in the almost wholesale rejection of the former.[12]

---

10   The other word for love encountered in the Bible and early Christian literature is *philia*, which is often compared to brotherly love, or friendship. It is interesting to note that the triumvirate of the great theological minds of late-nineteenth and early-twentieth-century Russian culture — Soloviev, Bulgakov, and Pavel Florenskii — were evenly split over which kind of love to regard as the most essential. If Soloviev gravitated toward *eros* and Bulgakov toward *agape*, Florenskii found the closest representation of his ideal in *philia*, which he saw as corresponding most exactly to the meaning of the Russian *liubit'*. See P. Florenskii, *The Pillar and Ground of the Truth*, Princeton, 1997, pp. 286-89.

11   'Even in the apostolic fathers we find only a single occurrence of eros (Ignatius, ad Rom. 7.2), and here it is used only to denote the love which the author declares that he has left behind him as crucified.' K. Barth, 'Agape and Eros,' in *Church Dogmatics: A Selection*, Louisville & London, 1994, pp. 173-93 (p. 177). In *Beyond Good and Evil*, Nietzsche saw the contemporary association of the erotic with sin as having its source in Christian tradition: 'Christianity gave Eros poison to drink; he did not die of it, certainly, but degenerated into vice.' F. Nietzsche, *Beyond Good and Evil*, New York, 1989, p. 131. Bulgakov, however, mentions Symeon the New Theologian and Gregory Palamas as later fathers who incorporated a positive interpretation of *eros* into their writings. See S. N. Bulgakov, *The Comforter*, Grand Rapids MI, 2004.

12   See, especially, A. Nygren, *Agape and Eros*, London, 1953. Karl Barth, though diverging from Nygren's antithetical juxtaposition of *agape* and *eros*, is just as categorical in his condemnation of *eros*, and its incompatibility with *agape*: 'Erotic love is a denial of humanity [...] *Agape* cannot change into *eros*, or *eros* into *agape*.' Barth, 'Agape and Eros,' p. 189.

Yet, as Soloviev demonstrates in his article on love for the Brockhaus-Efron Encyclopaedia, although the biblical lexicon avoids the term *eros*, there is a strong tradition of erotic symbolism in the biblical literature.[13] From the comparison of Israel's relation to God in the Hebrew Bible to that of lovers in the writings of prophets such as Hosea, the relation of the Church to Christ in the New Testament to that of bride to bridegroom in the book of Revelation, or the yet more overtly erotic language of the Song of Songs, the examples are many and wide-ranging. Christian mysticism, too, is abundant in erotic imagery, and one does not have to look far to find narrations of the mystic's erotic experience of God. Origen is one of the earliest such examples, and it is telling that Soloviev both in his lifetime and posthumously was compared with the early church father.[14] Yet, as Grace Jantzen points out, in Origen, as in the great majority of Christian mystics, 'the use of erotic imagery was at the expense of the valuation of real sexual relations. It used the language of passion, but forbade any actual physical passion in an effort to channel all desire away from the body and towards God.'[15] Even in contemporary attempts to recover the erotic and integrate human sexuality within a holistic vision of life based on a Christology open to the possibility of real passion, there remains an emphasis on the overcoming, or instrumentalization, of *eros* for purposes at least potentially incidental to its own vocation. Such an approach can be seen, for example, in Pope Benedict XVI's 2005 encyclical *Deus caritas est*, whose goal in large part was to reaffirm the rights of *eros* in Christian life. While he writes that the 'universal principle of creation — the *Logos*, primordial reason — is at the same time a lover with all the passion of a true love' wherein *eros* is 'supremely ennobled,' it is so precisely because 'at the same time it is so purified as to become one

---

[13] SS, x, pp. 236-37.

[14] Soloviev responded to real or imagined claims that he had, like Origen, castrated himself, in an obscene poem sent to Sergei Trubetskoi. 'K istorii odnoi druzhby,' pp. 20-21. In one of the earliest works on the philosopher (1st ed. 1902), Aleksandr Nikol'skii dubbed Soloviev the 'Russian Origen.' A. Nikol'skii, *Russkii Origen XIX veka Vl. S. Solov'ev*, St Petersburg, 2000.

[15] G. Jantzen, *Power, Gender and Christian Mysticism*, Cambridge, 1995, p. 91.

with *agape*.'¹⁶ Bulgakov himself, while positively reworking Soloviev's conception of *eros* as spiritual 'syzygy,' is extremely careful not to ignore the rights of *agape*. 'In the dual character of churchly love as *agape* and as *eros*,' he wrote in *The Comforter*, 'there is manifested the antinomic duality of the Christian path as ascesis and creative activity, of repentant humility and creative inspiration. Self-renunciation is realized in *agape*: an individual dies in his egoism in order to live in and by the whole. In *eros*, an individual, experiencing inspiration to the point of self-transcendence, ascends to creative self-revelation.'¹⁷ It was this path of Eastern ascesis that Nikolai Berdiaev believed Soloviev to have strayed from, seeing in the philosopher a model of Western mysticism, which he interprets negatively:

> Catholic mysticism is sensual [...] The imitation of the Lord's passion, the state of being in love with Christ — all this is possible only when Christ is an object outside and over the human being, an object of striving and not inwardly received [...] In the West, in Catholicism, there has always been not so much a marriage of humanity and God as the human being in love. And the great mission of the Catholic West has perhaps been to disclose the mystical truth about the state of being in love as a creative force.¹⁸

The most serious aspect of Berdiaev's accusation is not its numbering of Soloviev amongst the Catholic West — debate over the 'Orthodoxy' of the philosopher's thought is still very much a subject of debate —

---

16   Benedict XVI, 'Deus Caritas est,' 25 December 2005, <http://www.vatican.va/holy_father/benedict_xvi/encyclicals/documents/hf_ben-xvi_enc_20051225_deus-caritas-est_en.html> [accessed 18 July 2008]
17   Bulgakov, *The Comforter*, p. 322. Bulgakov's definition of prophecy earlier in the same work as the 'eros of the spirit' comes very close to Soloviev's own understanding of prophetic activity. But there are subtle differences. For Bulgakov, prophecy is an 'extremely active state of the spirit, in which the latter strives to meet the higher principle' and, for this reason, an 'extremely creative state of the human spirit' (p. 292). To turn into true divine-human activity, therefore, prophecy needs to accept the passivity given outside itself in the self-renunciation to God's agapeic love. Bulgakov's ideal thus lacks the particular concentration of the *entirety* of divine-human powers in the phenomenon of prophecy and theurgic creativity, with their indivisibility of active and passive components, that we find in Soloviev's work.
18   N. Berdiaev, 'Problema Vostoka i zapada v religioznom soznanii Vl. Solov'eva,' in *Kniga o Vladimire Solov'eve*, pp. 355-73 (pp. 365, 366).

but rather the judgment it makes on his theanthropic project. The kind of erotic mysticism pursued by Soloviev, argues Berdiaev, is by its very nature incapable of achieving that union between humanity and the divine on which his entire philosophy is premised.[19] The place of love, and most especially erotic love, in the theanthropic economy thus needs to be examined in detail to ascertain its precise character.

Soloviev's approach is notable not merely for its attempt, in his work *The Meaning of Love* (1892-94), to articulate a Christian philosophy of love that included its erotic and sexual aspects. It is so, primarily, for the extent that it actually diverges from the Christian model of love in favour of a modified Platonism centred on an eschatological interpretation of *eros*. Indeed, Soloviev does not even try to integrate *eros* into the broader landscape of agapeic love, and though in the early work there are nods to the need to purge love of its dæmonic energy, in the late work on eschatological and soteriological themes *eros* appears to act with autonomy. For Soloviev, the erotic was the highest incarnation of both human and divine love or, more exactly, of the divine-human love realized in Christ and, in the new era of the Holy Spirit, harnessed by a conscious humanity. His conception of love is thus almost wholly subsumed by its erotic aspect, with a role accorded to an agapeic residue only in its lower, less perfect manifestations.

Related to this, Soloviev's treatment of love is remarkable for its overwhelming emphasis on materiality. There may be times when Soloviev's discourse is inexact and contradictory, but his use of the phrase 'resurrection of the flesh' as opposed to 'resurrection of the body' to describe eschatological consummation is certainly not accidental. 'Only flesh is illumined and spiritualized; flesh is the necessary object of love,' he wrote in *The Meaning of Love*.[20] The only power that was capable of winning victory over death was a love that had as its object

---

[19] Ruth Coates largely follows Berdiaev in assigning Soloviev, again with negative ramifications, to the Catholic mystical tradition. See Coates, 'Mystical Union,' pp. 145-52. Adrian Pabst argues that the 'natural desire of all human and cosmic reality to surpass itself in the direction of the absolute,' far from being evidence of the object's location outside the desiring subject, is a 'sign that the absolute is always already related to the universe.' Pabst, 'Wisdom and the Art of Politics,' p. 126.

[20] S^1, II, p. 520.

that which was itself subject to death: the decaying, disintegrating flesh of the concrete human being. A love that directed itself at material phenomena in their ideal rather than actual materiality—that is, at the reality expressed by terms such as 'body,' which already contains a certain organization of spiritual forces over matter—might provide, in Soloviev's view, an ideal flight from death's fiat, but could never root it out at its core.[21]

In all Soloviev's writing on the nature and vocation of love, the importance of both the individual biography of Plato and his works, particularly the dialogues *Symposium* and *Phaedrus*, is impossible to overstate. His treatment of *eros* in *The Life Drama of Plato*, and the introduction to his translation of the Platonic dialogues, are thus key to an understanding of his philosophy of love and eschatology. He was drawn above all to the peculiar fact that, of all the many forms of love that were known to ancient Greece, Plato chooses the term *eros* for two of its seemingly most radically divergent manifestations.

> Greek is not lacking in words for love, and if such a master of thought and word as Plato, philosophizing on the highest manifestation of human life, uses an expression that relates to lower, animal passion, then it is clear that the whole contradiction in the direction of these two psychical movements—elemental-animal and spiritual-human—does not invalidate the real commonality of their foundation, immediate object, and material. Love, as erotic pathos—in its highest or lowest manifestation—is not at all like love for God, for humankind, for parents or homeland, for brothers or friends—it is essentially *love for corporeality*, and the only question is for what purpose? What is love really striving for in regard to corporeality: is it so that the same elemental facts of emergence and disappearance can be repeated without end, that same Hadean victory of chaos, death and decay? Or does it strive to introduce the corporeal into real life in beauty, immortality and sempiternity?[22]

---

[21] Soloviev's unenthusiastic description of *agape* as an 'ideal principle of spiritual and social union' in his encyclopaedia entry on 'Love' is illustrative of the general conclusion observed throughout his work: anything that is merely ideal, that is, which does not exert influence over the real, the material, is in essence powerless and unworthy of endorsement or praise. SS, X, p. 237.

[22] S¹, II, pp. 614-15.

The way in which Soloviev poses the question leaves one in no doubt that the proper response can only be the latter. All-encompassing love, love that carried out its mission to the end, could not reconcile itself with the inevitability of death; 'actually loving someone, it is impossible to reconcile oneself with the assurance of their destruction.'[23] Erotic love, as 'love for corporeality,' is the only love that can result in such radical realization.[24] Yet it holds within its essential nature the possibility of two radically divergent outcomes — death and immortality — and 'the contradiction between the two *erotes* is merely the contradiction between the moral and immoral relation to [corporeal] life and the corresponding contradiction between the goals and results of its activity in this life.'[25] In this way, the entire antinomic thrust of Soloviev's thought on spirit and matter is subsumed in *eros*, understood as both the source of their disunity and the potential source for their reunification. In the *eros* of humanity in its animal aspect, matter is uncoupled from spirit; in *eros* as spiritually ennobled, or as a moral rather than elemental power, it is spiritualized. If we cast an eye back to Soloviev's early metaphysics, we find that the desire for being-corporeality that he posited as the source of the Fall in the *materia prima* (Satan) turns out to be that same desire which, in its spiritualized form, restores the creation to wholeness and brings it to fulfilment. And it is that same 'flesh,' as the principle of sin, that Christ welcomes into his being (in both his eternal and historical kenoses) and then makes the foundation for the body of God.[26]

---

[23] Ibid., p. 520.
[24] 'The mediating energy of love,' writes Kornblatt, 'continually reenacts the Incarnation. Each act of erotic pathos is the incarnation of heavenly spirit into matter, creating, or "giving birth" to a new whole.' Kornbatt, 'Transifguration of Plato,' p. 44.
[25] S¹, p. 614. Compare Plato, *Symposium*, pp. 12-13.
[26] The parallels here between Soloviev and recent Catholic theology on this point are more than striking. See, especially, P. Riches, 'Deification as Metaphysics: Christology, Desire and Filial Prayer,' in P. M. Candler Jr and C. Cunningham (eds), *Belief and Metaphysics*, Nottingham, 2007, pp. 345-73. Riches, echoing Jean Daniélou's statement that Christ 'recapitulates' the sin of Adam 'on a higher plane,' writes: 'In the recapitulation of the Adamic-story, the reproduction of the false-sequela [sequela, here, means something like 'path' — OS] of death, becomes the Sequela of resurrection into deification by grace. The divinity Adam sought to take by force and by a misguided logic is, in Christ, revealed to be what God eternally wills the human to receive as gift' (p. 348). The distinction between Soloviev and theologians such as Henri de Lubac, whom Riches

Yet this ennobling of erotic love does not for Soloviev equate with its purification in *agape*. Rather, what we find in his work is not the instrumentalization of *eros* but its intensification, the realization of its essential nature, as such given fraudulently in the elemental thirst for corporeality. If it is to step into its true vocation, there is required of it a dual movement: firstly, the turning away from the purely corporeal and carnal to God as the source and rule of its being; and secondly, the turning back to the corporeal as the salvific object of divine love. If the ascending love of the human subject to God is erotic, the love of God uses this same human *eros* in its descent, only now working from its own centre through the medium of divinized humanity. It takes the moment of self-giving given in the winged movement of reverential love, and transforms it into another form of self-affirmation: still a desire to possess, but to possess absolutely, integrally and eternally. *Eros* for Soloviev is thus the environment for a multitude of movements and agencies; it is 'the transition, the means, and the bond between the two worlds: it combines within itself both ideal and sensual nature.'[27] It is that liminal creature whose duty it is to 'build a bridge between heaven and earth':[28] it is the first impulse to reach for heaven, the material of which the bridge is constructed, and the final bond itself. Most perplexingly, it is in *eros* too that the underlying impulse of Soloviev's philosophy—the kenotic giving away to the other, in Christian tradition associated above all with the agapeic function of love—is realized. The height of self-assertion coincides with the height of self-renunciation.[29]

The complexity of these movements consists in the fact that they are but one; 'true love is indivisibly *amor ascendens* and *amor descendens*,

---

focuses on, lies once more in the former's refusal to associate such desire with will, which for de Lubac was 'the fundamental depth of substance of the human human person, a depth in which desire and reason are united' (p. 349).

[27] SS, XII, p. 391.
[28] S¹, II, p. 611.
[29] Michael Meerson has noted the paradox involved in such movement. 'For Solovyov,' he writes, 'love is the self-negation of the subject, the assertion of the other, but through which he realizes his own supreme self-assertion, since true self-assertion is achieved only through self-negation.' M. A. Meerson, *The Trinity of Love in Modern Russian Theology: The Love Paradigm and the Retrieval of Western Medieval Love Mysticism in Modern Russian Trinitarian Thought (from Solovyov to Bulgakov)*, Quincy, IL, 1988, p. 31.

or those two Aphrodites which Plato did well to distinguish, but poorly to separate.'[30] Further, this unitary yet dual movement of the subject toward the other coincides with its goal: the ultimate destination of what Soloviev calls the 'erotic task'[31] is nothing other than *eros* itself, a dwelling in love that is the consciousness of itself in its own efficacy. It is to this identity of the various components of love, as well as their realization in an eschatological framework, that Soloviev gives the term 'erotic pathos' or the 'pathos of love.'

Although not abundantly present in the philosopher's discourse, the concept of pathos is surely the most crucial modification Soloviev brings to the Platonic theory of love, and has far-reaching consequences for his thought on human activity in the world. Although harking back to the division between pathos and ethos in Hellenistic thought,[32] it picks up elements of Hegel's treatment of pathos in his *Aesthetics*, and was certainly influenced by Belinskii's further development of the term.[33] The particular combination of pathos and love, however, seems to have emerged as strongly from the contingencies of the philosopher's

---

[30] S¹, II, p. 534. The idea that *eros* is an ontic unity rather than a duality, which manifests itself as a unitary agency operating from two directions, is developed by Proclus and Pseudo-Dionysius, for whom, as Nygren explains, Eros 'is no longer merely an ascending love, but also and primarily a love that *descends*.' There is thus a 'unitary force of Eros permeating the whole universe and holding all things together.' Nygren, *Agape and Eros*, pp. 570, 578; A. H. Armstrong, 'Platonic Eros and Christian Agape,' *Downside Review*, 1964, 79, 105-21 (pp. 115-17). In his encyclopaedia entry on Proclus, Soloviev signalled him out as unique among the Neoplatonists in that he did not follow them in regarding matter as 'an extreme weakening of divine emanation, something defective or nonexistent, [but] derived it from the intelligible principle of limitlessness.' SS, X, p. 486. John Rist suggests that Eros exhibited a distinctly agapeic function even earlier: 'in the tradition of Platonism from the time of Plato himself Eros is seen not only as an appetitive, self-centred power, but as expansive and generous.' J. Rist, 'A Note on Eros and Agape in Pseudo-Dionysius,' *Vigiliae Christianae*, 20, 1966, 4, pp. 235-43 (p. 235).

[31] S¹, II, p. 614. 'The principle of evil, i.e. exclusive self-affirmation, which had plunged everything that exists into primordial chaos,' wrote Soloviev in *Lectures*, 'now steps forward once again in a new form as the conscious, free activity of the individual human [...] Without the power of the self-affirming personality, without the power of egoism the very good in humanity is powerless and cold, only an abstract idea.' S², II, pp. 141-42, 150. 'The final goal is not the external limitation of evil, but its inner rebirth into good.' Ibid., p. 530.

[32] See Chapter III, note 134.

[33] See G. W. F. Hegel, *Aesthetics: Lectures on Fine Art*, 2 vols, Oxford, 1998, I, pp. 232-35.

biographical path, as well as his continuing reflection on the lessons to be taken from the lives of Plato and Pushkin, as it did from any purely intellectual influence.

In *Justification of the Good*, Soloviev writes that the 'pathos of love directs [humanity] onto the right path and the highest goal for that positive and abundant power that is contained within this pathos itself.'[34] In other words, such pathos not only leads its subject to a consciousness of the task but also gives her the necessary tools — itself — in order to realize it. Accordingly, if we associate love with feeling, as Soloviev does, pathos can be understood as a creative feeling whose motives are not blind to itself, a feeling not led by an elemental lust for the other but by a conscious desire for the other in God (or a desire for the other to be in God). In some of the last words he wrote, Soloviev pointed to the uniqueness of the pathos of love as spiritual-material event:

> The life of the soul is not exhausted by the interplay between ideal-theoretical strivings, raising it into the intelligible realm of pure forms, and material-practical stimuli, sinking it into the dark stream of deceptive 'flux' (*byvanie*). There is in the human being a fact and a factor, which cannot be reduced to the material nor the spiritual principle alone, but contains both indivisibly. Anyone who has experienced the quintessentially human pathos of personal love knows that one cannot attribute it in essence either to spiritual or to carnal needs, for both of these can be satisfied without this love, and that here we have to do with something particular, independent and intermediate, relating exactly neither to the one nor to the other aspect of our nature, but to its wholeness, or fullness.[35]

The pathos of love as state of consciousness has its own particular environment, reducible neither to the spiritual nor to the material, but containing both in their interaction, unity, or wholeness. Its strength as eschatological principle lies not in the universalization of its mandate, as if the object of human love could be a multitude of things simultaneously, but in its intensification.[36] 'The lover really sees

---

34 S¹, I, p. 230.
35 SS, XII, p. 390.
36 This represents a change from Soloviev's views on love in *Critique*, where he posits the need for the intensity of love to become correlated with the universality of its object. PSS, III, p. 43.

and visually perceives things which others do not,'[37] writes Soloviev; erotic love is therefore the 'most concentrated, most concrete, and thus the deepest and strongest: it is the true foundation and the general type of any other love.'[38] And it is this enhanced, concentrated vision, characteristic of individual love, that he posits as the condition for eschatological consummation. In adopting such a position, however, he is faced with the problem of explaining how this emphatically individual phenomenon relates not only to individual fulfilment but to that of the universe at a cosmic level.

If the meaning of the world is the 'inner unity of each with all,' writes Soloviev, then 'in the form of a living, personal power this unity is love.'[39] In other words, love is that determination at the core of the subject's being which positions it positively vis-à-vis the other, or unites its subject with the other. But this unity differs according to its kind. 'The quality of being-in-love differs from other types of individual human love — parental and childish, brotherly etc. — in particular,' writes Soloviev, 'by its indivisible unity of the spiritual and physical aspects.'[40] By this he means, firstly, that the object of erotic love is loved as much in its physical aspect as its spiritual aspect: the lover is 'attached to both with an identical intensity of feeling.'[41] Secondly, and most interestingly, he means that there is as much of the spiritual in the experience of erotic love as there is of the physical. To put it another way, in erotic pathos it is both the spirit ('God') and matter ('flesh') that are loving in equal measure; and, conversely, it is both spirit and matter that are being loved. Unlike the descending love of the parent toward child, which gives more than it receives, and the love of the child toward parent, which receives more than it gives, in erotic love the giving and the receiving are, as Soloviev puts it, 'balanced' (*uravnovesheno*). Thus, alongside the traditional conceptual pair *amor ascendens* and *amor descendens*, the philosopher introduces a third kind of love, representing their synthetic resolution: *amor aequalis*

---

[37] S¹, II, pp. 515-16.
[38] SS, XI, p. 346.
[39] Solov'ev, *Dukhovnye osnovy*, p. 87.
[40] S¹, I, p. 230.
[41] Ibid., p. 230.

(*equal love*).⁴² The significance of *amor aequalis*, which we submit as a synonym for the pathos of love, is that in it spirit and matter are united in human feeling.⁴³ Seen from this perspective, the pathos of love becomes the realization of the meaning of human nature as mediator between the spiritual and material realms, or the space of their concrete unity.⁴⁴

The most difficult question of all in regard to Soloviev's philosophy of love is how to characterize the ideal interaction between spirit and matter in erotic pathos taken in its eschatological aspect, and how this differs from the intensity of the erotic relationship as found in everyday life. The philosopher is insistent that his ideal does not involve a return to a purely ideal model of love outside sensuality.

> If *eros* is the striving of that which exists in material form toward ideal being, then this is not yet a striving to return to ideal being. In this latter everything is eternal and does not require fulfilment since it cannot lose

---

42   SS, x, p. 236. *Amor aequalis* appears to be a Solovievian innovation, although the phrase was used in connection with Emperor Valentinian I. See *The Jesuit Series*, ed. P. M. Daly and G. R. Dimler, 5 vols, Toronto, 2002, III, p. 94. It is possible that it had roots in early Gnosticism.

43   In this respect, Soloviev's erotic pathos differs from pathos in the Hegelian sense. For Hegel, pathos was 'an inherently justified power over the heart, an essential content of rationality and freedom of will [...] the essential rational content which is present in man's self and fills and penetrates his whole heart' or, as Geoffrey Mure has put it, 'a passionate absorption in fulfilling a one-sided ethical purpose.' Hegel, *Aesthetics*, p. 232; G. R. G. Mure, *The Philosophy of Hegel*, London, 1965, p. 192. Soloviev does not deny that pathos includes rationality, but argues that the heart is penetrated not by reason but by love. Further, this 'equal love' is the opposite of one-sided, subjective activity, representing instead the unity of opposing terms, the final break out of subjectivity.

44   Belinskii understood pathos precisely in terms of unity, both in the process of creation and as eternally realized. Pathos, he wrote in praise of Gogol''s *Dead Souls*, was what allowed the artist 'to let the phenomena of the external world pass through his *living soul*, thus breathing a *living soul* into them.' In an article on Lermontov, he spoke of that 'divine pathos which makes one's heart beat in unison with the cosmos [...] that divine pathos through which the terrestrial shines divine, the divine merges with the terrestrial, and all Nature appears in the brilliance of her wedding finery, an unriddled hieroglyph of the Spirit, now reconciled to her.' Cited in V. Terras, *Belinskij and Russian Literary Criticism: the Heritage of Organic Aesthetics*, Madison, WI, 1974, pp. 40, 84. Terras argues that Belinskii's concept of pathos is identical with Hegel's, 'though it somewhat overemphasizes the emotional side of artistic creation' (p. 137). This weight on the emotional aspect seems to us to be more important than Terras allows.

anything. The striving is not to find a way back to a form of ideal being but to realize the eternal form, the ideal essence in that material process from which this striving derives.[45]

Soloviev's great reproach to Plato was that the Greek philosopher had 'arrived with his mind and feeling at an understanding of the true task of life, both universal and personal,' but had turned out to be the 'greatest of the misfortunates' since 'he had not attached himself with his whole soul to the true task revealed to his mind,' preferring the contemplation of pure ideas to the exhortations of Eros. The extent to which Soloviev's ideal incorporated the physical aspect of human love can be seen from a sermon belonging to a Masonic priest in Aleksei Pisemskii's 1880 novel *Masons*, written by the philosopher at the novelist's request:

> Today, after the new Adam restored the spiritual union with the new Eve, that is, the Church, each separate person, becoming the image of this heavenly Adam, should even in his natural union with his wife have as its foundation the pure spiritual love which is in the union of Christ with the Church; then even in carnal togetherness not only will the heavenly light be retained, but the flesh itself will also be spiritualized, as the body of Christ was spiritualized. In this way we can channel and, through this, realize the union of God with nature that was restored in Christ in and through corporeal interaction itself, if only external union will be for us not a goal and not the first motive but only the extreme expression and final consummation of that inner spiritual unity of which the Lord himself said: 'that which God has joined, let no man separate.'[46]

Everything depended on this last condition, which guaranteed the purity of external, fleshly union as the 'final consummation' of the inner spiritual unity given in the pathos of love.[47] Soloviev's peculiar attitude toward the 'physiological aspect of the matter,'[48] as he squeamishly refers to it in *The Meaning of Love*, did not derive from any existential vacillation between the justification and repudiation

---

[45] Solov'ev, 'Lektsii po istorii filosofii,' p. 131.
[46] Solov'ev, *Pis'ma i prilozhenie*, Brussels, 1970, IV, pp. 308-308.
[47] Another important constituent to Soloviev's theory of love in its eschatological aspect is his development of Plato's myth of the androgyne, which was later taken up by the Kabbala, on which see J. D. Kornblatt, 'Solov'ev's Androgynous Sophia and the Jewish Kabbalah,' *Slavic Review*, 50, 1991, 3, pp. 487-496.
[48] S^1, II, p. 511.

of sexual union (as, for example, in the life and work of Leo Tolstoy), but rather from the very nature of his philosophical *eros*, which was both *summum malum*—the perpetuator of 'bad infinity,' the inflamer of carnal lust—and, at least potentially, *summum bonum*—the last fruit of spiritual-material consummation. It was this fateful proximity of good and evil that was to become embodied in his Antichrist, and it was, as we have argued, in the character of Antichristic love that he becomes known as such. There is thus an intrinsic contiguity between Soloviev's development of his philosophy of love and the apocalypticism of the last years. To become located in the pathos of love was to face the irreducible tension of a battle waged at a single pole: the pathos of love was the pathos of the end.

This concentration to an individual point of intensity, felt and intuited as pathos rather than attained by the mind, is the major change between Soloviev's middle and late periods. As is evident from an important letter of 1897 titled 'Two Streams,' the philosopher had indeed come to believe that the energies of his best years had been 'wasted on empty, or fantastical goals.'[49] Yet by this he did not mean theocracy per se but rather his previously held notion that any actual unity must be preceded by a realized social coherence on a universal level, a unified church or a theocratic society. This belief is shattered in the dénouement to *Short Story of the Antichrist* where a kind of radical disunity amongst temporal and spiritual powers, as well as amongst Christians themselves, is the backdrop to the apocalyptic realization of unity depicted in its last pages. By positing the locus of concrete unity in the pathos of erotic love, Soloviev reined in the circumference of the eschaton from the limits of the societal whole to a focus in the life of the individual. But this move away from expansive toward intensive realization, as he goes on to note in the 1897 letter, leads to great difficulties—the formulation of a 'paradoxical task,' the actualization of world meaning not only for the spirit, as it was in Hegel, but for a necessarily expansive material world. 'How is it,' Soloviev asks,

---

[49] SS, x, p. 47. The letter is the fifteenth in a series of twenty-two 'Sunday Letters,' written on different social and religious themes in 1897-98, and published as an appendix to *Three Conversations*.

'that by means of small powers an infinite, moral magnitude can be realized?'[50] He goes some way toward giving the answer by postulating the condition for the spiritualization, and resulting expansion, of the erotic impulse in an act on the part of the individual—described elsewhere as 'a spiritual-physical, theanthropic feat'[51]—which he characterizes in the following terms:

> That inner act, by which awakened passion is restrained from external expression, and the power of the soul, instead of dissipating itself in exteriority, is concentrated, absorbed within. Can this act, or this energy, really go nowhere? And, given that it has not turned into anything external, where then can it go except to the strengthening of the psychical being itself, food for its immortality [...] The external stream, which tries to take away our soul, should be counteracted not by stoic indifference but by a new feeling, answering good for evil and giving birth inside the soul to another, independent stream of movements and actions, ever more expanding and strengthening our being (*sushchestvo*).[52]

This may sound very much like a form of repression, but Soloviev is clear in *The Meaning of Love* that this act, identical with the energy of the pathos of love, is not only a subjective feeling—a turning inward—but also the beginning of an outward movement, the birth of a new, 'independent stream' of movements,[53] or 'real spiritual-

---

[50] SS, x, p. 47.
[51] S¹, II, p. 619.
[52] SS, x, pp. 49-50.
[53] Here Soloviev seems to part ways with Plato's theory of love, which Gregory Vlastos has described as 'fully sensual in its resonance, but denying itself consummation, transmuting physical excitement into imaginative and intellectual energy.' G. Vlastos, *Platonic Studies*, Princeton, 1973, pp. 22-23. In Soloviev, the energy produced from such movement is sensual both in resonance and effect. Aleksei Losev, however, saw a fundamental synchronization of views between Soloviev and the Plato of *Symposium* on the question of outer, physical consummation. 'Plato wants that kind of transfiguration of the world in which flesh would be pure, the flesh precisely of the spirit, and not an evil principle.' A. Losev, 'Eros u Platona,' in *Bytie, imia, kosmos*, Moscow, 1993, pp. 32-60 (p. 55). Olga Matich suggests that 'what Solov'ev prohibits is coitus, without, however, pathologizing sex. This is the paradoxical meaning of his erotic utopia and one of the fundamental causes of its unrealizability.' Olga Matich, *Erotic Utopia: The Decadent Imagination in Russia's Fin de Siècle*, Madison, WI, 2004, p. 71.

corporeal currents,'⁵⁴ as he calls them, where the philosopher returns to the biblical discourse around the image and likeness of God, this time linking the practice of love with the distance between the two:

> Apart from the material and empirical content of his life, each human being contains in itself the image of God, i.e. a particular form of absolute content. This image of God is known theoretically and abstractly to us in reason and through reason, but in love it is known concretely and vitally. And if this revelation of an ideal being (*sushchestvo*), ordinarily closed to material phenomena, is not limited to inner feeling alone but sometimes becomes sensible in the sphere of external feelings, then how much more significance should we accord love as the beginning of the visible restoration of the image of God in the material world, the beginning of the incarnation of true, ideal humanity (*chelovechnost'*). The power of love, transitioning into light, transforming and spiritualizing the form of external phenomena, reveals to us its objective might.⁵⁵

This was as far as Soloviev reached in his treatment of the subjective conditions for the spiritualization of matter. From the movement of love issuing from a divinized humanity, our attention must now turn to the outward realization of this love in an objective, spiritualized materiality, the eschatological idea as such — beauty.

BEAUTY

Many commentators have recognized that the core of Soloviev's aesthetics coincides with his eschatology. It provides the 'answer to the question that had long troubled the philosopher about the fate and meaning of matter [...] Beauty is the initiation of material being into the moral order through its illumination and spiritualization.'⁵⁶ As Irene Masing-Delic has noted, 'aesthetics is key to Soloviev's salvation program. Beauty corrects the fatal structural and textural

---

54   S¹, II, p. 546.
55   Ibid., p. 516.
56   V. Asmus, and others, 'Solov'ev, Vladimir Sergeevich,' in *Filosofskaia entsiklopediia*, ed. F. B. Konstantinov, 5 vols, Moscow, 1960-70, v, pp. 51-56 (p. 54).

flaw that Sophia's fall into materiality entailed.'[57] Less developed, however, has been the connection between Soloviev's philosophy of love and his aesthetics in the eschatological context. In his 1889 essay 'Beauty in Nature,' the philosopher writes about love and beauty as two sides of the same 'world meaning,' which together constitute a 'living balance':

> The true meaning of the universe — the individual incarnation of the life of the world, the living balance between the singular and the general, or the presence of all in one — this meaning, finding itself the most concentrated expression for inner feeling in sexual love, is the very same thing that for contemplation appears as the beauty of nature. In the feeling of love, annulling my egoism, I feel inside myself in the most intensive way the same Divine power that manifests itself outside me extensively in the creation of natural beauty, annulling material chaos, which is at its foundation that same egoism which works in me. The inner identity of these two manifestations of world meaning is clearly revealed to us in those poems where the poetic image of nature merges with the motif of love.[58]

In many ways this passage represents yet another formulation of the central idea of the Philosophy of All-Unity — the ontic correspondence between the individual and the universal, an idea found under other guises from the very earliest period of Soloviev's career. In his *Critique*, for example, he had written that 'to fully perceive one object, one being, i.e. to perceive it as it truly is, means to perceive everything; for in its true definition any object is connected with all in unity, or is a unity of itself and all.'[59] The legal philosopher and historian Boris Chicherin responded to the work, and in particular this idea, with a wide-ranging attack on Soloviev's argument in an article titled 'Mysticism in Science' (1880). His central accusation centred around the claim that Soloviev's so-called 'unity of substance excludes the independence of separate creatures, reducing them to the level of mere phenomena.'[60]

---

[57] Masing-Delic, *Abolishing Death*, p. 109.
[58] FI, p. 418.
[59] PSS, III, p. 306.
[60] Cited in Ibid., p. 465.

Uncharacteristically, Soloviev did not respond to the criticism, but it seems likely that it spurred him on to look for a more concrete link between individual and universal than the mere logical postulation of the 'all-one existent.' Such a link he found at the empirical level in the form of the pathos of love and the phenomenon of beauty, in which he intuited a 'living balance' between the one and the many. Returning to the above passage, we may note that this balance manifests itself in three ways: firstly, in the pathos of love as subjective feeling, or state of consciousness; secondly, in beauty as objective appearance, or the 'object of contemplation'; and thirdly, in the 'inner identity' of both. We have dealt with the balance of love in *amor aequalis*. Let us now deal briefly with the second point before moving on to the third.

In the same essay, Soloviev explains the peculiar beauty of the diamond in the following way:

> The play of light, captured and modified by this body, perfectly covers its coarsely material appearance and, though the dark material of carbon is present here too, as it is in coal, it is only as the bearer (*nositel'nitsa*) of another, luminous principle which, in this play of lights, reveals its own content.[61]

The beauty that arises from this 'play of light' is not only, in Soloviev's view, the production of the light, or 'luminous principle,' but just as strongly that of the material — carbon — in which this play takes place. 'Beauty, belonging neither to the material body of the diamond, nor to the ray of light refracted in it, is the product of both in their interaction.'[62] Beauty, as such, is thus the objective counterpart of erotic pathos, in which the spiritual and material aspects mutually fulfil each other: matter provides the foundation on which spirit ('light') can realize itself in concrete form, while spirit provides the principle of illumination itself, through which matter is transfigured.[63] Being

---

[61] Ibid., p. 37.
[62] Ibid., p. 37.
[63] In concrete terms, the 'spiritualization of matter' is always presented by Soloviev as the 'illumination of matter.' Light is also the constant background of his mystical experience. *Siiat'* — to shine — is the active verb used repeatedly to herald the entry of Sophia into his poetic framework. She is described as the 'radiant one' (*luchezarnaia*),

the activity of neither principle in its singular orientation toward its object, beauty becomes the space of true, prophetic freedom.⁶⁴ Most importantly, we have here a freedom that does not come into being by means of a break-through into the world of the in-itself, i.e. through a separation from the appearance of things. Rather, beauty is a '*phenomenological realization.*' It rests on the perception of the viewer which witnesses to the balance of its spiritual-material nature: 'visible beauty is the true, accomplished goal.'⁶⁵

Alongside this exaltation of natural beauty, however, which reaches its highest pitch in Soloviev's Lake Saimaa poems, his philosophy evinces a continuous disappointment in beauty's inability to retain, or reproduce, itself in an undying progression, to transfigure the world at its core. 'The beauty of nature is really only a cover thrown on evil life, and not the transformation of this life.'⁶⁶ Natural beauty is ephemeral; even the diamond fails to shine at night. Therefore, as we have seen, the 'aesthetic task' moves up a level to the human realm, where the artist contemplates the eternal ideas so that she may sow them in material form, and in which beauty reaches a new, conscious intensity. Even this, however, cannot satisfy Soloviev. 'In human life, artistic beauty is only a symbol of a better hope, a momentary rainbow on the dark backdrop of our chaotic existence.'⁶⁷ Indeed, his reader gets a sense that the externalization of spiritual content in artistic form is for him a kind of evasion tactic, a substitution of the true task for its close, yet ultimately insufficient, approximation. There always remained in the visionary-poet Soloviev a conviction that the

---

and it is precisely in her luminosity that her 'activity' is manifested. See my 'Sophianic Task,' pp. 173-74. See, also Bulgakov, who writes that 'spiritual beauty is not only the outward adornment by beauty but also the illumination by beauty from within; it is a question of incarnate spirit, not soulless body.' Bulgakov, *The Comforter*, p. 204.

64   Caryl Emerson writes in this connection that for Soloviev beauty is not the realization of some abstract ideal form' but a 'quality brought about through a dynamic, open, but at all times necessarily contested relation between an embodied and an unembodied force.' C. Emerson, 'Solov'ev, the late Tolstoi, and the Early Bakhtin on the Problem of Shame and Love,' *Slavic Review*, 50, 3, 1991, pp. 663-71 (p. 666).
65   V. V. Bychkov, *Russkaia teurgicheskaia estetika*, Moscow, 2007, pp. 62-63.
66   FI, p. 76.
67   Ibid., p. 31.

primacy of natural beauty as beheld in the eye of the aesthete is worth more than its reworking on canvas or verse. It was this conviction that had led him to place '*mistika*' as the highest of all the arts in *Philosophical Principles*,[68] and to describe his new art — 'theurgy' — as the transfiguration of natural reality itself.

In the context of aesthetics, the 'inner identity' of love and beauty did not only consist, in Soloviev's view, in the fact that what is revealed in the former intensively is the same thing that is revealed in the latter extensively. In artistic creation, the philosopher posits an interaction between the two principles so that the content of erotic pathos is in some respect *constitutive* of beauty: love, as subjective feeling, spills over into beauty. This 'spilling over' is the final realization of the vocation of Eros, who is 'love, as the striving to create in the beautiful, or love to give birth to the beautiful.'[69] In other words, love is both an engendering *of* the beautiful and the act of creating *in* the beautiful. In this way, love and beauty find themselves in the same relation to one another as spirit and matter in the individual case of the beauty of the diamond: they are mutually conditioning, engendering — a unity of giving and receiving. Here Soloviev follows almost exactly Diotima's argument in *Symposium*, which proceeds from the threefold contention, acknowledged by Socrates, that 'we love only what is beautiful; in loving it we desire to possess it in perpetuity'; and that 'we desire to possess it because it is good, and expect that its possession would make us happy,'[70] to the conclusion, which baffles Socrates, that to serve this end requires 'birth in beauty.' Gregory Vlastos interprets these words as follows: 'beauty stirs us so deeply, Plato is saying, because we have the power to create and only the beauty we love can release that power.'[71] Plato then proceeds to paint a picture of sexual love which, though it finds some resonance in Soloviev's work, ultimately left the latter with

---

[68] PSS, II, p. 196.
[69] Solov'ev, 'Lektsii po istorii filosofii,' p. 131. The idea is found in *Symposium* where, when Diotima is asked in what the activity of those who follow Eros consists, she answers: 'Love's function is giving birth in beauty both in body and in mind.' Plato, *Symposium*, p. 43.
[70] Ibid., p. 41.
[71] Vlastos, *Platonic Studies*, p. 21.

the feeling that something had remained unsaid. Even worse, he not only sees inadequacy in the articulation of Plato's ideal but, in the years that follow the writing of the two great dialogues on love, its betrayal: 'the momentary ascent of Plato's thought to the idea of Eros as a bridge connecting the world of the truly-existent with that of material reality remained without repercussions. The philosopher pointed the way to this bridge in enigmatic expressions, but proved unable to step onto it himself, or lead others across.'[72]

Despite this damning assessment, the 'fall' of Plato, seen in Soloviev's opinion in its most pitiful unravelling in the writing of the *Laws* at the end of his life, did not repel him from the Greek philosopher. If anything, it made him draw ever closer to the Platonic corpus, wishing to uncover its dynamism, its meaning, its tragedy, and its promise.[73] The drama of Plato's life was not a matter of academic interest to Soloviev: it was the archetype, the meta-narrative, of the prophetic-philosophical path — that concrete historical example in which philosophy had discovered the wings to ascend to the prophetic heights yet, like Icarus, had come crashing down to Earth. Plato had 'approached conceptually the creative task of Eros, understood it as the task of life — "birth in beauty" — but did not define the ultimate content of that task, not to speak of its fulfilment.'[74] Soloviev's aesthetics and philosophy of love should be seen not as an attempt to build an alternative model to that of Plato but rather to regain that height of erotic inspiration once attained

---

[72] S¹, II, p. 327.
[73] The introduction to Soloviev's translation of the Platonic dialogues exhibits a fascination, bordering on obsession, with determining their exact chronology. An interpretation of the dialogues themselves could only rest, in his view, on a proper understanding of the evolution of the individual who gave them life. Sergei Trubetskoi talked about the 'remarkable congeniality' that drew the philosopher to Plato, while for Losev, 'only Vladimir Soloviev [managed] to find in his soul real contact with Plato's philosophy, and was the first to realize a purely intuitive, spontaneous and living approach to the philosopher.' Trubetskoi, 'Predislovie,' p. 497; Losev, 'Eros u Platona,' p. 37. Soloviev believed the peak of Plato's creativity — the writing of *Symposium* and *Phaedrus* — to have coincided with an 'erotic crisis.' S¹, II, p. 608. This conclusion has ramifications not only for the way he wished his reader to interpret the 'fall' of Plato, but how we interpret the truly Platonic task that Soloviev sees himself as continuing.
[74] S¹, II, p. 619.

by the latter, to elucidate the content of the task there attained, and to realize it. It was thus a quintessentially Platonic endeavour; indeed, it was to be more Platonic than Plato himself.

We find a fascinating link between Soloviev's late re-immersion in Plato and the apocalypticism of *Short Story of the Antichrist* in the words spoken to the Antichrist by the 'metallic and completely soulless' voice the reader takes to be that of the devil near the beginning of the story: 'As before my spirit gave birth to you in *beauty*, so now it gives birth to you in *power*.' It is at the sound of these words that the Antichrist's mouth opens and a 'sharp, icy stream entered into him, and filled his whole being.'[75] The phrase acts as a kind of magical initiation into falsehood, and the scene as a whole is analogous to the biblical depictions of prophetic calling, yet whose agent is here the enemy of God rather than God herself. What does it mean for the devil to give birth to the Antichrist in beauty, and then power? It is hard not to see in these words a resonance with Soloviev's reflections on the life-drama of Plato. Having ascended in love to the striving for birth in beauty, Plato had been pulled back, writes Soloviev, by two opposing tendencies: the conviction that 'ideal truth can only be reflected or imprinted on the surface of real being, and not incarnate in it essentially,' and that the 'spirit is only connected to this reality in a transitory and external way.'[76] In the commission of the Antichrist by his master in *Short Story* we find a kind of narrative expansion of the existential decision taken by Plato to renounce the higher task of Eros. The devil, as hypostatized self-love, gives birth to the Antichrist in beauty. It is not love itself that births beauty but its opposite: the creativity of beauty does not arise from an inner erotic pathos but is enforced on its object by the will of the begetter. The Antichrist is 'Christ turned-inside-out,' to recall Soloviev's definition, insofar as his beauty is worn on the outside; it does not arise from the love in which he dwells but instead superficially covers his external form as the ultimate semblance of good. This point is expertly brought out by Lithuanian philosopher Antanas Matseina, who writes that satanic beauty for Soloviev 'is that clothing in which the

---

[75] Ibid., pp. 742-43.
[76] Ibid., p. 321.

devil arrays his supporters and their works so as to attract to himself members of Christ's Kingdom.'[77]

'Birth in power' is from this perspective the logical conclusion of such one-sided birth in beauty — beauty that arises not from the equal, divine-human love of *amor aequalis* but from the satanic will which finds in beauty not itself in rebirth but merely a means for power. It is the end point of that kind of beauty that stops at surface level, not resurrecting human nature from within but deceptively imposing itself on human form from without. Only the one whose image is set at the core of human inner being can give birth from within; the devil must work with externalities. It is also the end point of the drama of Plato's life in Soloviev's handling: the disintegration of beauty into power that characterizes the *Republic* and, most definitively, the *Laws*.

The theme of counterfeit beauty permeates the work of Soloviev's late period. While the philosopher found almost no attempt to describe in philosophical terms the actual transition of erotic pathos into birth in beauty in Plato, the tremendous value of the Hegelian dialectic for him consisted in its depiction of the inner dynamism of this process. Like Soloviev, Hegel, for whom the disclosure and self-discovery of inner consciousness in external form was the final realization of spirit, which in such recognition 'knows itself for the first time,'[78] wrote about the creative process in terms of the transition of an intensive pathos into an expansive externality.

> Now such 'pathos' essentially demands representation and graphic amplification. And at that it must be a soul inherently rich which puts into its 'pathos' the wealth of its inner being and does not merely concentrate itself in itself and remain intensive, but expresses itself extensively and rises to a fully developed form [...] In order to be concrete in itself, as ideal art requires, the 'pathos' must come into representation as the

---

[77] A. Matseina, *Taina bezzakoniia*, St Petersburg, 1999, p. 115. Soloviev makes a point of describing the 'beauty' and 'nobility' of the Antichrist. When he appears on stage as the president of the European United States, for example, Soloviev remarks on the 'brilliance of his superhuman young beauty and power.' S¹, II, pp. 740, 745.

[78] Consciousness 'must see how it has externalized itself in various objects, and in seeing this also cancelled the externalization. It must see all its objective forms as itself.' Hegel, *Phenomenology of Spirit*, p. 589.

'pathos' of a rich and total spirit [...] Feeling must completely either disclose itself on its own account or shine clearly and thoroughly through the external material in which it has enshrined itself.[79]

While Hegel's remarks follow very closely the thrust of Soloviev's aesthetics in its continual thirst for the external expression of inner content, there are several substantial differences between the two. The most crucial is the complete lack of anything approximating Solovievian balance (*ravnovesie*) in Hegel's account. For Hegel, spirit (*Geist*) is located in an emphatically one-sided relation to material form, which itself derives from the one-sidedness of his pathos: spirit forces its way into matter through the sheer energy of its own self-negating dialectic. Michael Meerson comments that the universal and eternal idea is for Hegel 'embodied' in beauty whereas for Soloviev beauty is itself 'the *interaction* between spiritual and material elements. Through this interaction, the material element is elevated to the eternal status of the spiritual.'[80] Soloviev writes:

> In Hegelian aesthetics, beauty is an incarnation of the universal and eternal idea in individual and transitory phenomena. Yet this is how they remain — transitory, vanishing like disconnected waves in the flow of the material process, reflecting only for a minute the radiance of the eternal idea. But this is possible only in an indifferent relation between the spiritual principle and material principle.[81]

It is this indifference, in Soloviev's eyes, of relation between the spiritual and material that produces the superficiality of Hegelian beauty.[82] The ideal glimmers in the object but is not brought to birth in it; the erotic pathos, in which spirit and matter are equalized in love, becomes the pathos of power — the idea dictates and, in its dominion, loses the path to its true freedom, for it is in slavery to the one who desires only himself.

---

[79] Hegel, *Aesthetics*, pp. 234-35, 290.
[80] Meerson, *Trinity of Love*, p. 35.
[81] FI, p. 81.
[82] The discussion here does not relate to natural or artistic beauty but to the perception, or consciousness, of that beauty, from which in any case it cannot be separated.

In Hegelianism the philosophical subject comes closer than it ever has to its authentic and ultimate definition as the becoming reason of truth (*razum istiny*). But, having risen to this height, its head spins and it insanely imagines that the principle of its understanding (*razumenie*) of the truth is the inception of the truth itself, and that the truth's growth and development is its own growth and development.[83]

This tragic substitution by the subject of itself in place of the being in which it is involved ('pathos')[84] is for Soloviev the downfall of Hegel and his system. He lacked that 'intent or that act of will in its giving itself over to its object that is the real principle of movement,'[85] imagining his own self to be the ultimate creator of that space in which alone his selfhood could find its ultimate realization. Soloviev concludes his evaluation of Hegel in *Theoretical Philosophy* in biblical tones, writing that 'amongst the philosophers who have *approached* the truth, there is none greater than Hegel, yet even the least amongst the philosophers *issuing* from the truth itself is greater than he.'[86]

Perhaps the most remarkable treatment of superficial beauty as the renunciation of the pathos of love is found in Soloviev's 1899 article on Mikhail Lermontov. While recognizing that love motifs predominate in Lermontov's verse, Soloviev writes that these 'only partly possess the personal self-feeling (*samochuvstvie*) of the poet, blunting the sharpness of his egoism, softening his cruelty, but not completely filling or covering his ego.'[87] The philosopher goes on to

---

[83] S¹, I, p. 829. *Razum istiny* (reason of truth) is the key technical term of Soloviev's late theoretical philosophy which, however, he did not manage to develop sufficiently before his death.

[84] The idea of participation as being-in-pathos resonates with the Platonic concept *methexis*, which Christopher Bigger describes as 'the name of the "relation" which accounts for the togetherness of elements of diverse ontological type in the essential unity of a single instance. In this sense it is real relation, one constitutive of the nexus qua nexus which arises from it.' C. P. Bigger, *Participation: A Platonic Inquiry* (Baton Rouge: Louisiana State Press, 1968), p. 8. Soloviev was surely aware of the term although he does not mention it. Bulgakov, however, writes: 'Methexis, the participation of matter in the idea is precisely Eros, the eros of "earth" to "heaven".' Bulgakov, *Svet nevechernii*, p. 211.

[85] S¹, I, p. 830.

[86] Ibid., p. 829. Compare Matthew 11.11.

[87] FI, p. 385.

intuit the 'victory of egoism' over the 'misfortunate effort of love' in every corner of Lermontov's poetry.

> One feels that real significance belongs here not to love, not what it makes of the poet, but what *he* makes of it, how *he* relates to it. When a huge glacier is lit by the sun, it is, they say, an entrancing sight. But this new beauty occurs not because the sun makes something new of the glacier (it cannot, after all, melt it) but from what the glacier, remaining unchangingly itself, makes of the sun's rays, reflecting and refracting them in various ways on its surface. Such is the peculiar charm (*prelest'*) of Lermontov's love poetry: an optical charm, the charm of a mirage.[88]

Taken together, the glacier and the diamond can be understood as symbols of the identity of radical difference in the Solovievian conception of beauty.[89] The glacier as the natural archetype of non-transfigurative beauty — a beauty that is but the concealment of the void — and the diamond as the natural archetype of its opposite — a beauty that penetrates to the core of its material, the birthing forth of an interior love that cannot set limits to itself — these two are the ambiguous poles of Soloviev's theory, the dual horizon of his aesthetic landscape.[90] It is in their light that we arrive at the final philosophical model against which Soloviev wished to differentiate his own.

---

[88] Ibid., p. 386.
[89] Although he does not speak of beauty, Desmond has written in a similar way of the 'radical equivocity' of the Antichrist, 'the fact that the "sameness" of Christ and anti-Christ is absolute difference.' Desmond, 'God Beyond the Whole,' p. 191.
[90] Despite Soloviev's rejection of Hegelian aesthetics, these two poles carry distinct echoes of Hegel's use of the terms *Schein* (semblance) and *Erscheinung* (appearance), both of which express the Essence (*Wesen*) of an object but in different respects. In much the same way that Soloviev uses light in his treatment of glacier, Hegel uses *Schein* to express an outward shining that appears to communicate Essence but which in actuality only masks or veils it. *Erscheinung*, to the contrary, 'forms a connected totality of the ways the Essence shows itself from within, a totality whose horizon is the world as the collection of all possible relationships between the Essence and other things.' See T. Ryba, 'Manifestation,' in W, Braun and R. T. McCutcheon (eds), *Guide to the Study of Religion*, London, 2006, pp. 168-189 (pp. 176-77). Soloviev, while preserving a similar distinction between counterfeit *Schein* and authentic *Erscheinung* focuses rather on the human-active component in the realization of each. In his article 'The Freedom of Will and Causality,' he posits the source of these differing

If Sergei Trubetskoi talked of the congeniality between the Russian philosopher and Plato, it is surely justifiable to discuss yet another correspondence, this time with a figure who lived at the same time as Soloviev, died just twenty-six days after him, and in many ways had just as immense an influence on Russian thought as Soloviev himself—Friedrich Nietzsche. Here it is no longer a matter of congeniality but of correspondence in inversion: in all major points, seeming proximity between the two thinkers is eclipsed by their essential, radical divergence. Soloviev understood perhaps more profoundly than any other thinker in late-nineteenth-century Europe the danger of the illusory beauty that found conscious and expansive articulation, and, as such, repudiation, in Nietzscheanism. In *Birth of Tragedy*, Nietzsche had summed up the purpose of beauty in the following terms:

> If we could imagine dissonance become man—and what else is man?—this dissonance, to be able to live, would need a splendid illusion that would cover dissonance with a veil of beauty. This is the true artistic aim of Apollo in whose name we comprehend all those countless illusions of the beauty of mere appearance that at every moment make life worth living at all and prompt the desire to live on in order to experience the next moment.[91]

Beauty for Nietzsche is thus the falsification of the real, the illusion that allows the weaker human being to go on living through believing the coddling lie of what Sonia Sikka has called the 'metaphysico-religious interpretation' of beauty, which Nietzsche seeks to expose.[92] In this understanding, beauty 'saves' not because it is true but because it is entirely delusory: 'the salvific power of the beautiful dream-vision resides entirely in its fraudulent character, in the fact that is an idealized,

---

products in activities he calls 'mechanism' and 'creativity' respectively: 'creativity is the realization or incarnation of the idea in matter; mechanism is the relative realization of the idea *by means of* (*posredstvom*) matter.' See Solov'ev, 'Freedom of Will and Causality,' p. 183.

91 F. Nietzsche, *The Birth of Tragedy*, New York, 1967, p. 25.
92 S. Sikka, 'On the Truth of Beauty: Nietzsche, Heidegger, Keats,' *Heythrop Journal*, 39, 1998, 3, pp. 243-63 (pp. 245-48).

and thus falsified, image of life.'[93] Nietzsche, then, in refusing to accept the beautiful illusion, is the first to rise to a level where, instead of the 'indication of connection in and through an ontological ground' that appears to be given in such illusions, surveys the new horizon and sees what is really true: the utter separation of the individual from the whole, and its irrevocable path to total destruction and decay. The myth of eternal beauty becomes the coward's way out of the total suffering of absolute transience.

In a number of articles of the 1890s Soloviev battled against what he saw as the devaluation of beauty — a 'pagan view of power and beauty,' as he characterized Nietzscheanism[94] — in the hands of contemporary Russian poets. In his 1894 'The Buddhist Disposition in Poetry,' he rails against the beauty he finds in the now barely known poetry of Arsenii Golenishchev-Kutuzov (1848-1913), 'powerless to rebirth its admirer to new life, promising him flight and oblivion alone,' and whose results were writ large in his verse: 'having become disillusioned in external and interior beauty, the author, naturally, loses faith in his own poetic vocation.'[95] Two months before his own death, Soloviev wrote an obituary for Vasilii Preobrazhenskii (1864-1900), the first Russian writer to undertake a systematic exposition of Nietzsche's philosophy, and translator and popularizer of the latter's ideas in Russian society. Preobrazhenskii's 1892 article, 'Friedrich Nietzsche, Critique of the Morality of Altruism,'[96] may have provided Soloviev with his first introduction to the German existentialist.[97] To say that Soloviev did not share Preobrazhenskii's positive interpretation of Nietzsche is to

---

[93] Ibid., p. 245.
[94] S^2, II, p. 612.
[95] FI, p. 457.
[96] V. P. Preobrazhenskii, 'Fridrikh Nitsshe, kritika morali al'truizma,' *Voprosy filosofii i psikhologii*, 1892, 15, pp. 115-60.
[97] It is likely that Soloviev, who for many years took an active role in the running of the journal *Voprosy filosofii i psikhologii*, had a part in writing the editorial note published at the head of Preobrazhenskii's article, which seeks to undercut the latter's positive assessment of Nietzsche's philosophy by reminding the reader what a 'great and meaningful lesson is given us in the fate of this misfortunate proud man, who ended up in a mental asylum as a consequence of an *idée fixe* that he was the Creator of the world.' Ibid., p. 115. The same idea occurs in similarly immoderate wording in Soloviev's 1897 'Sunday Letter' 'Philology or Truth?.' See SS, X, p. 29.

put it mildly. In his obituary, however, Soloviev lays out his critique of Nietzsche while withholding judgement from his Russian admirer: 'only the truly beautiful (*istinno-prekrasnoe*) is worthy of love, and the truly beautiful is first of all the truly good. I had reason to think that even this "aesthete" recognized that the *ultimate* benchmark for all judgement resided in the ethical.'[98]

The, in essence, Platonic idea that beauty is the only true object of love in which the good, far from ceding its ground to the aesthetic, finds its ultimate realization[99] lies at the heart of Soloviev's work, particularly of the late period. For him, good was 'justified' precisely in beauty, or, to recall his celebrated triadic formulation, 'through truth in beauty.' His refusal to acknowledge 'aesthetic separatism' (the separation of the principle of beauty from other fields, particularly ethics)[100] was the very crux of his conflict with Nietzsche and the Russian Nietzscheans. Yet more interesting, however, is the question of where such divergent convictions had their source, that is, which intuitions or foundational principles created the energy for his particular worldview. Here we return, finally, to a discussion of Nietzschean 'dissonance,' a term which, like so much in Nietzsche, contains a certain amount of ambiguity.

For Nietzsche, dissonance was a sensation containing within itself a kind of 'tragic pleasure.' Since it seeks not to deny the suffering of the world, which Nietzsche equated with the denial of life, the conscious living-through of dissonance coincides with the 'highest state of affirmation of existence,' which does not exclude even the 'highest degree of pain.'[101] On the basis of *Birth of Tragedy*, Daniel Came has argued that there are at least two possible interpretations of the principle in Nietzsche's thought: firstly, that it refers to something which is pleasurable in itself, as a 'pleasure *in* dissonance'; and secondly, that 'it is not intrinsically pleasurable' but instead 'causally linked to something which *is*,' since 'dissonance causes the resolution that

---

[98] Ibid., IX, p. 430.
[99] The Greek word *kalos* can be translated as either good or beautiful.
[100] The term occurs in the 1894 'First Step Toward a Positive Aesthetics' in relation to the kind of art that separates itself from all other spheres, thinking itself self-sufficient and self-defining. FI, p. 91.
[101] F. Nietzsche, *Will to Power*, New York, 1968, p. 453.

follows to sound more agreeable.'[102] Nevertheless, Came had due cause to settle on the first interpretation since, as he argues, dissonance must be understood as the 'aesthetic significance of the problematic aspects of existence' which, in themselves, according to Nietzsche, can and should receive no resolution.[103] Resolution in beauty is the illusion of resolution; the dissonance between the individual and the whole, between the hope for eternity and the reality of unending death and decay, is itself evidence of their absolute non-contiguity and non-correspondence. Only she who lives out the 'tragic pleasure' had in the feeling of dissonance aligns herself with what is true, where truth coincides with the negation of all good and truth, and the attainment of a position 'beyond good and evil.'

Soloviev was not afraid of dissonance, and did not seek to deny it. Indeed, as we have argued, the great impulse for his work was the distance between the world 'as it is' and the world 'as it should be' according to our desires.[104] Yet for him the feeling, or experience, of beauty was not the irrevocable evidence of primal and absolute dissonance but the concrete, realized unity of the spiritual and material principles, not as a kind of spiritual *diktat*, as in Hegel, but as their living interaction as birth in beauty. On the other hand, anyone who reads Soloviev's *Short Story*, or any number of works of the middle and late periods, will be convinced of the philosopher's belief in the existence of that illusory beauty of which Nietzsche speaks. The apocalyptic turn in Soloviev's late period gives the lie to the words spoken in that early manifesto letter to Katia Romanova ('I do not believe in the devil')[105] when, like Ivan Karamazov, he could no longer deny the personal agency of evil in the world. But, in regarding such beauty as false, he at the same time

---

[102] D. Came, 'Nietzsche's Attempt at a Self-Criticism: Art and Morality in *The Birth of Tragedy*,' in *Nietzsche-Studien*, ed. M. Montinari, Berlin, 1974, pp. 37-67 (p. 57).

[103] Ibid., p. 57.

[104] Soloviev's *Spiritual Foundations of Life* begins with an unflinching expression of existential dissonance: 'The two great desires — immortality and truth — are counterposed by two great facts — the inevitable dominion of death over all flesh and the invincible rulership of sin over all souls. We only desire to rise above the rest of nature; death equates us with the entire earthly creation, and sin makes us worse than it.' Solov'ev, *Dukhovnye osnovy*, p. 24.

[105] Solov'ev, "Nepodvizhno," p. 173.

acknowledged the existence of an authentic beauty of which the other was the counterfeit. While both beauties were for him equally 'true' from a phenomenal perspective — insofar as they were both experienced as such — the truly beautiful is so only by dint of its connection with the truly good. Ultimately, the place of discernment can only rest in the subjective feeling involved in the emergence of the beautiful or, more exactly, the pathos that informs the differing experiences. While, for Nietzsche, beauty is merely an imagined resolution of ontic dissonance, for Soloviev it is the *result*, the ultimate fruit of an equally primary, ontic consonance between the individual and universal, in which the former develops on the path outlined in the previous sections, from faith through reverence to the attainment of the pathos of love. The difference is, however, that while there is nothing that can ultimately prove or disprove the Nietzschean assertion of absolute dissonance, for Soloviev the consonance of the divine and the human in *amor aequalis* does not, or should not, remain merely an interior pathos but should rather spills over into the birth of immortality in material form. As he writes in the introduction to the third edition of his collected poems (1900):

> The more perfect and intimate the revelation of true beauty which clothes the Godhead and by Her power frees us from suffering and death, the narrower is the boundary separating it from its false image, from that illusory, powerless beauty which merely continues the kingdom of suffering and death.[106]

The uniqueness of Soloviev's late approach to this problem consists not only in the overcoming of evil by the good in beauty but also in the proximity between its two poles: as he writes, the more intimate and complete the manifestation of the truly beautiful, the less clear the boundary between counterfeit and authentic beauty becomes. By this he means, as we have said, that the final conflict between good and evil, waged in beauty, is not one of opposites but of superficial identity. But there is also a sense in Soloviev that the illusory beauty, which Nietzsche so reviled, itself becomes the place of transition to authentic beauty, by

---

[106] SS, XII, p. 4.

dying to itself and rebirthing. This removal of the border between true and false beauty, which does not equate with their 'merging,' comes through most strikingly in Soloviev's 'Sunday Letter,' *Christ is Risen!*, where the philosopher begins by developing a distinctly Nietzschean argument on the dominion of death, which 'knows that the beauty of nature is only a colourful and bright veil thrown on a continuously decomposing corpse.'[107] Beauty '*appears* eternal to the external eye, from the side, to the observer accepting this new, momentary life for the continuation of what came before.' But 'if what is born today is not the same as that which died yesterday but something else, then what cause have we to speak of rebirth?'[108]

Soloviev, like Nietzsche, accepted that the eternity of beauty is but a seeming eternity, that what it announces to the human spirit and soul is a message at odds with its real efficacy. But he had no wish to embrace the illusion, or even to renounce it in the name of the universal suffering of dissonance: 'No! This seeming life is only a symbol and the beginnings of true life; the organization of visible nature is not the decisive victory of the living spirit over death, but only its *preparation for real actions*.'[109] This 'no' would be interpreted by Nietzsche as the cowardly return to the comfortable illusion, yet it is clear that for Soloviev such an act was far from comfortable. At the end of his life, amidst his growing fears in the presentness of the end, a side of his Christology which, while not ignored, had hitherto been, so to speak, subsumed in the power revealed in the Resurrection, comes to the fore. What he had once described as 'the inner theosis through the experience of the cross'[110] is re-emphasized, and the moral power revealed in the cross moved to central place. As Soloviev writes in the same letter:

> If physical power is inevitably conquered by death, the power of the mind is not enough to conquer death: only the limitlessness of moral power gives life its absolute fullness, excludes any dualism and, consequently, does not allow the definitive fall of a living being into two separate parts:

---

[107] Ibid., X, p. 34.
[108] Ibid., p. 34.
[109] Ibid., p. 35.
[110] S², II, p. 228.

fleshless spirit and decomposing matter. The crucified Son of Man and Son of God, having felt himself abandoned by both people and God and yet praying for his enemies, clearly had no limits to his spiritual power, and no part of his being could become death's trophy.[111]

Christ's ability to continue to love, even in a situation in which the very heights of dissonance between the individual, his environment, and the absolute itself, are reached and felt as such,[112] is here presented as the condition for his Resurrection, and the connection made between the true eternity of beauty and such love. Thus, alongside the importance of reverence, which had possessed him during his blissful solitude at the side of Lake Saimaa, there appears another feeling in late Soloviev: the descent into the very pit of Nietzschean abandonment, a feeling through of death as the destroyer of all relation yet, at the same time, the breaking through of such radical abandonment by the limitless moral power of love. The pathos of love, the pathos of the end, and the pathos of the cross become different ways of expressing the same thing. There is a dissonance that only love can overcome, and there is a love that can only fully overcome by descending into dissonance. That Soloviev, who for so long had hoped for the gradual realization in the historical order of that consonance between spirit and matter announced to him in his sophianic visions, should late in life embrace the tragic dissonance of the pathos of the end, yet at the same time remain convinced of the saving power of beauty brought to birth by love, was perhaps not the only possible dénouement to his life's drama, but it is surely a fitting one.

---

[111] SS, X, p. 36.
[112] We recall Soloviev's definition of the prophet as one 'in whom the contradiction with the social environment that surrounds him reaches absolute incommensurability.' See p. 153.

Conclusion
ON SPIRITUAL-MATERIAL UNITY

Vladimir Soloviev's legacy to twentieth-century Russian thought was to prove far from straightforward. Symbolism, sophiology, neo-idealism, humanism, neo-Leibnizianism, and many others, all claimed him as their own, and developed his ideas in directions that he could barely have foreseen. Soloviev's ideal of spiritual-material unity became the object of heated debate, not so much over what it was an attempt to unify — the answers to that question, though manifold, were always guided by the universal pretensions of the 'All' — as over the character of such unity. The sheer range of interpretations can perhaps be explained by the fact that the philosopher's key articulations of spiritual-material unity — the monad, the all-one substance, Sophia, the resurrected flesh of the God-man, prophecy, the pathos of the love, beauty — are all characterized by a certain fissure at their heart, in which the antinomic constituents of their being are contested and balanced, finding resolution in the whole only to emerge once more at the height of their conflict. The question that would occupy Soloviev's successors is whether, in his vision of 'spiritualized matter,' the balance between the two opposing principles should be understood as one of resolved or of antinomic unity.[1] In other words, does this balance manifest itself in an eternal, Schellingian 'debasement to the All,'[2] or does it exhibit, to the contrary, an irreducible antinomy that becomes the very force of its unity?

---

[1] Bulgakov would later speak of the 'antinomic unity' of the two natures of Christ in the case of the Chalcedonian definition. See S. N. Bulgakov, *The Lamb of God*, Grand Rapids, MI, 2008, pp. 33-34.

[2] See p. 69, note 136.

Conclusion

The battle over Solovievian unity continued to be waged, as it was in the philosopher's own later years, in the landscape of Christian eschatology. In a 1914 review article of an early version of Pavel Florenskii's magnum opus, *The Pillar and Ground of Truth*, Evgenii Trubetskoi objects to what he sees as two irreconcilable propositions: on one hand, he writes, Florenskii presents antinomicity as the essence of the sinful character of human reason while, on the other, he argues that the truth itself is antinomic by its very nature. 'To assert that antinomicity is the mark of the sinful fissure within our reason and, at the same time, to think that it is precisely in such antinomicity that the power which saves us consists, is to fall into a contradiction of a kind that has no place in rigorous thought.'[3] Trubetskoi goes on to oppose such a view with the dominant Eastern Christian theme of the transfigured light of Christ on Mount Tabor, when the apparent conflict of opposing forces are reconciled in an overarching, resolved unity.

> Antinomy and antinomicity are rooted in a rational (*rassudochnyi*) understanding of the world's mysteries. When we are elevated above the rational, the antinomies are resolved and the contradictions transformed into the union of opposites (*coincidentia oppositorum*).[4]

On just which side of this debate Soloviev falls depends very much on how one interprets the body of his work. Anna Lisa Crone suggests an alignment with Trubetskoi when she makes a parallel between Soloviev and twentieth-century psychology, writing that his 'campaign in favor of restoring balance to the divine and human aspects of Christ *and* man anticipates Jung's advocacy of a balanced flesh-spirit, a *unio oppositorum*.'[5] We find a similar unfolding of paradoxical union, or sophianic mediation, between two opposite terms in the work of Semen Frank, another follower of Soloviev. In his *God with us* (1946), Frank cites the use of the terms *complexio contrariorum* (combination of contradictories) and *coincidentia oppositorum* (coincidence of opposites) by Nicholas of Cusa while developing his own, biblically grounded

---

[3] E. N. Trubetskoi, 'Svet Favorskii i preobrazhenie uma,' *Voprosy filosofii*, 12, 1989, pp. 112-29 (p. 117).
[4] Ibid., p. 118.
[5] Crone, *Eros and Creativity*, p. 231.

approach to what he calls the 'all-embracing unity of concrete realities.'⁶ While Frank regards the terms as synonymous, however, German political theorist and philosopher Carl Schmitt draws a sharp distinction between the two. By *coincidentia* he suggests that 'opposites converge in the transcendent infinitude of God,'⁷ whila at the same time reserving no such resolution for *complexio*. In his 1923 essay 'Roman Catholicism and Political Form,' he wrote that the Church

> understands little of the dualisms of nature and spirit, nature and intellect, nature and art, nature and machine, and their varying pathos. The synthesis of such antitheses remains as foreign as the antithesis of empty form and formless matter. The Catholic Church is categorically something higher than the (in any case, always absent) "higher third" of the German philosophy of nature and history. To it belong neither the despair of the antitheses nor the illusory optimism of their synthesis.⁸

Although Schmitt's understanding of *complexio* is 'resolutely this-worldly' and 'conceived strictly with respect to the finite world of phenomena'⁹ — a circumstance that takes his concept of 'Church' some distance from that of Soloviev — there is room to draw parallels between the visions of unity we find in these two, otherwise very different, thinkers. Soloviev, like Schmitt, had no intention of pursuing a finalized resolution of spirit and matter in a 'higher third.' His Sophia is who she is not because she elevates herself to a position equal, or above, the unity of the Godhead but precisely because she reduces herself, allowing the elements that move through her to exceed themselves in self-discovery in otherness.¹⁰ Sophia, in looking away from herself, becomes less about the matrix of relation in which the antinomy is overcome and more about that which is related. The two — spirit and matter — remain in the irreducible tension of their unique identity

---

6   See S. L. Frank, *God with us: three meditations*, London, 1946, p. 124.
7   Cited in S. Weber, *Targets of Opportunity: On the Militarization of Thinking*, New York, 2005, pp. 27-30.
8   C. Schmitt, *Roman Catholicism and Political Form*, Westport CT, 1996, p. 11.
9   Weber, *Targets of Opportunity*, p. 27.
10 'Sophia entreats God to allow her to decrease, to surrender the infinite speed of divine companionship and enact her love for God ('at her own pace'). Divine excess is the eternal rapture in God that contains this plea for a created sphere, a world of decelerated excess.' Baker and Gangle, 'Ecclesia: The Art of the Visual,' p. 273.

yet without becoming principles of mutual exclusion. 'True union presupposes the true separation of what is unified, i.e. a separation where they do not exclude but mutually presuppose each other.'[11] This kind of thinking prefigures, albeit in a less self-conscious way, William Desmond's 'metaxological path,' which seeks to 'avoid both reduction and absorption, with a sense of the One and the plural beyond both dualism and self-mediating totality.'[12]

The spiritualization of matter is not, in Soloviev, a harmonious chord progression directed toward an inescapable cadence. As Kornblatt has pointed out, 'the process by which the mediator "enters" an object is not always an easy one in Solov'ev's philosophy, whether in the case of Socrates in the minds of Ancient Athenians, or light in the diamond. The transformation of passive object to active subject often involves struggle — both physical and spiritual.'[13] In his late article on the poetry of Tiutchev, Soloviev would write of this struggle as occurring both within nature itself and within the poet, in his attempt to capture it in concrete expression.

> Chaos, i.e. negative limitlessness, the yawning abyss of all madness and formlessness, demonic impulses that rise up against everything positive and all that should be — this is the deepest essence of the world soul and the universe [...] This presence of a chaotic, irrational principle at the depth of being endows the various phenomena of nature with that freedom and power without which there would be no life and beauty. Life and beauty in nature are a battle and identity between light and darkness, but this necessarily presupposes that darkness is an actual force [...] This is in no way contradicted by the transparent, spiritualized character of Tiutchev's poetry. To the contrary, we find that the more illumined and spiritual a poetic creation, the more deeply and fully has that dark, non-spiritual element, which requires illumination and spiritualization, been felt through (*prochuvstvovano*) and experienced.[14]

The resolution between good and evil in itself is not that in which life consists. Rather, the moving power of being is found in their very

---

11 S^1, II, p. 544.
12 W. Desmond, *God and the Between*, Malden, MA, 2008, p. 232.
13 Kornblatt, 'Transformation of Eros,' p. 49.
14 FI, p. 475.

tension, the illumination of darkness, the play of shadows, the revelation of beauty. 'If in me there was no evil passion as a hidden power, as potential energy, I would be as impassive as a corpse, which decomposes as easily as a log, costing nothing to destroy; like a handful of sand that the first breeze blows away.'[15] The prophetic activity of the human being thus consists in the deepest possible participation in a being that is both duality and oneness. In this feeling through of the depths, this antinomic experience, the soul becomes a mediator that reveals, not itself, but the infinite excess of a divine love that makes even the formless its beloved. It balances in the present what in essence may never be definitively and finally balanced as the *result* of an activity, or as past event.

The elemental striving of the World Soul — that desire for corporeality which Soloviev was later to associate with erotic love, the very principle of individuation — becomes the paradoxical ground on which material separation and decay is overcome in the power of the spirit. His kenotic metaphysics, and his kenotic model of human being-in-the-world, do not involve an abrogation of self but the (re-)discovery of true selfhood in the mutuality of the pathos of love. Renunciation of will in Soloviev, therefore, does not amount to a Dionysian disappearance in being, but a conscious immersion in the pathos of the One who loves enough never to allow otherness to dissolve in identity. There are prefigurations here of Mikhail Bakhtin's concept of 'answerability': the goal of the human being is understood not merely as the creation of unity 'at any cost' but the preservation of the receptivity found in a dialogic relation to the world. 'Participation in the being-event of the world in its entirety does not coincide,' Bakhtin stated, 'with irresponsible self-surrender to Being, with being-possessed by Being.'[16] The peculiarity of Soloviev's conception consists in the fact that the principle which works toward the cessation of such dialogic relation — the desire to possess the whole

---

[15] SS, X, p. 49.
[16] M. M. Bakhtin, *Toward a Philosophy of the Act*, Austin, TX, p. 49. Bakhtin compares this approach of 'self-surrender' to Nietzsche's philosophy, which he describes as 'one-sided participation.' See Alan Jacobs' revealing treatment of love and kenosis in Bakhtin's thought: A. Jacobs, *A Theology of Reading: the Hermeneutics of Love*, Boulder, CO, 2001, pp. 105-07. Clowes writes that 'what is remarkable in Solov'ev's thinking is the promise of reciprocity and dialogue between self and other that is to lead to a fuller notion of selfhood.' See Clowes, 'Solov'ev's 'Language of Syzygy,' p. 559.

for oneself—becomes in his handling its paradoxical guarantor. The cosmic fall of Sophia is recapitulated in the Christ-event through the spiritualization of the product of this fall—his human flesh, matter self-transcendent in perfected human consciousness. The darkness of sin hides within itself the beacon of light.

Whether, as in the words to the introduction of the first edition of the philosophical journal *Logos* in 1910, 'chaos, dark and irrational, has been set by the dark will of fate to watch everlastingly over the Russian synthesis,'[17] or whether, beyond the exigencies of time, Soloviev imagined that the pathos of the end could be replaced by an indwelling in God in which the antinomies of being would find resolution, is impossible to answer definitively. Soloviev's own vacillations between the resolved unity of his sophianic poetry and the antinomic unity that characterizes much of his philosophy, particularly that of the late period, seem to point to the fundamental fissure that must of necessity subsist in any attempt to articulate the nature of a god who interacts in her deepest essence with the world of temporality and becoming. After the mysterious appearance of the 'Woman Clothed in Sun,' and the procession of the newly unified remnant of Christians and Jews toward Sinai, the manuscript of *Short Story of the Antichrist* breaks off; the monk Pansophius (its fictional author), we are told, died before he was able to finish it, and so Z (its reader) must paraphrase what he remembers in broad outline. This is a cunning literary device, to be sure, but it is more that that. The 'end' in Soloviev turns out to be not so much about finality as ambiguity, an embodiment of the maximum of tension in otherness amidst the strongest desire for union. A spiritualized matter is one in which, if the material is to retain the freedom which is its gift, resolution must eternally give way to antinomy, just as antinomy eternally gives way to resolution. In the taut equilibrium that results, Soloviev's Kingdom of God 'everywhere peers through and pierces the senselessness that encircles it.'[18]

---

[17] Cited in J. West, 'Art as Cognition in Russian Neo-Kantianism,' *Studies in East European Thought*, 47, 3/4, 1995, pp. 195-223 (p. 218).
[18] Solov'ev, *Dukhovnye osnovy*, p. 75.

BIBLIOGRAPHY

Primary Sources

Collected Works

Solov'ev, V. S., *Sobranie sochinenii*, ed. E. L. Radlov and S. M. Solov'ev, 12 vols, Brussels, 1966-70.

---, *Pis'ma i prilozhenie*, ed. E. L. Radlov, 4 vols, Brussels, 1970.

---, *Stikhotvoreniia i shutochnye p'esy*, ed. Z. G. Mints, Leningrad, 1974.

---, *Sochineniia*, ed. A. F. Losev and A. V. Gulyga, 2 vols, Moscow, 1989.

---, *Sochineniia v 2-kh t.*, ed. N. V. Kotrelev, 2 vols, Moscow, 1989.

---, *"Nepodvizhno lish' solntse liubvi." Stikhotvoreniia; Proza; Pis'ma; Vospominaniia sovremennikov*, ed. A. A. Nosov, Moscow, 1990.

---, *Filosofiia iskusstva i literaturnaia kritika*, ed. R. Gal'tseva and I. Rodnianskaia, Moscow, 1991.

---, *Filosofskii slovar' Vladimira Solov'eva*, ed. G. B. Beliaev, Rostov-na-Donu, 1997.

---, *Polnoe sobranie sochinenii i pisem*, ed. A. A. Nosov, 3 vols, Moscow, 2000-01.

Individual Works

Solov'ev, V. S., 'Reformatsiia v Germanii po noveishemu issledovaniiu,' *Pravoslavnoe obozrenie*, Aug 1885, pp. 698-742.

---, 'Svoboda voli i prichinnosti,' *Mysl' i slovo*, 2, 1918-21, pp. 176-77.

---, 'Lektsii po istorii filosofii,' *Voprosy filosofii*, 1989, 6, pp. 76-132.

---, 'Zhiznennyi smysl khristianstva,' *Filosofskie nauki*, 1991, 3, pp. 51-64.

---, 'Pis'ma A. A. Kireevu,' *Simvol*, 27, 1992, pp. 191-254.

---, *Dukhovnye osnovy zhizni*, St Petersburg, 1995.

---, 'Ob istinnoi nauke,' in A. P. Kozyrev, *Solov'ev i gnostiki*, Moscow, 2007, pp. 239-67.

Secondary Sources

---, 'K istorii odnoi druzhby. V. S. Solov'ev i S. N. Trubetskoi. Novye materialy,' *De visu*, 3, 1993.

ed. Abramovich, D. I. *Pis'ma russkikh pisatelei k A. S. Suvorinu*, Leningrad, 1927.

Allen, P. M., *Vladimir Soloviev: Russian Mystic*, Blauvelt, NY, 1978.

Antonov, K. M., *Filosofiia religii v russkoi metafizike XIX — nachala XX veka*, Moscow, 2009.

Asmus, V., and others, 'Solov'ev, Vladimir Sergeevich,' in *Filosofskaia entsiklopediia*, ed. F. B. Konstantinov, 5 vols, Moscow, 1960-70, v, pp. 51-56.

Avdeeva, L. P., 'Personalizm,' in *Russkaia filosofiia: Slovar'*, ed. M. A. Maslin, Moscow, 1999, pp. 367-69.

Averintsev, S. S., 'Ontologiia pravdy kak vnutrenniaia pruzhina mysli Vladimira Solov'eva,' in *Sofiia — Logos: Slovar'*, Kiev, 2001, pp. 413-16.

Balthasar, H. U., *The Glory of the Lord: A Theological Aesthetics*, San Francisco, 1996.

Bar-Yosef, H., 'Sophiology and the Concept of Femininity in Russian Symbolism and in Modern Hebrew Poetry,' *Journal of Modern Jewish Studies*, 2, 2003, 1, pp. 59-78.

Berdiaev, N. A., 'Osnovnaia ideia Vl. Solov'eva,' in *Sobranie sochinenii*, 5 vols, Paris, 1983-97, III, pp. 205-13.

---, 'Vladimir Solov'ev i my,' *Sovremennye zapiski*, 1937, 63, pp. 368-73.

---, 'Problema Vostoka i zapada v religioznom soznanii Vl. Solov'eva,' in *Kniga o Vladimire Solov'eve*, ed. B. V. Averin, Moscow, 1991, pp. 355-73.

---, *Filosofiia svobody — Istoki i smysl russkogo kommunizma*, Moscow, 1997.

Bibikhin, V. V., 'Dve legendy, odno videnie: inkvizitor i antikhrist,' *Iskusstvo kino*, 1994, 4, pp. 6-11.

---, 'Dobro, istina i nesushchestvovanie u Vladimira Solov'eva,' in A. P. Ogurtsov (ed), *Blago i istina: klassicheskie i neklassicheskie reguliativy*, Moscow, 1998, pp. 71-95.

J. Billington, *The Icon and the Axe: An Interpretive History of Russian Culture*, New York, 1970.

Bobro, M. E., *Self and Substance in Leibniz*, Dordrecht, 2004.

Bulgakov, S. N., 'Chto daet sovremennomu soznaniiu filosofiia Vl. Solov'eva,' in *Kniga o Vladimire Solov'eve*, ed. B. V. Averin, Moscow, 1991, pp. 389-447.

---, *Towards a Russian Political Theology*, ed. R. Williams, Edinburgh, 1999.

---, *Svet nevechernii: Sozertsaniia i umozreniia*, Moscow, 1994.

---, 'Priroda v filosofii Vl. Solov'eva,' in *Vl. Solov'ev: Pro et Contra*, ed. T. L. Samsonova, 2 vols, St Petersburg, 2002, pp. 618-43.

---, 'Muzhskoe i zhenskoe v Bozhestve,' in *Religioznyi-filosofskii put'*, ed. A. P. Kozyrev, Moscow, 2003, pp. 343-65.

Burmistrov, K., Vladimir Solov'ev i Kabbala,' *Issledovaniia po istorii russkoi mysli (Ezhegodnik)*, Moscow, 1998, pp. 7-104.

Bychkov, V. V., *Russkaia teurgicheskaia estetika*, Moscow, 2007.

Cioran, Samuel D., *Vladimir Solov'ev and the Knighthood of the Divine Sophia*, Waterloo, Ontario, 1977.

Coates, R., 'Mystical Union in the Philosophy of Vladimir Solovev,' in J. Andrew, D. Offord, R. Reid (eds), *Turgenev and Russian Culture: Essays to Honour Richard Peace*, Amsterdam, 2008, pp. 135-56.

Copleston, Frederick C., 'V. S. Solov'ev,' in *Russian Religious Philosophy: Selected Aspects*, Notre Dame, IN, 1988, pp. 201-40.

Courten, Manon de, *History, Sophia and the Russian Nation: A Reassessment of Vladimir Solov'ëv's Views on History and his Social Commitment*, Bern, Switzerland, 2004.

Crone, A. L., *Eros and Creativity in Russian Religious Renewal: The Philosophers and the Freudians*, Leiden and Boston, 2010.

Davidson, P., 'Vladimir Solov'ev and the Ideal of Prophecy,' *The Slavonic and East European Review*, 78, 2000, 4, pp. 643-70.

---, 'The Moral Dimension of the Prophetic Ideal: Pushkin and His Readers,' *Slavic Review*, 61, 2002, 3, pp. 490-518.

Desmond, W., 'God Beyond the Whole: Between Solov'ev and Shestov,' in *Is There a Sabbath for Thought? Between Religion and Philosophy*, New York, 2005, pp. 167-99.

Emerson, C., 'Solov'ev, the late Tolstoi, and the Early Bakhtin on the Problem of Shame and Love,' *Slavic Review*, 50, 3, 1991, pp. 663-71.

Evdokimov, P., *The Sacrament of Love: The Nuptial Mystery in the Light of the Orthodox Tradition*, trans. A. P. Gythiel and V. Steadman, Crestwood NY, 1985.

Evlampiev, I. I., *Istoriia russkoi metafiziki v XIX-XX vekakh. Russkaia filosofiia v poiskakh absoliuta*, 2 vols, Saint Petersburg, 2000.

---, 'Shopengauer i "Kritika otvlechennych nachal" v filosofii Vl. Solov'eva,' in *Issledovaniia po istorii russkoi mysli: Ezhegodnik*, M. A. Kolerov and N. S. Plotnikov (eds), Moscow, 2004/05, pp. 45-70.

Fateev, V. A., *S russkoi bezdnoi v dushe: zhizneopisanie Vasiliia Rozanova*, St Petersburg, 2002.

Fedotov, G. P., 'Ob antikhristovom dobre,' in *Litso Rossii: Sbornik statei (1918-1931)*, Paris, 1967, pp. 31-48.

Filaret, Mitropolit Minskii i Slutskii, 'Privetstvennoe slovo,' in *Rossiia i Vselenskaia Tserkov,*' ed. V. Porus, Moscow, 2004, pp. 7-9.

Florenskii, P., *The Pillar and Ground of the Truth*, trans. B. Jakim, Princeton, 1997.

Florovsky, G., *Ways of Russian Theology*, 2 vols., Vaduz, 1987.

Gaidenko, P., 'Gnosticheskie motivy v ucheniiakh Shellinga i Vl. Solov'eva,' in I. Surat (ed), *Vittorio: mezhdunarodnyi nauchnyi sbornik, posviashchennyi 75-letiiu Vittorio Strady*, Moscow, 2005, pp. 68-93.

Gallaher, G., 'The Christological Focus of Vladimir Solov'ev's Sophiology,' *Modern Theology*, 25, 4, 2009, pp. 617-46.

Gardner, Clinton, 'Vladimir Solov'ev: From Theism to Panentheism,' in *Vladimir Solov'ëv: Reconciler and Polemicist: Selected Papers of the International Vladimir Solov'ëv Conference held at the University of Nijmegen, the Netherlands, in September 1998*, ed. Wil van den Bercken, Manon de Courten and Evert van der Zweerde, Leuven, 2000, pp. 119-29.

Gavrilyuk, P. L. 'The Reception of Dionysius in Twentieth-Century Eastern Orthodoxy,' in S. Coakley (ed), *Re-Thinking Dionysius the Areopagite*, Malden, MA, 2009, pp. 177-94.

Grillaert, Nel, 'A Short Story about the Übermensch: Vladimir Solov'ëv's Interpretation of and Response to Nietzsche's Übermensch,' *Studies in East European Thought*, 55, 2003), 2, 157-84.

Gustafson, R. F., 'Soloviev's Doctrine of Salvation,' in *Russian Religious Thought*, Madison, WI, 1996, pp. 31-48.

Hamburg, G. M., and R. A. Poole, 'Introduction: The humanist tradition in Russian philosophy,' in *A History of Russian Philosophy 1830-1930: Faith, Reason and the Defense of Human Dignity*, Cambridge, 2010, pp. 1-26.

Helleman, W. E., 'The World Soul and Sophia in the Early Work of Solov'ev,' in *Vladimir Solov'ev: Reconciler and Polemicist. Selected Papers of the International Solov'ev Conference held in Nijmegen, September 1998*, ed. Wil van den Bercken, Manon de Courten and Evert van der Zweerde, Leuven, 2000, pp. 163-84.

Ianzhul, I. I., 'Vospominaniia o perezhitom,' *Russkaia starina*, 3, 1910, pp. 477-500.

Ivanova, I. I., 'Rol' obshchestvennykh organizatsii filosofov v obespechenii ikh vliianiia na obshchestvo,' in *Vyzovy sovremennosti i otvetstvennost' filosofa: materialy «Kruglogo stola», posviashchennogo vsemirnomu Dniu filosofii*, ed. I. I. Ivanova, Biskek, 2003, pp. 32-38.

Khoruzhii, S., 'V. Solov'ev i mistiko-asketicheskaia traditsiia Pravoslaviia,' in *O starom i novom*, St Petersburg, 2000, pp. 182-206.

---, 'Solov'ev i Nitsshe v krizise evropeiskogo cheloveka,' in *Opyty iz russkoi dukhovnoi traditsii*, Moscow, 2005, pp. 249-86.

Kline, G. L., 'Hegel and Solovyov,' in *Hegel and the History of Philosophy*, ed. J. J. O'Malley, K. W. Algozin and F. G. Weiss, The Hague, 1974, pp. 159-70.

Kornblatt, J. D., 'Solov'ev's Androgynous Sophia and the Jewish Kabbalah,' *Slavic Review*, 50, 1991), 3, pp. 487-96.

---, 'The Transfiguration of Plato in the Erotic Philosophy of Vladimir Solov'ev,' *Religion and Literature*, 24, 2, 1992, pp. 35-50

---, 'Russian Religious Thought and the Jewish Kabbala,' in *The Occult in Soviet and Russian Culture*, ed. B. G. Rosenthal, Ithaca, NY, 1997, pp. 75-95.

---, *The Wisdom Writings of Vladimir Solovyov*, Ithaca & London, 2009.

Kotrelev, N., "Blagonamerennost' ne spasaet cheloveka." Neizdannye avtografy Vladimira Solov'eva,' *Nashe nasledie*, 2000, 55, pp. 64-73.

---, 'Eskhatologiia u Vladimira Solov'eva («k istorii Trekh razgovorov»),' in *Eskhatologicheskii sbornik*, St Petersburg, 2006, pp. 238-57.

Kozyrev, A. P. 'Gnosticheskie vliianiia v filosofii Vladimira Solov'eva,' unpublished doctoral thesis, Moskovskii gosudarstvennyi universitet, Moscow, 1996.

---, *Solov'ev i gnostiki*, Moscow, 2007.

Krasitskii, Ia., *Bog, chelovek i zlo: Issledovanie filosofii Vladimir Solov'eva*, Moscow, 2009.

Krylov, D. A., *Evkharisticheskaia chasha: Sofiinye nachala*, Moscow, 2006.

Lavrin, J., 'Note on Solovyev,' in V. S. Solovyev, *Plato*, trans. R. Gill, London, 1935, pp. 1-21.

Lindblom, J., *Prophecy in Ancient Israel*, Oxford, 1962.

Lopatin, L. M., 'Filosofskoe mirovozzrenie V. S. Solov'eva,' in *Filosofskie kharakteristiki i rechi*, Minsk & Moscow, 2000, pp. 145-91.

Losev, Aleksei, *Vladimir Solov'ev i ego vremia*, Moscow, 2000.

N. A. Maksheeva, 'Vospominaniia o Vl. S. Solov'eve,' in *Vl. Solov'ev: pro et contra*, ed. D. K. Burlaka, 2 vols, 2000, I, pp. 360-72.

Masaryk, T. G., *Spirit of Russia: Studies in History, Literature and Philosophy*, trans. W. R. and Z. Lee, 3 vols, London, 1955.

Masing-Delic, I., *Abolishing Death: A Salvation Myth of Russian Twentieth Century Literature*, Stanford, CA, 1992.

---, '«Nasha liubov' nuzhna Rossii...»: Perepiska E. N. Trubetskogo i M. K. Morozovoi,' *Novyi mir*, 1993, 9, pp. 172-229.

Matich, Olga, *Erotic Utopia: The Decadent Imagination in Russia's Fin de Siècle*, Madison, WI, 2004.

Matseina, A., *Taina bezzakoniia*, St Petersburg, 1999.

Meerson, M. A., *The Trinity of Love in Modern Russian Theology: The Love Paradigm and the Retrieval of Western Medieval Love Mysticism in Modern Russian Trinitarian Thought (from Solovyov to Bulgakov)*, Quincy, IL, 1988.

Men', Aleksandr, 'Vladimir Solov'ev,' in *Russkaia religioznaia filosofiia*, Moscow, 2003, pp. 25-47.

Milbank, J., 'Sophiology and Theurgy: the New Theological Horizon,' *The Centre of Theology and Philosophy: Online Papers, University of Nottingham* (2007), <http://www.theologyphilosophycentre.co.uk/papers/Milbank_SophiologyTheurgy.doc> [accessed 16 June 2008]

Mints, Z., 'Vladimir Solov'ev — poet,' in *Stikhotvoreniia i shutochnye p'esy*, Moscow, 1974, pp. 5-56.

---, 'K genezisu komicheskogo u Bloka (Vl. Solov'ev i A. Blok),' in *Aleksandr Blok i russkie pisateli*, St Petersburg, 2000, pp. 389-442.

Mochul'skii, Konstantin, *Vladimir Solov'ev. Zhizn' i uchenie*, Paris, 1936.

Moss, Walter G., 'Vladimir Soloviev and the Jews in Russia,' *Russian Review*, 1970, 2, pp. 181-91.

Motroshilova, N. V., 'Vl. Solov'ev o F. Nitsshe: Poisk novykh filosofskikh paradigm,' in *Fridrikh Nitsshe i filosofiia v Rossii: sbornik statei*, St Petersburg, 1999, pp. 46-57.

Müller, Ludolf, 'Nietzsche und Solovjev,' *Zeitschrift für philosophische Forschung*, 1, 1947, 4, pp. 499-520.

Munzer, Egbert, 'Solovyev and the Meaning of History,' *The Review of Politics*, 11, 1949, 3, pp. 281-93.

Nethercott, F., *Russian Legal Culture Before and After Communism: Criminal justice, politics and the public sphere*, London and New York, 2007.

Nikol'skii, A., *Russkii Origen XIX veka Vl. S. Solov'ev*, St Petersburg, 2000.

A. Pabst, 'Wisdom and the Art of Politics,' in A. Pabst and C. Schneider (eds), *Encounter Between Eastern Orthodoxy and Radical Orthodoxy: Transfiguring the World Through the Word*, Farnham, Surrey, 2009, pp. 109-40.

Pild, L., 'Geine v literaturnom dialoge K. Sluchevskogo i Vl. Solov'eva,' in *Sbornik statei v chest' Tat'iany Vladimirovny Tsiv'ian*, ed. L. Zaionts, Moscow, 2007, pp. 156-65.

Polovinkin, S. M. 'V. S. Solov'ev i russkoe neoleibnitsianstvo,' *Voprosy filosofii*, 2, 2002, pp. 90-96.

Poulin, F., 'Vladimir Solov'ev's *Rossiia i vselenskaia tser'kov*, Early Slavophilism's Pneumatic Spirit, and the Pauline Prophet,' *Russian Review*, 52, 1993, 4, pp. 528-39.

Preobrazhenskii, V. P., 'Fridrikh Nitsshe, kritika morali al'truizma,' *Voprosy filosofii i psikhologii*, 1892, 15, pp. 115-60.

Rashkovskii, E. B., *Smysli v istorii: Issledovaniia po istorii very, poznaniia, kul'tury*, Moscow, 2008.

---, 'Bibleiskii realizm, ili "opravdanie" istorii v trudakh pozdnego Solov'eva (vmesto poslesloviia),' in Ia. Krasitskii, *Bog, chelovek i zlo: Issledovanie filosofii Vladimira Solov'eva*, Moscow, 2009, pp. 427-44.

Rotsinskii, S. B., *Vladimir Solov'ev i zapadnaia mysl': Kritika, Primirenie, Sintez*, Moscow, 1999.

Rozanov, V. V., 'Khristianstvo passivno ili aktivno?' in *Religiia. Filosofiia. Kul'tura*, Moscow, 1992, pp. 143-53.

---, 'Avtoportret Vl. S. Solov'eva,' in *Okolo narodnoi dushi: Stat'i 1906-08 gg.*, Moscow, 2003, pp. 392-99.

Schrooyen, Pauline, 'The Resolution of the "Great Controversy": The Debate between Vladimir Solov'ëv and Aleksandr Kireev on the Question of Church (Re)Union (1883-1897),' *Journal of Eastern Christian Studies*, 57, 2005, 1-2, pp. 67-90.

Seiling, J. 'Soloviev's Early Idealism and the Birth of Sophia,' *Conference of the Association for the Study of Eastern Christian History and Culture (ASEC)*, October 2005 (received through personal correspondence), p. 11 of 32.

Semenova, S., *Filosof budushchego veka: Nikolai Fedorov*, Moscow, 2004.

Shchegolev, P., ed., 'Sobytie 1-ogo marta i Vladimir Solov'ev: Novye dokumenty,' in *Byloe*, 1918, 4-5, pp. 330-36.

Shestov, L., 'Umozrenie i Apokalipsis,' in *Vladimir Solov'ev: Pro et Contra*, ed. D. K. Burlaka, 2 vols, Saint Petersburg, 2002, II, pp. 467-530.

Silakova, D. V., '«Nesladnykh virshei polk za polkom nam shlet Vladimir Solov'ev»: Poeziia Vladimira Solov'eva v zhurnale "Vestnik Evropy",' *Aktsenty*, 2004, 1-2, pp. 50-54.

Solov'ev, S. M., *Vladimir Solov'ev: Zhizn' i tvorcheskaia evoliutsiia*, Moscow, 1997.

Strémooukhoff, Dimitri, *Vladimir Solov'ev and His Messianic Work*, trans. E. Meyendorff, Belmont, MA, 1979.

Sutton, J., 'The Centenary of the Death of Vladimir Solov'ëv,' *Studies in East European Thought*, 2000, 52, pp. 309-26.

---, *The Religious Philosophy of Vladimir Solovyov — Towards a Reassessment*, Basingstoke, 1988.

Suvorin, A, ed., 'V filosofskom obshchestve,' *Novoe vremia*, 13 Oct 1898, no. 8126, p. 3.

Swiderski, E., 'Vladimir Solov'ëv's "Virtue Epistemology",' *Studies in East European Thought*, 1999, 53, pp. 199-218.

Tikholaz, A. G., 'Platon v filosofii vseedinstva Vladimira Solov'eva,' in *Platon i platonizm v russkoi religioznoi filosofii vtoroi poloviny XIX — nachala XX vekov*, Kiev, 2003, pp. 149-200.

Trubetskoi, E. N., *Mirosozertsanie Vl. Solov'eva*, 2 vols, Moscow, 1995.

Trubetskoi, S. N., 'Predislovie,' in *Sobranie sochinenii*, ed. E. L. Radlov and S. M. Solov'ev, 12 vols, Moscow, 1966, XII, pp. 496-99.

Valliere, P., 'Vladimir Solov'ev (1853-1900): Commentary,' in *The Teachings of Modern Orthodox Christianity: On Law, Politics, & Human Nature*, ed. J. Witte Jr and F. S. Alexander, New York, 2007, pp. 33-68.

Valliere, Paul, 'Sophiology as the Dialogue of Orthodoxy with Modern Civilization,' in *Russian Religious Thought*, ed. J. D. Kornblatt and R. F. Gustavson, Madison, WI, 1996, pp. 176-192.

---, *Modern Russian Theology: Bukharev, Soloviev, Bulgakov: Orthodox Theology in a New Key*, Edinburgh, 2000.

Zen'kovskii, V. V., 'Vladimir Solov'ev,' in *Istoriia russkoi filosofii*, 2 vols, Paris, 1950, pp. 11-72.

---, 'Russkie mysliteli i Evropa,' Moscow, 1996, pp. 114-40.

---, 'Esteticheskie vozzreniia Vl. Solov'eva,' in *Russkie mysliteli i evropa*, Moscow, 1997, pp. 278-87.

Zernov, Nicolas, *Three Russian Prophets: Khomiakov, Dostoevskii, Soloviev*, London, 1944.

---, *The Russian Religious Renaissance of the Twentieth Century*, London, 1963.

Other Works Consulted

Aquinas, T., *Aquinas on Creation*, trans. S. E. Baldner and W. E. Carroll, Toronto, 1997.

Armstrong, A. H., 'Platonic Eros and Christian Agape,' *Downside Review*, 1964, 79, pp. 105-21.

Athanasius, *On the Incarnation*, trans. and ed. a religious of C. S. M. V., Crestwood, NY, 1998.

Augustine, 'Psalm XXXVIII,' in *Expositions of the Book of Psalms*, London, 1848, pp. 68-94.

---, *The Greatness of the Soul; The Teacher*, trans. J. Colleran, New York, 1949.

---, *The Enchiridion on Faith, Hope and Love*, trans. H. Paolucci, Washington, DC, 1996.

Aune, D., 'Apocalyptic,' in *Westminster Dictionary of New Testament and Early Christian Literature*, Louisville, KY, and London, 2003, pp. 46-50.

Baker, A., and R. Gangle, 'Ecclesia: The Art of the Visual,' in C. Davis, J. Milbank and S. Žižek (eds), *Theology and the Political: The New Debate*, Durham and London, 2005, pp. 267-80.

Barth, K., 'Agape and Eros,' in *Church Dogmatics: A Selection*, Louisville & London, 1994, pp. 173-93.

Belinskii, V. G., *Sochineniia Aleksandra Pushkina*, Moscow, 1995.

Boehme, Jacob, *The Signature of All Things*, trans. J. Sparrow, London, 1934.

---, *Mysterium Magnum, or an Exposition of the First Book of Moses Called Genesis*, trans. John Sparrow, 2 vols, London, 1965.

---, *Essential Readings*, ed. Robin Waterfield, Wellingborough, 1989.

Boland, V., *Ideas in God according to Saint Thomas Aquinas*, Leiden, 1996

Bonhoeffer, D., ed. E. Bethge, *Letters and Papers from Prison*, New York, 1971.

Bowie, A., *Schelling and Modern European Philosophy: an Introduction*, London and New York, 1993.

Boyd, James, *Notes to Goethe's Poems*, 2 vols, Oxford, 1944-49.

Brueggemmann, W., *The Prophetic Imagination*, Minneapolis, 2001.

Bulgakov, S. N., *The Comforter*, trans. B. Jakim, Grand Rapids, MI, 2004.

---, *The Lamb of God*, Grand Rapids, MI, 2008.

Bultmann, R., *Theology of the New Testament*, trans. K. Grobel, 2 vols, London, 1965.

The Jesuit Series, ed. P. M. Daly and G. R. Dimler, 5 vols, Toronto, 2002, III.

Clayton, P., *Mind and Emergence: From Quantum to Consciousness*, Oxford, 2006.

Collins, P., *Partaking in Divine Nature: Deification and Communion*, London, 2010.

Derrida, J., 'Faith and Knowledge: The Two Sources of "Religion" at the Limits of Reason Alone,' in *Acts of Religion*, ed. G. Anidjar, New York, 2002, pp. 40-101.

Descartes, R., *The Philosophical Writings of Descartes*, trans. J. Cottingham, R. Stoothoff and D. Murdoch, 3 vols, Cambridge, 1984-91.

Dostoevskii, F. M., *Polnoe sobranie sochinenii*, 30 vols, Leningrad, 1972-88.

Dupuis, J., *Toward a Christian Theology of Religious Pluralism*, Maryknoll, NY, 1997.

---, 'The Truth will Make you Free,' *Louvain Studies*, 24, 1999, 3, pp. 211-63.

Ellacuría, I., 'Utopia and Prophecy in Latin America,' in *Mysterium liberationis: fundamental concepts of liberation theology*, ed. I. Ellacuría and J. Sobrino, New York, 1993, pp. 289-328.

Evans, Frederick, *Autobiography of a Shaker, and Revelation of the Apocalypse with an Appendix*, New York, 1889.

Fechner, G. T., *Über die physikalische und philosophische Atomenlehre. Zweite vermehrte Auflage*, Leipzig, 1864.

Filaret, 'Beseda po osviashchenii khrama Sviatago Blagovernago Velikago Kniazia Aleksandra Nevskago, pri dome Kommercheskoi Akademii,' in *Sochineniia Filareta Mitropolita Moskovskago i Kolomenskago: slova i rechi*, ed. A. I. Mamontova, 5 vols, Moscow, 1873-85, v, pp. 136-40.

Freitheim, T. E., 'Nature's Praise of God in the Psalms,' *Ex Auditu*, 1987, 3, pp. 16-30.

Gameleia, S. N., *Pis'ma*, Moscow, 4 vols, 1856-60.

Garber, Daniel, 'Leibniz, Gottfried Wilhelm,' *Routledge Encyclopedia of Philosophy* (1998) <http://www.rep.routledge.com/article/DA952SECT11> [accessed 12 January 2006]

Garber, D., *Leibniz, Body, Substance, Monad*, Oxford and New York, 2009, p. 199.

Gavrilyuk, P. L., *The Suffering of the Impassible God: the Dialectics of Patristic Thought*, Oxford, 2005.

Gill, C., 'The Ēthos/Pathos Distinction in Rhetorical and Literary Criticism,' *The Classical Quarterly*, 34, 1984, 1, pp. 149-66.

Goethe, *Faust: Part One*, trans. D. Luke, Oxford, 1998.

Golubinskii, F. A., and D. G. Levitskii, *Premudrost' i blagost' Bozhiia v sud'bakh mira i cheloveka (o konechnykh prichinakh)*, St Petersburg, 1907.

Hampshire, Stuart, *Spinoza and Spinzoism*, Oxford, 2005.

Hegel, G. W. F., *Aesthetics: Lectures on Fine Art*, trans. T. M. Knox, 2 vols, Oxford, 1998.

---, *Phenomenology of Spirit*, trans. A. V. Miller, Oxford, 1977.

---, *The Encyclopaedia Logic*, trans. T. F. Geraets, W. A. Suchting and H. S. Harris, Indianopolis, 1991.

---, *Hegel's Phenomenology of spirit: selections*, ed. Howard P. Kainz, University Park, PA, 1994.

Heidegger, M., 'The Word of Nietzsche: "God is Dead",' in *The Question Concerning Technology and Other Essays*, New York, 1977, pp. 53-112.

Heschel, A., *The Prophets*, New York, 2001.

Hölscher, G., *Die Profeten*, Leipzig, 1914.

Hoyles, J., *The Edges of Augustinianism: the Aesthetics of Spirituality in Thomas Ken, John Byrom and William Law*, The Hague, 1972.

Iurkevich, P. D., 'Serdtse i ego znachenie v dukhovnoi zhizni cheloveka, po ucheniiu slova Bozhiia,' in *Filosofskie proizvedeniia*, ed. A. I. Abramov and I. V. Borisova, Moscow, 1990, pp. 69-103.

Jantzen, G., *Power, Gender and Christian Mysticism*, Cambridge, 1995.

Jones, P. D., 'Barth and Anselm: God, Christ and the Atonement,' *International Journal of Systematic Theology*, 12, 2010, 3, pp. 257-82.

Theological Dictionary of the New Testament, Kittel, G., and G. Friedrich (eds.), Grand Rapids MI, 1985.

Kahn, C. H. 'Sensation and Consciousness in Aristotle's Psychology,' in *Articles on Aristotle. Vol. IV Psychology and Aesthetics*, London, 2003, pp. 1-31.

Kierkegaard, S., *Papers and Journals: A Selection*, London, 1996.

Knorr von Rosenroth, Christian, *Kabbala Denudata*, ed. S. L. M. Mathers, London, 1887.

Losev, A., 'Eros u Platona,' in *Bytie, imia, kosmos*, Moscow, 1993, pp. 32-60.

Louth, A., 'The Place of *Theosis* in Orthodox Theology,' in *Partakers of the Divine Nature: The History and Development of Deification in the Christian Traditions*, ed. M. J. Christensen and J. A. Wittung, Madison, 2007, pp. 32-44.

Majercik, R., 'Introduction,' in *The Chaldean oracles: text, translation, and commentary*, Leiden, 1989, pp. 1-46.

Maritain, J. M., *True Humanism*, trans. M. R. Adamson, London, 1941.

Mathers, S. L. M., 'Introduction,' in *Kabbala Denudata*, London, 1887, pp. 4-35.

McGuckian, M., 'The Sacramental Sacrifice,' in *The Holy Sacrifice Of The Mass: A Search For An Acceptable Notion Of Sacrifice*, Mundelein IL, 2005, pp. 107-33.

McHugh, J. F., 'The sacrifice of the mass at the Council of Trent,' in *Sacrifice and Redemption: Durham Essays in Theology*, ed. S. W. Sykes, Cambridge, 2007, pp. 157-81.

McMullin, E., 'Introduction,' in *The Concept of Matter in Greek and Medieval Philosophy*, ed. E. McMullin, Notre Dame IN, 1965, pp. 1-23.

McNamara, K. (ed.), *Dogmatic Constitution on the Church — Vatican II: The Constitution of the Church*, Chicago, 1968.

Moberly, W., *Prophecy and discernment*, Cambridge, 2006.

Moltmann, Jürgen, *God in Creation: An Ecological Doctrine of Creation*, London, 1985.

Mure, G. R. G., *The Philosophy of Hegel*, London, 1965.

Nietzsche, F., *The Birth of Tragedy*, trans. W. Kaufmann, New York, 1967.

---, *Will to Power*, trans. W. Kaufmann, New York, 1968.

---, *Beyond Good and Evil*, trans. H. Zimmern, New York, 1989.

Nygren, A., *Agape and Eros*, London, 1953.

Plato, *Symposium*, trans. C. Gill, London, 1999.

---, *Phaedrus*, trans. C. J. Rowe, Warminster, 2000.

Pushkin, A. S., *Pis'ma*, ed. B. L. Modzalevskii, 3 vols, Moscow, 1989.

Rahner, K., *The Practice of Faith*, ed. K. Lehmann and A. Raffelt, London, 1985.

Riches, P. 'Deification as Metaphysics: Christology, Desire and Filial Prayer,' in P. M. Candler Jr and C. Cunningham (eds), *Belief and Metaphysics*, Nottingham, 2007, pp. 345-73.

Rist, J., 'A Note on Eros and Agape in Pseudo-Dionysius,' *Vigiliae Christianae*, 20, 1966, 4, pp. 235-43.

Robinson, J. A. T., *The Body: A Study in Pauline Theology*, London, 1966.

Rudolf, K., *Gnosis: the nature and the history of gnosticism*, trans. R. M. Wilson, San Francisco, 1983.

Russell, B., *A Critical Exposition of the Philosophy of Leibniz*, London, 2005.

Ryba, T., 'Manifestation,' in W. Braun and R. T. McCutcheon (eds), *Guide to the Study of Religion*, London, 2006, pp. 168-89.

Schelling, F. W. J. *The Ages of the World*, Albany, NY, 2000.

---, *Philosophical Investigations into the Essence of Human Freedom*, Albany, NY, 2006.

Schmitt, C., *Roman Catholicism and Political Form*, Westport, CT, 1996.

Scholem, G., 'Schöpfung aus Nichts und Selbstverschränkung Gottes,' *Eranos Jahrbuch*, 1956, 25, pp. 87-119.

---, *Kabbalah*, Jerusalem, 1974.

Schopenhauer, A., *On the Basis of Morality*, trans. E. F. J. Payne, Providence RI, 1995.

Schwartz, S., *Judaism and Justice: the Jewish Passion to Repair the World*, Woodstock VT, 2006.

Sherman, R. L., *King, Priest and Prophet*, New York, 2004.

Shestov, L., *Afiny i Ierusalim*, Paris, 1951.

---, *Potestas clavium*, trans. B. Martin, Athens, OH, 1968.

Sikka, S., 'On the Truth of Beauty: Nietzsche, Heidegger, Keats,' *Heythrop Journal*, 39, 1998, 3, pp. 243-63.

Sobrino, J., 'Communion, Conflict and Ecclesial Solidarity,' in *Mysterium Liberationis: Fundamental Concepts of Liberation Theology*, ed. I. Ellacuria and J. Sobrino, Maryknoll, NY, 1993, pp. 615-36.

Stern, R., *Routledge philosophy guidebook to Hegel and the phenomenology of spirit*, London, 2002.

Stoeber, M., 'Dostoevsky's Devil: The Will to Power,' *Journal of Religion*, 74, 1994, 1, pp. 26-44.

Tanner, K., *God and Creation in Christian Theology: Tyranny and Empowerment?*, Oxford, 1988.

Terada, R., *Feeling in theory: emotion after the "death of the subject,"* Cambridge, MA, 2001.

Terras, V., *Belinskij and Russian Literary Criticism: the Heritage of Organic Aesthetics*, Madison, WI, 1974.

Trismogin, S., *Splendor Solis: Alchemial Treatises of Solomon Trismogin*, London, 1920.

Trubetskoi, E. N., 'Svet Favorskii i preobrazhenie uma,' *Voprosy filosofii*, 12, 1989, pp. 112-29.

Vlastos, G., *Platonic Studies*, Princeton, 1973.

von Rad, G., *Old Testament Theology*, trans. D. M. G. Stalker, 2 vols, London, 1979.

Waltzburger, W. S., 'Prophets and Prophecy,' in *Encyclopaedia Judaica*, 16 vols, 1973, XIII, pp. 1150-1182.

Ward, G., 'Death, Discourse and Resurrection,' in L. Gardner, D. Moss, B. Quash and G. Ward (eds), *Balthasar at the End of Modernity*, 1999, pp. 15-68 (p. 52).

Ware, T., *The Orthodox Church*, Harmondsworth, 1972.

Warminski, A., 'Reading for Example: "Sense-Certainty" in Hegel's Phenomenology of Spirit,' *Diacritics*, 11, 1981, 2, pp. 83-95.

Weber, S., *Targets of Opportunity: On the Militarization of Thinking*, New York, 2005, p. 27.

Williams, L. L., 'Will to Power in Nietzsche's Published Works and the Nachlass,' *Journal of the History of Ideas*, 57, 1996, 3, pp. 447-63.

Williams, R., *Dostoevsky: Language, Faith & Fiction*, Waco, TX, 2008.

Zöller, G., 'Schopenhauer on the Self,' in *Cambridge Companion to Schopenhauer*, Cambridge, 1999, pp. 18-43.

Zubiri, X., *Nature, History, God*, trans. T. B. Fowler, Washington D. C., 1981.

PRINCIPAL WORKS CITED

1874 The Crisis of Western Philosophy: Against the Positivists
1876 Sophie/La Sophia
1877 Filosofskie nachala tsel'nogo znaniia (Philosophical Principles of Integral Knowledge)
1877-81 Chteniia o Bogochelovechestve (Lectures on Theanthropy)
1880 Kritika otvlechennykh nachal (Critique of Abstract Principles)
1880-81 Lektsii po istorii filosofii (Lectures on the History of Philosophy)
1881 Tri rechi v pamiat' Dostoevskogo (Three Speeches in Honour of Dostoevsky)
1882-84 Dukhovnye osnovy zhizni (The Spiritual Foundations of Life)
1883 Velikii spor i khristianskaia politika (The Great Schism and Christian Politics)
1884 Evreistvo i khristianskii vopros (The Jews and the Christian Question)
1886 Istoriia i budushchnost' teokratii (The History and Future of Theocracy)
1888 *La Russie et l'église universelle* (Russia and the Universal Church)
1890 Obshchii smysl iskusstva (The General Meaning of Art)
1891 Ob upadke srednevekovogo mirosozertsaniia (On the Decline of the Mediaeval Worldview)
1891 O poddelkakh (On Counterfeits)
1892-94 Smysl liubvi (The Meaning of Love)
1894 Pervyi shag k polozhitel'noi estetike (First Step toward a Positive Aesthetics)
1894 Opravdanie dobra (Justification of the Good)
1897 Sud'ba Pushkina (Pushkin's Fate)
1897-98 Voskresnye pis'ma (Sunday Letters)
1897-99 Teoreticheskaia Filosofiia (Theoretical Philosophy)
1898 Zhiznennaia drama Platona (The Life Drama of Plato)
1899 Znachenie poezii v stikhotvoreniiakh Pushkina (The Meaning of Poetry in the Verse of Pushkin)
1899 Ideia sverkhcheloveka (The Idea of the Superman)
1899 Krasota v prirode (Beauty in Nature)
1900 Tri razgovora (Three Conversations), inc. Kratkaia povest' ob antikhriste (Short Story of the Antichrist)

Appendix
GLOSSARY

БОГОЧЕЛОВЕЧЕСТВО n. (adj. богочеловеческий, n. богочеловек) = Theanthropy. Together with всеединство (see below), one of the key terms of Soloviev's philosophical discourse. Jonathan Seiling has demonstrated that, far from being a heterodox innovation or a Gnostic borrowing, the conceptual cluster *theanthropia — theandria — theandropos*, from which it is all but certain Soloviev derived the exact Russian counterparts богочеловечество and богочеловек, is encountered throughout the patristic writings, most notably in Maximus the Confessor and John of Damascus.[1] Paul Valliere, however, considers these terms to be atypical of the patristics.[2]

ВСЕЕДИНСТВО n. (adj. всеединый) = All-Unity. Alongside sophiology, the term most often used to describe Soloviev's philosophy as a whole ('Philosophy of All-Unity'). It is very likely that Soloviev developed the term from the Greek formula εν και παν ('one and all'), which dates back to Heraclitus, and can be found in many of Soloviev's early works. It features in the treatises of Hermes Trismegistus ('Thrice-Great Hermes'), which Soloviev may have read during his time in London. Later, it became the slogan of the Jena Romantics, including Schelling, Novalis and Hölderlin, and is the title of the Goethe poem quoted by Soloviev in *Critique of Abstract Principles*.[3]

НЕПОСРЕДСТВЕННЫЙ adj. = direct. A word of vital importance in Soloviev's thought, which does not have a precise equivalent in English. Its root, посредство, means 'mediation,' and непосредственный carries the meaning of 'without mediation,' i.e. that which is primary, and is thus the equivalent of the German philosophical term *unmittelbar*.

СУЩЕЕ n. = the substantial. Истинно сущее, абсолютно сущее, безусловное сущее, сущее всеединое, and всеединое are all terms that Soloviev applies

---

[1] J. Seiling, 'Soloviev's Early Idealism and the Birth of Sophia,' *Conference of the Association for the Study of Eastern Christian History and Culture (ASEC)*, October 2005 (received through personal correspondence), p. 11 of 32.
[2] See n. 12 in Paul Valliere, *Modern Russian Theology: Bukharev, Soloviev, Bulgakov: Orthodox Theology in a New Key*, Edinburgh, 2000, p. 13.
[3] PSS, III., pp. 338-39.

to the absolute, or God, in its full manifestation. The Russian word сущее, an adjectival noun, has the same root as существо, meaning 'essence,' or 'being.' It is possibly the most crucial of all terms in Soloviev's early philosophy but also one of the hardest to translate. He uses it to express the totality of reality, in all its forms, as a living organism, i.e. God as both the foundation and living form of all. It is Soloviev's response to the Kantian *Ding an sich* ('the thing in-itself'), and in many ways corresponds to Hegel's *die Sache selbst* ('the Thing itself,' or 'the really real'). But it is profoundly dissimilar to this latter in one important respect: whereas for Hegel *die Sache selbst* is that which is absolutely *known*, for Soloviev абсолютно сущее is that which absolutely *is*. The moment of being is stressed over and against the moment of knowing. Since Soloviev means to introduce a qualitatively new understanding of *substance*, which combines elements of Christian theology with modern philosophy, he avoids the Latinized term субстанция. In the Liturgy of St John Chrystostom, the Greek word *homoousios*, which was intended by the early church fathers to safeguard the unity of the Christian Godhead, is translated into Russian as единосущна, with which сущее shares its root. Soloviev's readers would have been familiar with the word's usage in this religious context, as well as its everyday meaning of 'existing,' or 'that which is.' *Homoousios* is commonly rendered in English-language rites as '(being) of one substance.' *Substance* in English thus has a philosophical *and* a religious application, both of which express a total-unity, and seems the best choice here. Unless otherwise stated, wherever абсолютно, or безусловно сущее occurs, it is translated as 'the absolute substance' (сущее всеединое = 'the all-one substance'). Сущее by itself is translated as 'the substantial.' In the rare cases that Soloviev uses the word субстанция, this has been indicated.

СУЩНОСТЬ n. = essence. Related to his thought on Sophia, Soloviev's use of the word includes elements from the philosophy of both Plato and Aristotle, as well as later scholastic thinkers.

УМОПОСТИГАЕМЫЙ adj. = intelligible. Умопостигаемый, which occurs regularly in Soloviev's discourse, is used in a similar way to Kant's *verständlich*, usually translated *intelligible*.

INDEX

Absolute, the, 22, 35-36, 49-77, 84, 86-88, 93, 174 n. 89, 214 n. 12, 220 n. 30, 221, 242, 246 n. 19
aesthetics, 206, 223, 257-58, 261, 262, 265-67
Aksakov, Ivan Sergeevich, 148, 149 n. 4
alchemy, 214 n. 12
Alexander II, Tsar of Russia, 150
Alexander III, Tsar of Russia, 147, 149-50, 156, 158 n. 32
All-Unity (*vseedinstvo*), 11, 13, 14 n. 36, 34, 39 n. 60, 46, 78, 87, 89, 95, 100, 103-04, 132 n. 104, 179, 183-86, 258
androgyne, 254 n. 47
anthropology, 13, 36, 93-95, 101-05, 113, 120-21, 140-41, 229
antichrist, 147, 157, 168-74, 175, 182, 183-85, 193, 255, 263, 264 n. 77, 267 n. 89
Aphrodite, 241, 250
Aquinas, Thomas, St, 57 n. 102, 87
Aristotle, 211 n. 4
Arnold, Gottfried, 75 n. 157
Athanasius, St, 128 n. 89
atomism, 36-37, 40-46, 81, 83
Augustine of Hippo, St, 69 n. 135, 191 n. 131, 210, 216, 221 n. 34
Averintsev, Sergei, 6-7

Bakhtin, Mikhail, 281
Barth, Karl, 123 n. 75, 142, 243 n. 11
Belinskii, Vissarion, 181-82, 188-90, 250, 253 n. 44
Benedict XVI, Pope, 244
Berdiaev, Nikolai, 153
    Soloviev as viewed by, 175-76 n. 94, 177-78, 245-46
Bibikhin, Vladimir, 15 n. 38, 182, 184-85

Bible, 1, 2, 5, 6, 13, 87, 96-97, 99, 101, 104, 109, 113, 117, 122, 133, 159, 162, 169-70 n. 74, 196, 211 n. 4, 214 n. 12, 243-44, 257, 266, 278-79
    Soloviev as translator/interpreter of, 142, 244
    exegesis, 141 n. 130,

Blok, Aleksandr, 164 n. 49

body, 203 n. 166, 244, 246
    relation to soul, 38, 39 n. 61, 40, 81, 209, 210, 211, 213

Boehme, Jacob, 25 n. 16, 30, 40 n. 65, 48 n. 85, 53 n. 92, 58 n. 106, 59 n. 108, 61, 75 n. 157, 86, 173, 191 n. 131, 214 n. 12

Bonhoeffer, Dietrich, 116

Bulgakov, Sergii, 16 n. 40, 49 n. 86, 116 n. 60, 164, 243 n. 10, 245, 260 n. 63, 277 n. 1
    Soloviev as viewed by, 57 n. 103, 59 n. 108, 96 n. 8, 240

Calvin, John, 197

Catholic theology, 136 n. 117, 164 n. 51, 245, 246 n. 19, 248 n. 26, 279

Chalcedon, Council of, 122 n. 70, 277 n. 1

Charlemagne, 194 n. 140

Chicherin, Boris, 258

Constantine the Great, Emperor, 194 n. 140

christology
    Theanthropy (*bogochelovechestvo*), 13, 93, 95, 111, 116-18, 119, 132, 134-37, 187, 198, 156
    resurrection body, 13, 126-31, 135-38, 140, 143-44, 254
    as second person of trinity, 137

Church (ecclesiology), 2 n. 3, 107, 116 n. 57, 122-24, 131-38, 143-44, 187, 196, 254, 279
    as Body of Christ, 32, 133, 134 n. 109, 135-38, 204
    reconciliation of, 155-56, 183

Comte, Auguste, 22 n. 6, 107 n. 36

creation, 49, 66, 84 n. 175, 87, 95, 96-97, 99, 101-04, 109 n. 42, 110-111, 112, 114-15, 116 n. 60, 118, 123 n. 75, 131, 143 n. 137, 206 n. 170, 221, 223, 229, 242, 248

Daniel, Book of, 190-91

Dante Alighieri, 194 n. 140

Darwin, Charles, 96-97, 99

de Condillac, Étienne Bonnot, 212

de Lubac, Henri, 248-49 n. 26

demiurge, 83-84, 90, 98

INDEX

Democritus, 46 n. 79
Derrida, Jacques, 137 n. 119,
Descartes, René, 38, 39, 212 n. 7
Desmond, William, 17, 26 n. 21, 184-86, 189, 235, 267 n. 89, 280
Dionysius the Areopagite, 49 n. 86, 250 n. 30
Dostoevsky, Fedor, 105, 128 n. 89, 150, 175, 182, 222-23
Duns Scotus, Blessed John, 214 n. 12, 232 n. 64
Dupuis, Jacques, 124

Ellacuría, Ignatio, 110 n. 45
emergence, 21, 48 n. 85, 49, 80, 97, 100-01, 112-14, 118, 121, 128, 143-44, 223,
en-soph, 59-62, 63-64, 66, 74, 210
Erdmann, Johann, 26 n. 21
eros, 180, 243-50, 253-55, 261-63, 266 n. 84
eschatology, 99 n. 14, 102-03, 190 n. 130, 193, 202-03, 205, 239-42, 246-67, 251-52, 255-56, 257-58, 278
ethics, 7, 21, 79-80, 84, 161, 167-68, 172-73, 192 n. 134, 209, 229-31, 270
    relation to ontology, 48, 102, 105
Eucharist, 134-37, 148-51

Fechner, Gustav, 44 n. 75
Fedorov, Nikolai, 33 n. 49, 108
Fedotov, Grigorii, 169-70, 172
feeling, 61, 66, 173 n. 87, 186-87, 189, 209-13, 214, 229-36, 242, 251, 253, 281
    relation to will/representation, 62, 78, 212 n. 9, 215
    and creativity, 218-21, 225, 227-28
    and love, 258, 259, 261
    and prophecy, 228-29
Fichte, Johann Gottlib, 213
Filaret (Drozdov), Metropolitan of Moscow, 191 n. 131
Florenskii, Pavel, 78 n. 162, 243 n. 10, 278,
    Soloviev as viewed by, 25 n. 16
Florovsky, Georges, 49 n. 87
    Soloviev as viewed by, 163-64, 196 n. 147
Frank, Semen, 278-79

Gamaleia, Semen, 191 n. 131
Genesis, Book of, 57 n. 102, 60, 64 n. 119, 66, 99, 101

Gets, Faivel', 159

Gichtel, Georg, 75 n. 157

Gnosticism, 26, 27, 82-83 n. 171, 84 n. 175, 85, 87, 89 n. 185, 94, 113, 141, 241, 253 n. 42

Goethe, Johann Wolfgang von, 45 n. 75, 46 n. 80, 170, 219

Gogol', Nikolai, 253 n. 44

Golenishchev-Kutuzov, Arsenii, 269

Golubinskii, Fedor, 25 n. 16, 78 n. 162, 141 n. 130

Grazhdanin (journal), 68

Hannaniah, false prophet, 158

Hegel, Georg Wilhelm Friedrich, 5 n. 11, 26, 32, 33 n. 46, 48 n. 85, 50-52, 70-73, 77 n. 159, 95 n. 6, 200, 214 n. 12, 218 n. 23, 220 n. 30, 232 n. 64, 234, 239, 250, 253 n. 43, 255, 263-66, 267 n. 50, 271

Heidegger, Martin, 174 n. 90,

Hermes Trismegistus, 89

Hippolytus of Rome, St, 27, 82 n. 71, 169

Hosea, Book of, 244

Ianzhul, Ivan, 27-28

incarnation,

Irenaeus of Lyons, St, 169

Isaiah, Book of, 64 n. 121

Iurkevich, Pamfil, 25, 26, 41 n. 66, 211 n. 4, 216

Izvestiia slavianskogo obshchestva (journal), 157

Janssen, Johannes, 170 n. 74

John, Gospel of, 66 n. 125, 121, 133 n. 108, 143, 181 n. 112

Judaism, 160-62
    reconciliation with Christianity, 154, 155, 160

Kabbala, 27-28, 59, 60 n. 110, 88-89, 107 n. 36, 159, 214 n. 12, 254 n. 47

Kant, Immanuel, 5, 32, 44, 47, 102

Katkov, Mikhail, 149 n. 5, 158

Ken, Thomas, 191 n. 131

kenosis (self-emptying), 69, 85, 122, 127, 136-37, 143, 216, 218, 248-49, 281

Kern, Anna, 241 n. 6

Khoruzhii, Sergei,
    Soloviev as viewed by, 95 n. 6, 163-64
Kierkegaard, Søren, 192 n. 132
Kingdom of God, 2, 11, 105-13, 117, 178, 195, 196, 201, 202, 241
Kireev, Aleksandr, 158-59

Leibniz, Gottfried Wilhelm, 36, 39-45, 46 n. 79, 47-48, 53 n. 92, 69 n. 136, 140 n. 126
Leontiev, Konstantin, 128 n. 89
Lermontov, Mikhail, 173, 253 n. 44, 266-67
liberation theology, 110-11 n. 45
light, 60, 64 n. 119, 84, 192 n. 132, 227, 257, 259, 267 n. 90, 278, 280
Liubimov, Nikolai, 149 n. 5
Logos (see also christology), 57 n. 102, 63-64, 66-70, 74-77, 81-82, 85, 89, 116 n. 60, 117, 121, 142-43, 186, 210, 244
Logos (journal), 282
Lord's Prayer, 110
Loris-Melikov, Mikhail, 149
Lopatin, Lev, 22 n. 4, 25 n. 14, 212 n. 9
Losev, Aleksei, 16, 22 n. 4, 270 n. 53, 276 n. 73
Lubac, Henri de, 248-49 n. 26
Luther, Martin, 197, 198

Maine de Biran, 211-13, 217
Maksheeva, Natal'ia, 181
Maritain, Jacques, 164 n. 51, 172, 206 n. 170
Marx, Karl, 105, 172
Mary (*Theotokos*), 174 n. 81
materia prima, 53-55, 56-58, 63, 67, 69-70, 80, 81, 83 n. 173, 100, 140 n. 127, 248
materia secunda, 53 n. 92
Maximus Confessor, 105
metaphysics, 30, 35, 36, 39, 42, 43-44, 46-50, 61, 81, 93, 102, 113, 161 n. 42, 173, 109, 218, 227-28, 268, 281
methexis, 266 n. 84
Milbank, John, 116
Moskovskie vedomosti (journal), 158

Moltmann, Jürgen, 123 n. 75

monadology, 36-37, 39-48, 52-53, 69 n. 135/136, 83-84

Morozova, Margarita, 177

Moses, 160 n. 377, 199, 203

mysticism, 23 n. 9, 33 n. 46, 123 n. 71, 214 n. 12, 244-46, 261

Neo-Leibnizianism, Russian, 42, 277

Neo-Patristic Synthesis, 49

Nietzsche, Friedrich, 168, 169 n. 74, 172-76, 183, 243 n. 11, 268-74, 281 n. 16

Neoplatonism, 28, 125 n. 79, 250 n. 30

Nicholas, of Cusa, 278

Old Testament, 160-61

ontology, 21 n. 1, 36-37, 43-44, 46 n. 80, 50, 81, 95, 102-04, 173-75, 190, 234, 235 n. 74, 269

Origen, 244

Orthodoxy theology, 105, 118, 122 n. 89, 163-64, 245-46,

Palamas, Gregory, St, 243 n. 11

panentheism, 22 n. 4

pantheism, 22 n. 4, 50

Paracelsus, 30, 53 n. 92, 89

pathos, 188-90, 192-94, 228-29, 239, 247, 248 n. 24, 250-51, 252-53, 254-55, 256, 259, 261, 264-66, 272, 274, 281

Paul, St, 4, 107 n. 36, 122-23, 133 n. 108, 135 n. 115, 138, 140-43, 159 n. 34, 169 n. 73, 236

Philo of Alexandria, 74 n. 155

Pico della Mirandola, Giovanni, 28

Pisemskii, Aleksei, 254

Plato, 4-5, 35, 46 n. 79, 78 n. 162, 83 n. 173, 84 n. 175, 88, 140 n. 126, 165, 178, 179-81, 183 n. 116, 188, 189, 192-93 n. 135, 223-24, 225, 239, 241, 247-48, 250, 251, 254, 256, 261-64, 268

Platonism, 49 n. 86, 57 n. 102, 67, 176 n. 94, 179, 181 n. 112, 210, 215 n. 15, 218, 246, 250 n. 30, 262-63, 266 n. 84

Plotinus, 116 n. 60, 125 n. 79

Pobedonostsev, Konstantin, 158 n. 32

Pordage, John, 75 n. 157

positivism, 22, 26 n. 6, 37

Pravoslavnoe obozrenie, 142, 170 n. 74

Preobrazhenskii, Vasilii, 269

prophecy, 5, 8, 147-62, 178, 190, 223, 226, 227, 228, 245 n. 17, 274, 281
    and authenticity, 164-68, 171-72, 175-76, 187, 191
    biblical, 64 n. 121, 147, 159, 165, 187, 234 n. 72, 244, 263
    in theocracy, role of, 194-206
    Soloviev as prophet, 182-83, 186, 192-94

Psalms, Book of, 234 n. 72

Pushkin, Alexander, 179, 189, 219, 220, 223, 224, 225-26, 241, 251

Radlov, Ernst, 17

Rahner, Karl, 121

reason, 30, 34, 36, 56, 72-73, 77 n. 159, 100, 103-04, 114, 116-18, 121, 128, 130, 132, 135, 165, 190, 210, 244, 257, 266, 278

Revelation, Book of, 172 n. 81, 244

reverence, 48, 230-31, 233-36, 242, 249, 272, 274

Romanova, Ekaterina, 24 n. 13, 25, 31, 152 n. 14, 271

Rousseau, Jean-Jacques, 232 n. 64

Rozanov, Vasilii, 169 n. 72
    Soloviev as viewed by, 175 n. 94, 224 n. 43

Rus', 128 n. 89

Russkii vestnik (journal), 31

Saimaa, Lake, 176, 260, 274

Saint-Martin, Louis-Claude, 191 n. 131

Satan, 81, 83-85, 86, 89-90, 140 n. 127, 169 n. 73, 173, 248, 264

Schelling, Friedrich Wilhelm Joseph, 5 n. 11, 32 n. 44, 40 n. 65, 48 n. 85, 53 n. 92, 54, 57 n. 104, 69 n. 135, 88, 95 n. 6, 173, 218, 277

Schmitt, Carl, 279

Schopenhauer, Arthur, 26, 173, 174 n. 89, 209, 221

sex, 240, 244, 246, 254-55, 256 n. 53, 258, 261

Shakerism, 28

Shekhinah, 89, 214 n. 12

Shestov, Lev
    Soloviev as viewed by, 165-66

Slavophilism, 148-49, 152-53, 157, 158,

sobornost', 153

Sobrino, Jon, 134 n. 109

Socrates, 46 n. 78, 180, 192 n. 132, 261, 280
Soloviev, Sergei (father of Soloviev), 29 n. 34
Soloviev, Sergei (nephew of Soloviev), 17, 35 n. 53
Soloviev, Vladimir
    life of, 24-31, 93-94, 147-49, 151-57, 159-60, 163, 168-69, 176-77, 178-79, 181-83, 186-89, 192-94, 239, 258-59, 273-74
    works of: *Crisis of Western Philosophy: Against the Positivists*, 12, 26, 36-38, 40, 46, 47, 48, 80, 174 n. 89, 209; *Sophie/La Sophia*, 28-31, 34-35, 42, 46, 47, 48, 50, 53, 54, 57, 74, 75 n. 156, 78, 79, 80-83, 86, 97 n. 10, 98, 240; *Philosophical Principles of Integral Knowledge*, 12, 13 n. 34, 30-31, 33 n. 46, 47, 48, 53-65, 73-78, 79, 80, 81, 86, 89 n. 185, 93, 209, 211, 261; 'Faith, Reason and Experience', 66, 77 n. 159; 'Three Forces', 152; *Lectures on Theanthropy*, 18, 93-94, 97-98, 113, 122, 142 n. 133, 160-62, 181 n. 112, 217, 223, 250 n. 31; *Lectures on the History of Philosophy*, 98, 125-26; *Critique of Abstract Principles*, 6, 23, 30-31, 32, 33, 34-35, 36, 40-47, 48, 51, 60 n. 113, 67, 80, 81, 83, 86-87, 157, 187, 214-15, 218, 219, 232 n. 65, 251 n. 36, 258; *Three Speeches in Honour of Dostoevsky*, 222-23; *Lived Meaning of Christianity*, 24 n. 11, 142; 'A Critique of Modern Education and the Crisis of the World Process' (speech against capital punishment), 147-51; 'Ob istinnoi nauke', 33; *The Spiritual Foundations of Life*, 4, 24 n. 11, 141, 143 n. 135, 221-22, 229-30, 234 n. 71, 271 n. 104; *The Great Schism and Christian Politics*, 187; *The Jews and the Christian Question*, 155, 160; 'The Slavic Question', 157; Review article on Janssen's *Geschichte des deutschen Volkes*, 170 n. 74, 171 n. 78; *The History and Future of Theocracy*, 6 n. 12, 101-02, 132 n. 104, 133, 156 n. 59, 160 n. 37, 162 n. 44, 177 n. 97, 113 n. 51, 178, 195-96, 198, 217; 'The Talmud and Recent Polemical Literature about it in Austria and Germany', 161 n. 42, 162;'Prorok budushchego', 153; *La Russie et l'église universelle*, 128 n. 90, 134-35, 152, 155, 159 n. 34, 177 n. 97, 194-95, 198, 204-05, 236, 242; *The General Meaning of Art*, 218; 'Primitive Paganism and its Dead Remnants', p. 158 n. 29; 'On Lyrical Poetry', 219 n. 26; 'Ex Oriente Lux', 155; *On Counterfeits*, 158; *The National Question in Russia*, 157 n. 28; 'Privet ministram', 151 n. 12; 'Freedom of the Will and Causality', 212 n. 9; *The Meaning of Love*, 115 n. 54, 227-28, 246-47, 254-55, 256-57; *First Step toward a Positive Aesthetics*, 270 n. 100; *Justification of the Good*, 48, 96, 140 n. 125, 174 n. 91, 178 n. 103, 179, 180, 190 n. 130, 200, 229-36, 251; 'The Buddhist Disposition in Poetry', 269; 'Russian Symbolists', 225 n. 47; 'The Poetry of Count A.K. Tolstoi', 144 n. 139, 218-19, 224; 'The Poetry of F.I. Tiutchev', 224-25, 280; *Pushkin's Fate*, 224 n. 43; 'Conception of God', 233; *Sunday Letters*, 139, 255 n. 49; 'When did the Hebrew Prophets Live?', 162; *Theoretical Philosophy*, 216-17, 230 n. 59, 239, 266; *The Life Drama of Plato*, 4, 179-80, 183 n. 116, 239, 247, 262, 264; 'The Idea of Humanity in Auguste Comte', 22 n. 6, 107 n. 36; 'Three Meetings', 3, 23, 27, 28; *The Idea of the Superman*, 172, 175-76; *Beauty in Nature*, 98 n. 12, 258; 'Lermontov', 173, 253 n. 44; 266-67;

'Speech in Honour of Belinskii', 181-82, 188-89, 190; Three *Conversations*, 10, 140 n. 125, 172, 177 n. 97, 186, 239, 255 n. 49; *Short Story of the Antichrist*, 6, 10, 12, 113, 167 n. 66, 168-72, 175, 182-84, 192-94, 235, 239, 255, 263-64, 282; encyclopaedia entries: 'Duns Scotus', 214 n. 12, 'Faith', 216 n. 17, 'Hegel', 72 n. 144, 214 n. 12, 218 n. 23, 'Love', 236 n. 75, 244, 247 n. 21, 'Maine de Biran', 212 n. 7, 'Proclus', 250 n. 30; 'Our Nicodemuses', 181 n. 112; 'Articles on Questions of Religion, Morality and Philosophy: Odd Pages (archive), 211

Solovieva, Poliksena, 29 n. 34

soteriology, 21, 35, 106 n. 35, 108-09, 110 n. 44, 112, 124-25, 131-32, 246

soul, 40, 45-46, 74-75, 77-78, 82-85, 210-215, 217, 219, 220-21, 227, 251, 281
    of the world (World Soul), 37 n. 56, 54, 71 n. 171, 84 n. 175, 85, 98, 100, 241, 280, 281
    immortality of, 140 n. 126
    relation to body, see *body*

Sophia (Divine Wisdom), 9-10, 23, 25 n. 16, 27, 28, 29, 45 n. 78, 54, 58 n. 107, 75 n. 157, 76, 77 n. 160, 78, 79, 81-83, 116 n. 60, 128, 138 n. 120, 176 n. 96, 192 n. 132, 200 n. 156, 210, 241, 258, 259-60 n. 63, 277, 278, 279, 282

Spinoza, 38-9, 40, 48, 233

Stasiulevich, Mikhail, 156 n. 26

Strakhov, Nikolai, 26

Strossmayer, Josip, Bishop, 152 n. 14

Swedenborg, Emmanuel, 25 n. 16, 30

Symbolism, Russian, 164, 225, 277

Symeon the New Theologian, St, 243 n. 11

syzygy, 245

Talmud, 159, 161 n. 42

tertium quid (third power), 15, 45, 152, 198-99, 201 n. 159, 209, 213, 231, 252-53

theocracy, 111, 158, 177-79, 194-96, 198-99, 203 n. 166, 206, 255

theosis, 2, 128 n. 89, 273

theosophy, 8, 75 n. 157, 191 n. 131

theurgy, 8, 24 n. 11, 35 n. 53, 206, 218, 221-23, 229, 261

Tillich, Paul, 142 n. 134, 191 n. 132

Tiutchev, Fedor, 182, 224-25, 280

Tolstaia (Bakhmateva), Sof'ia, 30, 75 n. 157

Tolstoi, Aleksei (poet), 144 n. 139, 218, 224

Tolstoi, Dmitrii, 158 n. 32

Tolstoy, Leo, 105, 172, 255
    Soloviev as viewed by, 26
Trent, Coucil of, 136 n. 117, 137
trinity, 59 n. 108, 64, 80-81, 88, 89, 116-117 n. 60
Trismogin, Solomon, 28
Trubetskoi, Evgenii, 7, 8, 10, 11, 16 n. 40, 177-78, 278
Trubetskoi, Sergei, 174 n. 91, 192, 193, 244 n. 14, 262 n. 73, 268
Tsertelev, Dmitrii, 29, 30

Valentinian I, Emperor, 253 n. 42
Vestnik Evropy, 156 n. 26, 158
von Balthasar, Hans Urs, 85, 136 n. 117
von Hartmann, Eduard von, 26, 174 n. 89, 209
Voprosy filosofii i psikhologii (journal), 269 n. 97
Vul'f, Aleksei, 241 n. 6

will (voluntarism), 26, 37 n. 56, 40 n. 65, 41, 53 n. 93/94, 54 n. 87, 56-58, 60-63, 66-67, 69-70, 76, 77, 78, 83-84, 103, 104, 120, 122, 125, 135-36, 142 n. 133, 160, 171-76, 183, 209 n. 1, 210, 212, 216, 217-18, 223-24, 249 n. 26, 263-64, freedom of the, 137 n. 119, 172, 174 n. 81, 217, 253 n. 43
Woman Clothed in Sun, 282

Zohar (see also Kabbala), 27-28
Zubiri, Xavier, 6

www.ingramcontent.com/pod-product-compliance
Lightning Source LLC
Chambersburg PA
CBHW071401300426
44114CB00016B/2145